# WHOOPS

This is the back of the book!

You're looking at the last page, not the first one.

MEGA MAN GIGAMIX is a comic originally published in Japan (known as manga). Traditional manga is read in a 'reversed' format, starting on the right and heading towards the left. The story begins where English readers expect to find the last page because the spine of the book is on the opposite side.

Preserving the original artwork, we've decided to leave the Japanese format intact. Check the examples below to see how to read the word balloons in proper order.

Now head to the front of the book and enjoy MEGA MAN GIGAMIX!

MEGA MAN GIGAMIX Vol. 1

Manga: HITOSHI ARIGA

Assistant: YUSUKE SUZUKI
TAMA TSUCHIYA
YOU MURAOKA

Old Assistant: RYOUMA NOMURA
TAKANORI YAMAZAKI
TAKASHI MATSUYAMA
RIE TAKAHASHI
YASUYO SATOU

ENGLISH EDITION:
Translation: M. KIRIE HAYASHI
Localization & Editing: ASH PAULSEN
Lettering: MARSHALL DILLON

UDON STAFF
Chief of Operations: ERIK KO
Managing Editor: MATT MOYLAN
Project Manager: JIM ZUBKAVICH
Market Manager: STACY KING
Editor, Japanese Publications: M. KIRIE HAYASHI

SPECIAL THANKS:
KENJI KUDOU
SATOSHI NAKAI
AYANO KOSHIRO

RYUJI HIGURASHI
INAFKING
CAPCOM

First published in Japan in 2009 by Wedge Holdings.
English translation rights arranged with Wedge Holdings

English edition of MEGA MAN GIGAMIX Vol. 1
©2010 UDON Entertainment Corp.

English language version produced and published by UDON Entertainment Corp.
P.O. Box 5002, RPO MAJOR MACKENZIE Richmond Hill, Ontario, L4S 0B7, Canada

www.UDONentertainment.com

Third Printing: May 2013
ISBN-13: 978-1-926778-23-5 ISBN-10 : 1-926778-23-5

Printed in Canada

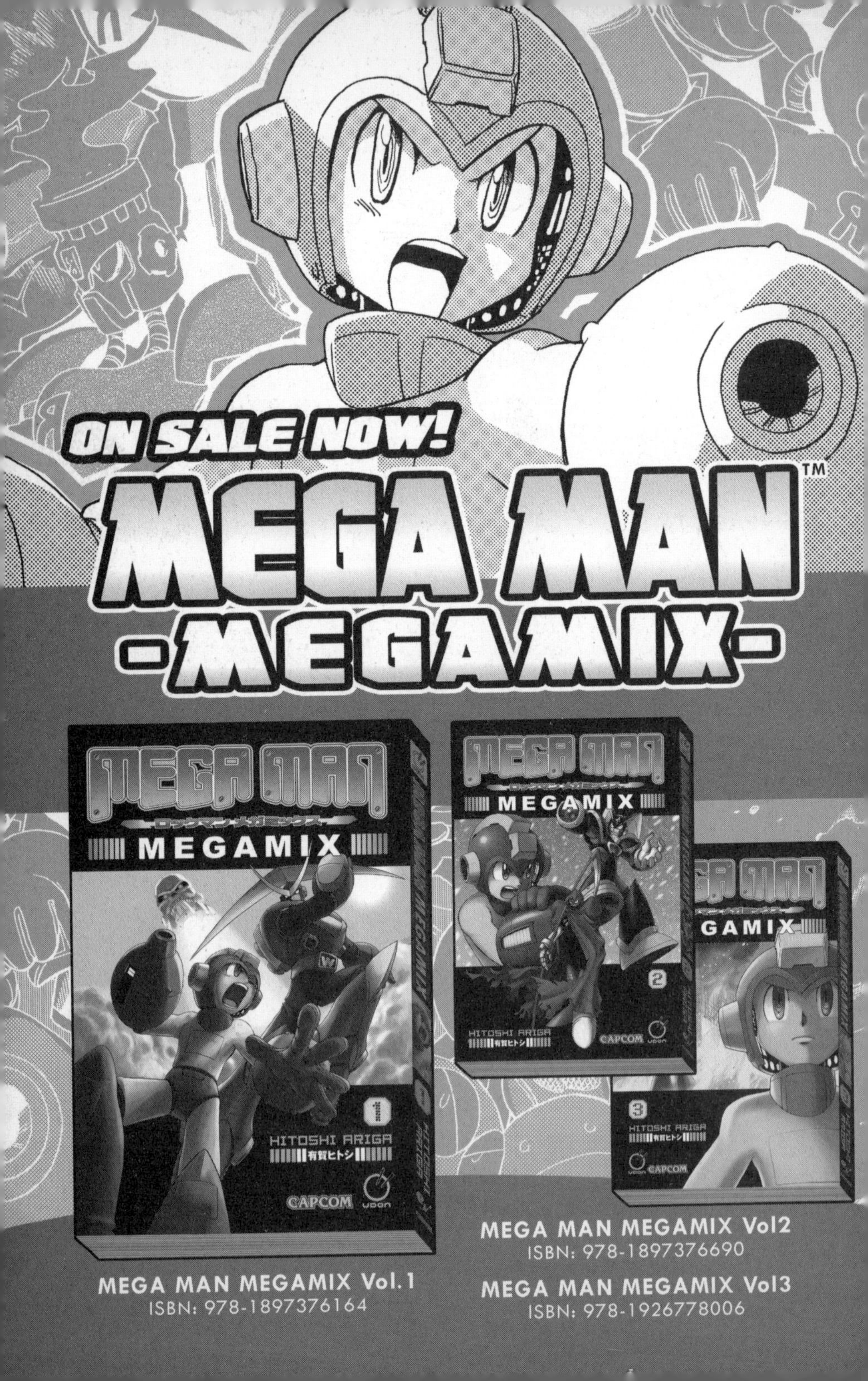
ON SALE NOW!
MEGA MAN™
-MEGAMIX-
MEGA MAN
MEGAMIX
HITOSHI ARIGA
有賀ヒトシ
CAPCOM
MEGA MAN MEGAMIX Vol.1
ISBN: 978-1897376164
MEGA MAN MEGAMIX Vol2
ISBN: 978-1897376690
MEGA MAN MEGAMIX Vol3
ISBN: 978-1926778006

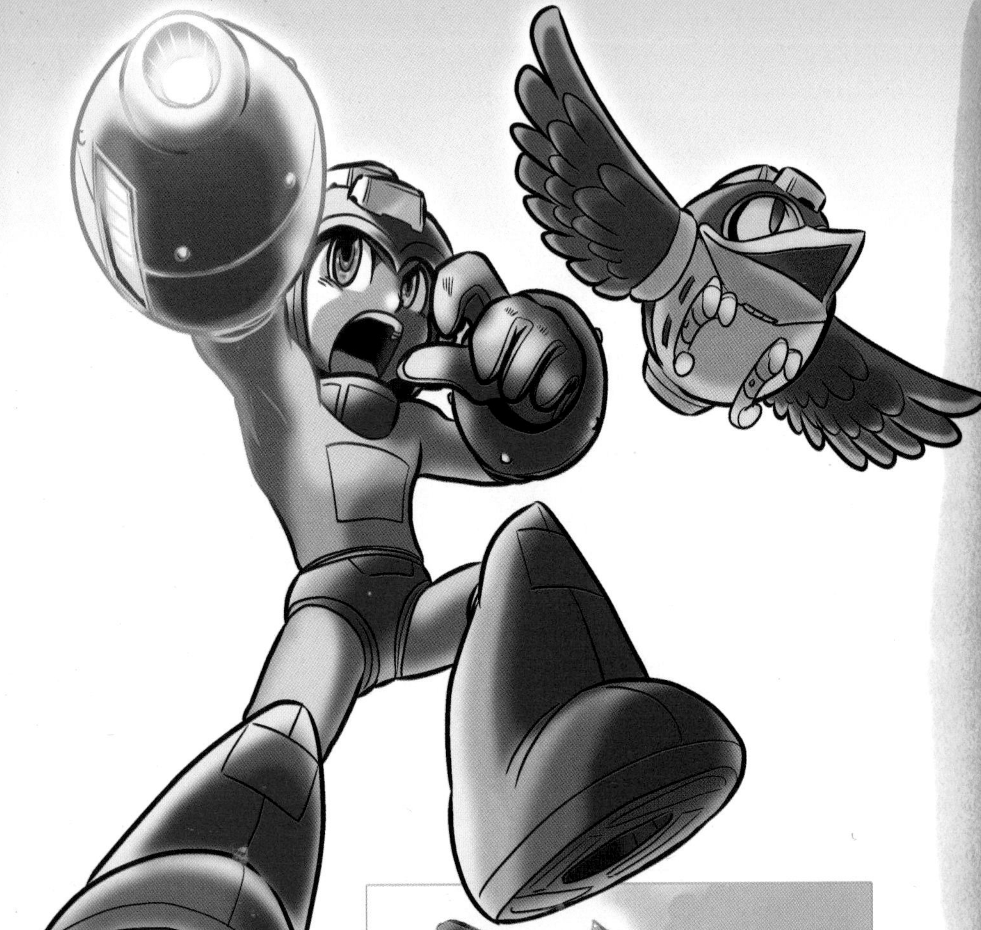

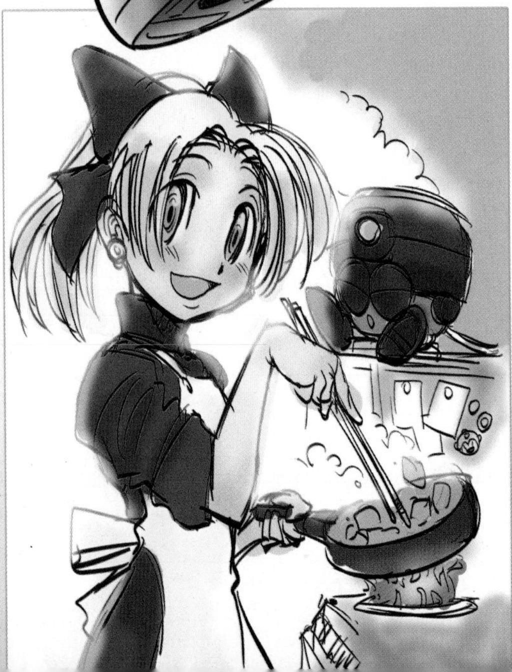

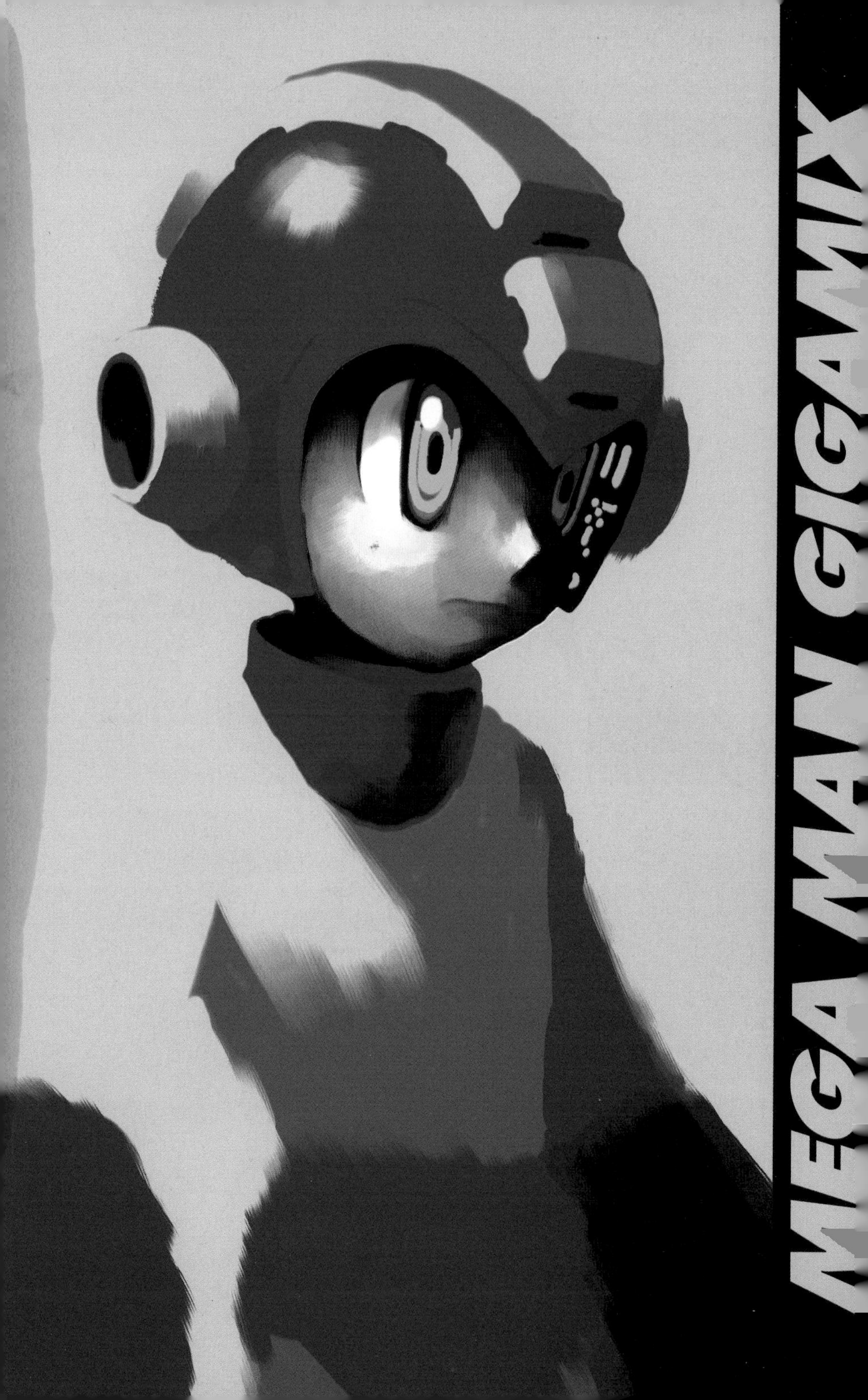
MEGA MAN GIGAMIX

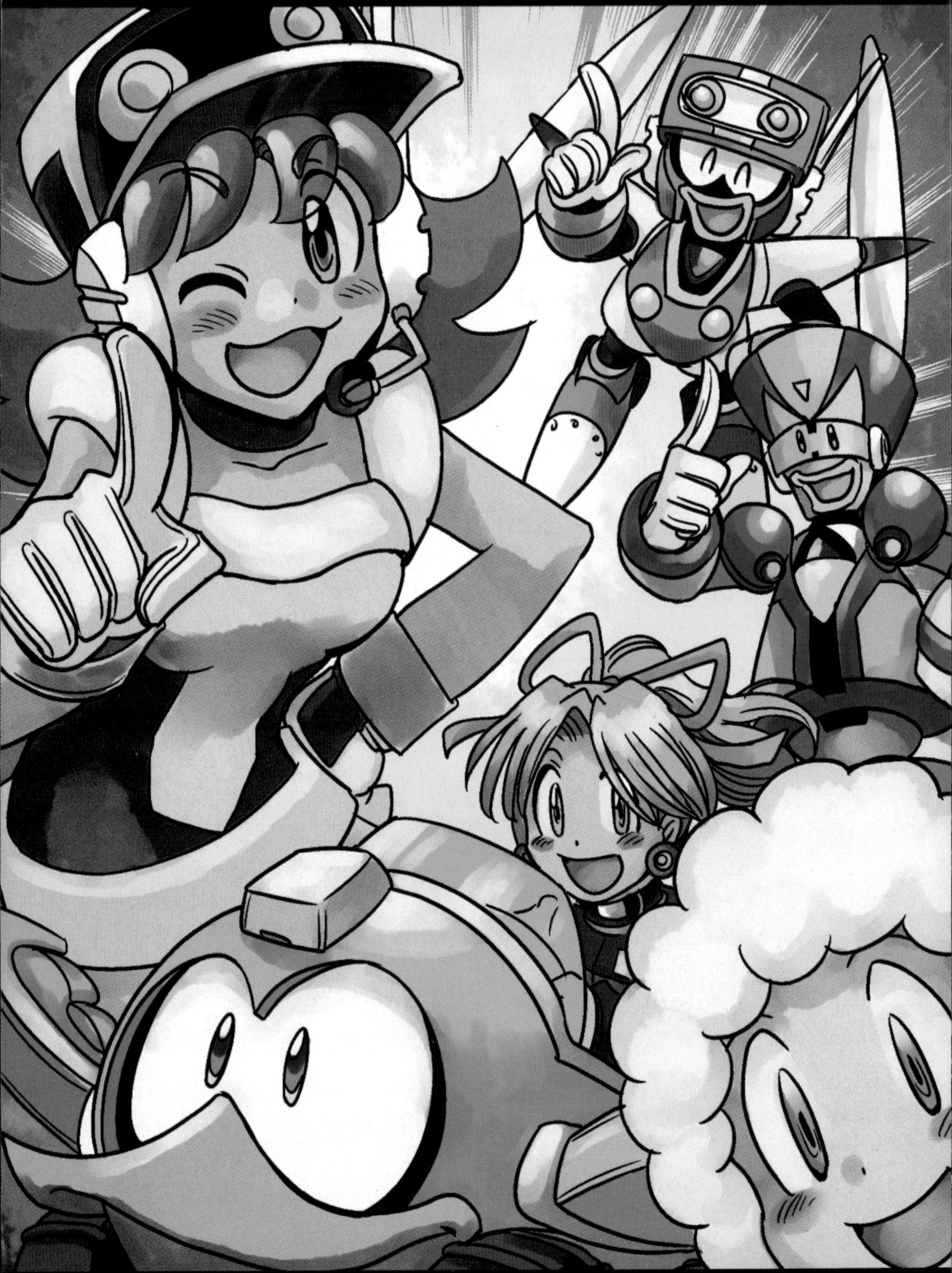

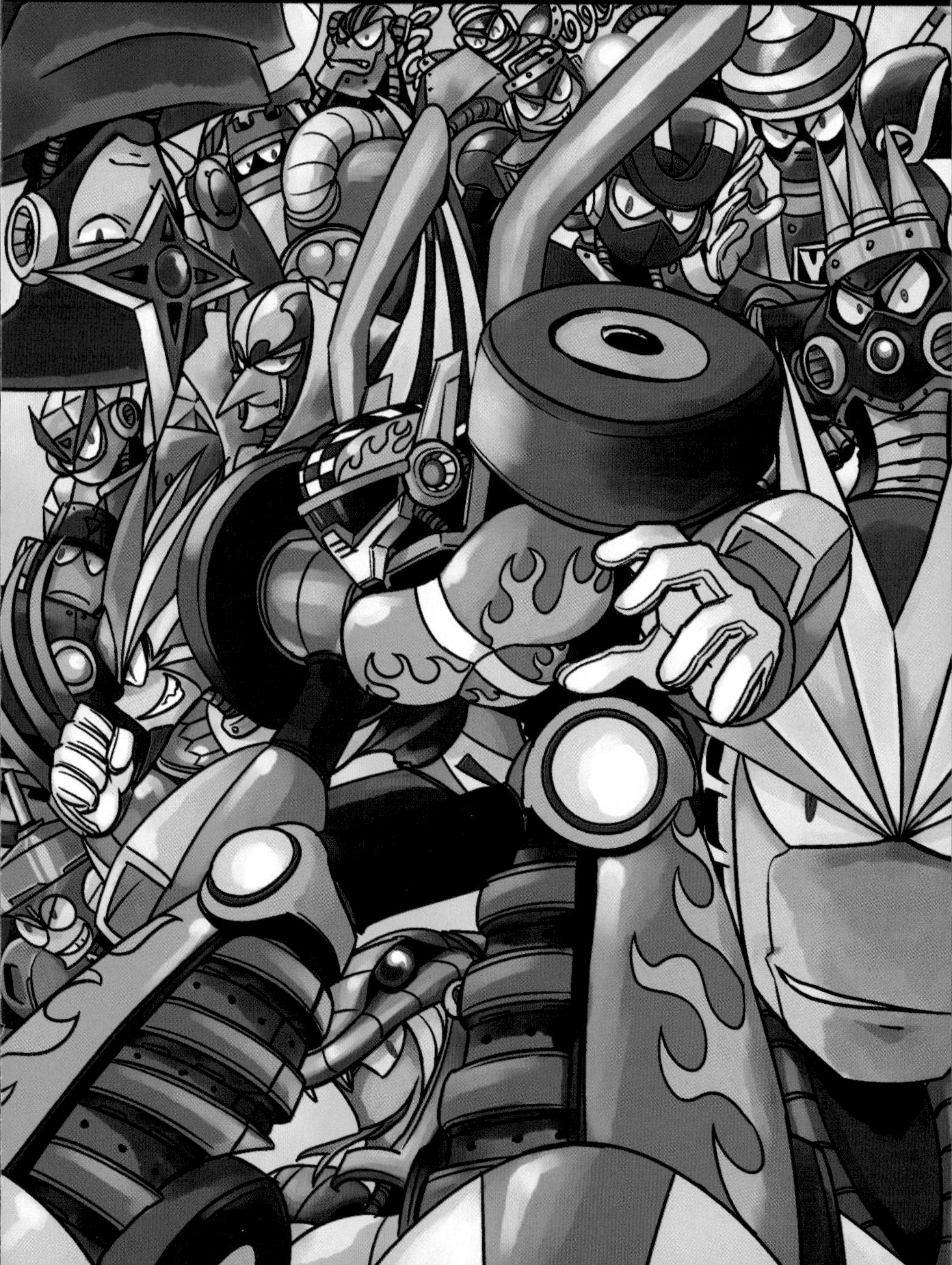

VOLUME 1

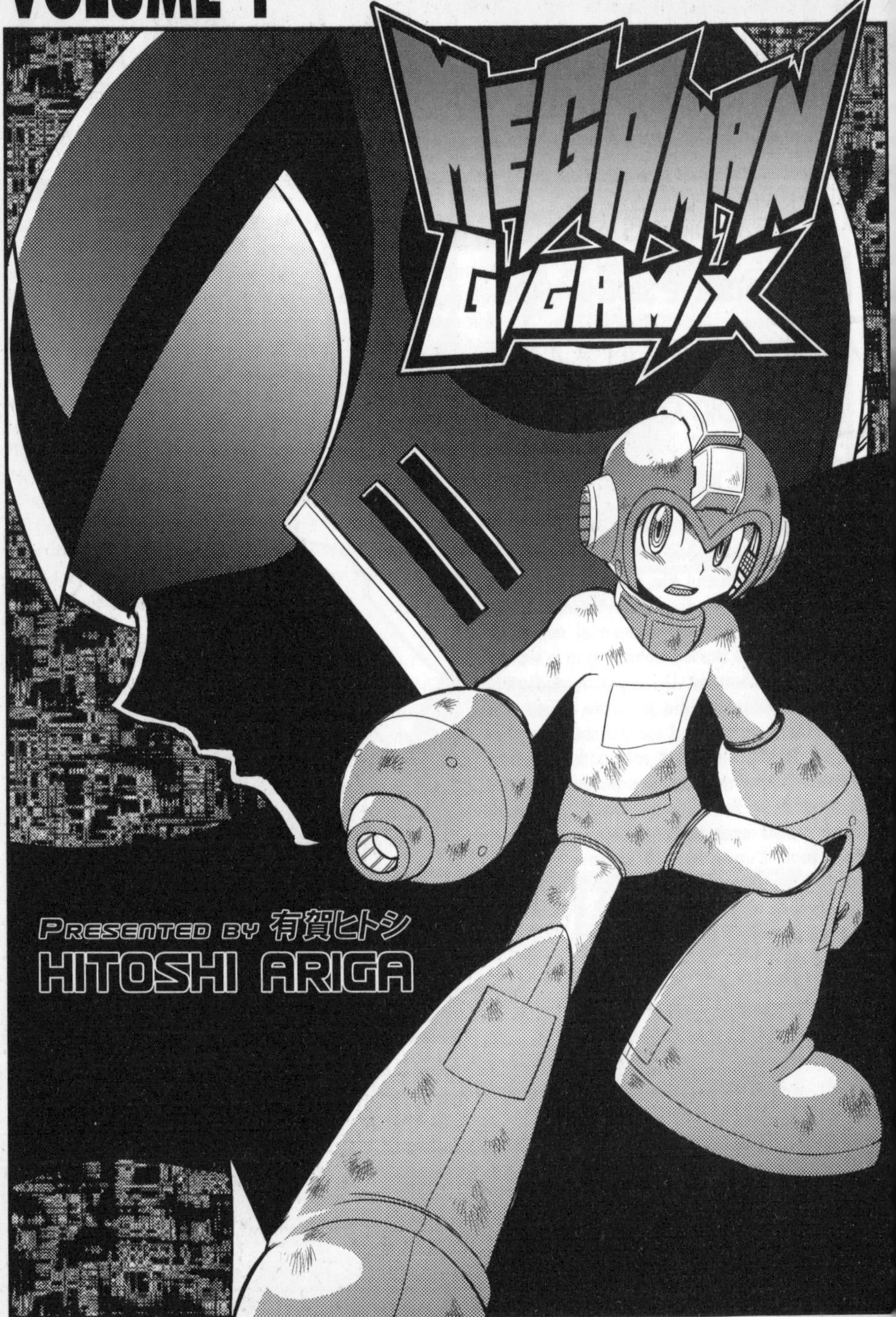
MEGAMAN GIGAMIX
PRESENTED BY 有賀ヒトシ
HITOSHI ARIGA

This book is a faithful translation of the boo
released in Japan on October 4, 2009.

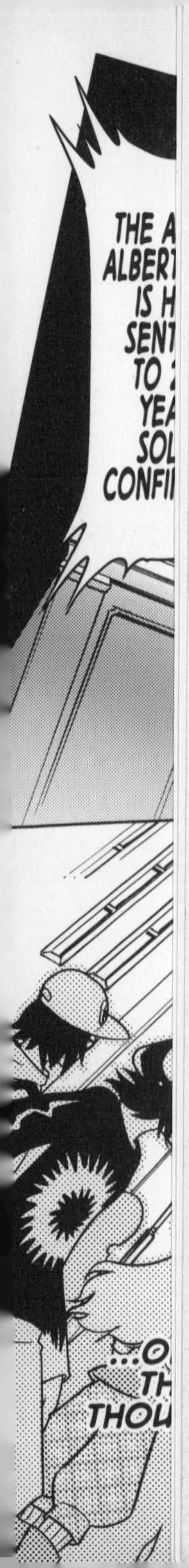
THE A
ALBERT
IS H
SENT
TO 2
YEA
SOL
CONFI
...O
TH
THOU

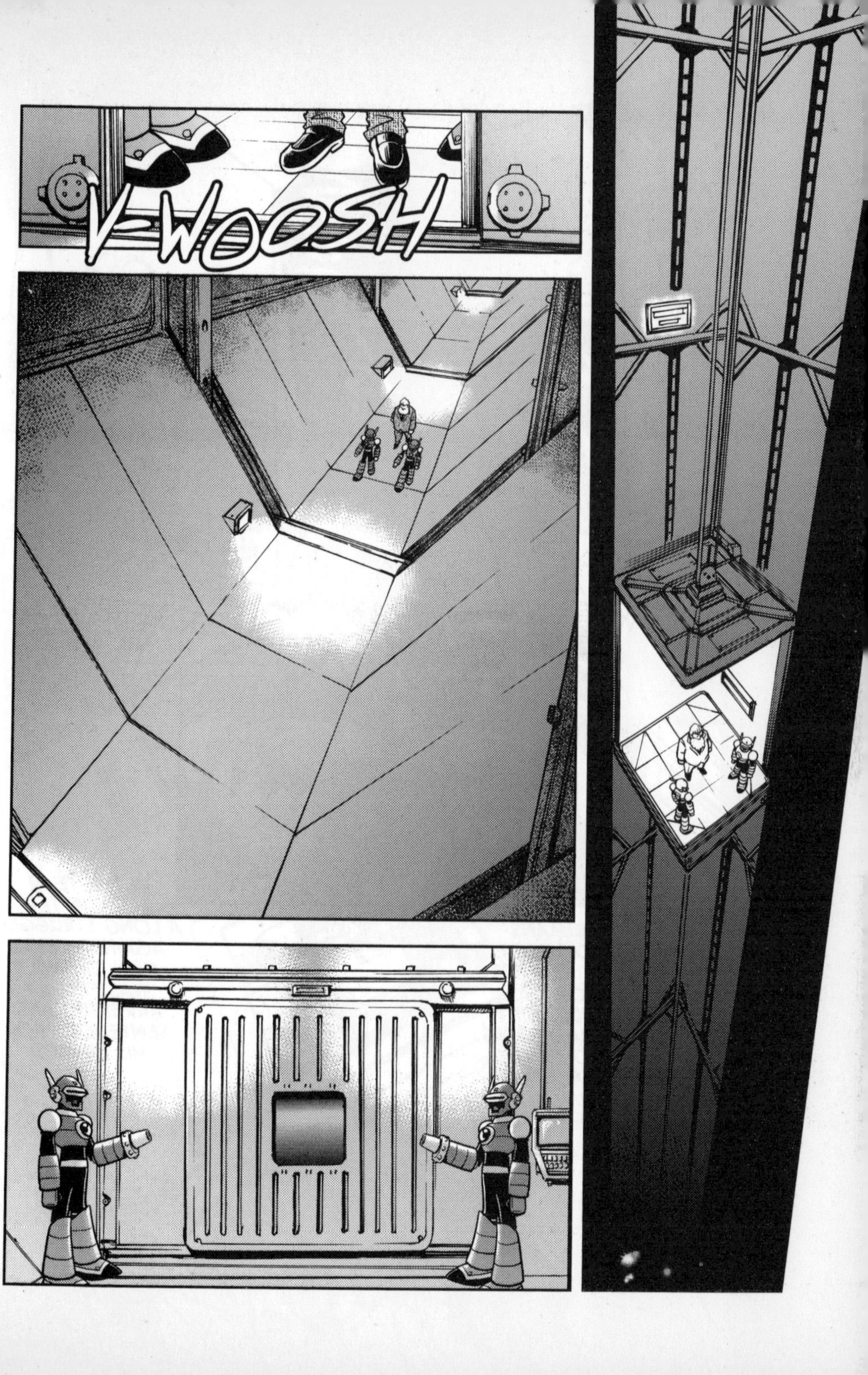
V-WOOSH

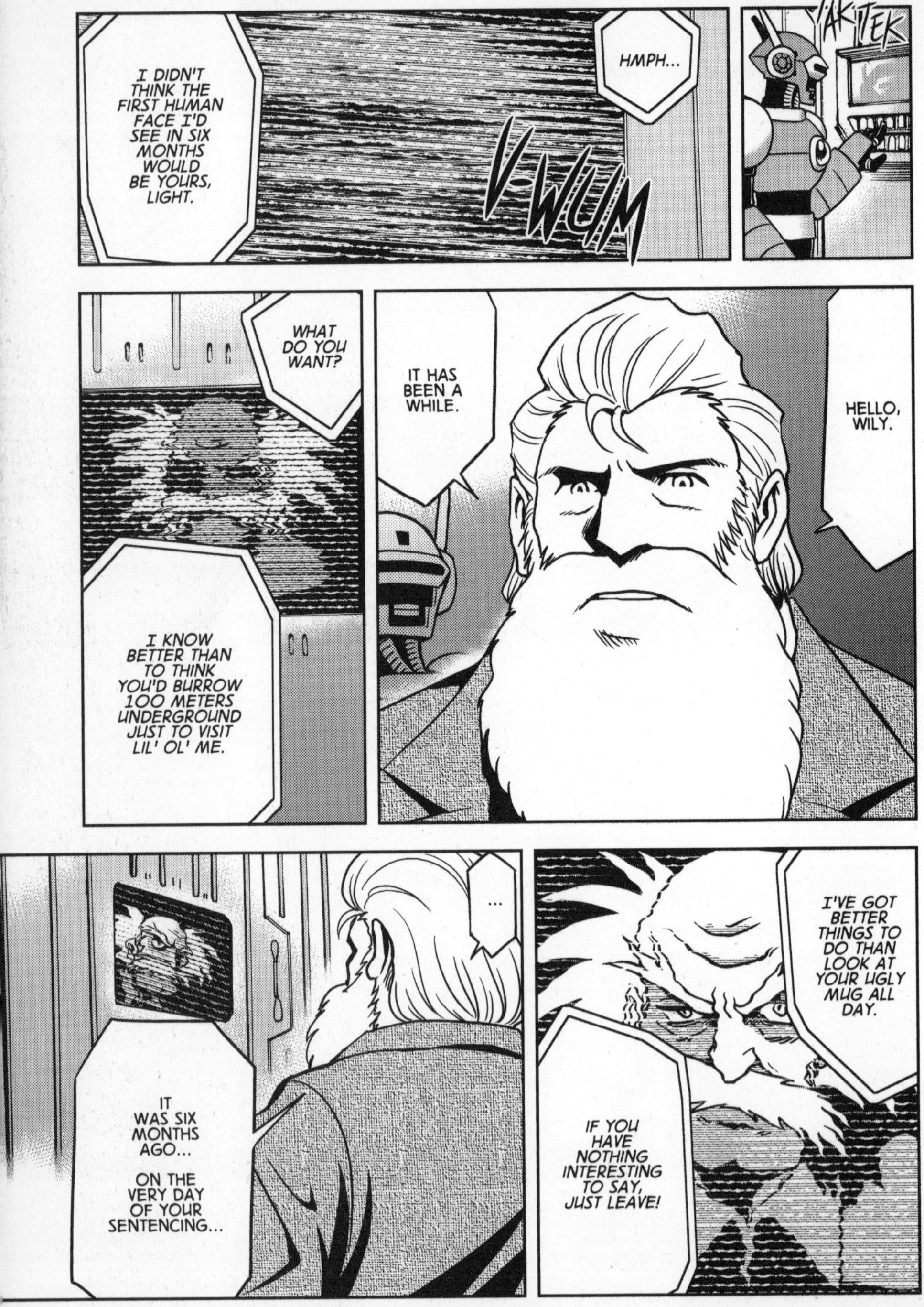
TAK TEK
HMPH...
V-WUM
I DIDN'T THINK THE FIRST HUMAN FACE I'D SEE IN SIX MONTHS WOULD BE YOURS, LIGHT.
HELLO, WILY.
IT HAS BEEN A WHILE.
WHAT DO YOU WANT?
I KNOW BETTER THAN TO THINK YOU'D BURROW 100 METERS UNDERGROUND JUST TO VISIT LIL' OL' ME.
I'VE GOT BETTER THINGS TO DO THAN LOOK AT YOUR UGLY MUG ALL DAY.
IF YOU HAVE NOTHING INTERESTING TO SAY, JUST LEAVE!
...
IT WAS SIX MONTHS AGO...
ON THE VERY DAY OF YOUR SENTENCING...

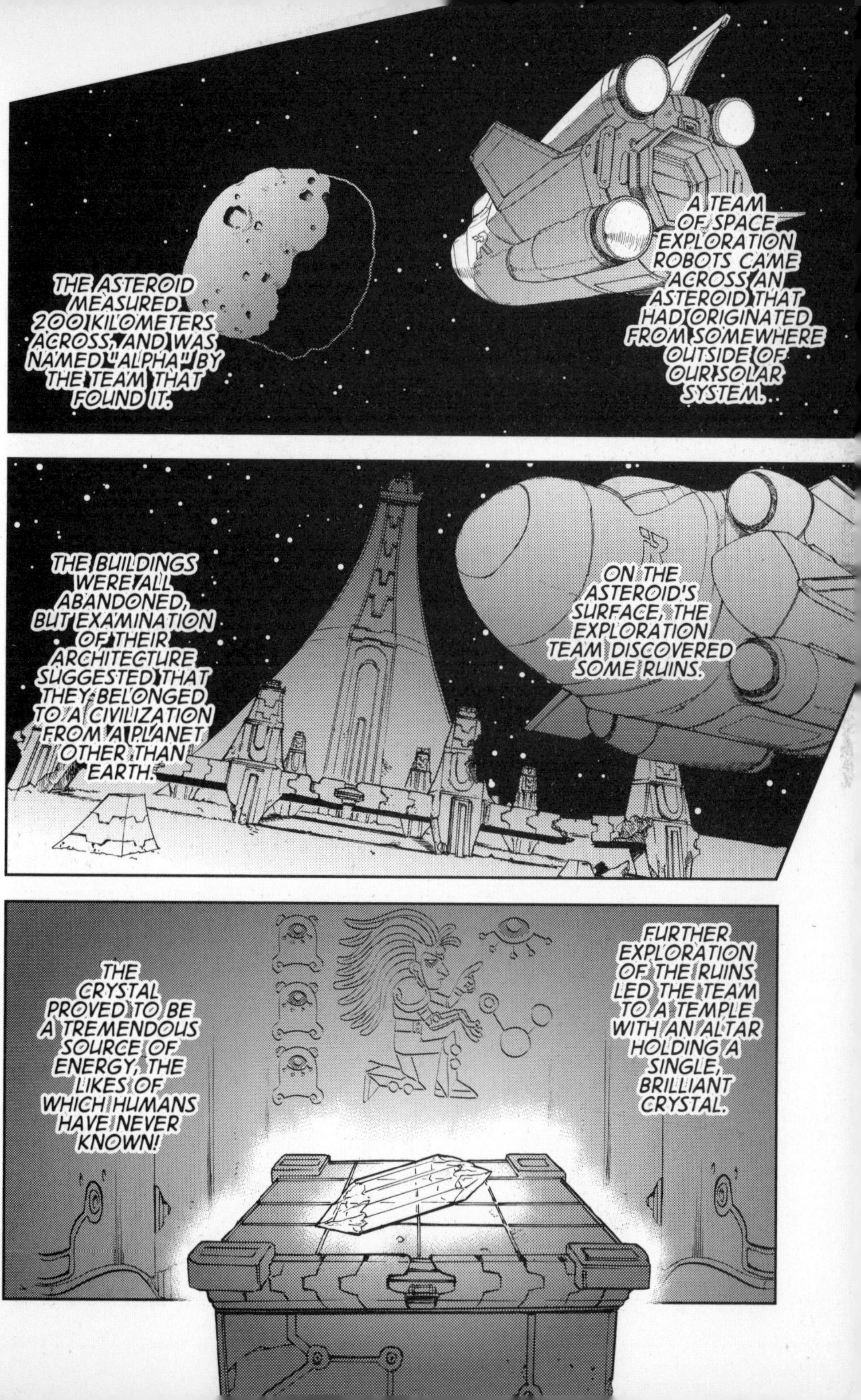
A TEAM OF SPACE EXPLORATION ROBOTS CAME ACROSS AN ASTEROID THAT HAD ORIGINATED FROM SOMEWHERE OUTSIDE OF OUR SOLAR SYSTEM.
THE ASTEROID MEASURED 200 KILOMETERS ACROSS, AND WAS NAMED "ALPHA" BY THE TEAM THAT FOUND IT.
ON THE ASTEROID'S SURFACE, THE EXPLORATION TEAM DISCOVERED SOME RUINS.
THE BUILDINGS WERE ALL ABANDONED, BUT EXAMINATION OF THEIR ARCHITECTURE SUGGESTED THAT THEY BELONGED TO A CIVILIZATION FROM A PLANET OTHER THAN EARTH.
FURTHER EXPLORATION OF THE RUINS LED THE TEAM TO A TEMPLE WITH AN ALTAR HOLDING A SINGLE, BRILLIANT CRYSTAL.
THE CRYSTAL PROVED TO BE A TREMENDOUS SOURCE OF ENERGY, THE LIKES OF WHICH HUMANS HAVE NEVER KNOWN!

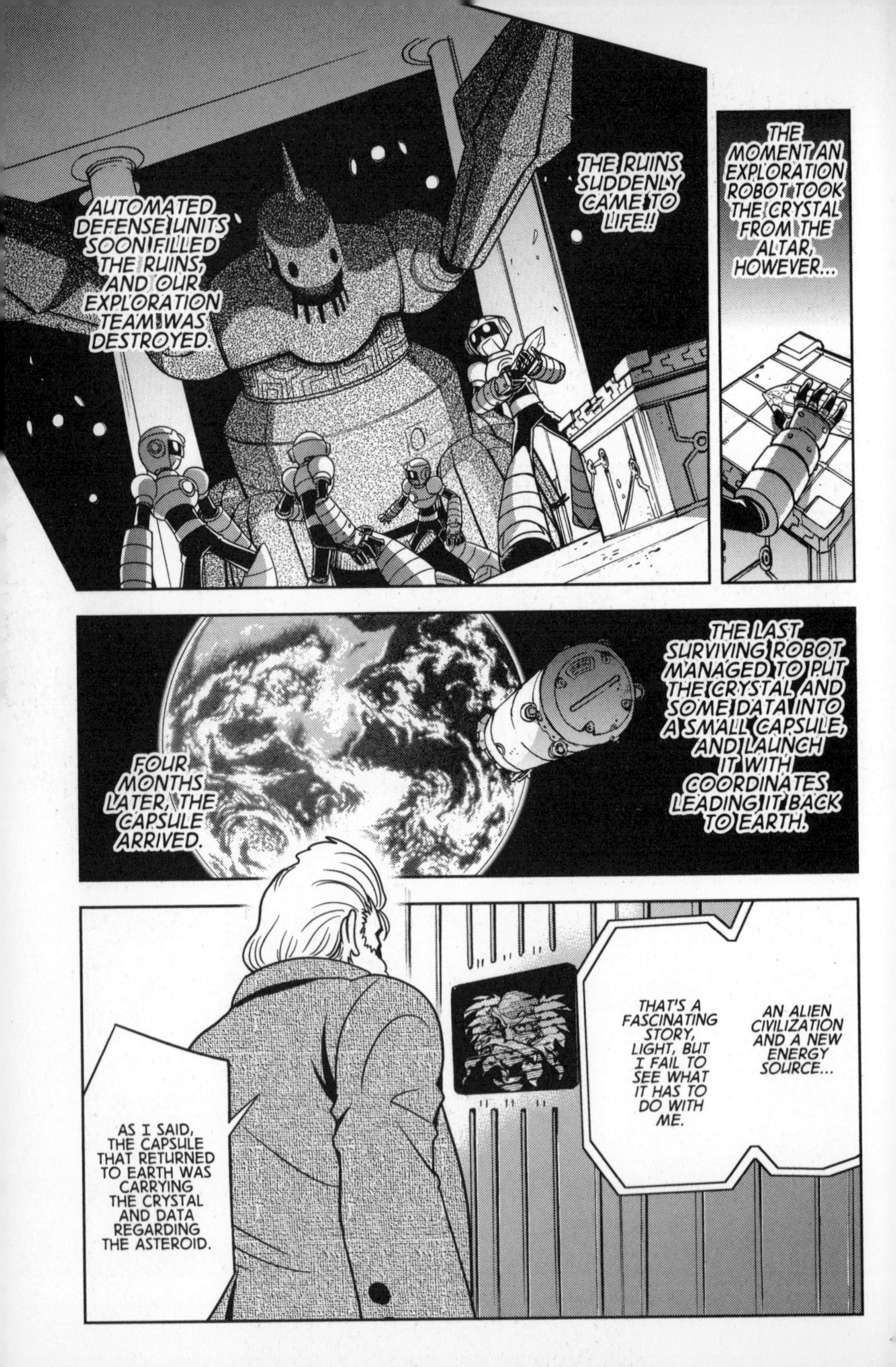
THE MOMENT AN EXPLORATION ROBOT TOOK THE CRYSTAL FROM THE ALTAR, HOWEVER...
THE RUINS SUDDENLY CAME TO LIFE!!
AUTOMATED DEFENSE UNITS SOON FILLED THE RUINS, AND OUR EXPLORATION TEAM WAS DESTROYED.
THE LAST SURVIVING ROBOT MANAGED TO PUT THE CRYSTAL AND SOME DATA INTO A SMALL CAPSULE, AND LAUNCH IT WITH COORDINATES LEADING IT BACK TO EARTH.
FOUR MONTHS LATER, THE CAPSULE ARRIVED.
AN ALIEN CIVILIZATION AND A NEW ENERGY SOURCE...
THAT'S A FASCINATING STORY, LIGHT, BUT I FAIL TO SEE WHAT IT HAS TO DO WITH ME.
AS I SAID, THE CAPSULE THAT RETURNED TO EARTH WAS CARRYING THE CRYSTAL AND DATA REGARDING THE ASTEROID.

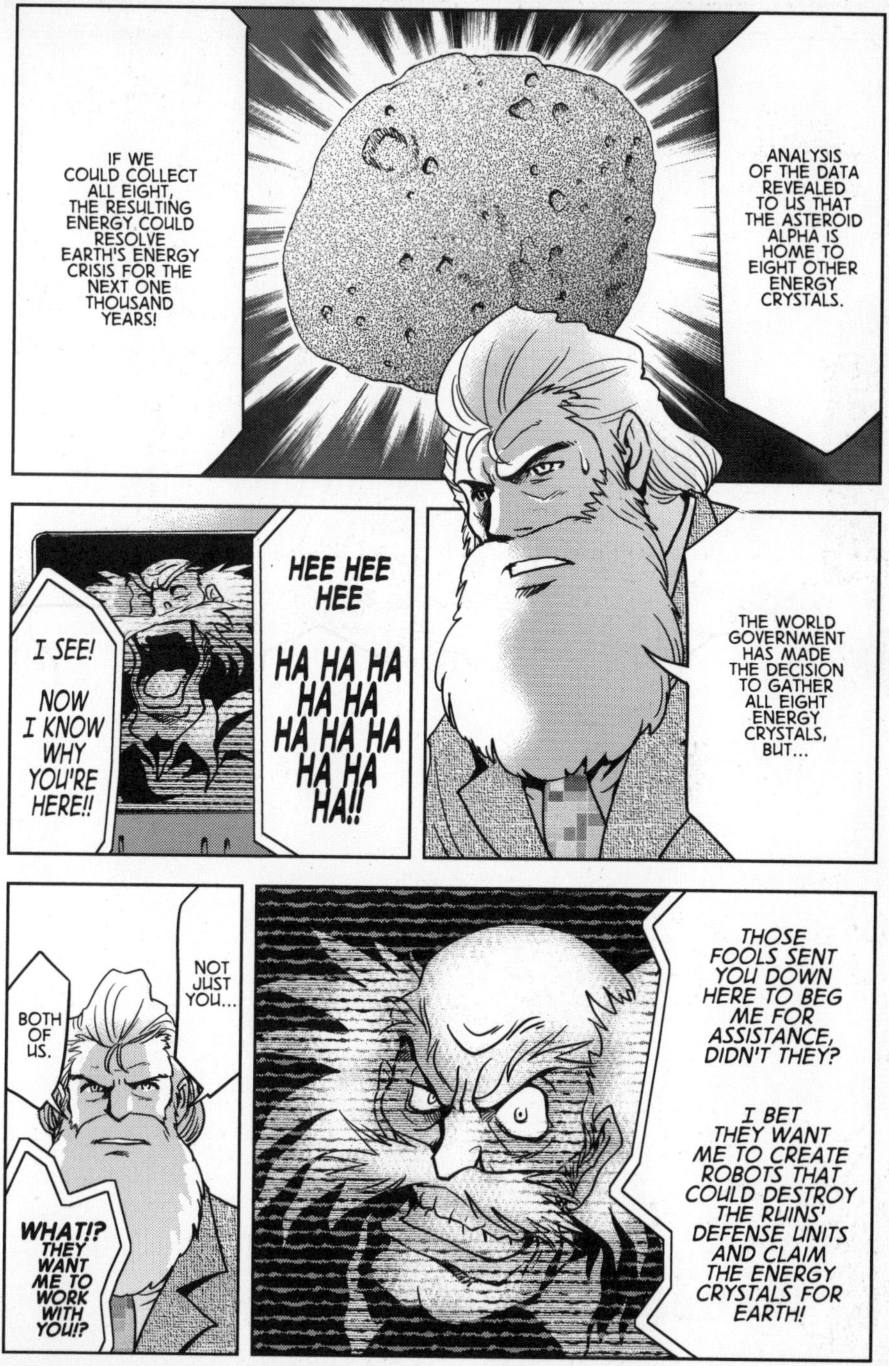
ANALYSIS OF THE DATA REVEALED TO US THAT THE ASTEROID ALPHA IS HOME TO EIGHT OTHER ENERGY CRYSTALS.
IF WE COULD COLLECT ALL EIGHT, THE RESULTING ENERGY COULD RESOLVE EARTH'S ENERGY CRISIS FOR THE NEXT ONE THOUSAND YEARS!
THE WORLD GOVERNMENT HAS MADE THE DECISION TO GATHER ALL EIGHT ENERGY CRYSTALS, BUT...
HEE HEE HEE
HA HA HA HA HA HA HA HA HA HA HA!!
I SEE!
NOW I KNOW WHY YOU'RE HERE!!
THOSE FOOLS SENT YOU DOWN HERE TO BEG ME FOR ASSISTANCE, DIDN'T THEY?
I BET THEY WANT ME TO CREATE ROBOTS THAT COULD DESTROY THE RUINS' DEFENSE UNITS AND CLAIM THE ENERGY CRYSTALS FOR EARTH!
NOT JUST YOU...
BOTH OF US.
WHAT!? THEY WANT ME TO WORK WITH YOU!?

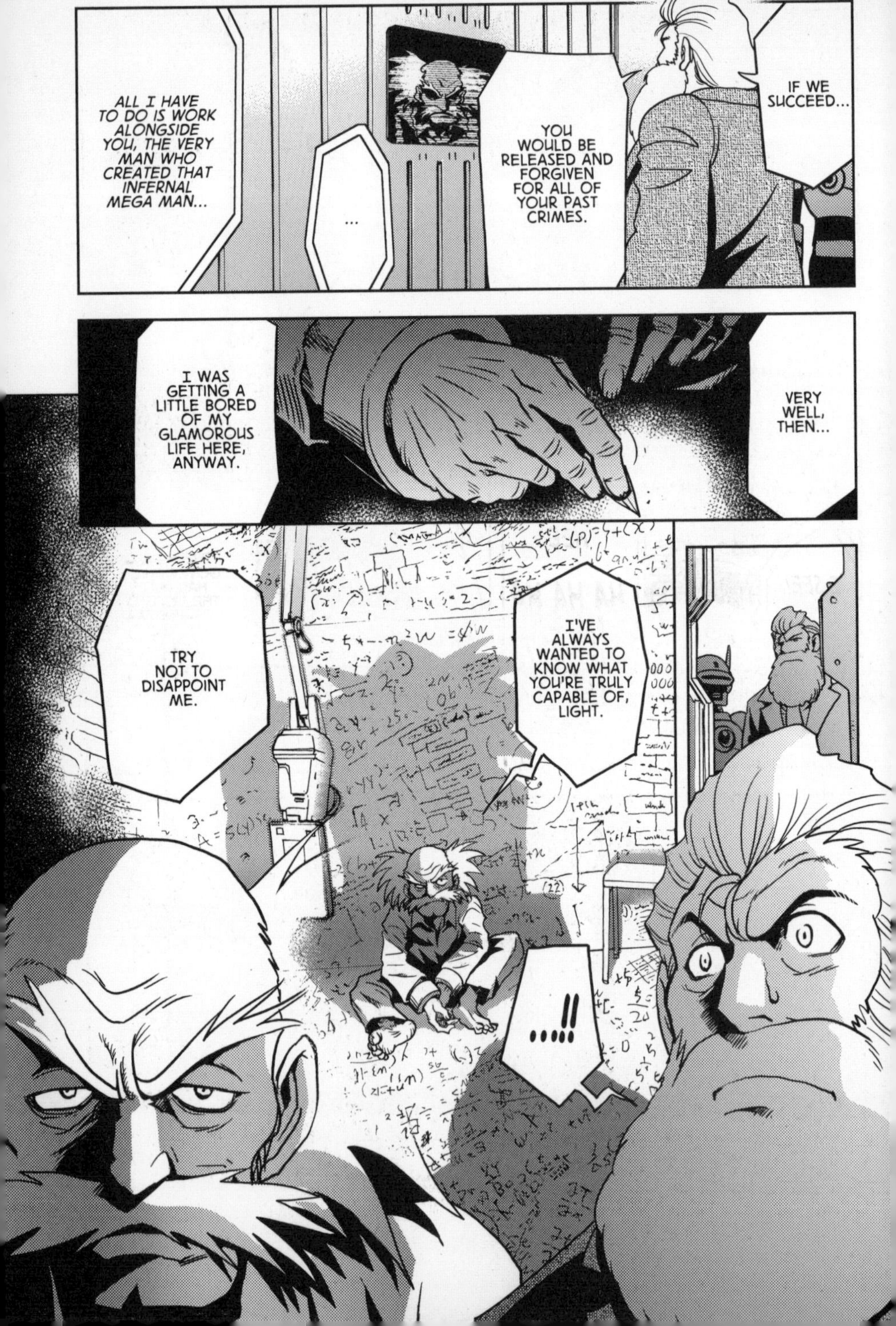
IF WE SUCCEED...
YOU WOULD BE RELEASED AND FORGIVEN FOR ALL OF YOUR PAST CRIMES.
...
ALL I HAVE TO DO IS WORK ALONGSIDE YOU, THE VERY MAN WHO CREATED THAT INFERNAL MEGA MAN...
VERY WELL, THEN...
I WAS GETTING A LITTLE BORED OF MY GLAMOROUS LIFE HERE, ANYWAY.
I'VE ALWAYS WANTED TO KNOW WHAT YOU'RE TRULY CAPABLE OF, LIGHT.
TRY NOT TO DISAPPOINT ME.
....!!

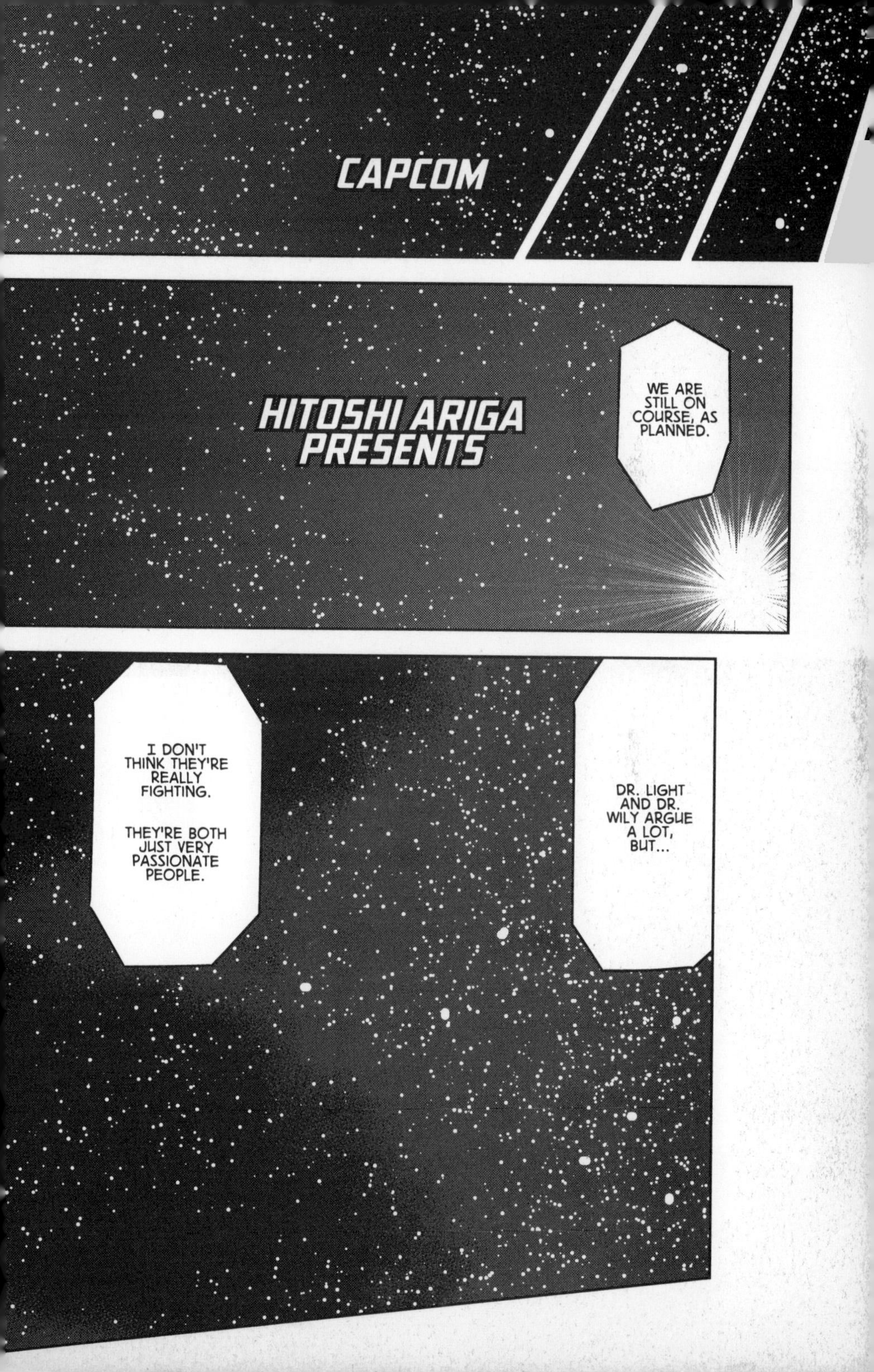
CAPCOM
WE ARE STILL ON COURSE, AS PLANNED.
HITOSHI ARIGA PRESENTS
DR. LIGHT AND DR. WILY ARGUE A LOT, BUT...
I DON'T THINK THEY'RE REALLY FIGHTING.
THEY'RE BOTH JUST VERY PASSIONATE PEOPLE.

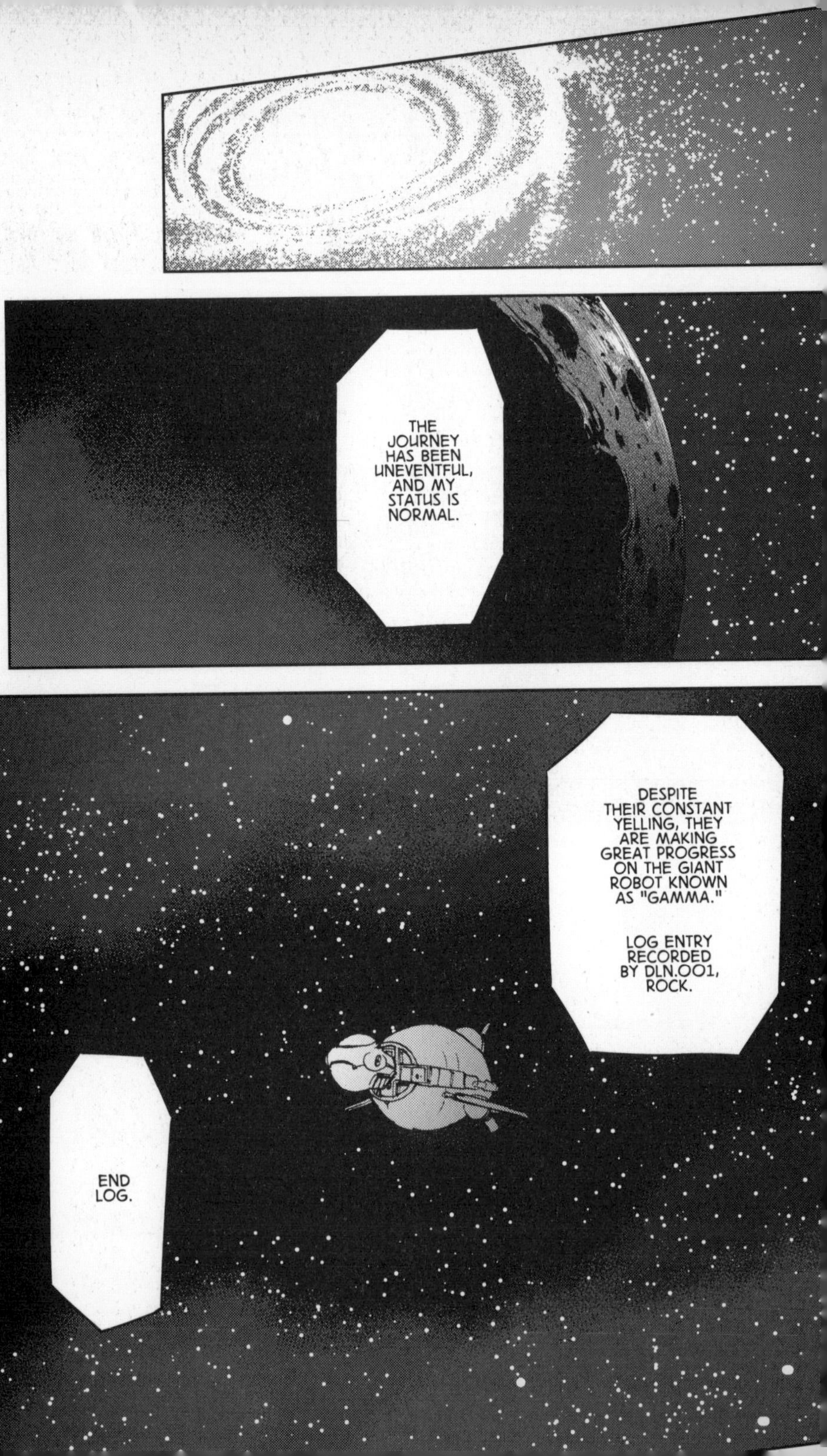
THE JOURNEY HAS BEEN UNEVENTFUL, AND MY STATUS IS NORMAL.
DESPITE THEIR CONSTANT YELLING, THEY ARE MAKING GREAT PROGRESS ON THE GIANT ROBOT KNOWN AS "GAMMA."
LOG ENTRY RECORDED BY DLN.001, ROCK.
END LOG.

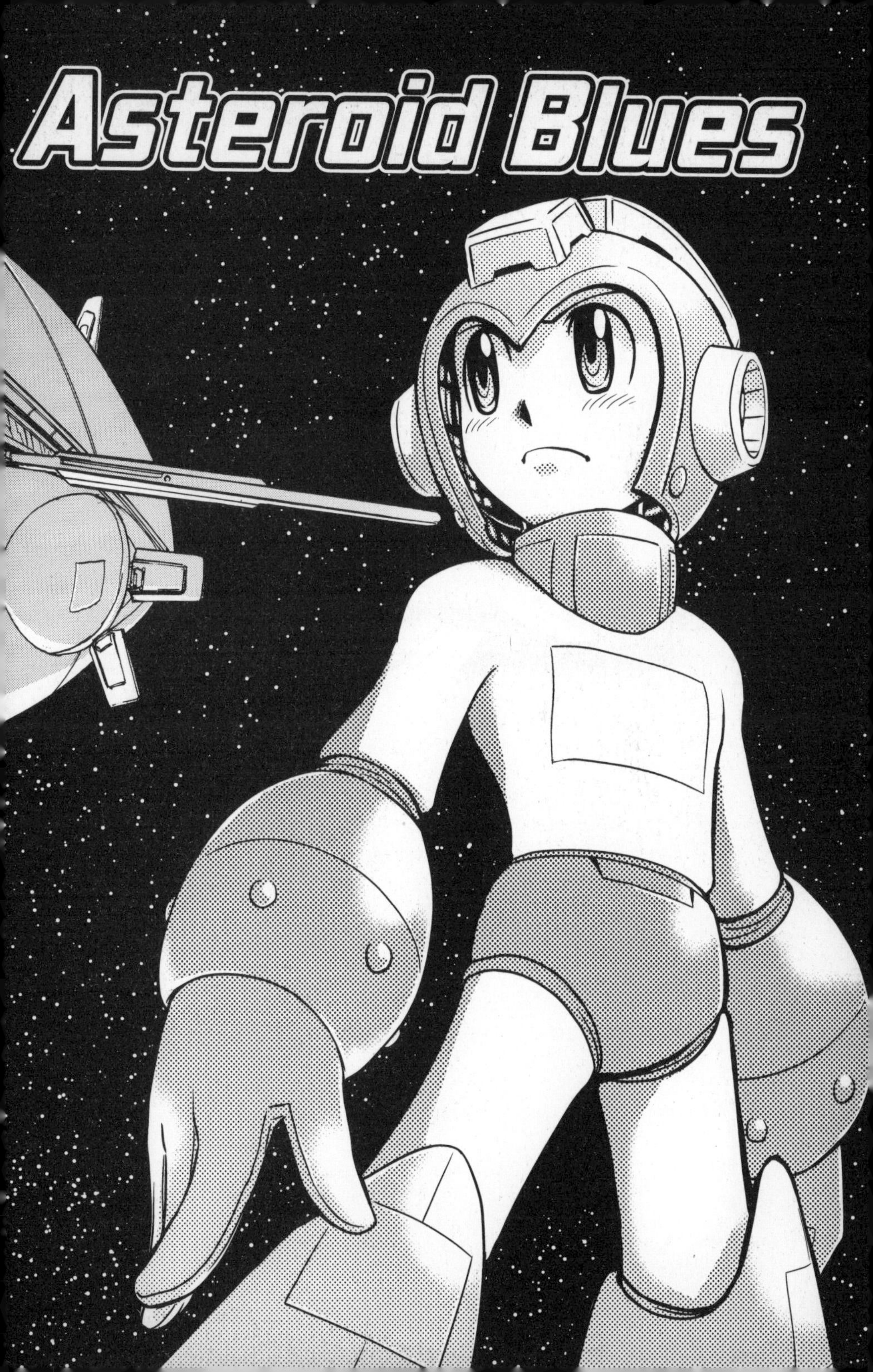
Asteroid Blues

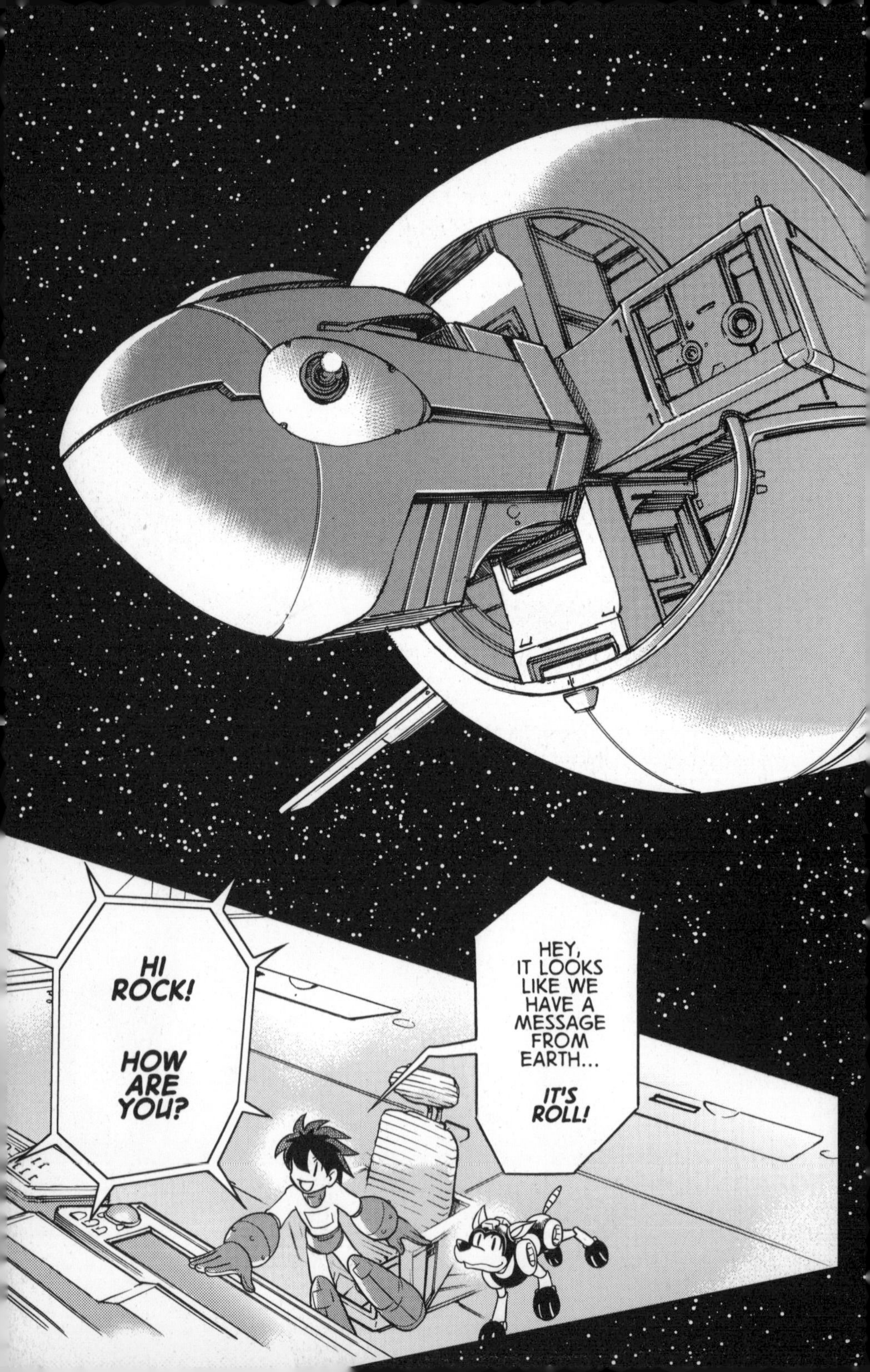
HEY, IT LOOKS LIKE WE HAVE A MESSAGE FROM EARTH... IT'S ROLL!
HI ROCK! HOW ARE YOU?

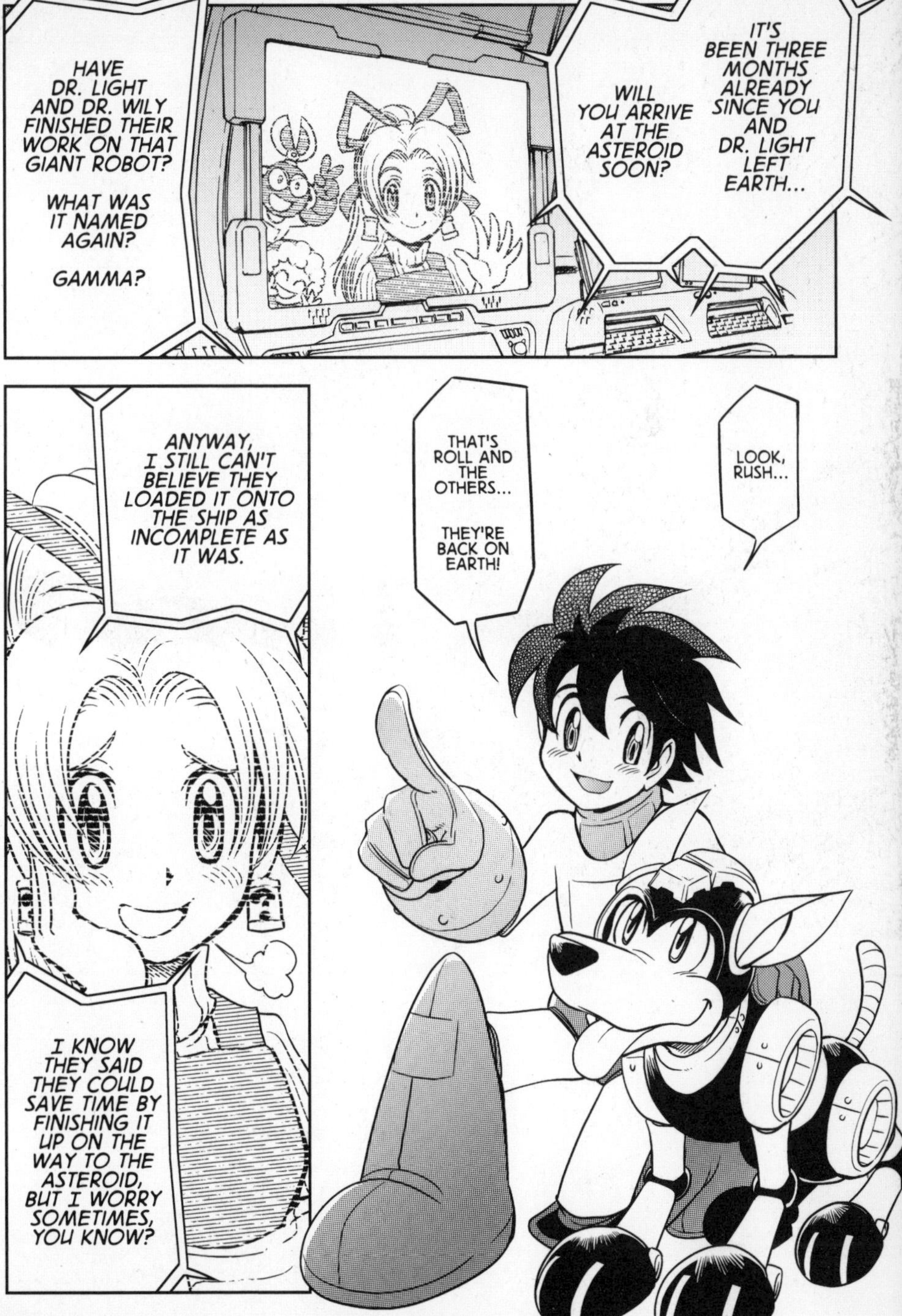
IT'S BEEN THREE MONTHS ALREADY SINCE YOU AND DR. LIGHT LEFT EARTH...
WILL YOU ARRIVE AT THE ASTEROID SOON?
HAVE DR. LIGHT AND DR. WILY FINISHED THEIR WORK ON THAT GIANT ROBOT? WHAT WAS IT NAMED AGAIN? GAMMA?
LOOK, RUSH...
THAT'S ROLL AND THE OTHERS... THEY'RE BACK ON EARTH!
ANYWAY, I STILL CAN'T BELIEVE THEY LOADED IT ONTO THE SHIP AS INCOMPLETE AS IT WAS.
I KNOW THEY SAID THEY COULD SAVE TIME BY FINISHING IT UP ON THE WAY TO THE ASTEROID, BUT I WORRY SOMETIMES, YOU KNOW?

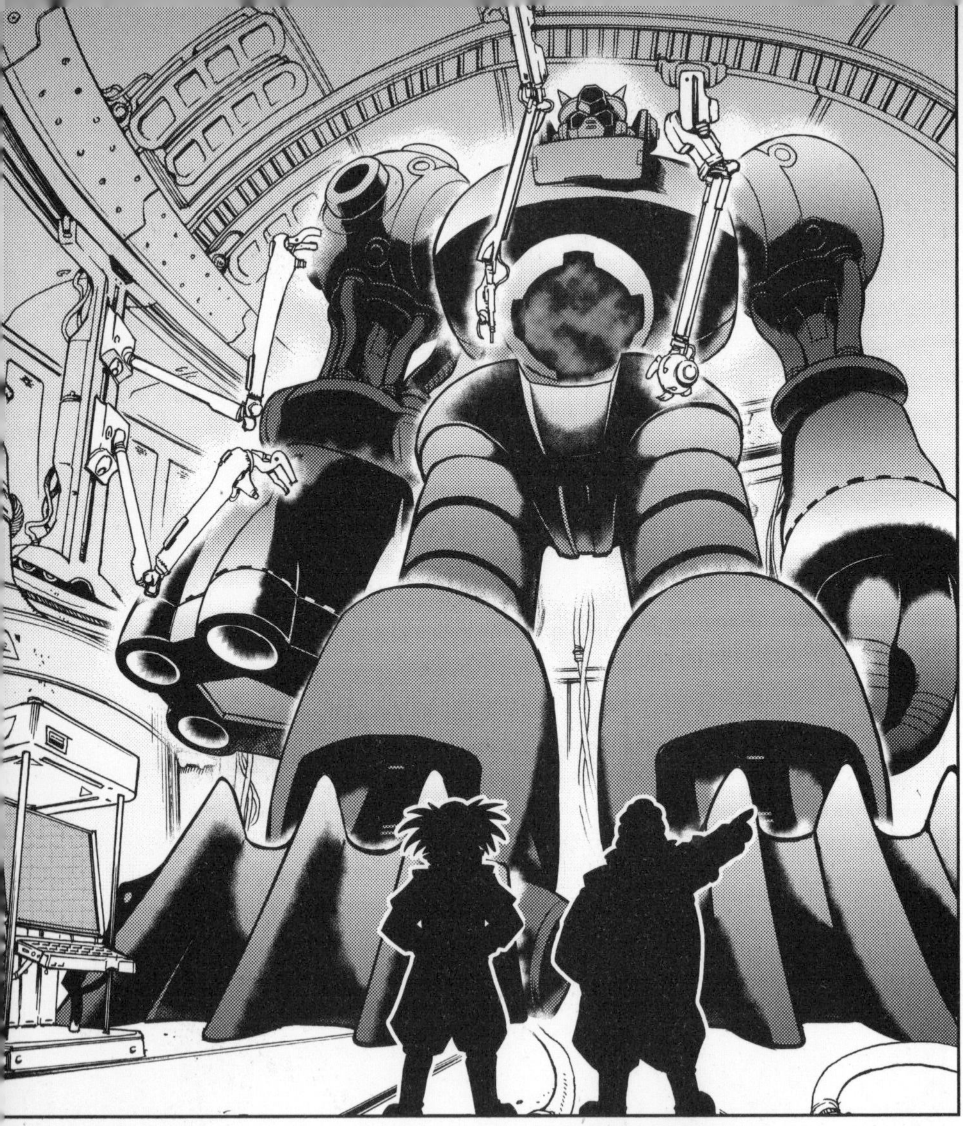

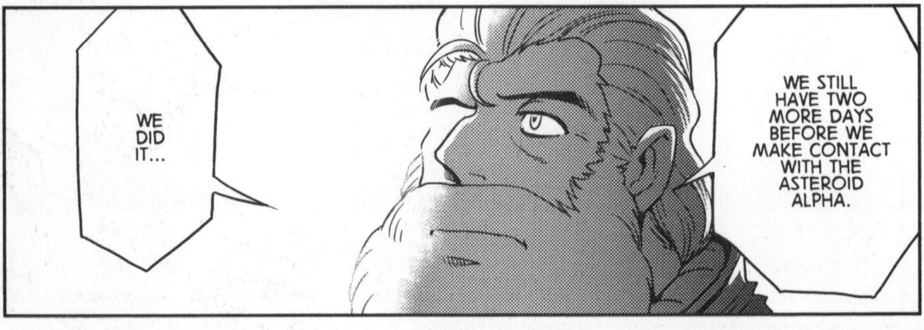
WE STILL HAVE TWO MORE DAYS BEFORE WE MAKE CONTACT WITH THE ASTEROID ALPHA.
WE DID IT...

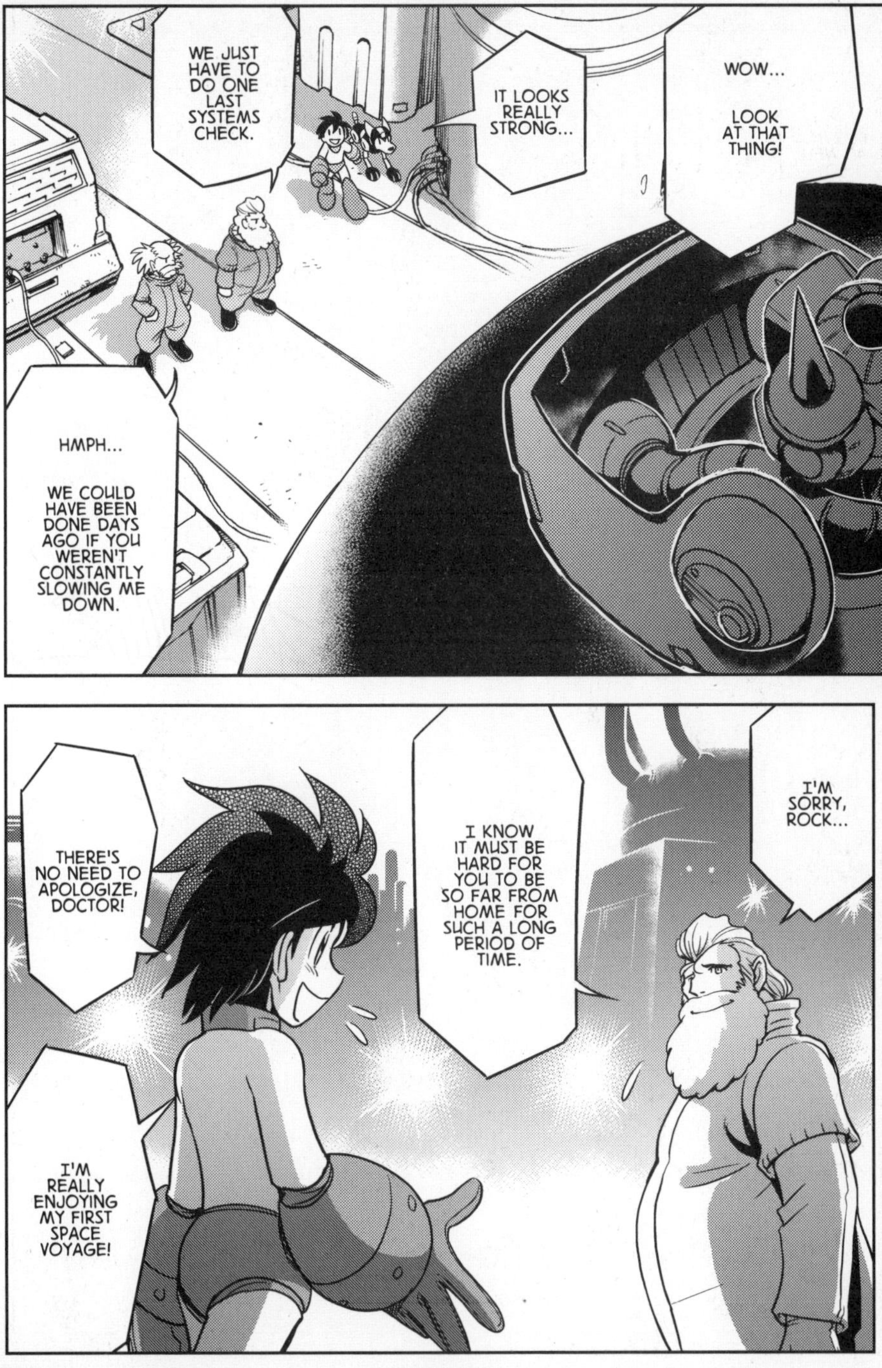
WOW... LOOK AT THAT THING!
IT LOOKS REALLY STRONG...
WE JUST HAVE TO DO ONE LAST SYSTEMS CHECK.
HMPH... WE COULD HAVE BEEN DONE DAYS AGO IF YOU WEREN'T CONSTANTLY SLOWING ME DOWN.
I'M SORRY, ROCK...
I KNOW IT MUST BE HARD FOR YOU TO BE SO FAR FROM HOME FOR SUCH A LONG PERIOD OF TIME.
THERE'S NO NEED TO APOLOGIZE, DOCTOR!
I'M REALLY ENJOYING MY FIRST SPACE VOYAGE!

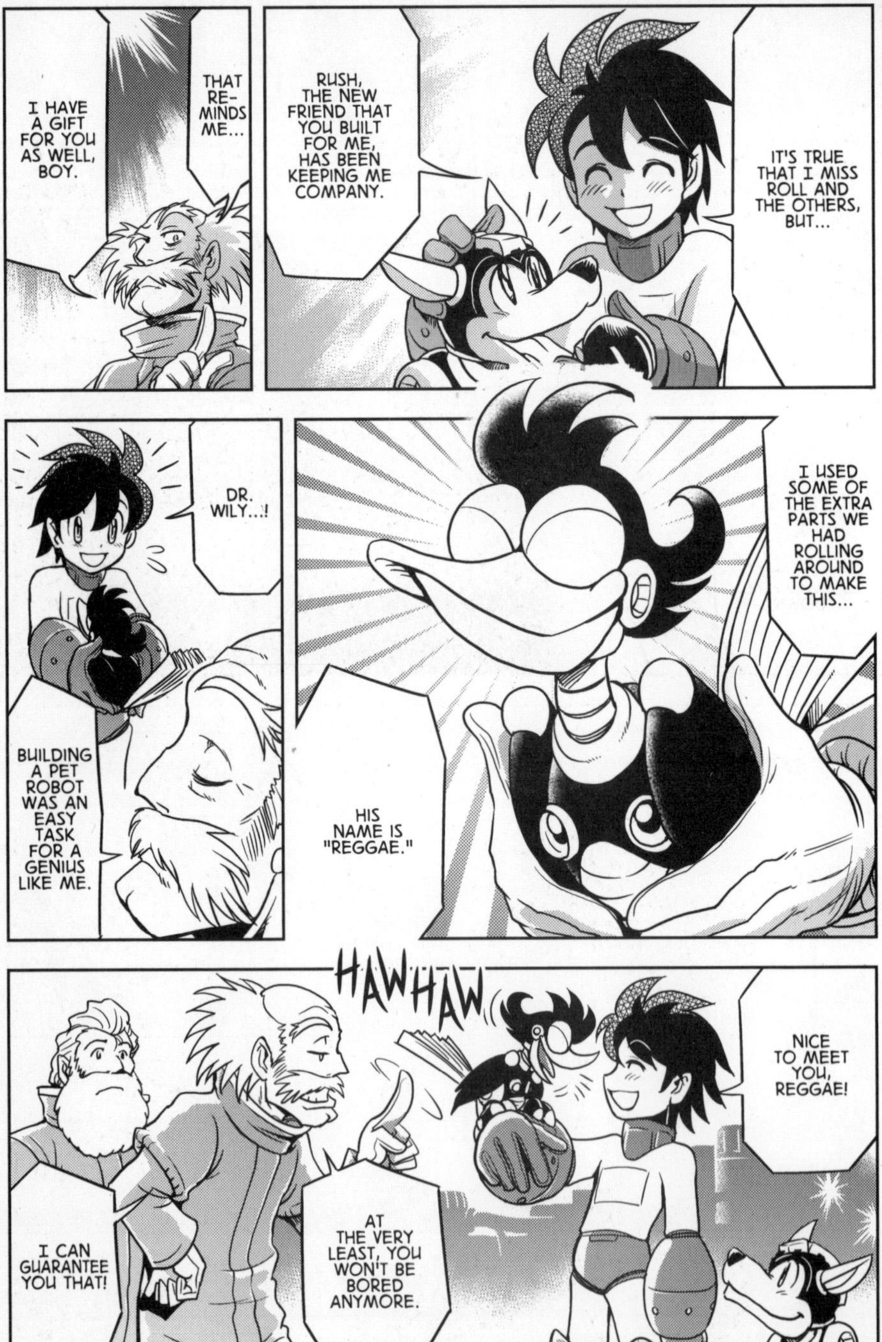
IT'S TRUE THAT I MISS ROLL AND THE OTHERS, BUT...
RUSH, THE NEW FRIEND THAT YOU BUILT FOR ME, HAS BEEN KEEPING ME COMPANY.
THAT RE-MINDS ME...
I HAVE A GIFT FOR YOU AS WELL, BOY.
I USED SOME OF THE EXTRA PARTS WE HAD ROLLING AROUND TO MAKE THIS...
HIS NAME IS "REGGAE."
DR. WILY...!
BUILDING A PET ROBOT WAS AN EASY TASK FOR A GENIUS LIKE ME.
NICE TO MEET YOU, REGGAE!
HAWHAW
AT THE VERY LEAST, YOU WON'T BE BORED ANYMORE.
I CAN GUARANTEE YOU THAT!

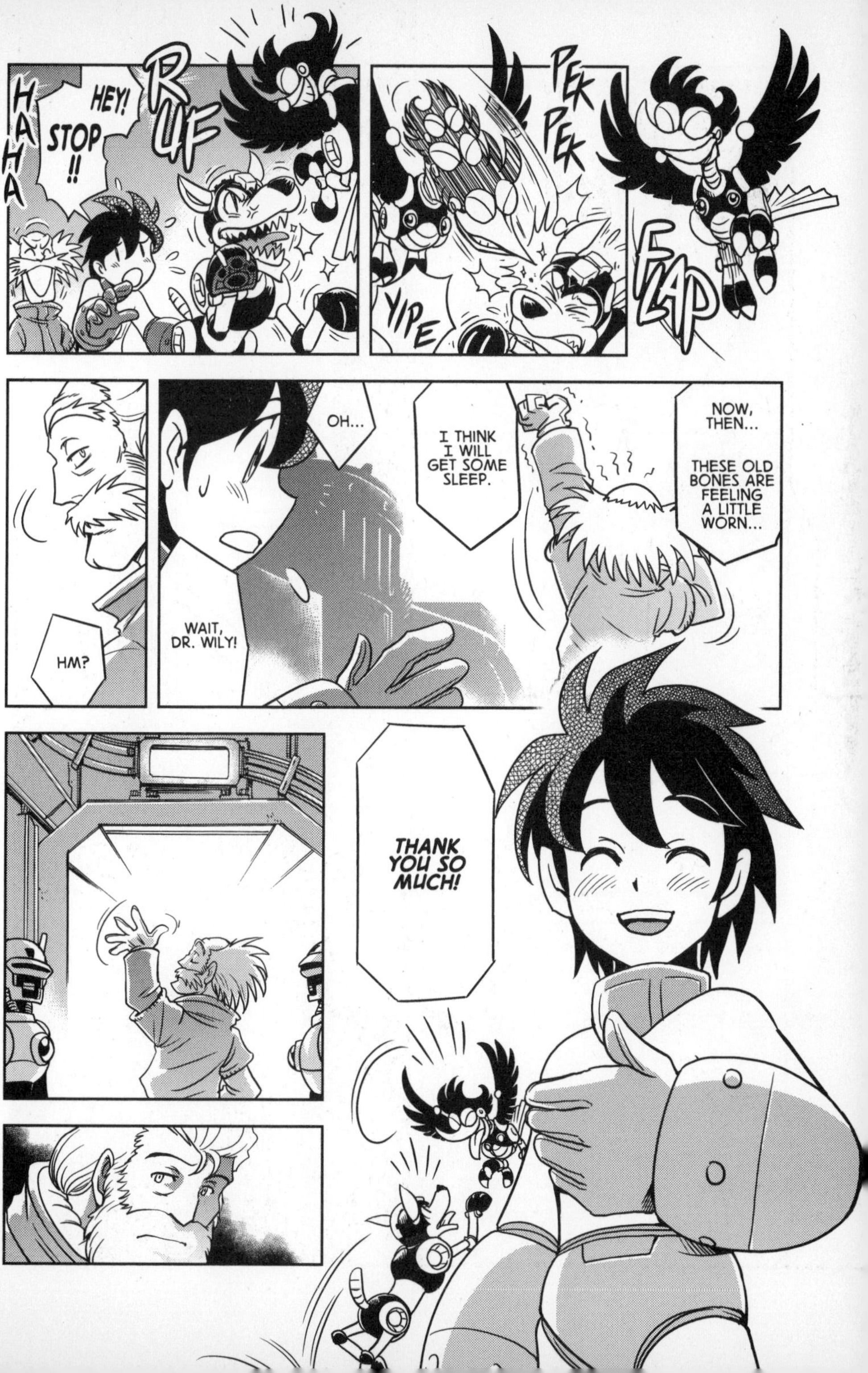
PEK PEK
FLAP
YIPE
RUF
HEY!
STOP !!
HAHA
NOW, THEN...
THESE OLD BONES ARE FEELING A LITTLE WORN...
I THINK I WILL GET SOME SLEEP.
OH...
WAIT, DR. WILY!
HM?
THANK YOU SO MUCH!

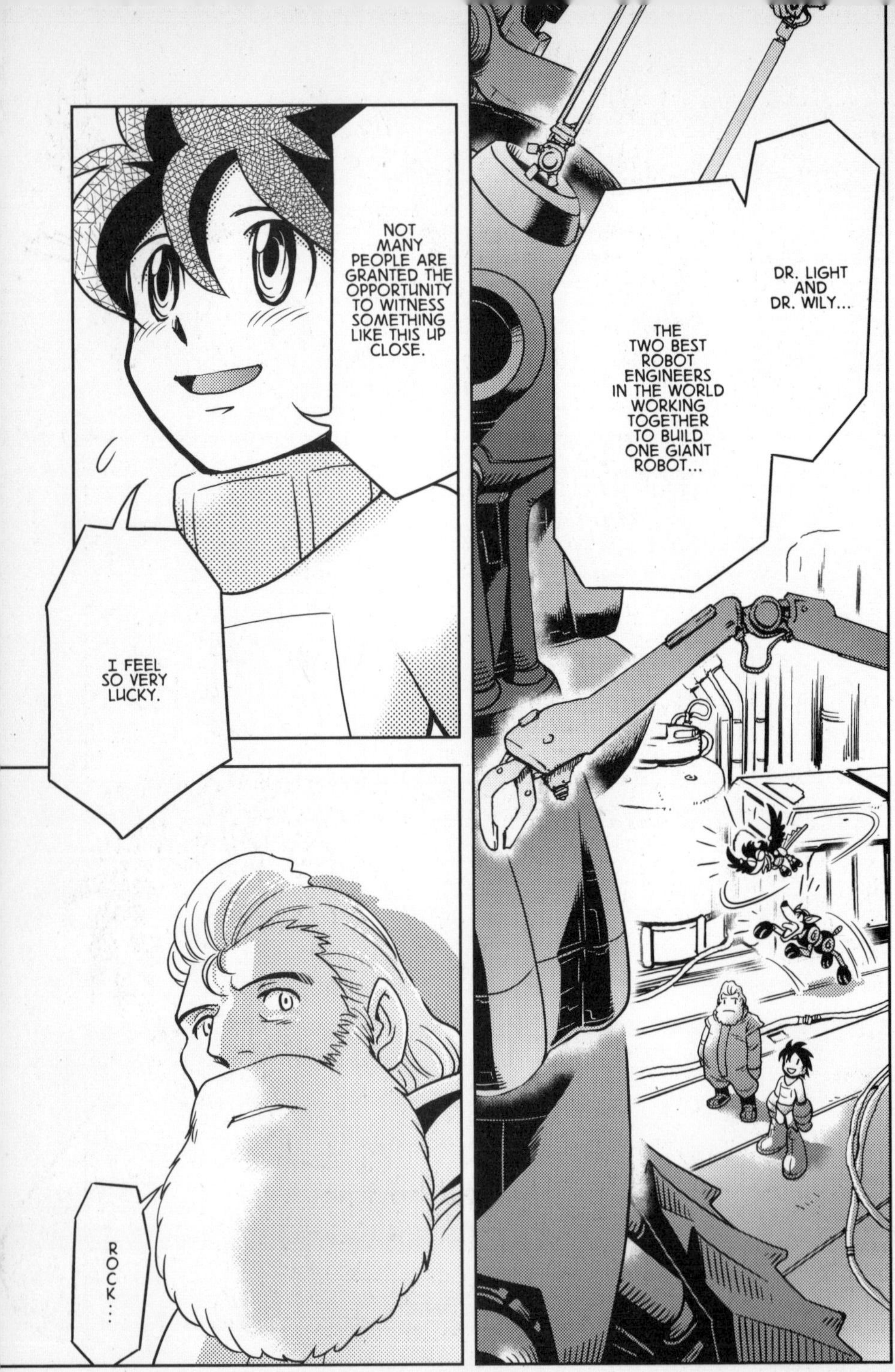
DR. LIGHT AND DR. WILY...
THE TWO BEST ROBOT ENGINEERS IN THE WORLD WORKING TOGETHER TO BUILD ONE GIANT ROBOT...
NOT MANY PEOPLE ARE GRANTED THE OPPORTUNITY TO WITNESS SOMETHING LIKE THIS UP CLOSE.
I FEEL SO VERY LUCKY.
ROCK...

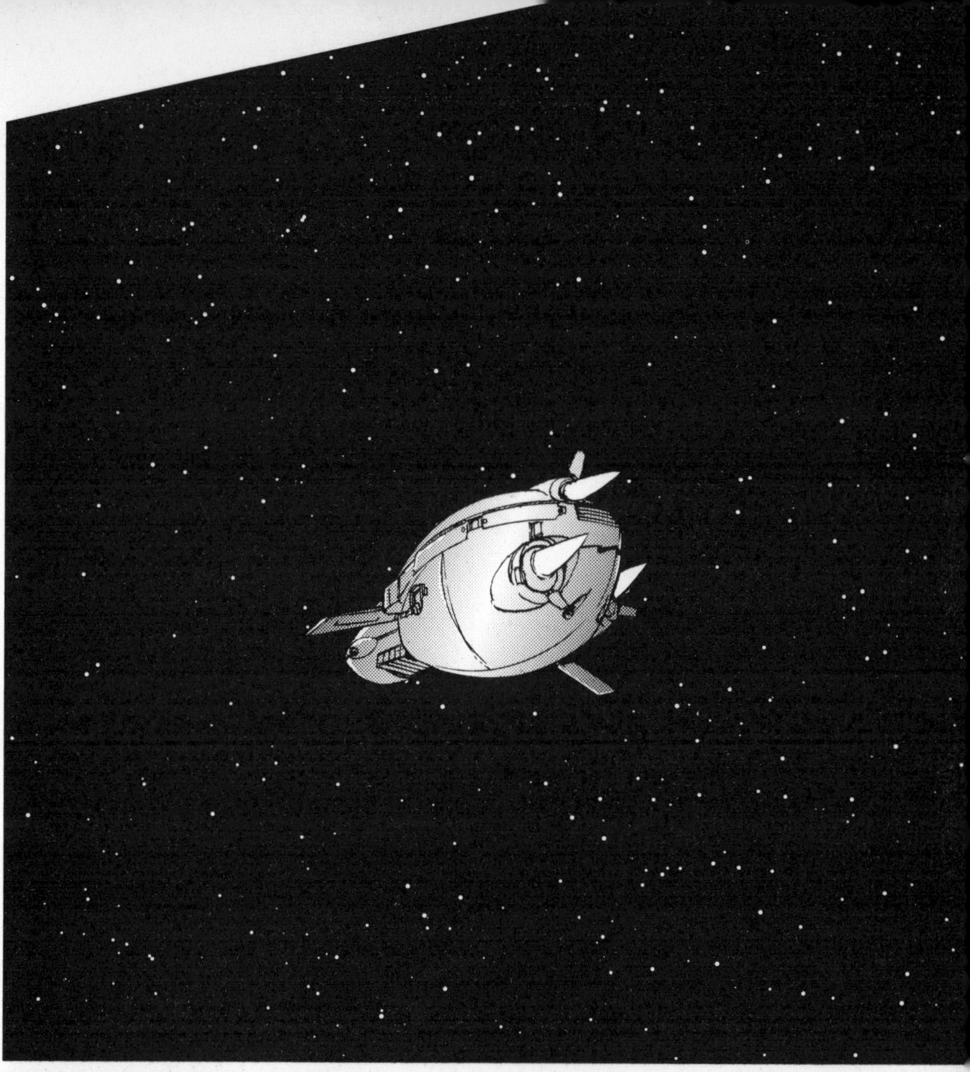
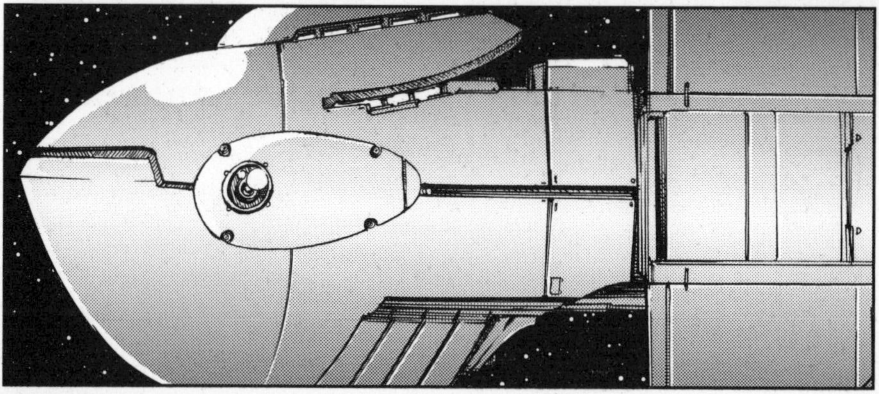

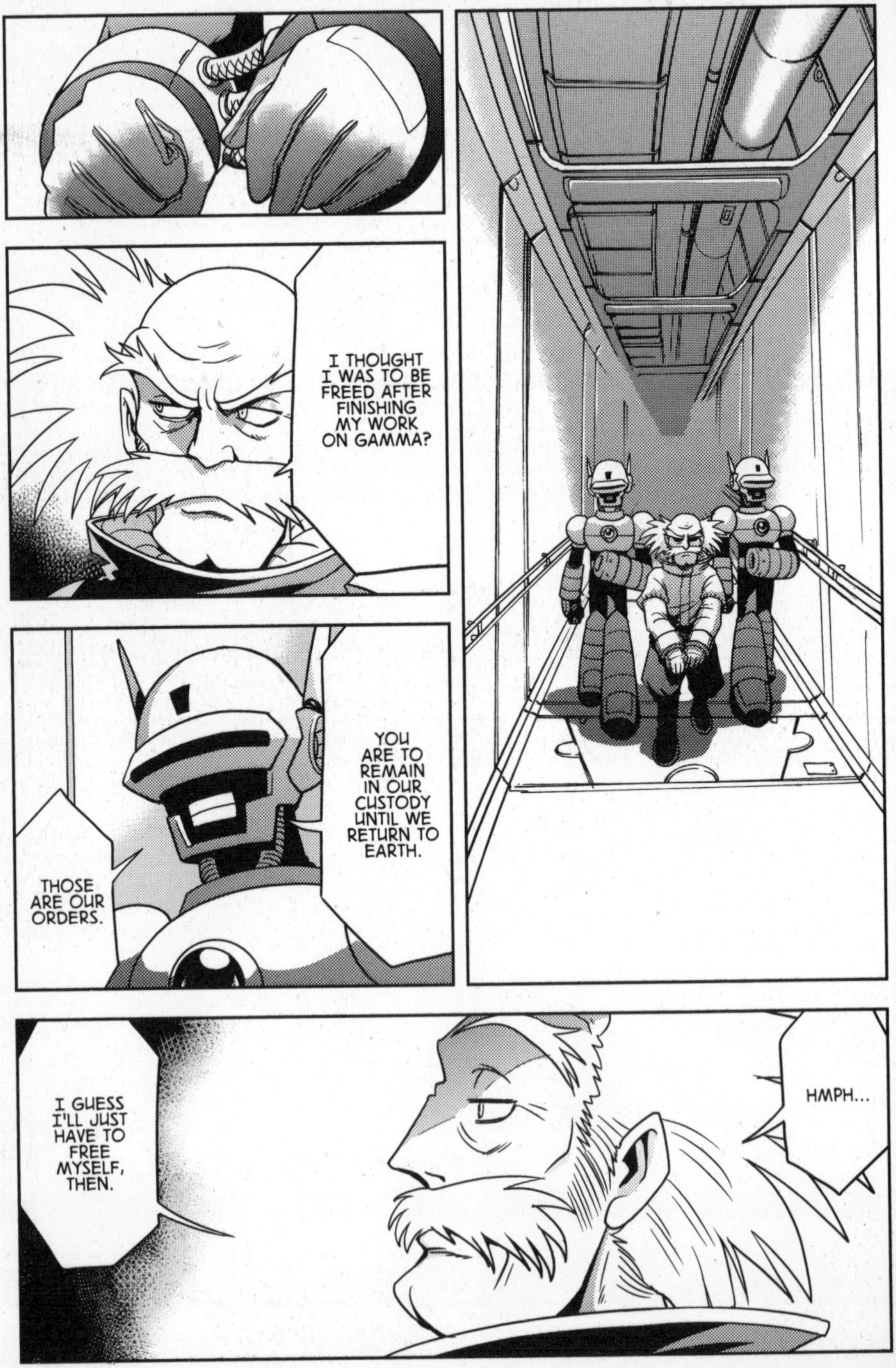
I THOUGHT I WAS TO BE FREED AFTER FINISHING MY WORK ON GAMMA?
YOU ARE TO REMAIN IN OUR CUSTODY UNTIL WE RETURN TO EARTH.
THOSE ARE OUR ORDERS.
HMPH...
I GUESS I'LL JUST HAVE TO FREE MYSELF, THEN.

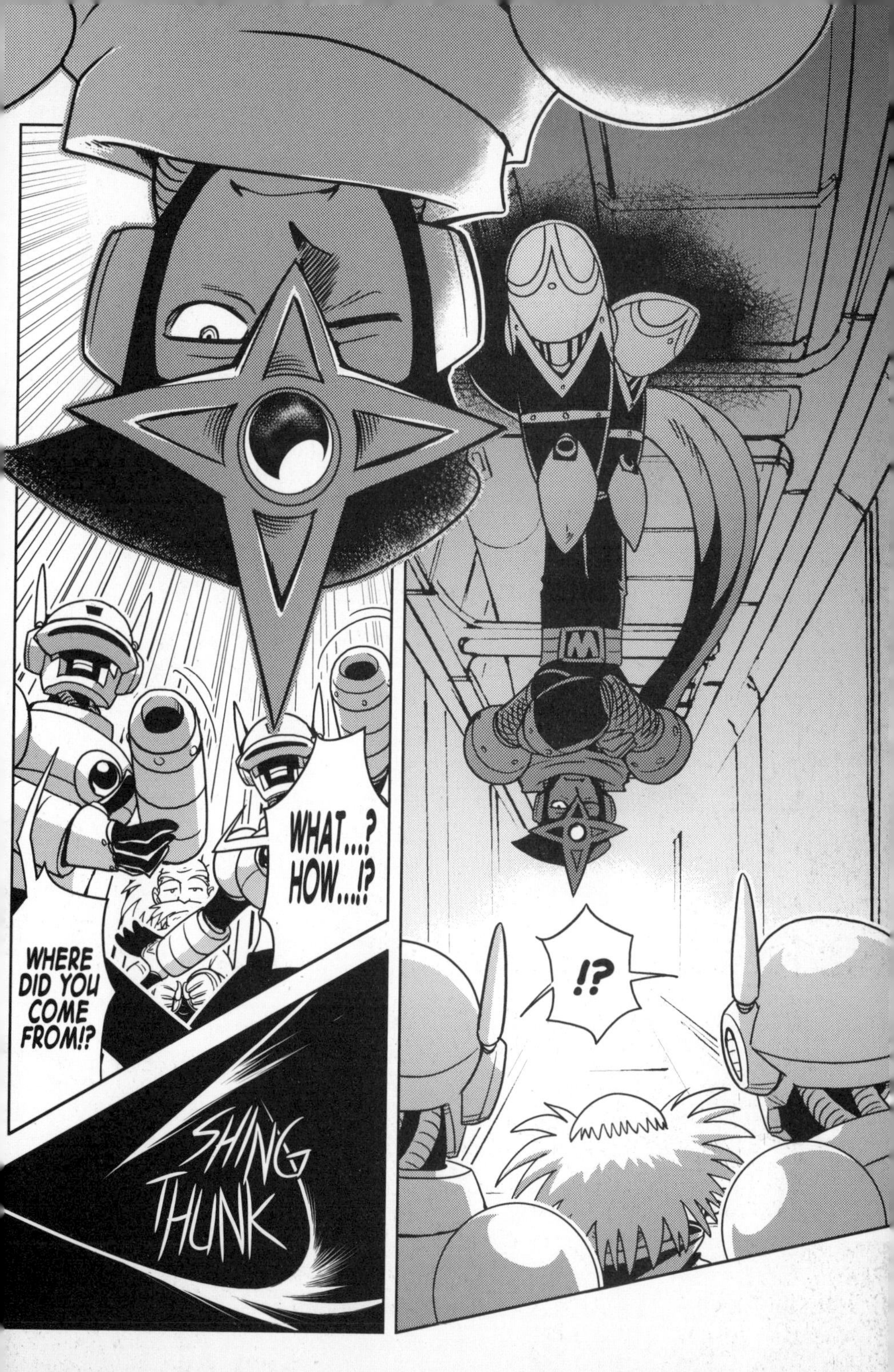
!?
WHAT...? HOW...!?
WHERE DID YOU COME FROM!?
SHING
THUNK

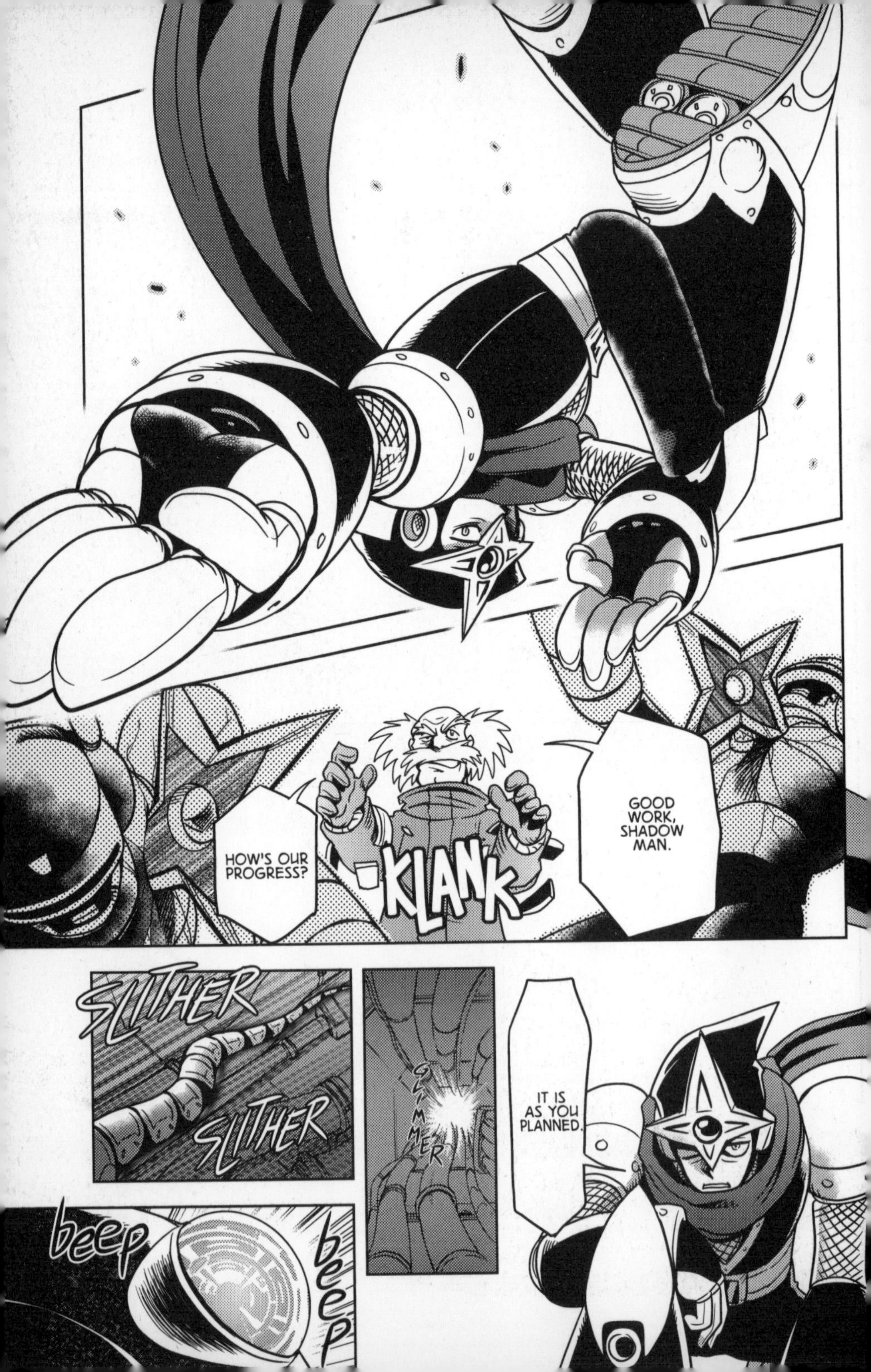
GOOD WORK, SHADOW MAN.
HOW'S OUR PROGRESS?
KLANK
IT IS AS YOU PLANNED.
GLIMMER
SLITHER
SLITHER
beep
beep

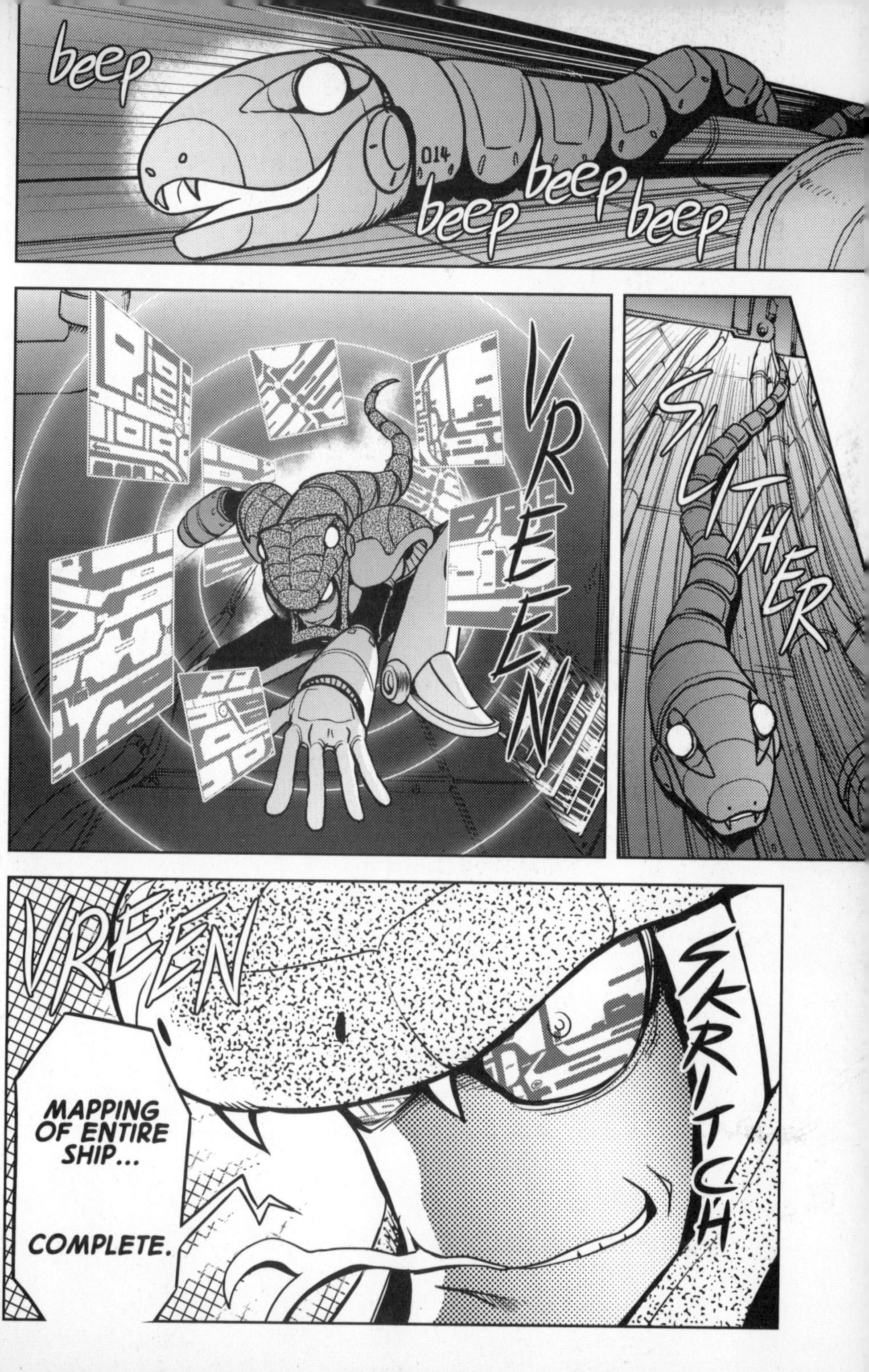
beep
014
beep beep
beep beep
SLITHER
VREEEN
SKRITCH
VREEN
MAPPING OF ENTIRE SHIP...
COMPLETE.

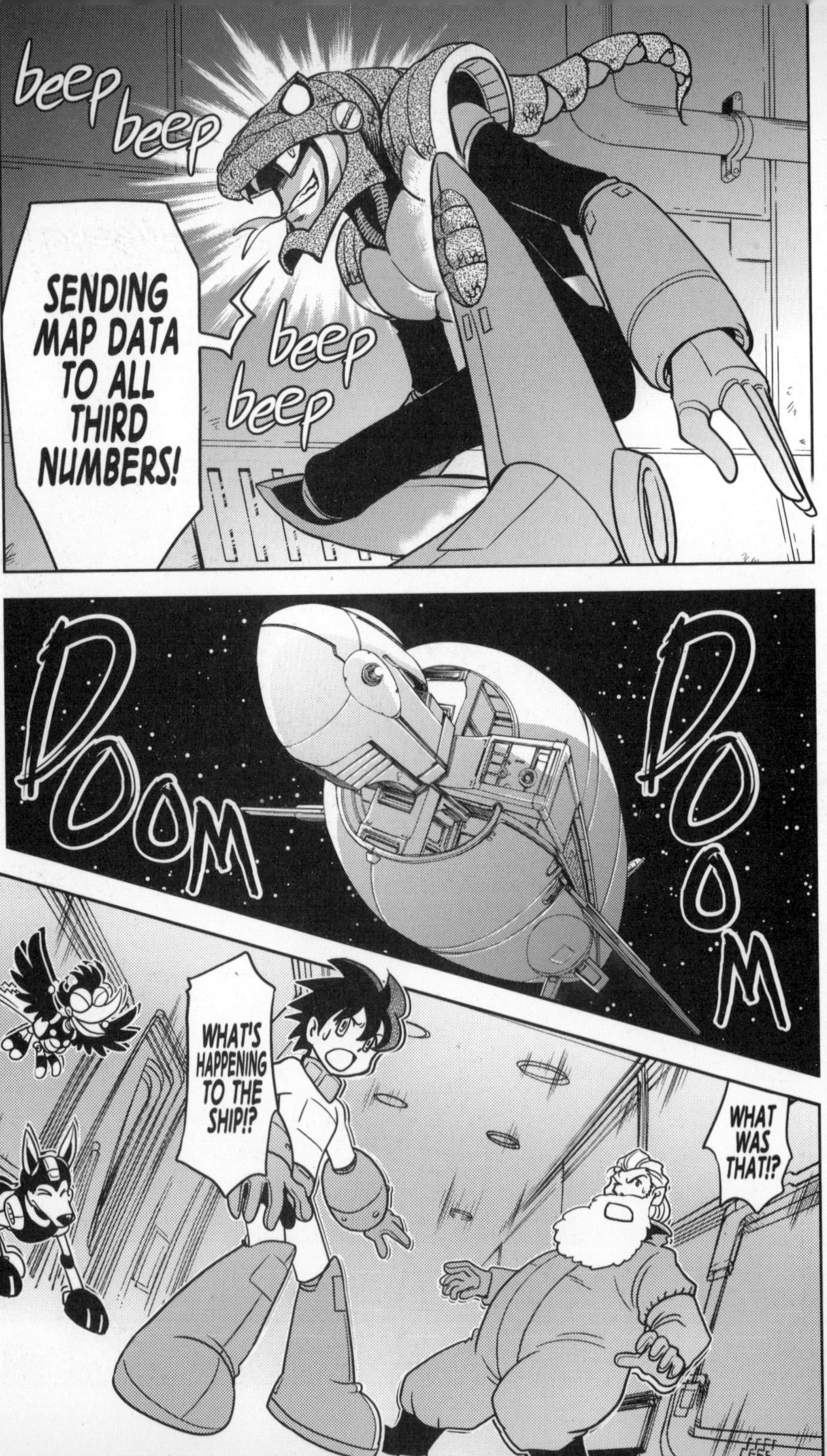
beep beep
SENDING MAP DATA TO ALL THIRD NUMBERS!
beep beep
DOOM
DOOM
WHAT WAS THAT!?
WHAT'S HAPPENING TO THE SHIP!?

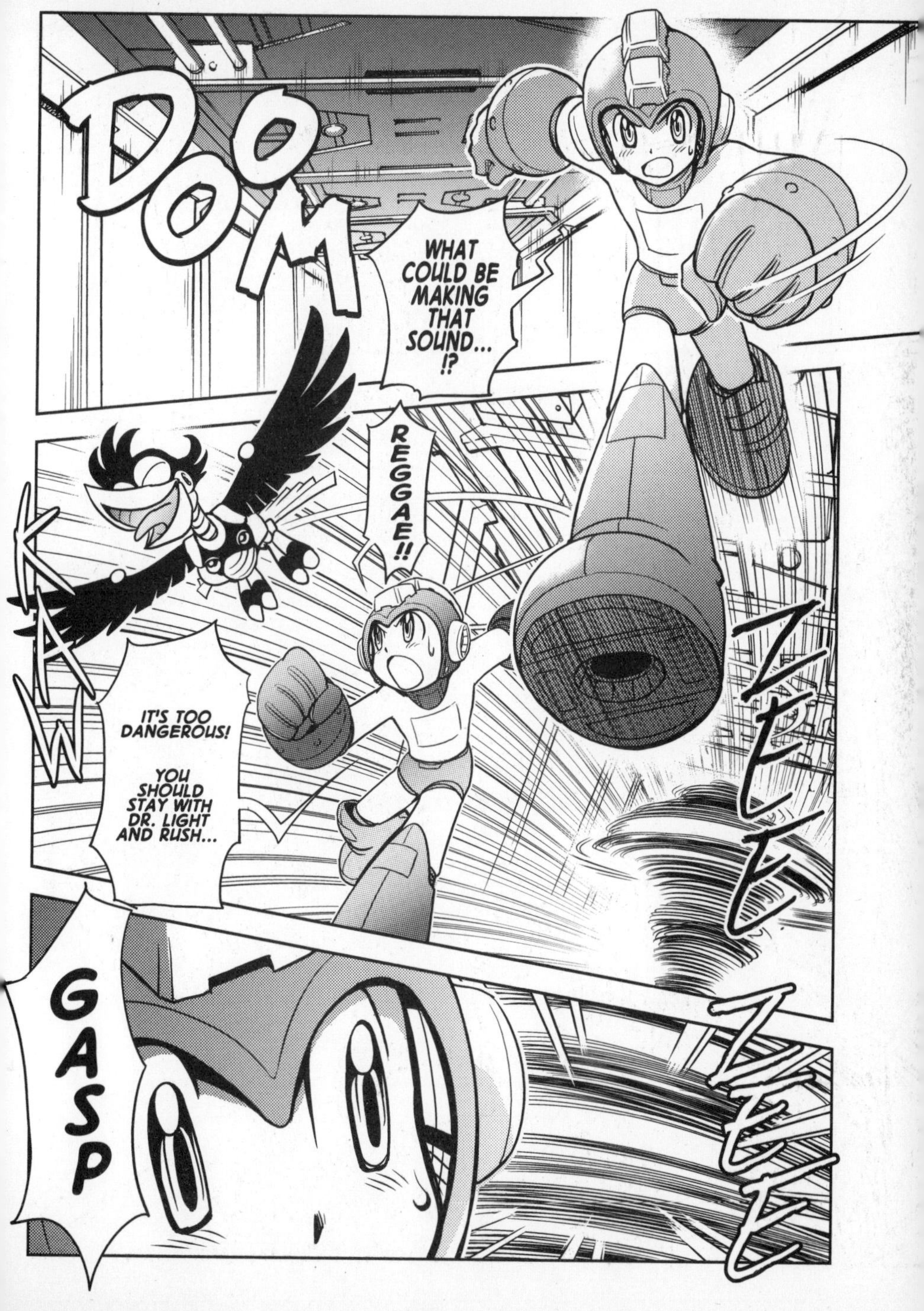
DOOM
WHAT COULD BE MAKING THAT SOUND...!?
ZEEE
REGGAE!!
KAW
IT'S TOO DANGEROUS!
YOU SHOULD STAY WITH DR. LIGHT AND RUSH...
ZEEEE
GASP

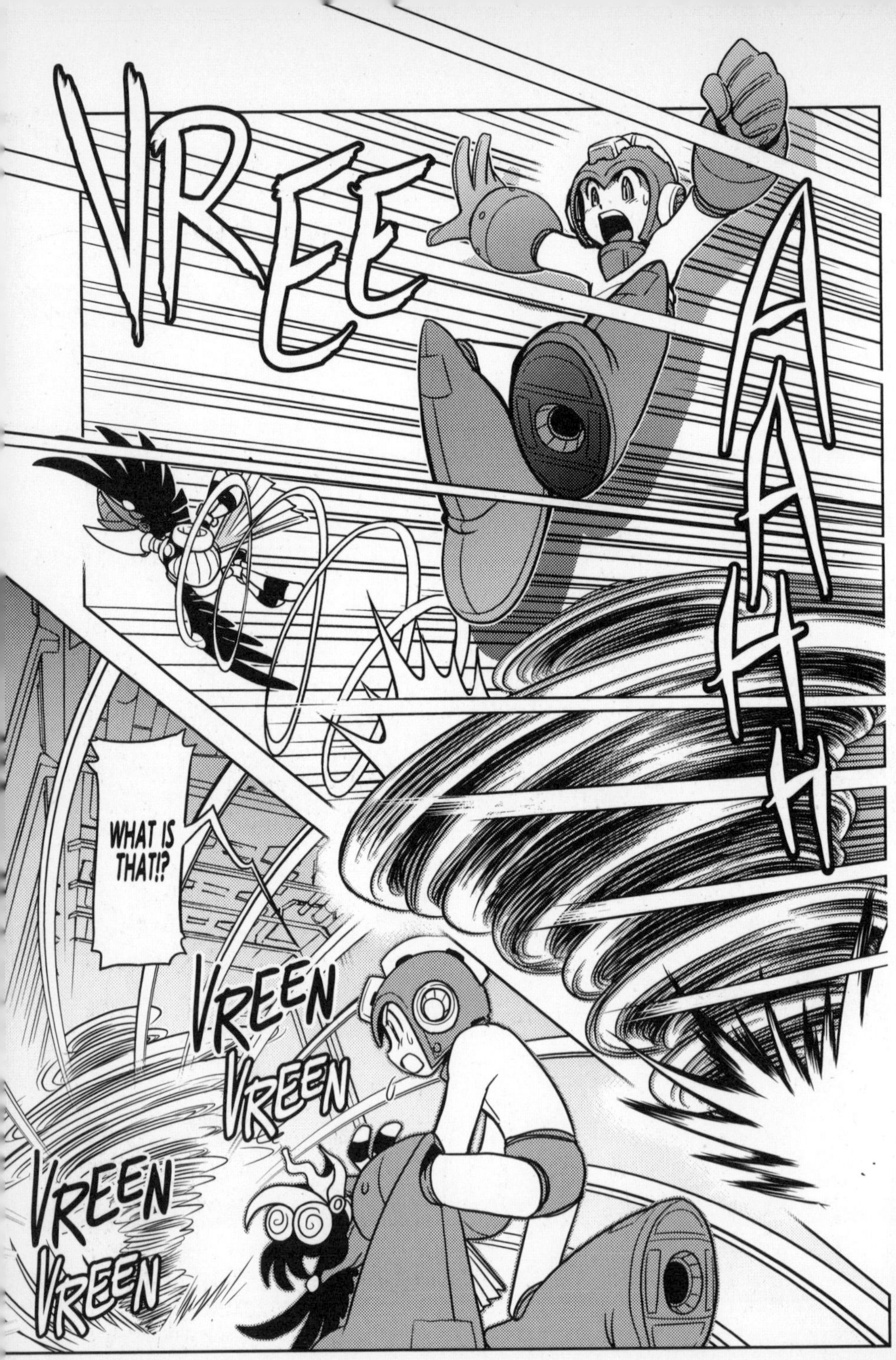
VREE
AAAHHH
VREEN
VREEN
WHAT IS THAT!?
VREEN
VREEN

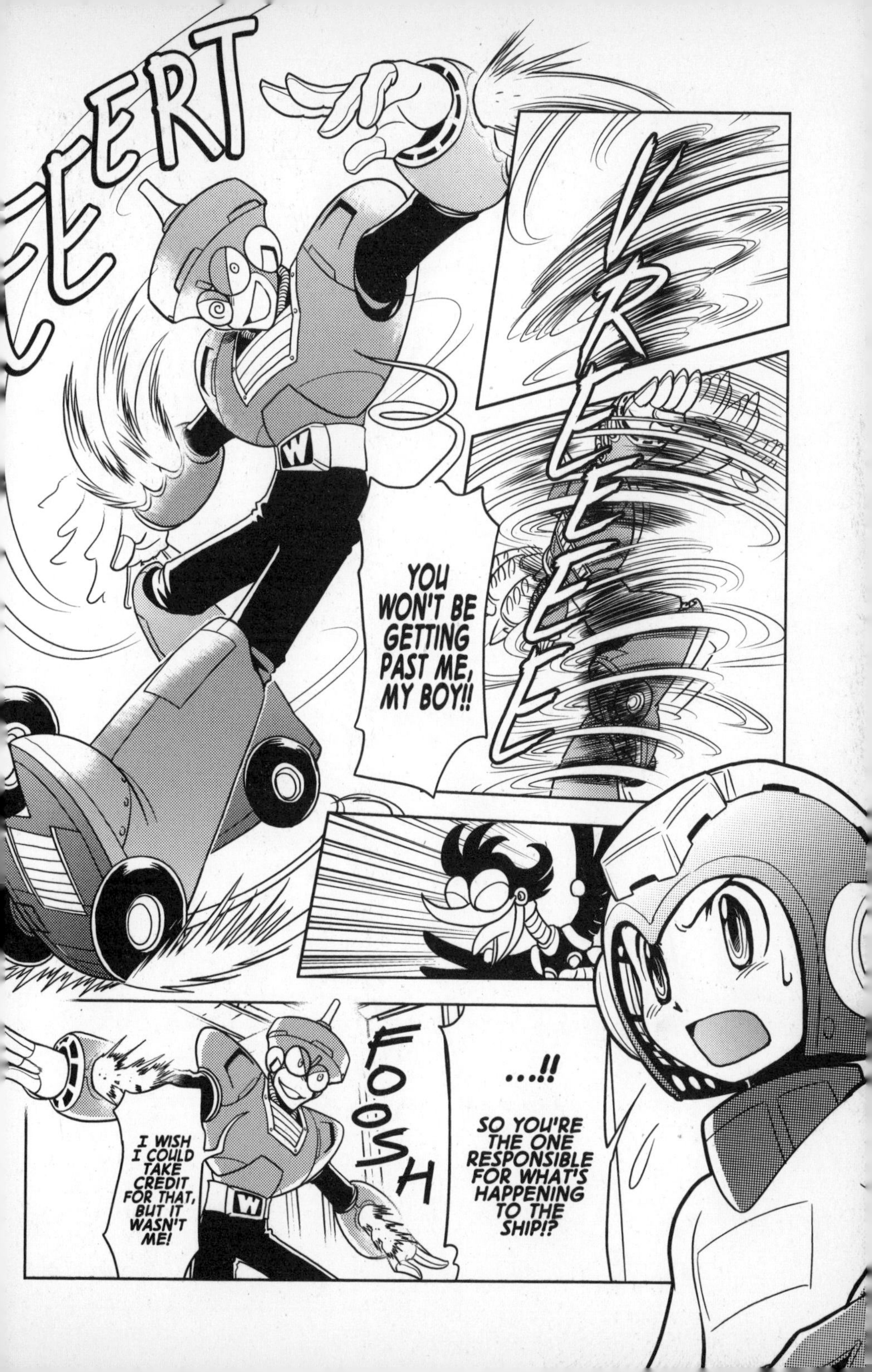
VREEEEEE
EEERT
YOU WON'T BE GETTING PAST ME, MY BOY!!
...!!
SO YOU'RE THE ONE RESPONSIBLE FOR WHAT'S HAPPENING TO THE SHIP!?
FOOSH
I WISH I COULD TAKE CREDIT FOR THAT, BUT IT WASN'T ME!

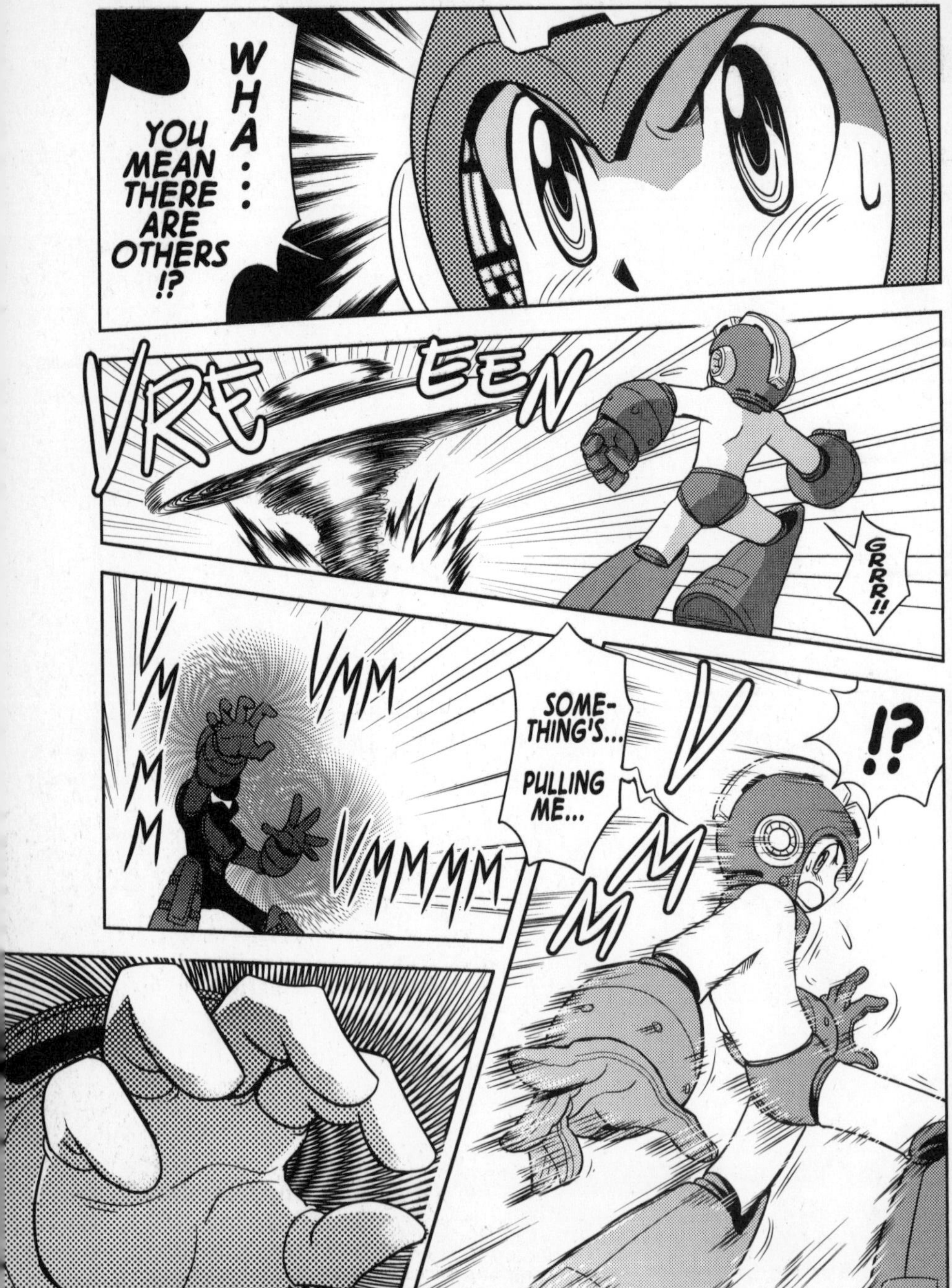
WHA...
YOU MEAN THERE ARE OTHERS!?
VRE—EEN
GRRR!!
!?
SOME-THING'S... PULLING ME...
VMMM
VMM
VMMMM
VMMMMM

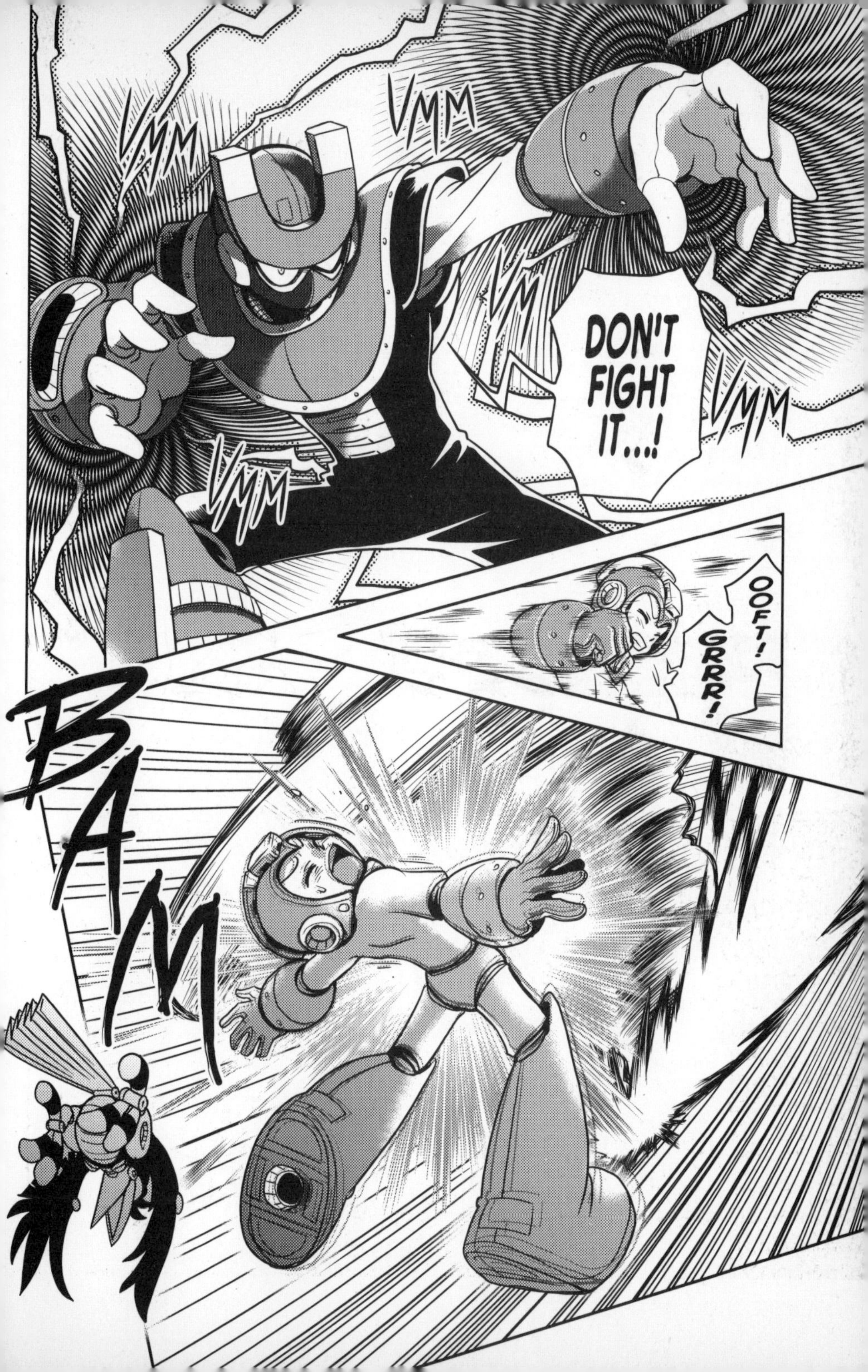
VMM
VMM
DON'T FIGHT IT...!
VMM
VMM
VMM
OOFT!
GRRR!
BAM

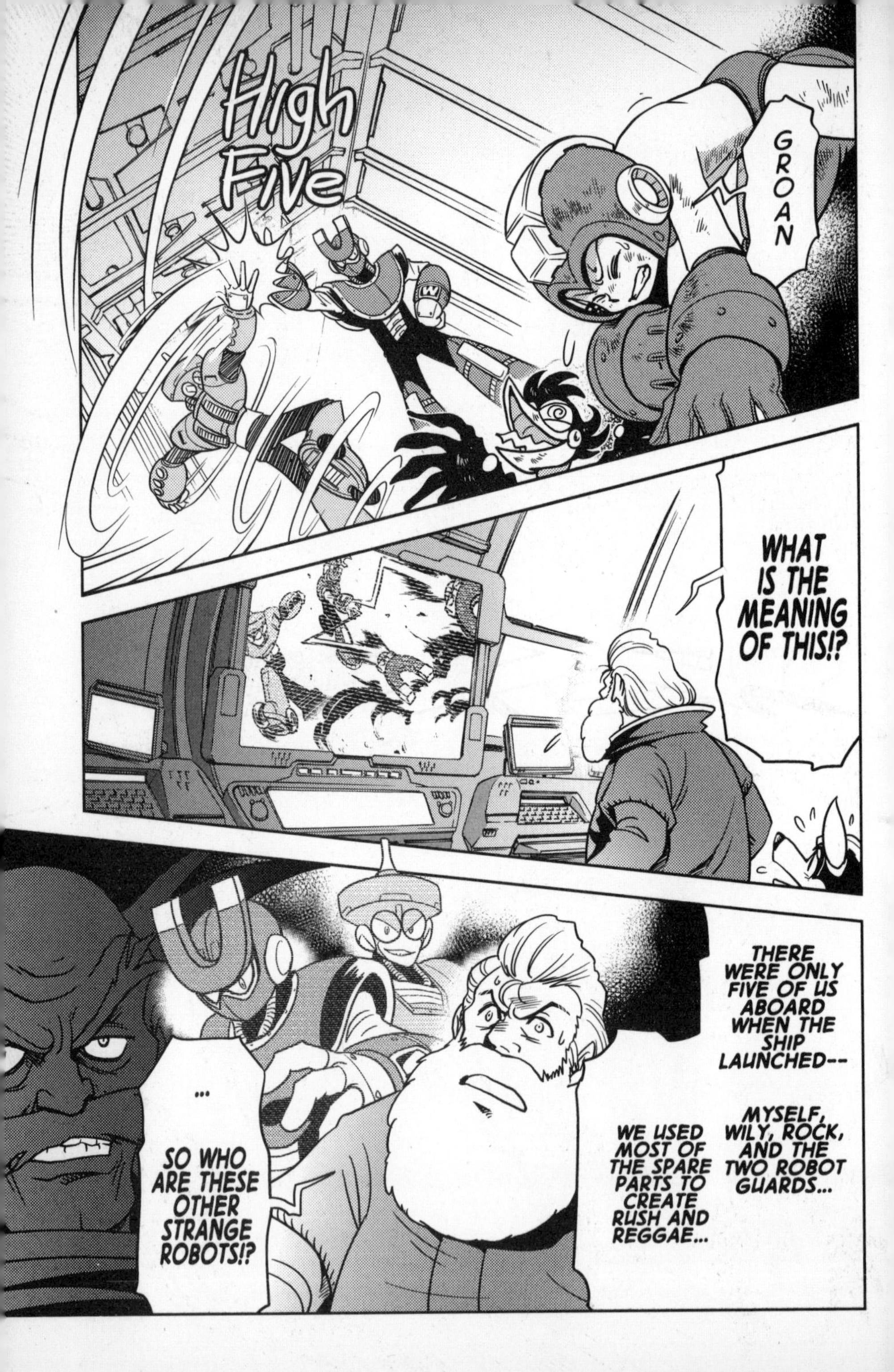
GROAN
High Five
WHAT IS THE MEANING OF THIS!?
THERE WERE ONLY FIVE OF US ABOARD WHEN THE SHIP LAUNCHED--
MYSELF, WILY, ROCK, AND THE TWO ROBOT GUARDS...
WE USED MOST OF THE SPARE PARTS TO CREATE RUSH AND REGGAE...
SO WHO ARE THESE OTHER STRANGE ROBOTS!?
...

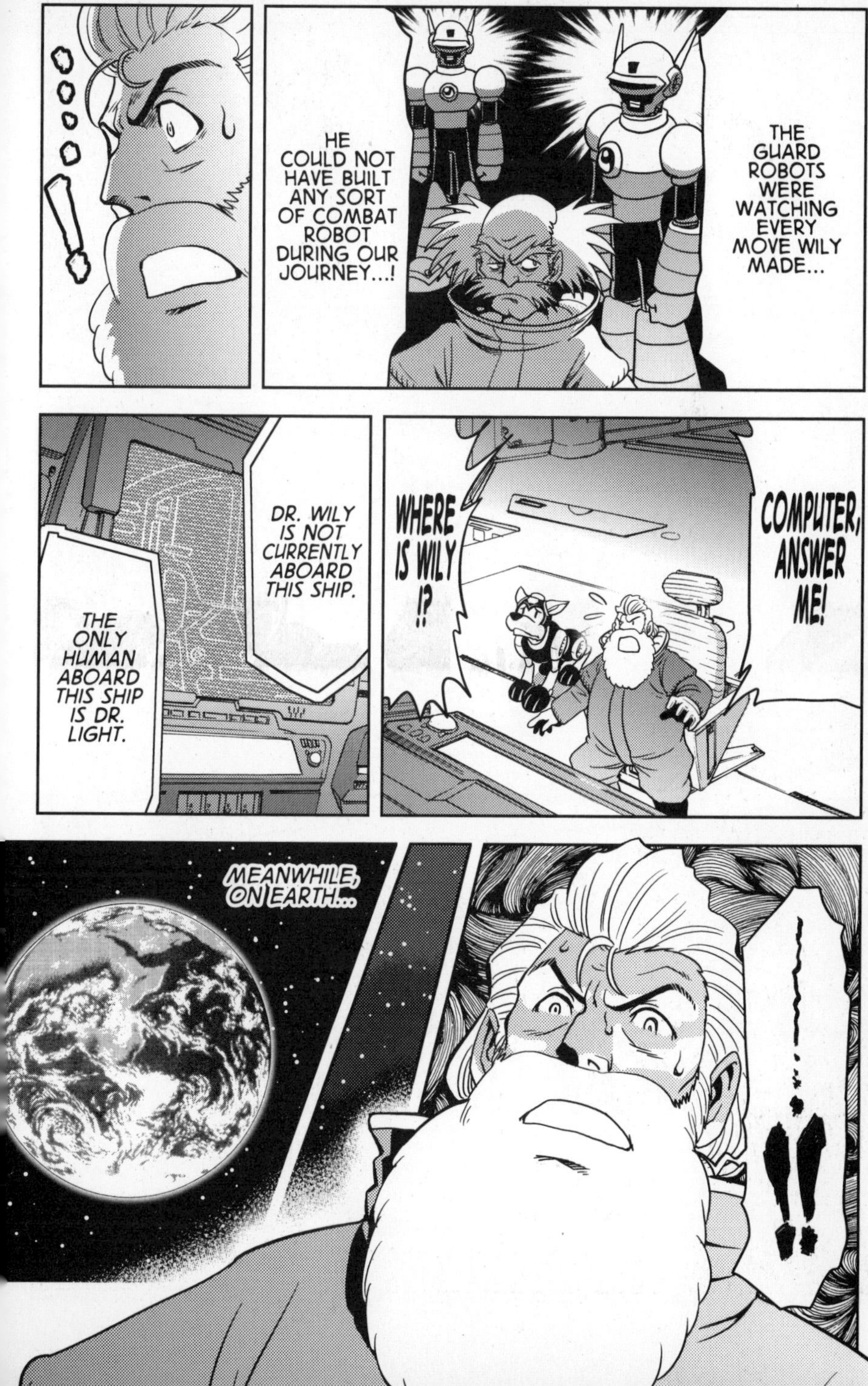
THE GUARD ROBOTS WERE WATCHING EVERY MOVE WILY MADE...
HE COULD NOT HAVE BUILT ANY SORT OF COMBAT ROBOT DURING OUR JOURNEY...!
COMPUTER, ANSWER ME!
WHERE IS WILY !?
DR. WILY IS NOT CURRENTLY ABOARD THIS SHIP.
THE ONLY HUMAN ABOARD THIS SHIP IS DR. LIGHT.
!!
MEANWHILE, ON EARTH...

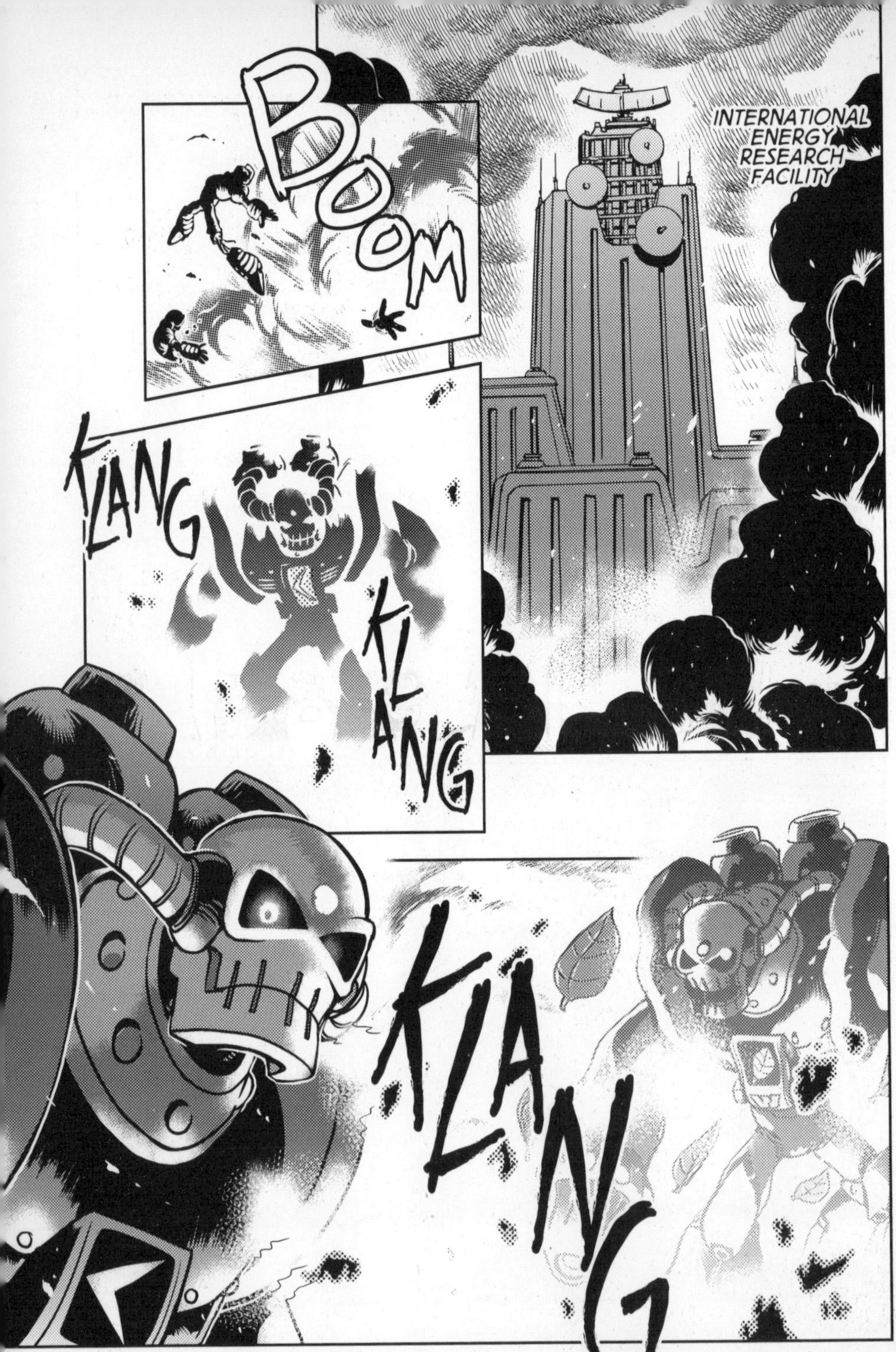

INTERNATIONAL ENERGY RESEARCH FACILITY
BOOM
KLANG
KLANG
KLANG

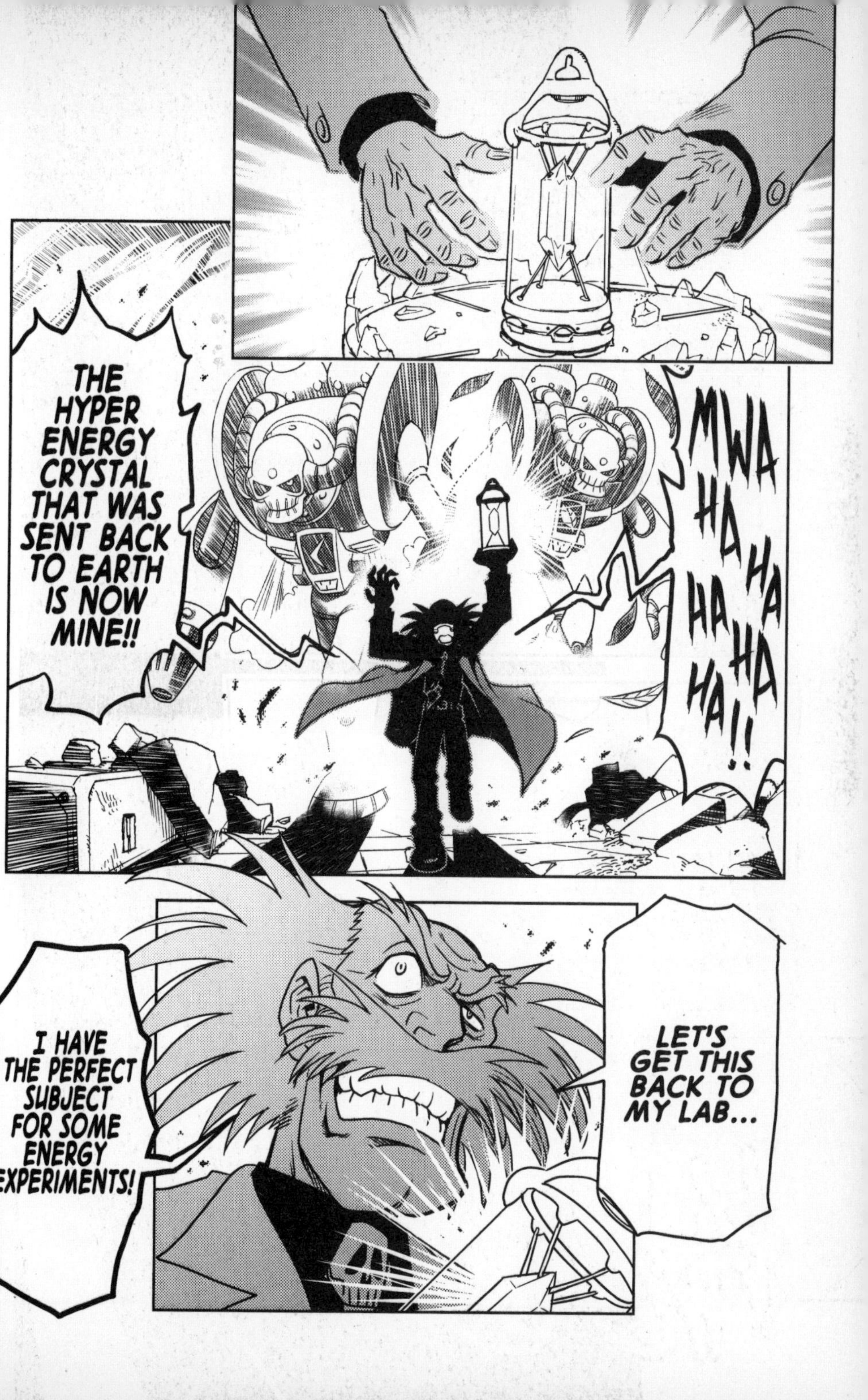
MWA HA HA HA HA HA HA!!
THE HYPER ENERGY CRYSTAL THAT WAS SENT BACK TO EARTH IS NOW MINE!!
LET'S GET THIS BACK TO MY LAB...
I HAVE THE PERFECT SUBJECT FOR SOME ENERGY EXPERIMENTS!

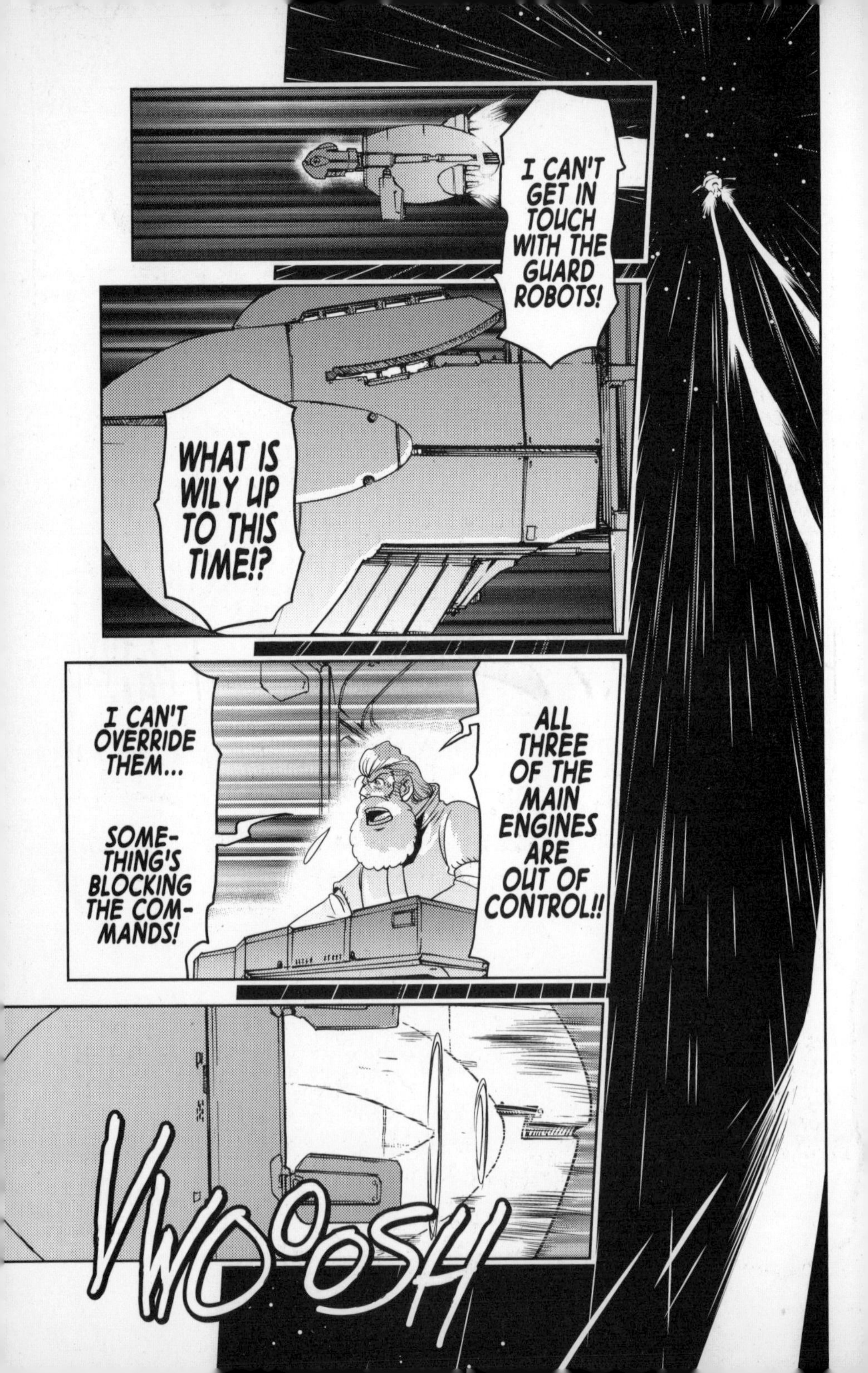
I CAN'T GET IN TOUCH WITH THE GUARD ROBOTS!
WHAT IS WILY UP TO THIS TIME!?
ALL THREE OF THE MAIN ENGINES ARE OUT OF CONTROL!!
I CAN'T OVERRIDE THEM...
SOME-THING'S BLOCKING THE COM-MANDS!
VWOOOSH

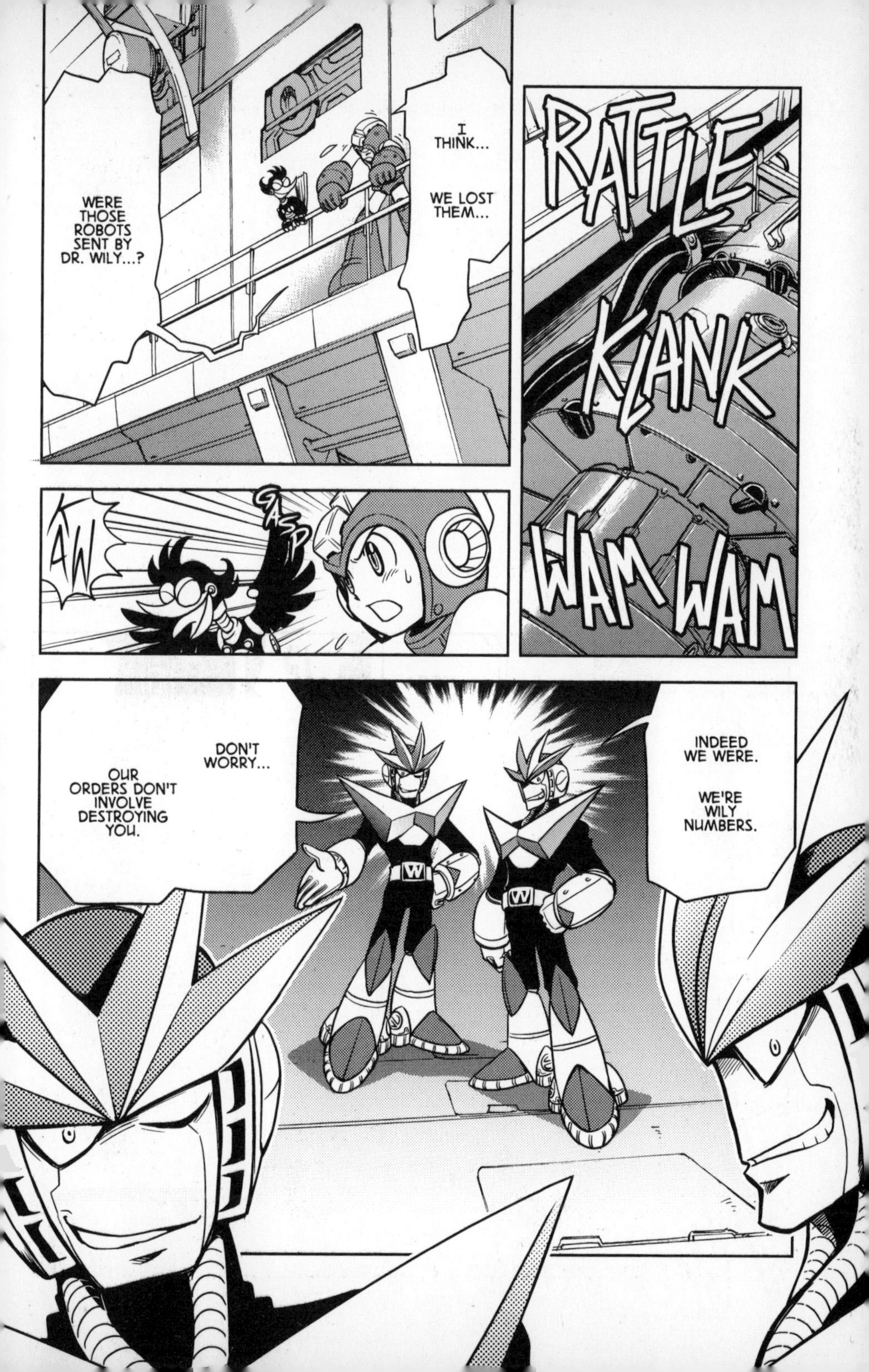
RATTLE
KLANK
WAM WAM
I THINK...
WE LOST THEM...
WERE THOSE ROBOTS SENT BY DR. WILY...?
GASP
KAW
INDEED WE WERE.
WE'RE WILY NUMBERS.
DON'T WORRY...
OUR ORDERS DON'T INVOLVE DESTROYING YOU.

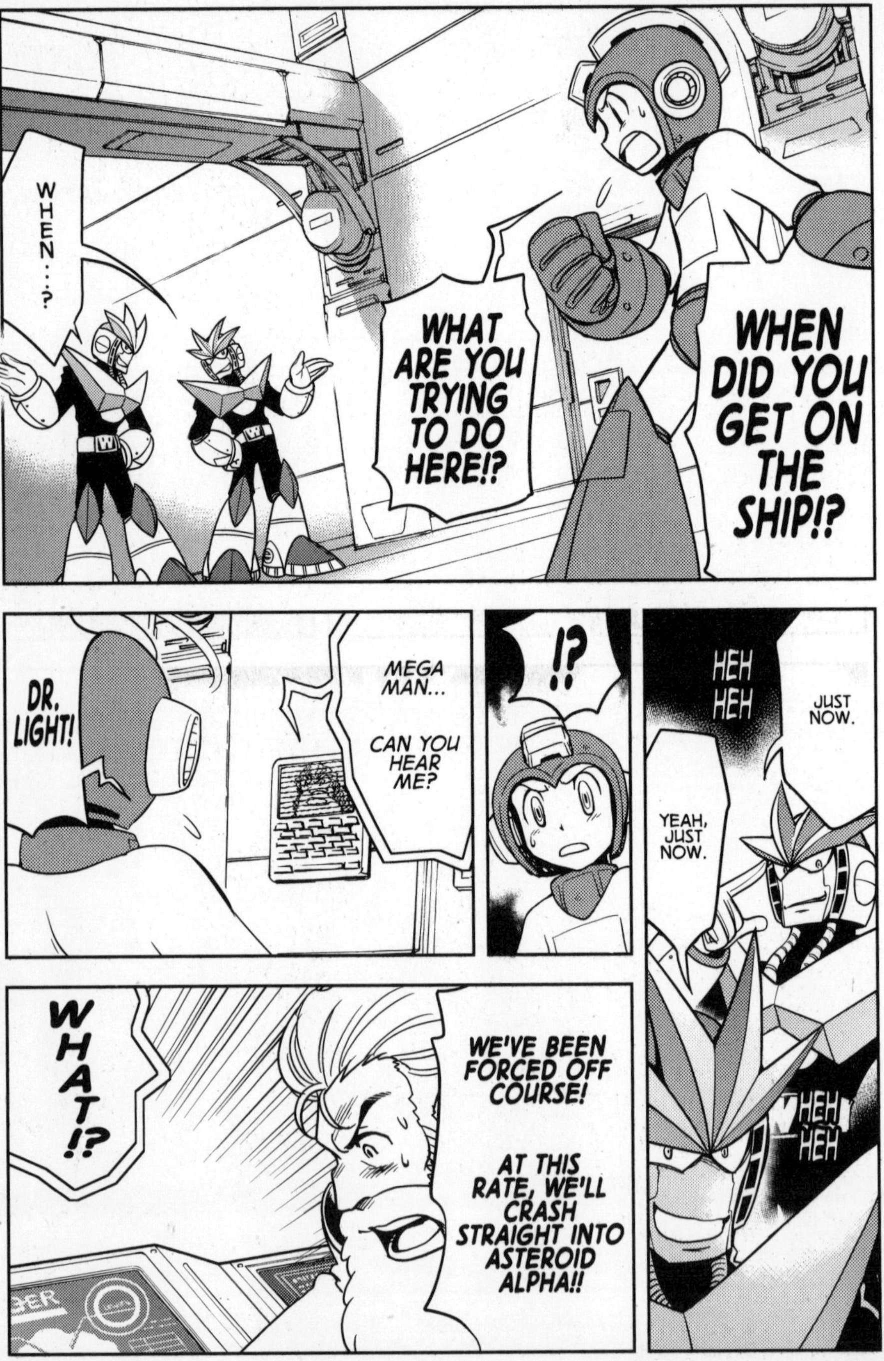
WHEN DID YOU GET ON THE SHIP!?
WHAT ARE YOU TRYING TO DO HERE!?
WHEN...?
HEH HEH
JUST NOW.
YEAH, JUST NOW.
HEH HEH
!?
MEGA MAN...
CAN YOU HEAR ME?
DR. LIGHT!
WE'VE BEEN FORCED OFF COURSE!
AT THIS RATE, WE'LL CRASH STRAIGHT INTO ASTEROID ALPHA!!
WHAT!?

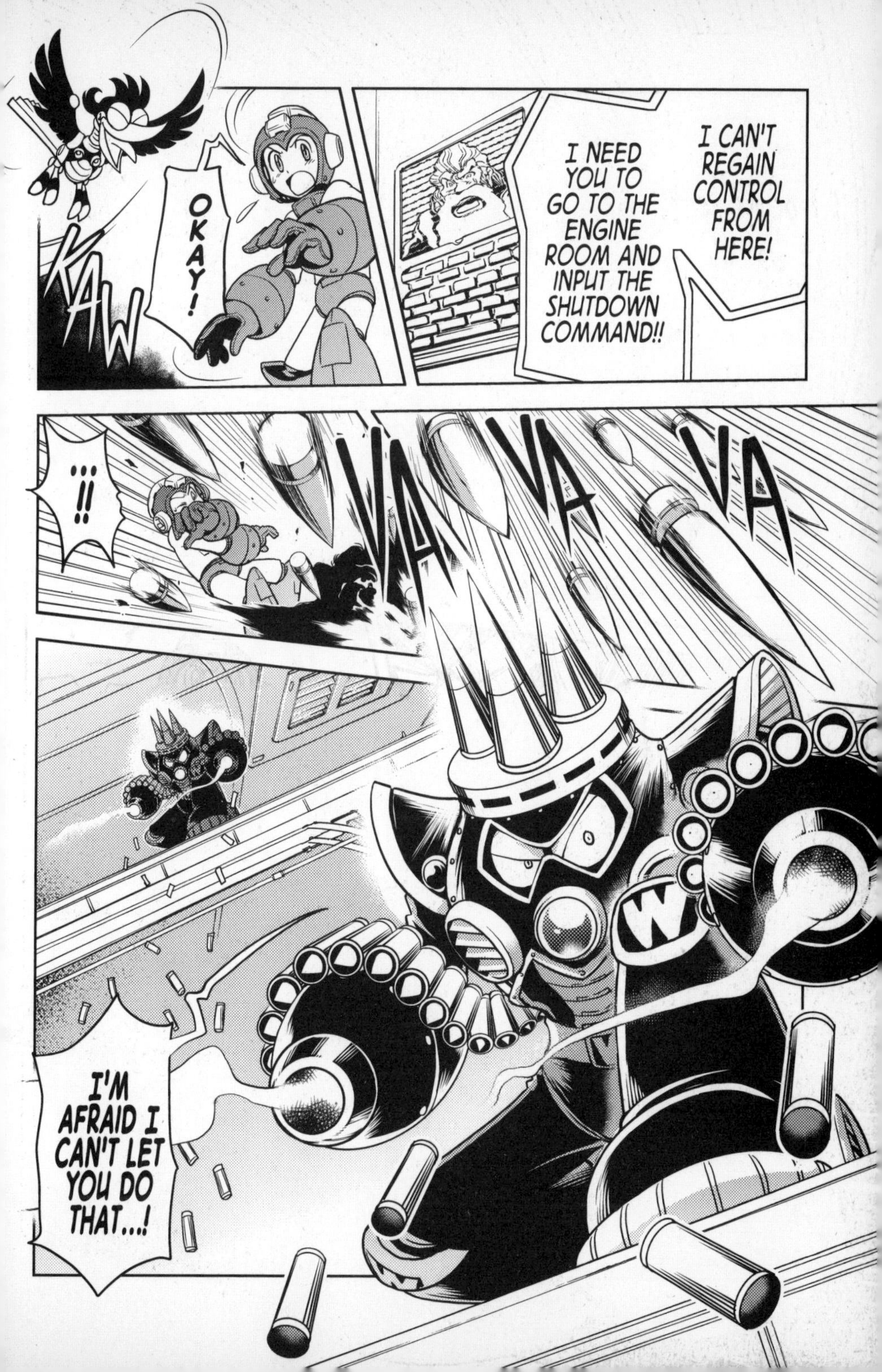
I CAN'T REGAIN CONTROL FROM HERE!
I NEED YOU TO GO TO THE ENGINE ROOM AND INPUT THE SHUTDOWN COMMAND!!
OKAY!
KAW
VA VA VA
...!!
I'M AFRAID I CAN'T LET YOU DO THAT...!

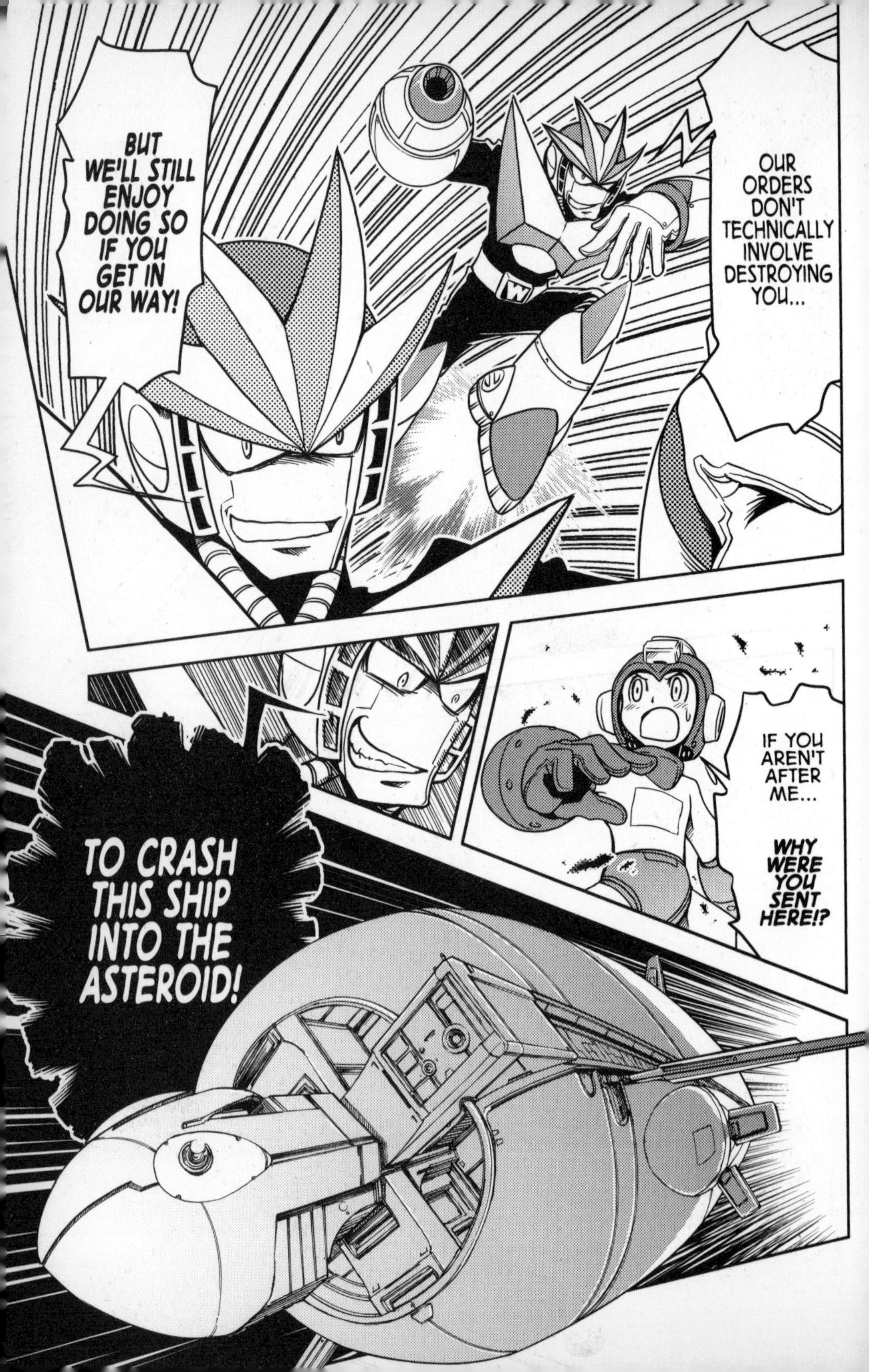
OUR ORDERS DON'T TECHNICALLY INVOLVE DESTROYING YOU...
BUT WE'LL STILL ENJOY DOING SO IF YOU GET IN OUR WAY!
IF YOU AREN'T AFTER ME...
WHY WERE YOU SENT HERE!?
TO CRASH THIS SHIP INTO THE ASTEROID!

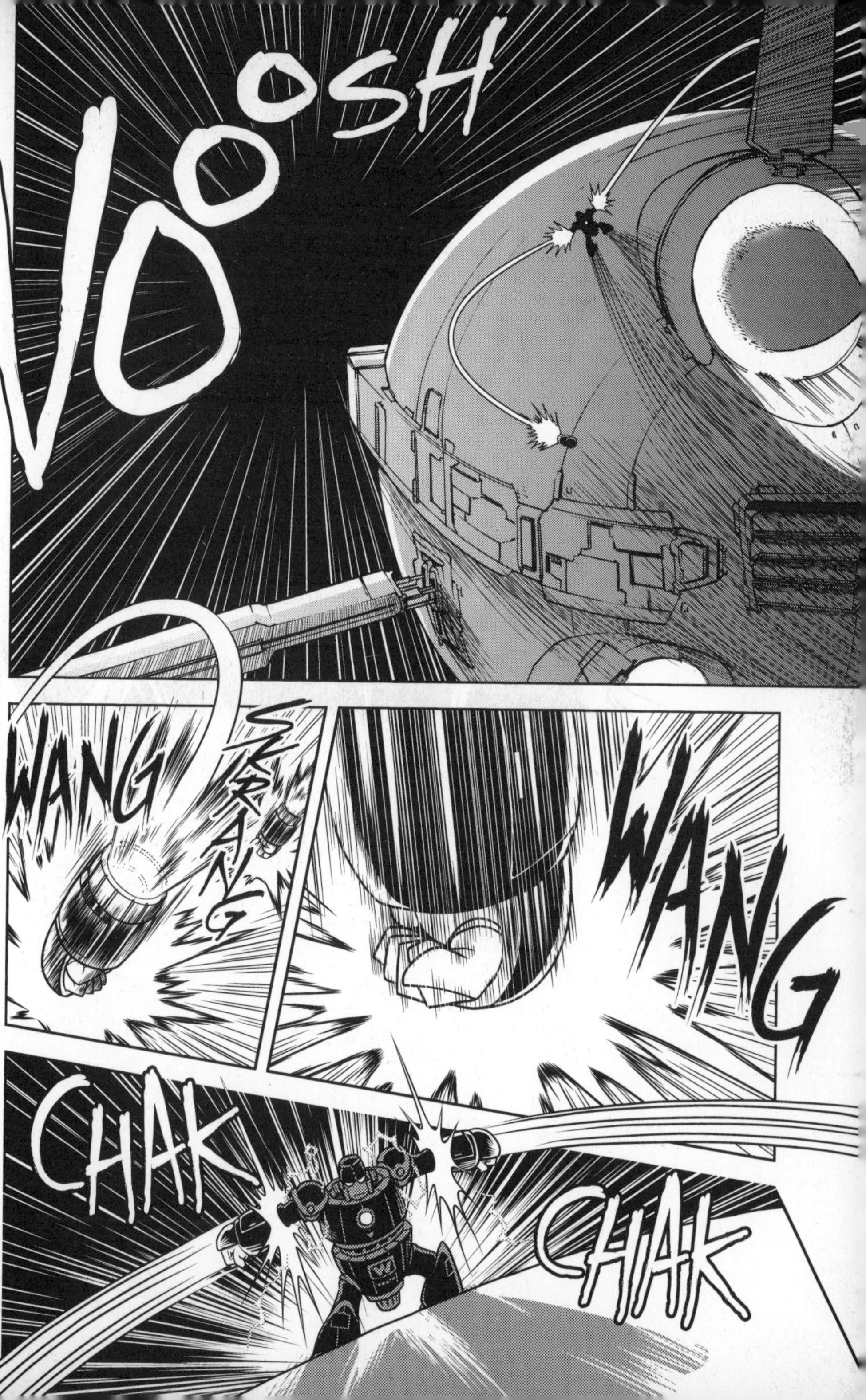
VOOOSH
WANG
SKRANG
WANG
CHAK
CHAK

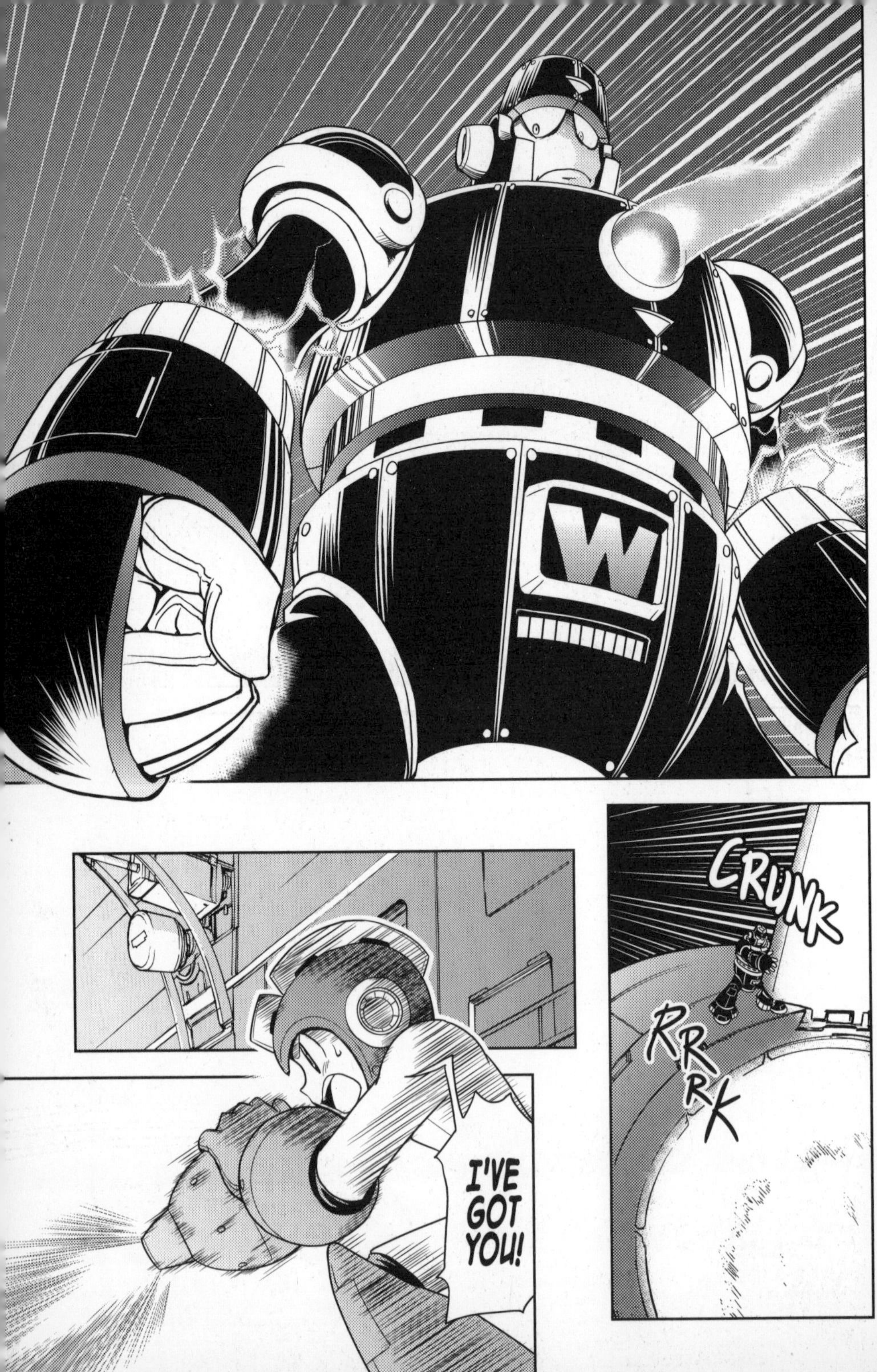
CRUNK
RRRK
I'VE GOT YOU!

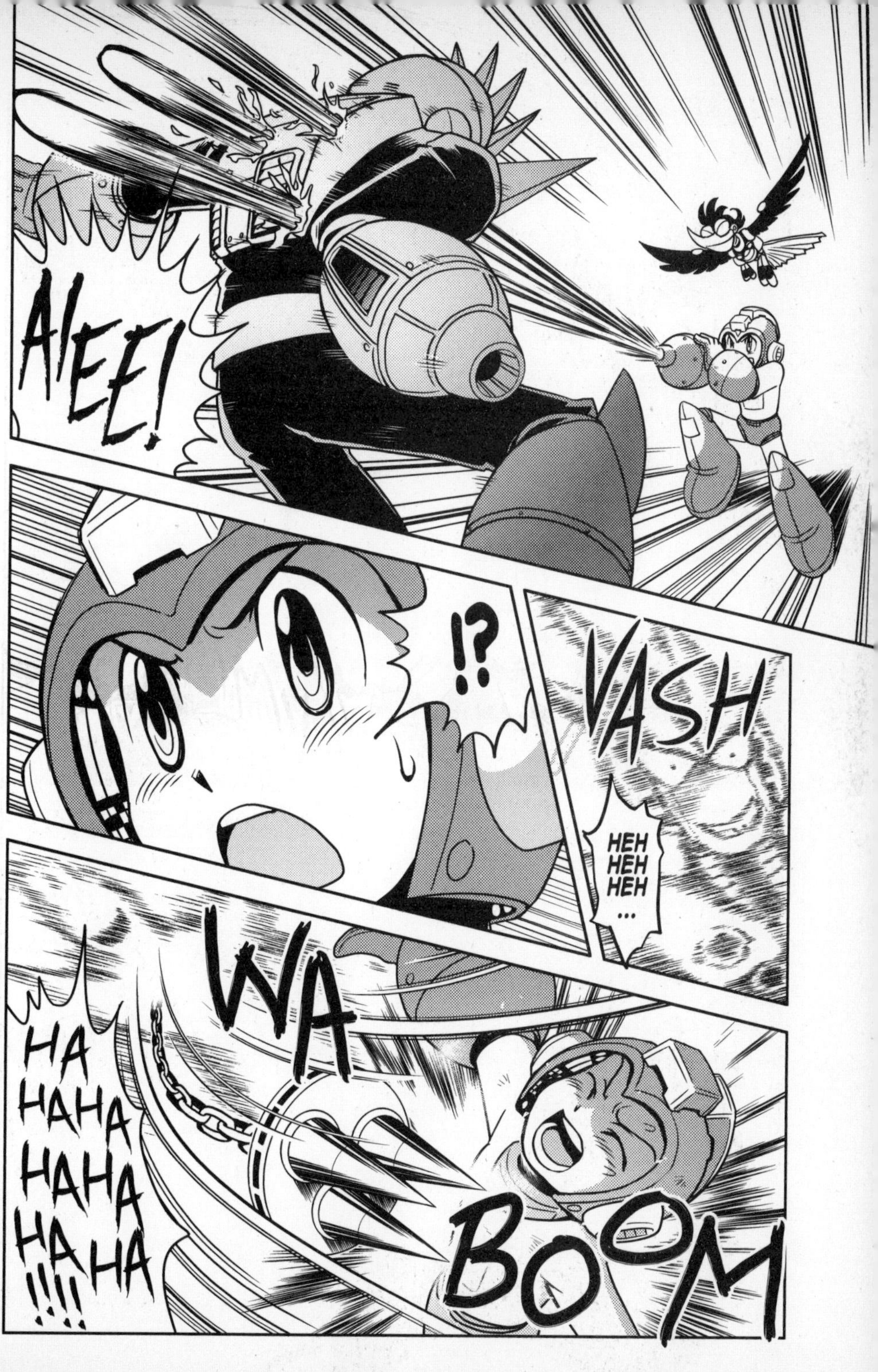
AIEE!
VASH
HEH HEH HEH ...
!?
WA
HA HAHA HAHA HAHA !!!!
BOOM

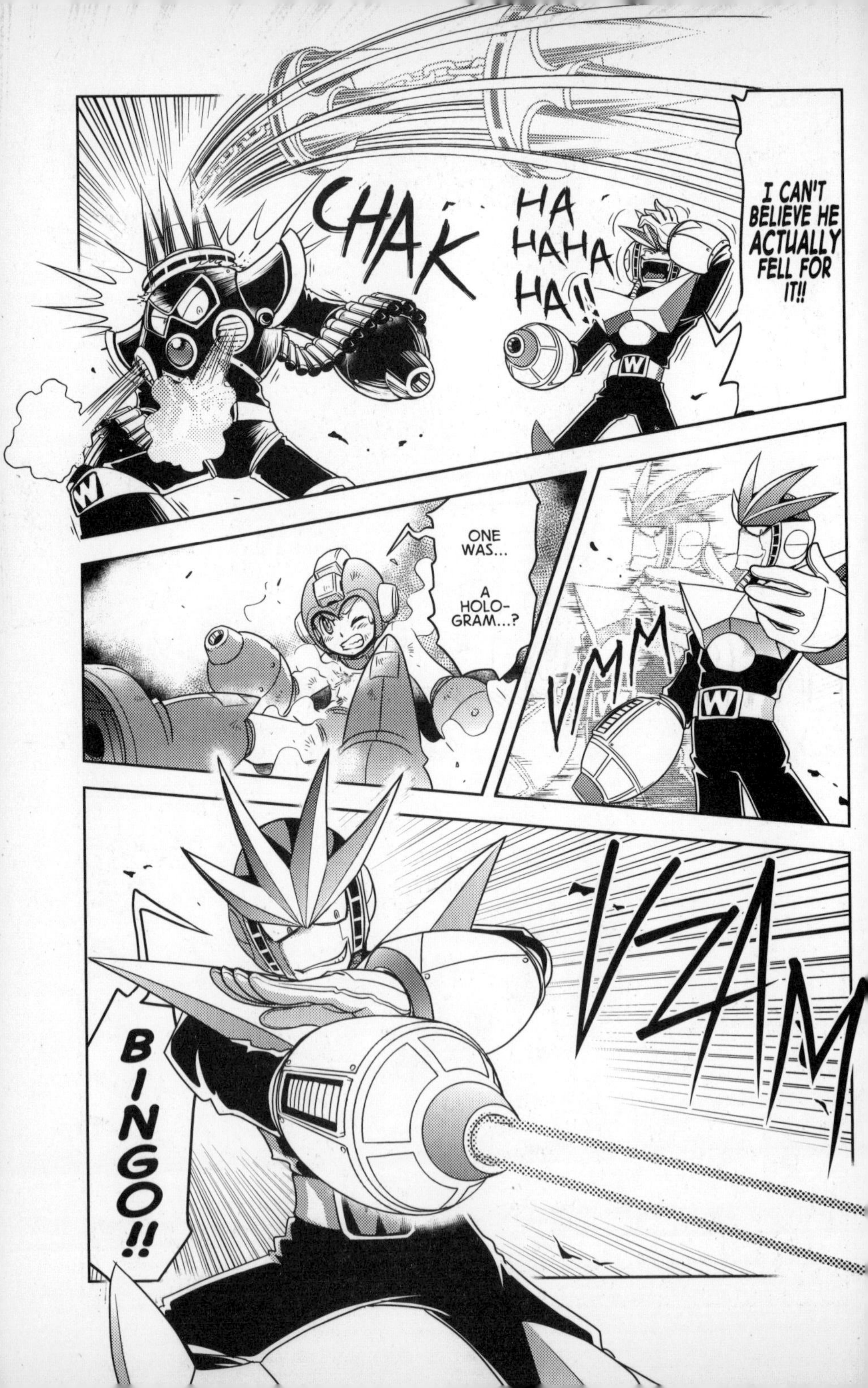
I CAN'T BELIEVE HE ACTUALLY FELL FOR IT!!
HA HAHAHA HA!!
CHAK
VMM
ONE WAS...
A HOLO-GRAM...?
VZAM
BINGO!!

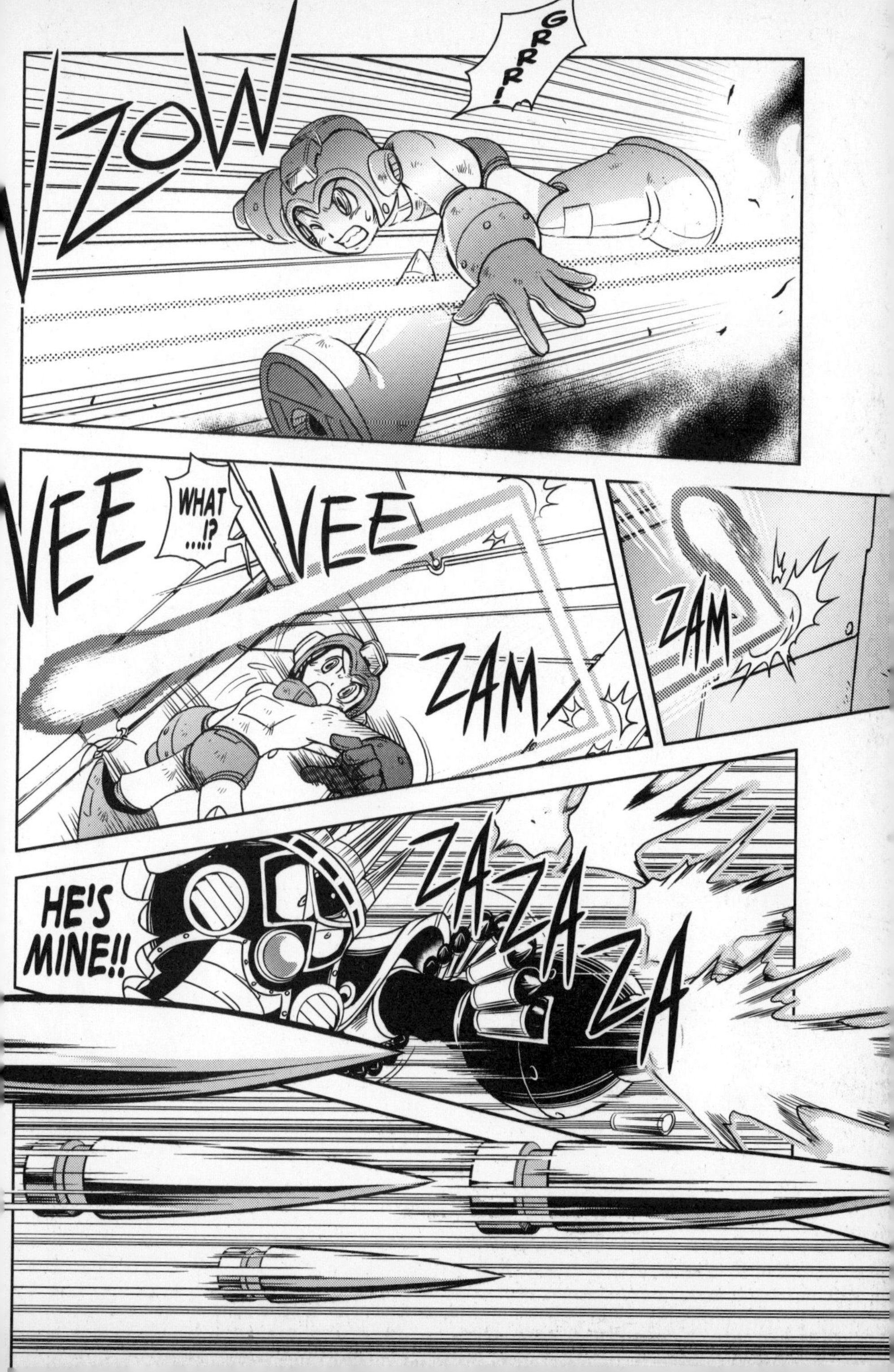
GRRR!
VZOW
ZAM
VEE
WHAT ...!?
VEE
ZAM
ZA ZA ZA ZA
HE'S MINE!!

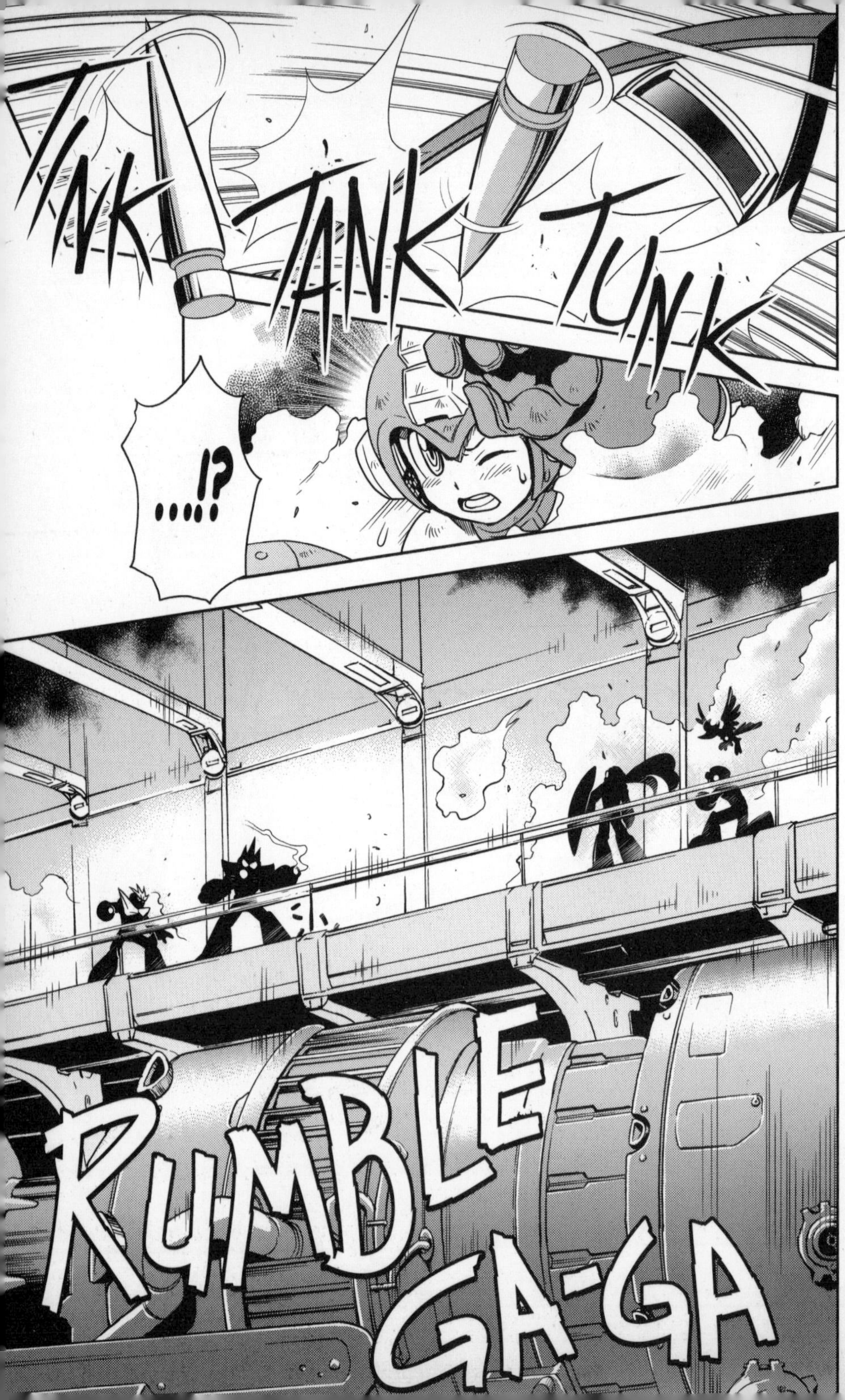
TINK TANK TUNK
...!?
RUMBLE
GA-GA

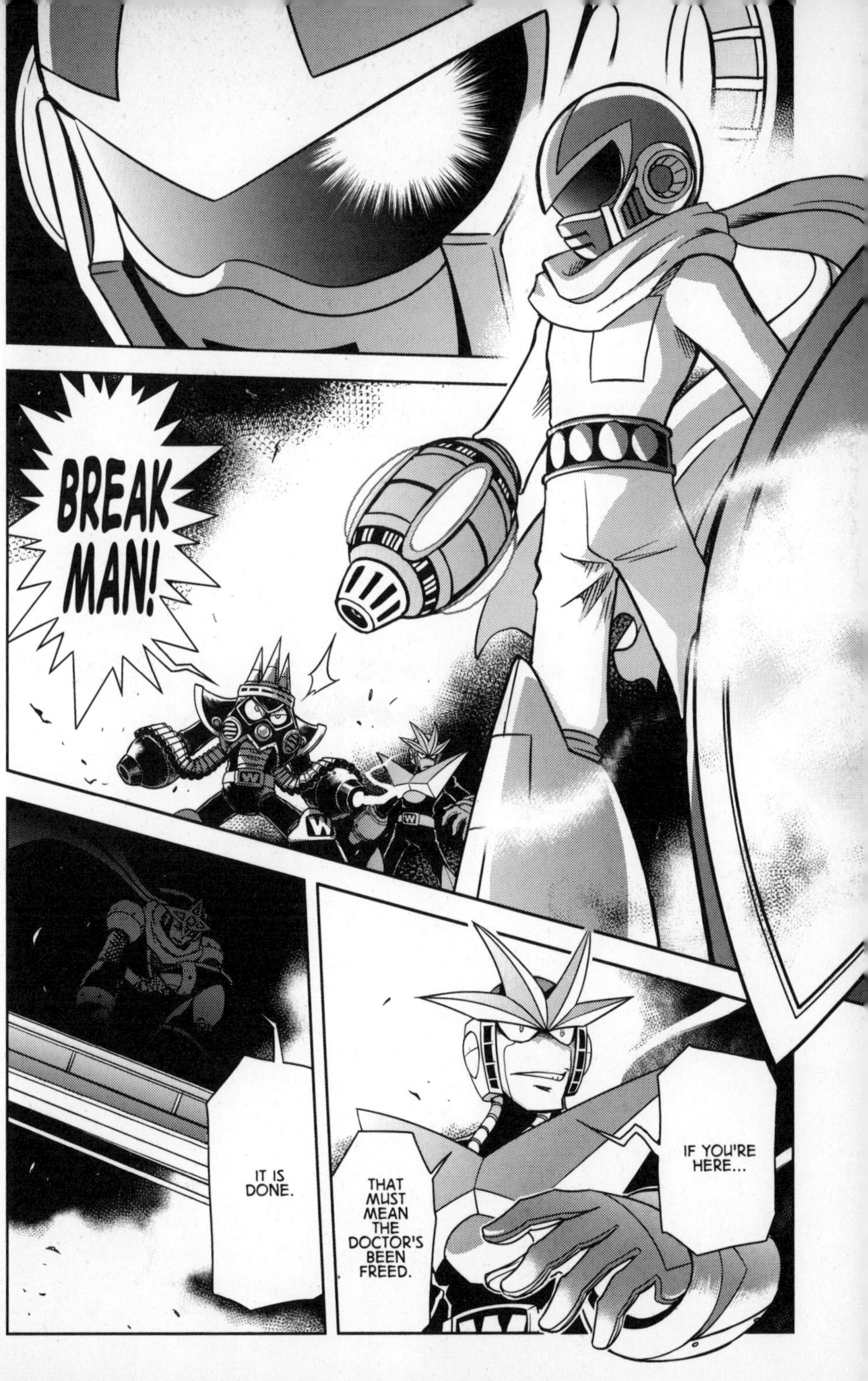
BREAK MAN!
IF YOU'RE HERE...
THAT MUST MEAN THE DOCTOR'S BEEN FREED.
IT IS DONE.

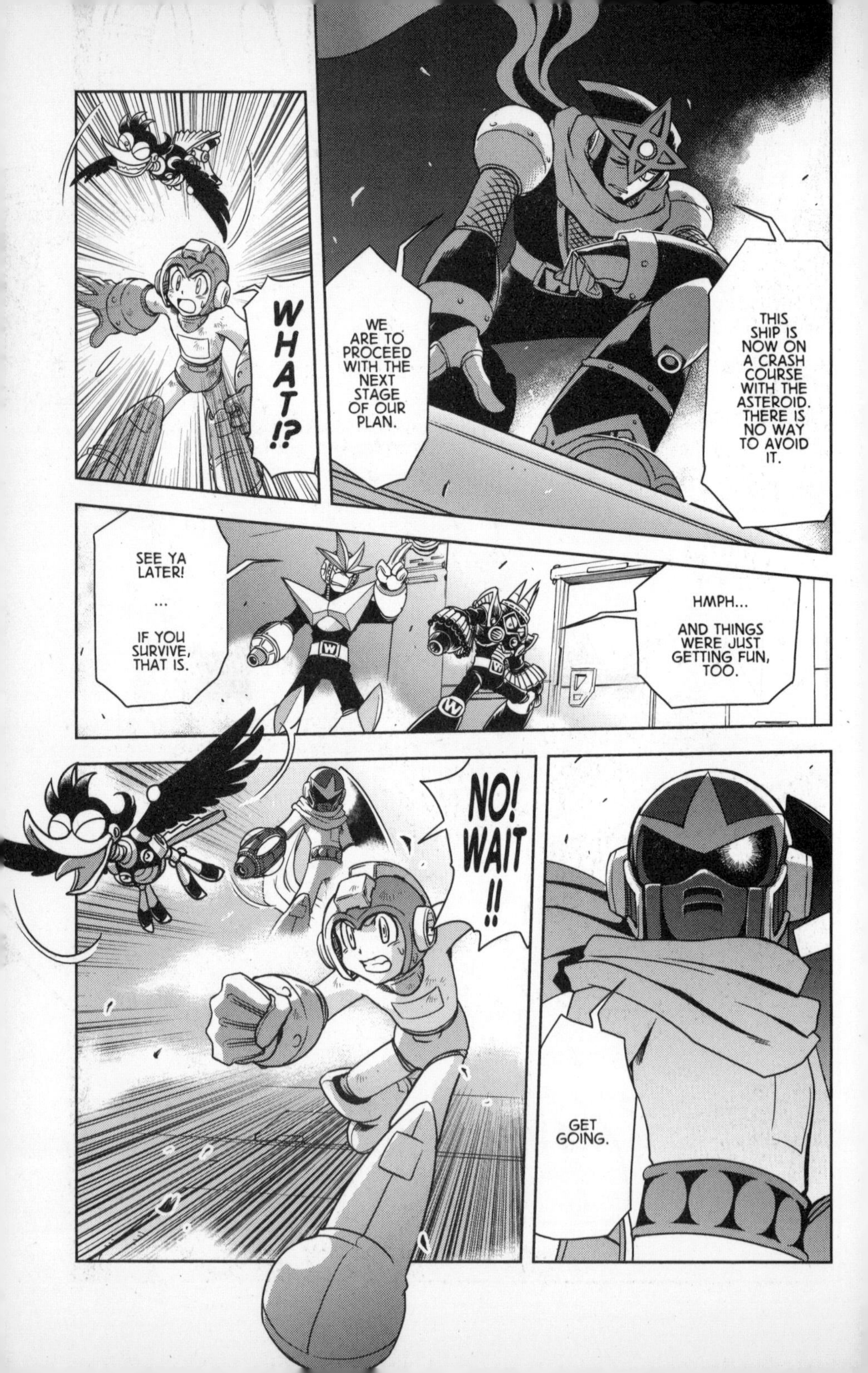
THIS SHIP IS NOW ON A CRASH COURSE WITH THE ASTEROID. THERE IS NO WAY TO AVOID IT.
WE ARE TO PROCEED WITH THE NEXT STAGE OF OUR PLAN.
WHAT!?
HMPH... AND THINGS WERE JUST GETTING FUN, TOO.
SEE YA LATER! ... IF YOU SURVIVE, THAT IS.
GET GOING.
NO! WAIT!!

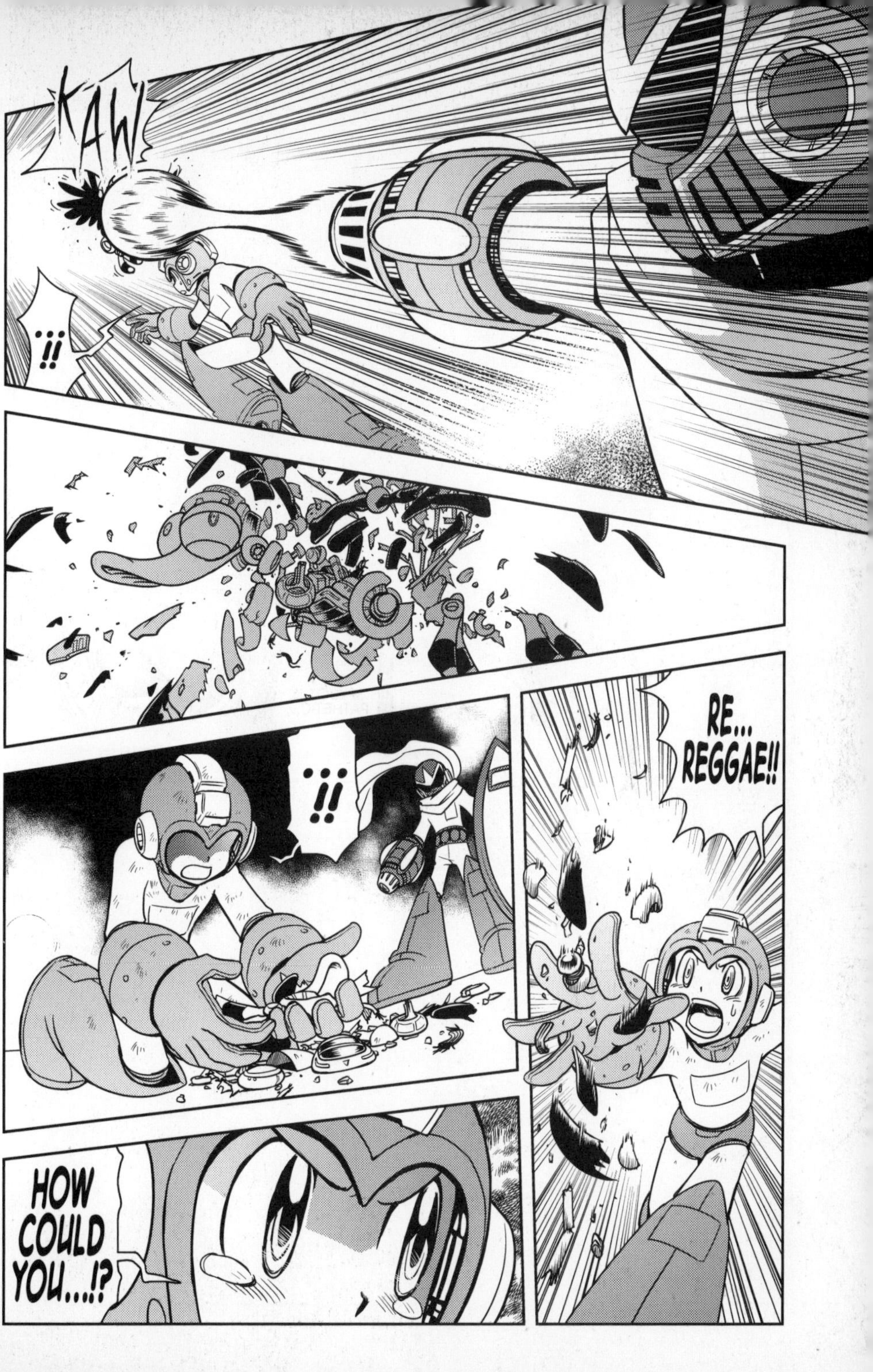
KAW
...!!
RE... REGGAE!!
...!!
HOW COULD YOU...!?

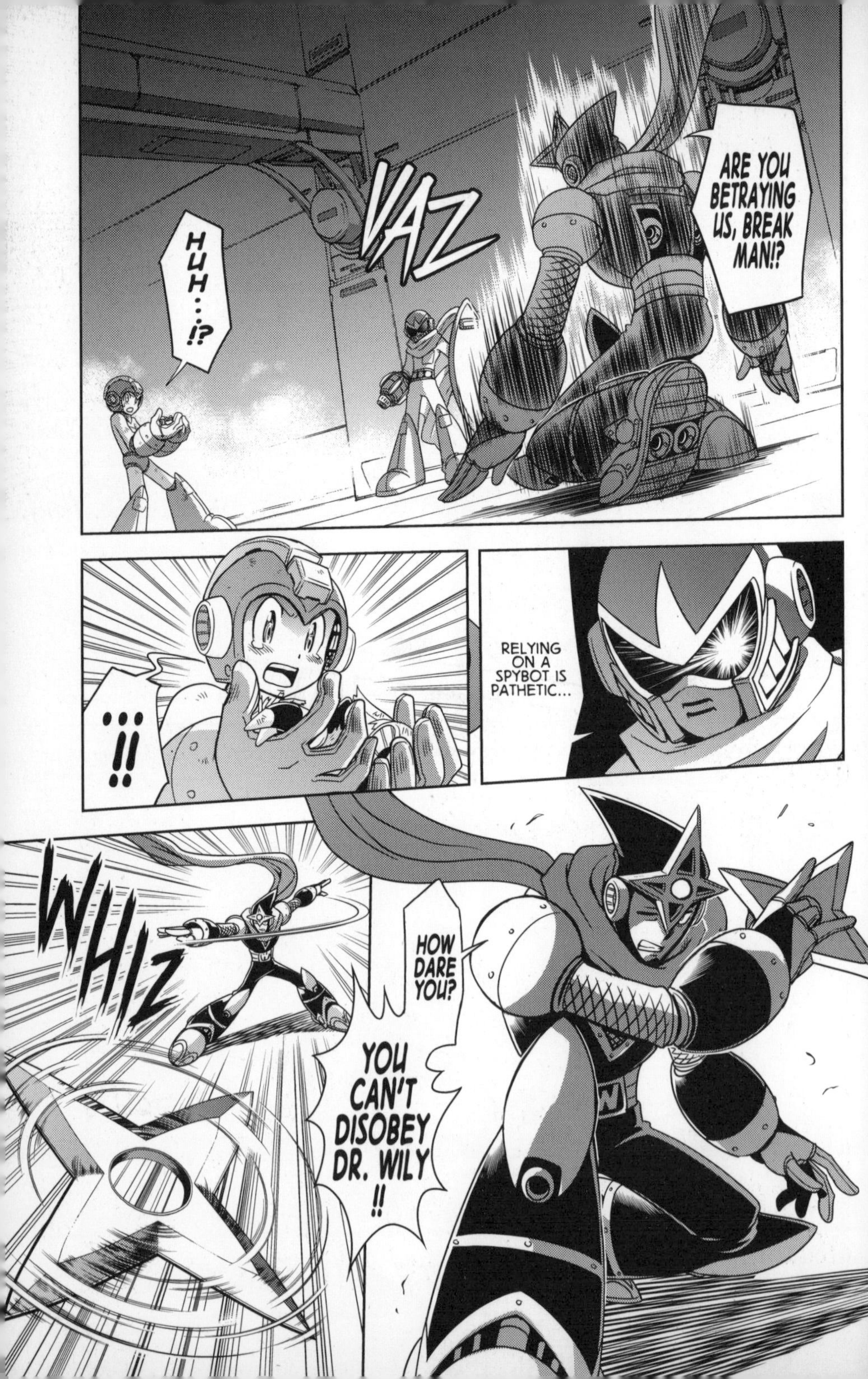
ARE YOU BETRAYING US, BREAK MAN!?
VAZ
HUH...!?
RELYING ON A SPYBOT IS PATHETIC...
...!!
HOW DARE YOU?
YOU CAN'T DISOBEY DR. WILY !!
WHIZ

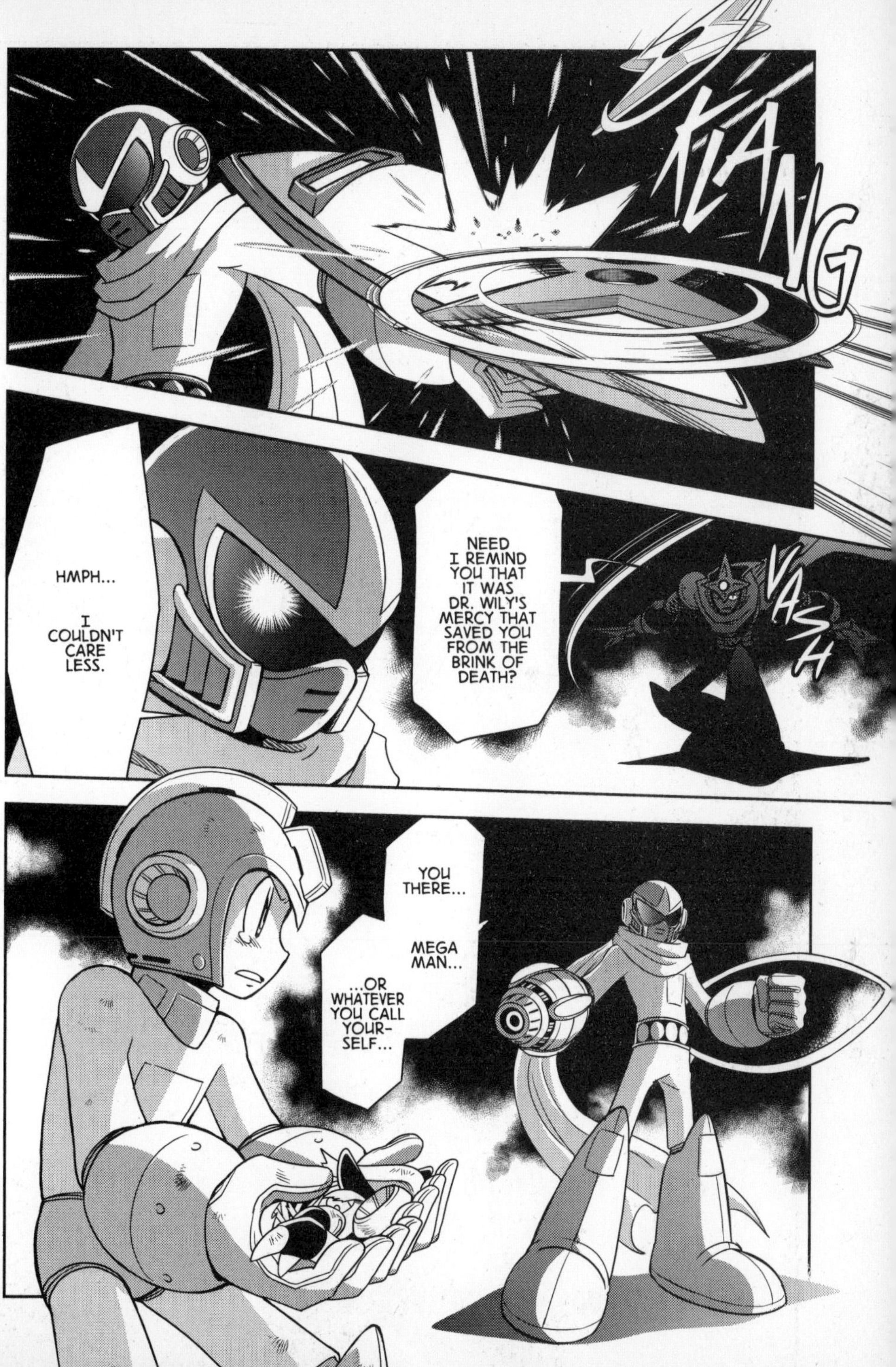
KLANG
VASH
NEED I REMIND YOU THAT IT WAS DR. WILY'S MERCY THAT SAVED YOU FROM THE BRINK OF DEATH?
HMPH... I COULDN'T CARE LESS.
YOU THERE...
MEGA MAN...
...OR WHATEVER YOU CALL YOUR-SELF...

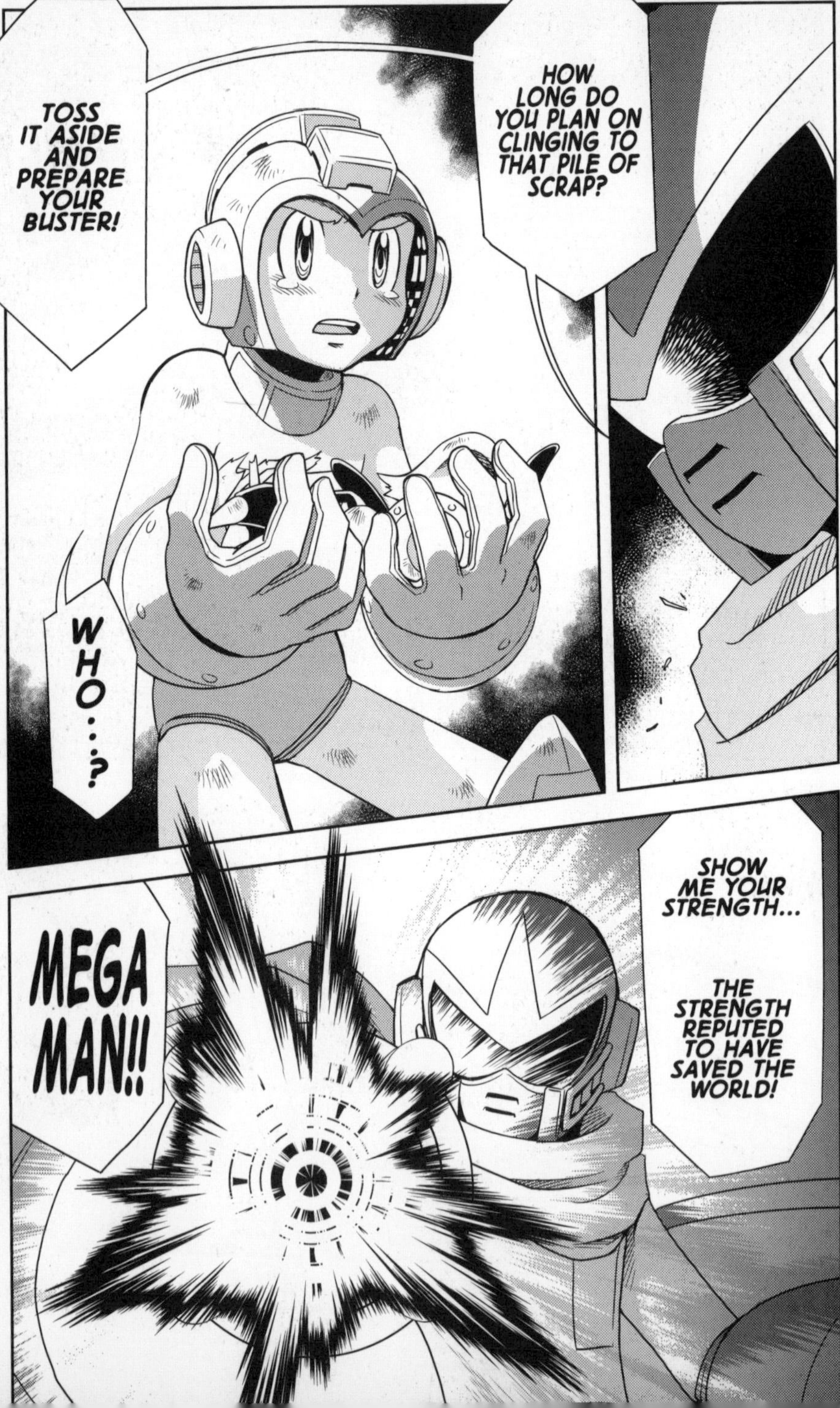
HOW LONG DO YOU PLAN ON CLINGING TO THAT PILE OF SCRAP?
TOSS IT ASIDE AND PREPARE YOUR BUSTER!
WHO...?
SHOW ME YOUR STRENGTH...
THE STRENGTH REPUTED TO HAVE SAVED THE WORLD!
MEGA MAN!!

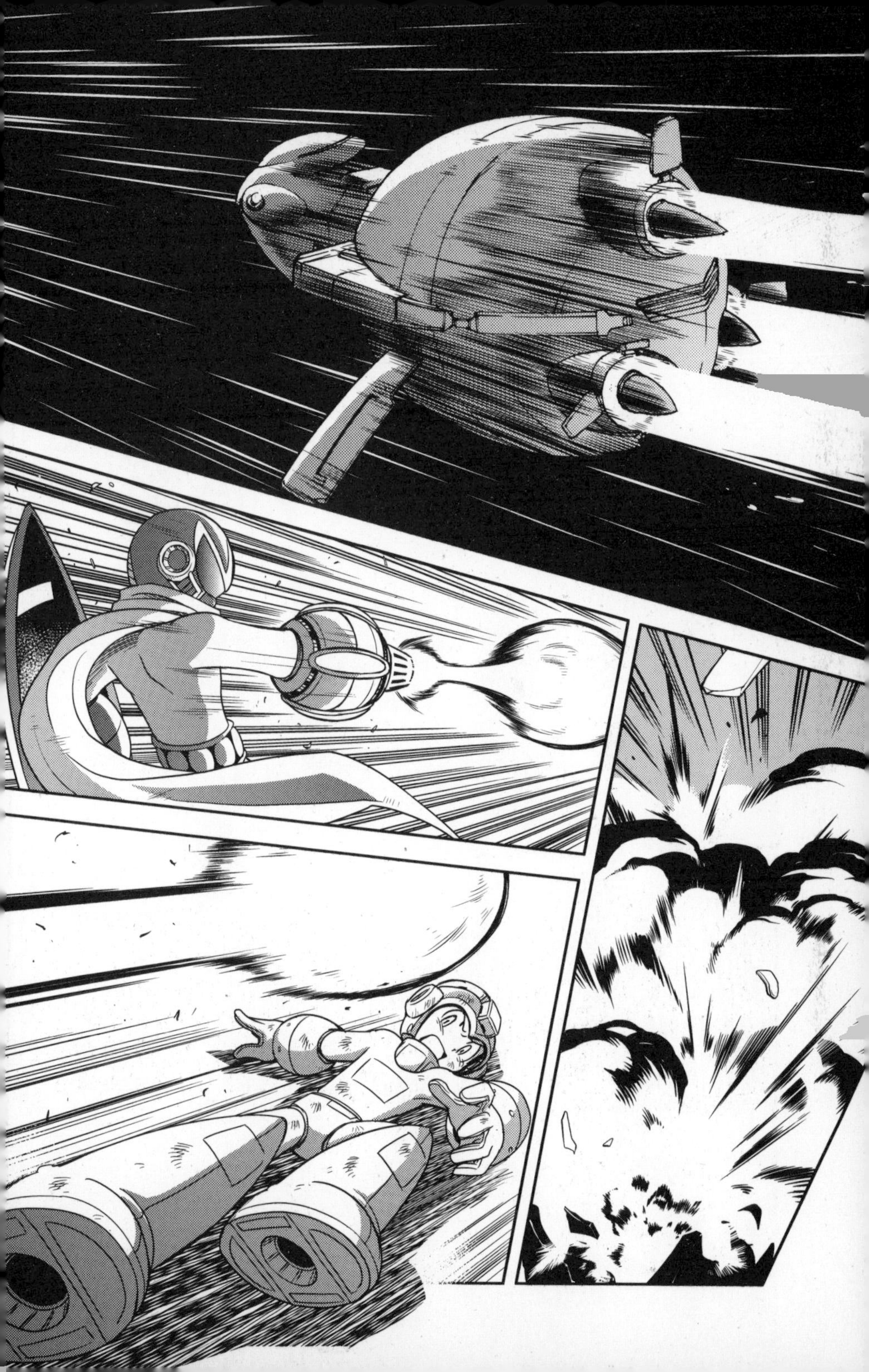

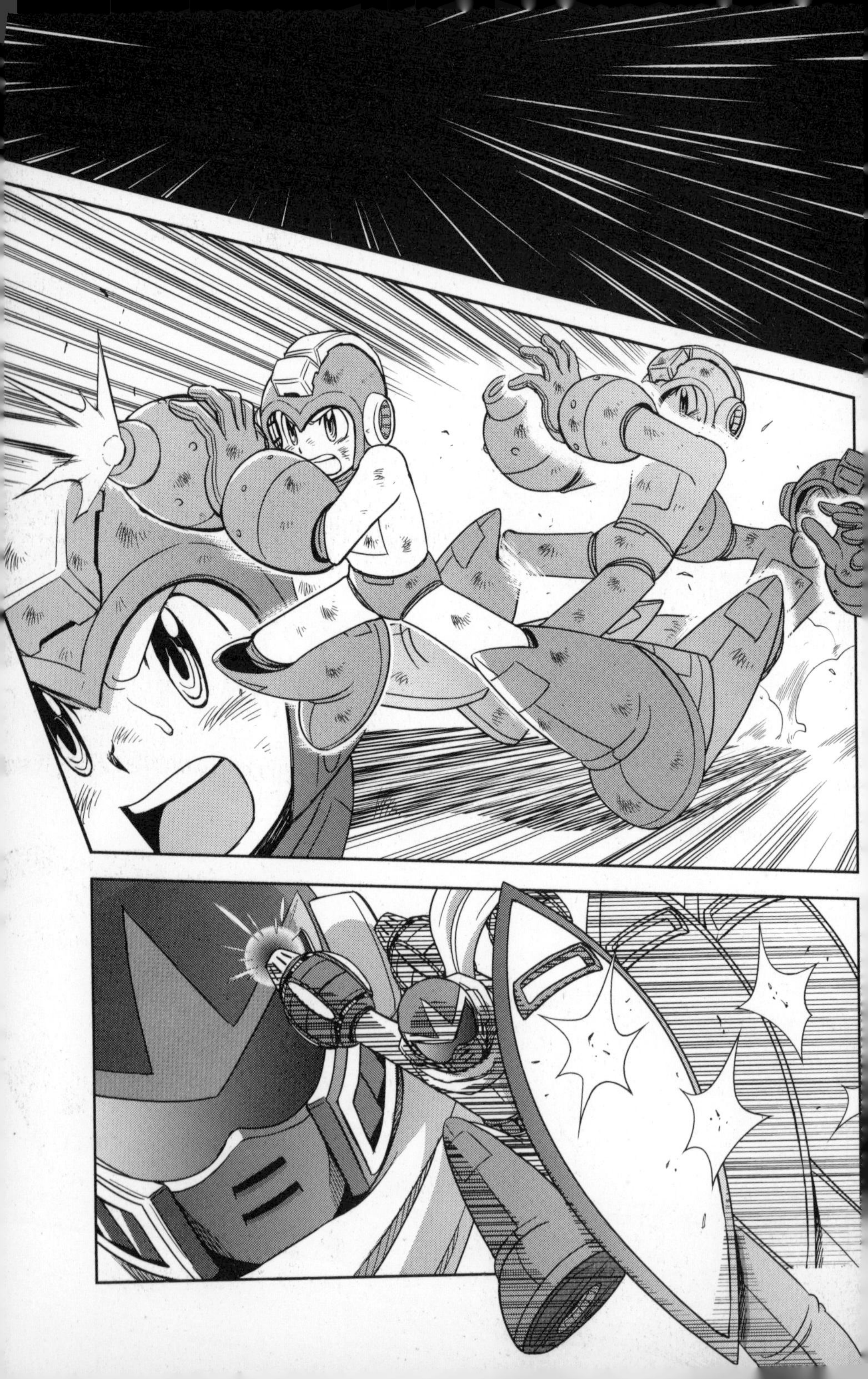

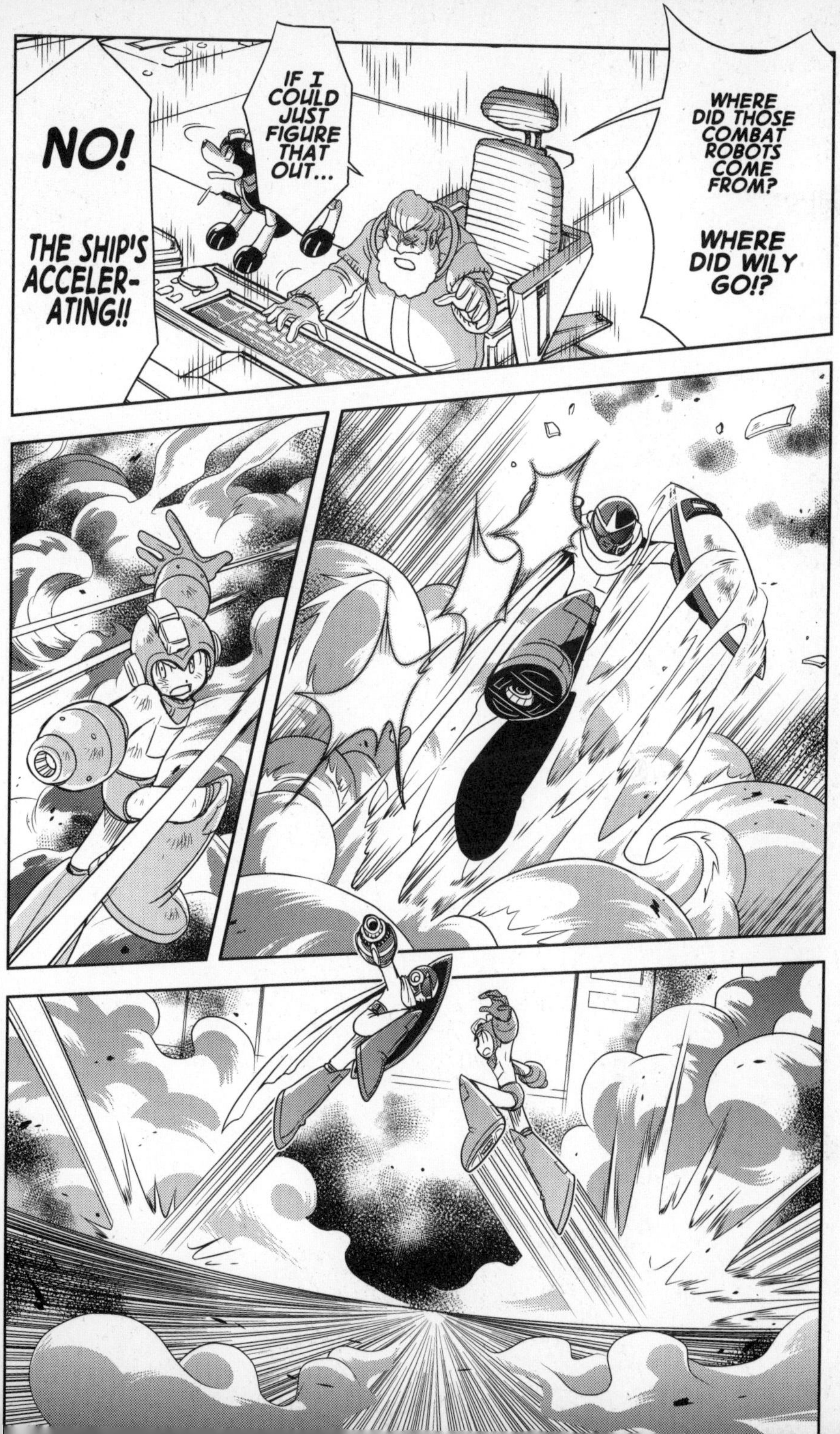
WHERE DID THOSE COMBAT ROBOTS COME FROM?
WHERE DID WILY GO!?
IF I COULD JUST FIGURE THAT OUT...
NO!
THE SHIP'S ACCELER-ATING!!

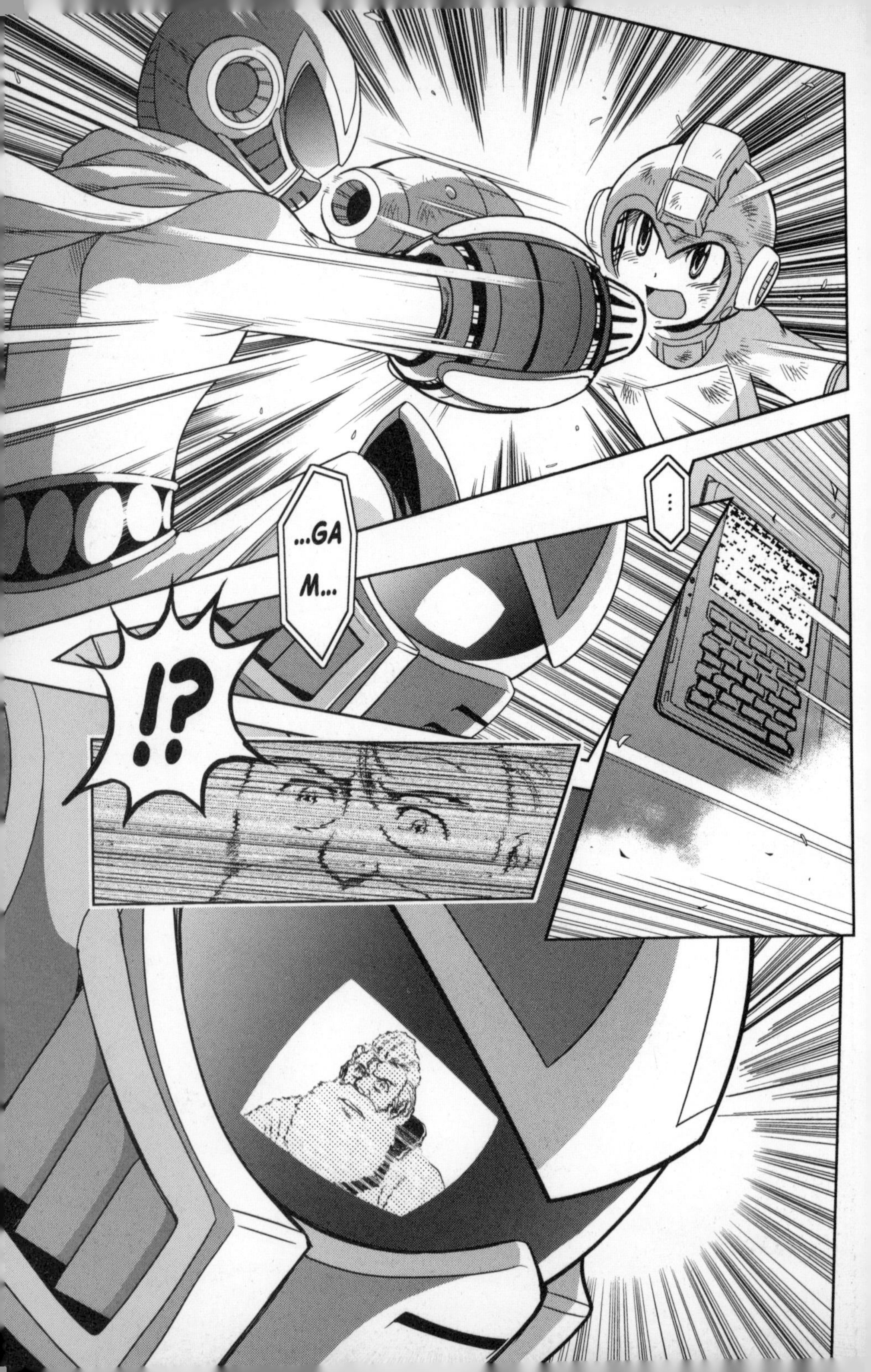
...
...GA M...
!?

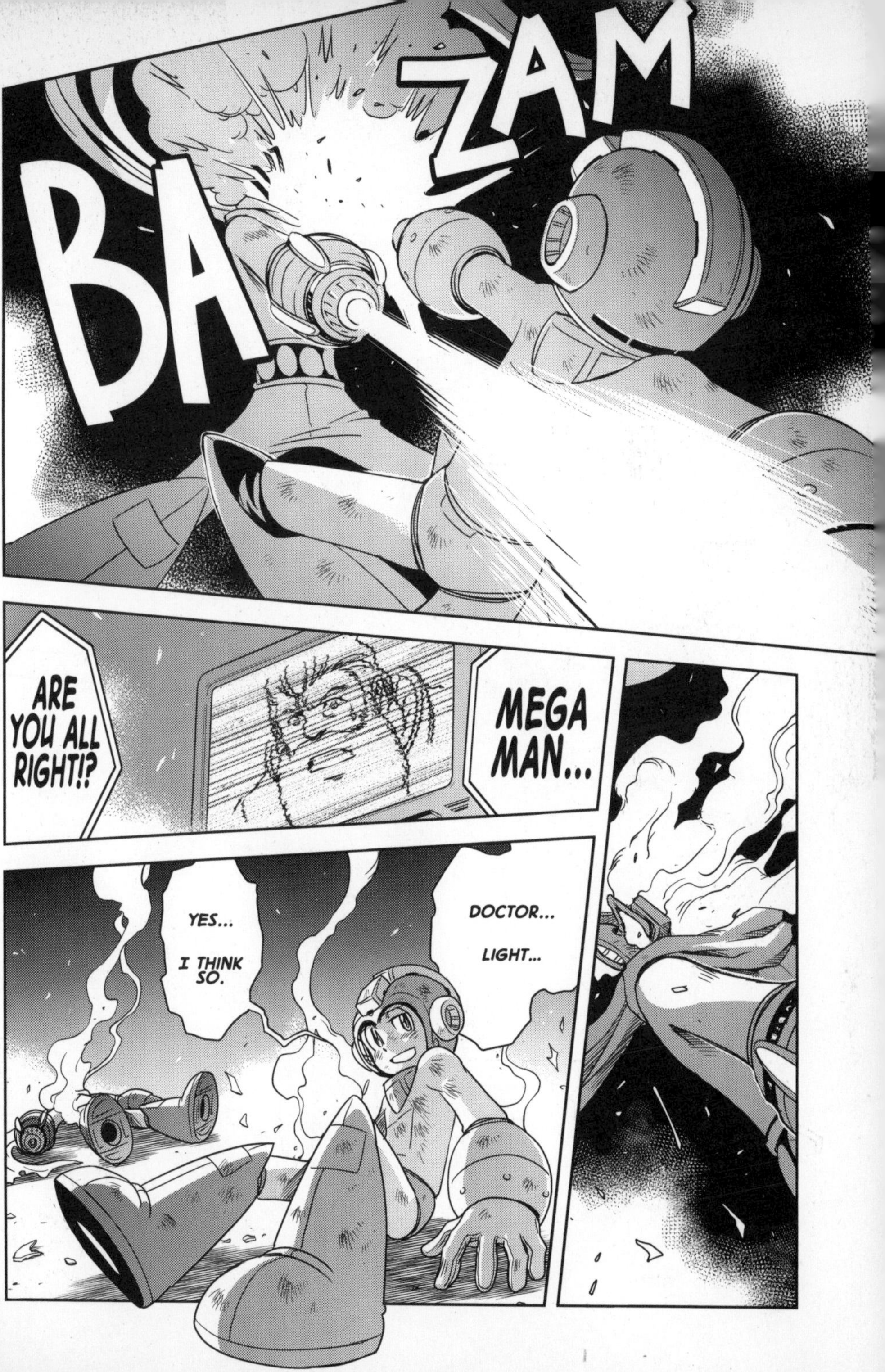
BAZAM
MEGA MAN...
ARE YOU ALL RIGHT!?
DOCTOR... LIGHT...
YES... I THINK SO.

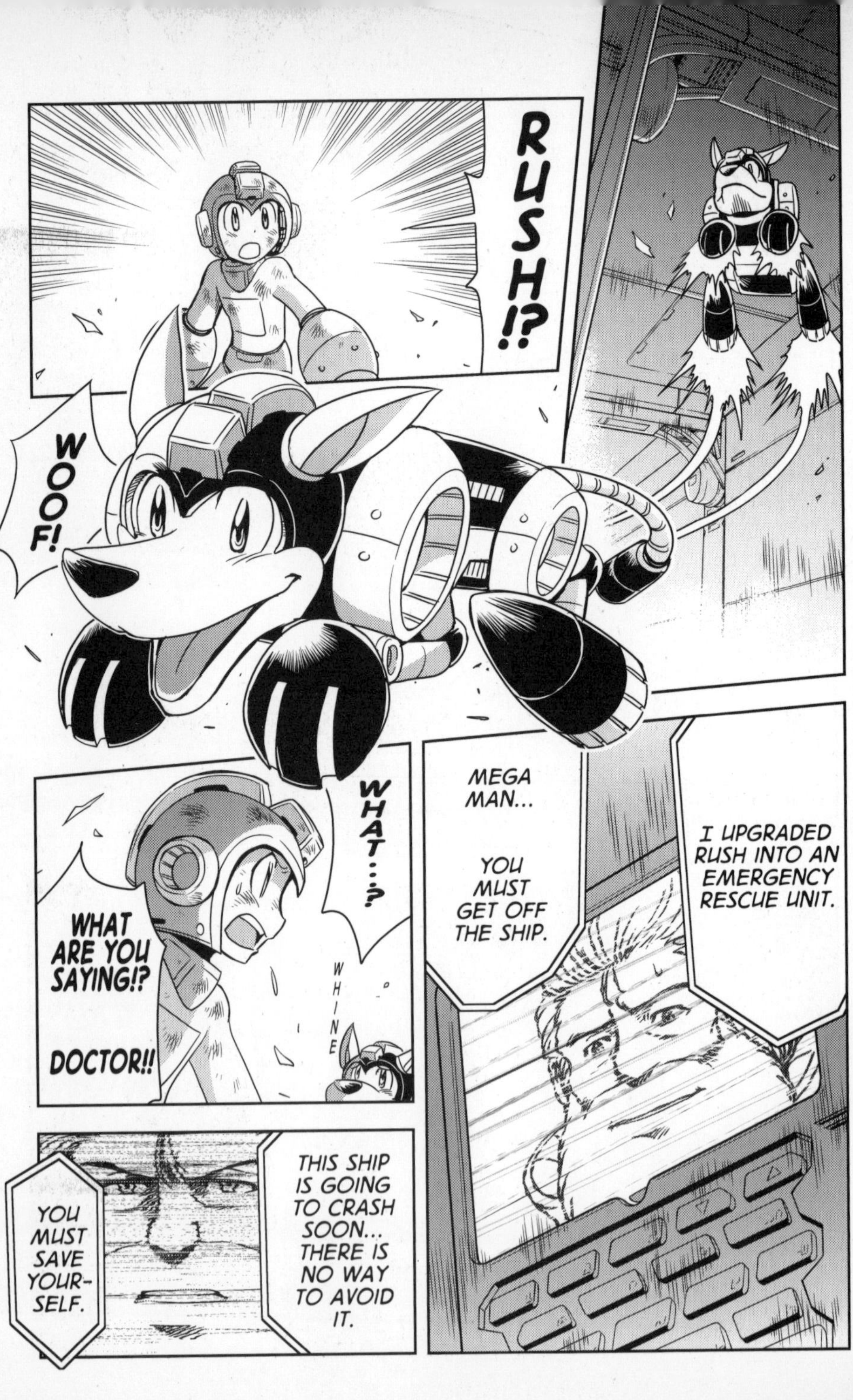
RUSH!?
WOOF!
I UPGRADED RUSH INTO AN EMERGENCY RESCUE UNIT.
MEGA MAN...
YOU MUST GET OFF THE SHIP.
WHAT...?
WHINE
WHAT ARE YOU SAYING!?
DOCTOR!!
THIS SHIP IS GOING TO CRASH SOON... THERE IS NO WAY TO AVOID IT.
YOU MUST SAVE YOUR-SELF.

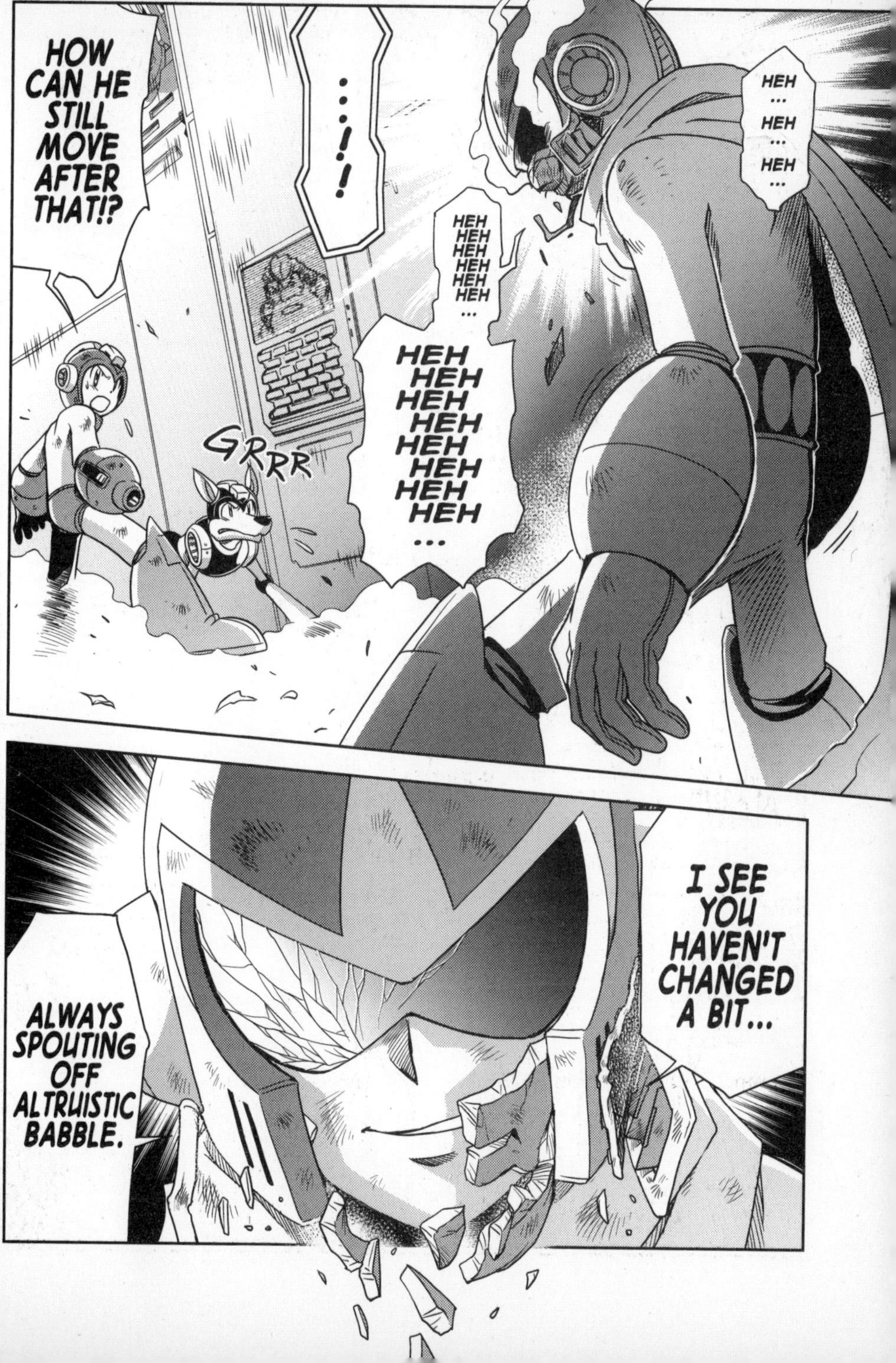
HEH... HEH... HEH...
HEH HEH HEH HEH HEH HEH...
...!!
HOW CAN HE STILL MOVE AFTER THAT!?
HEH HEH HEH HEH HEH HEH HEH HEH...
GRRR
I SEE YOU HAVEN'T CHANGED A BIT...
ALWAYS SPOUTING OFF ALTRUISTIC BABBLE.

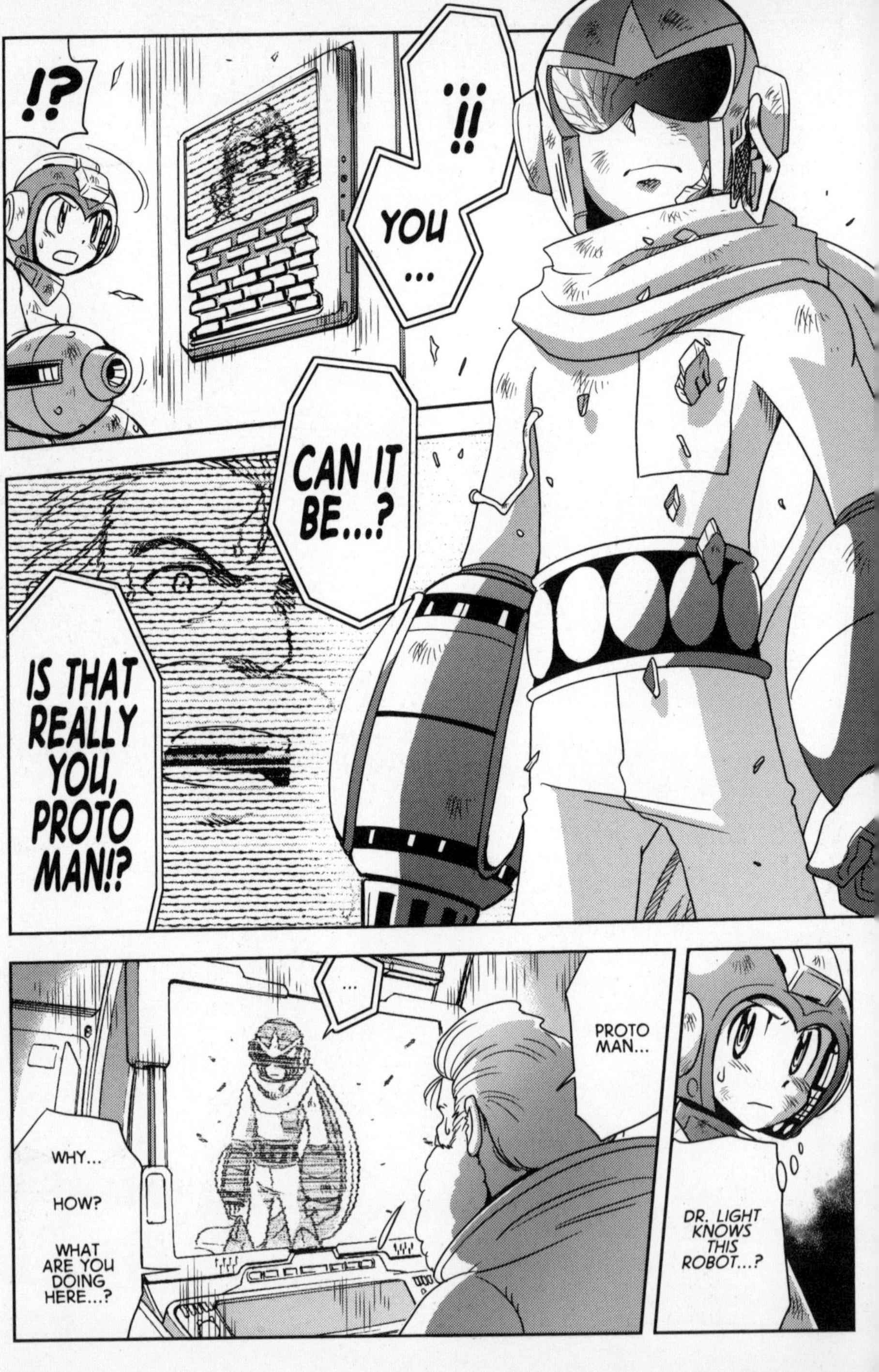

...!!
YOU ...
!?
CAN IT BE...?
IS THAT REALLY YOU, PROTO MAN!?
DR. LIGHT KNOWS THIS ROBOT...?
...
PROTO MAN...
WHY...
HOW?
WHAT ARE YOU DOING HERE...?

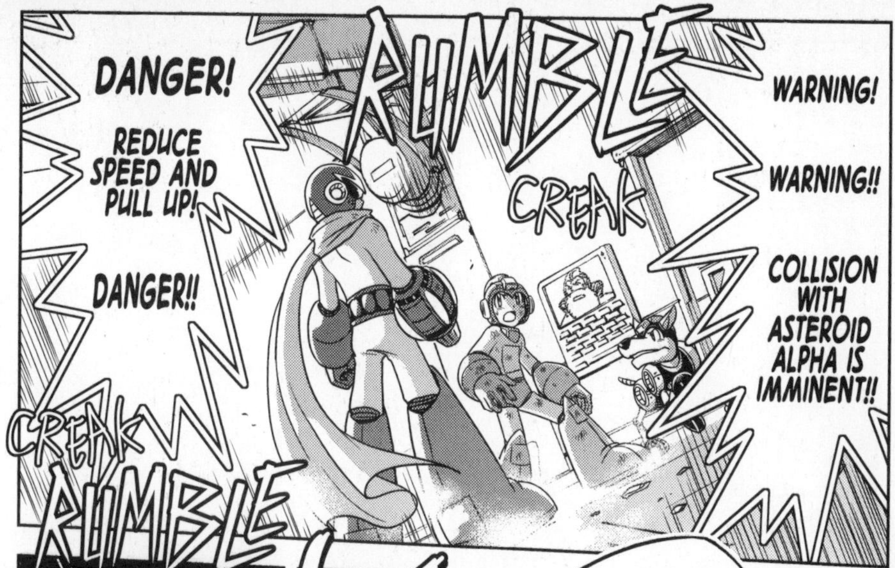
WARNING!
WARNING!!
COLLISION WITH ASTEROID ALPHA IS IMMINENT!!
RUMBLE
CREAK
DANGER!
REDUCE SPEED AND PULL UP!
DANGER!!
CREAK
RUMBLE

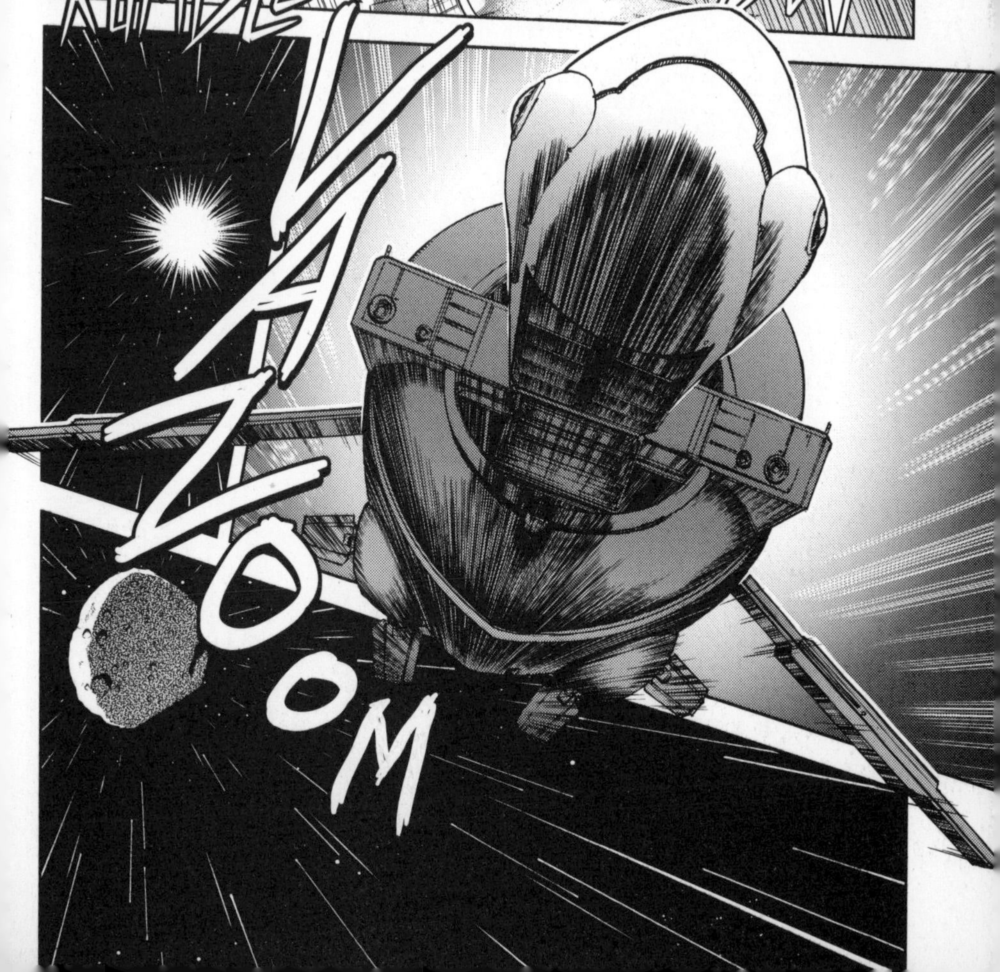
VVAZOOOM

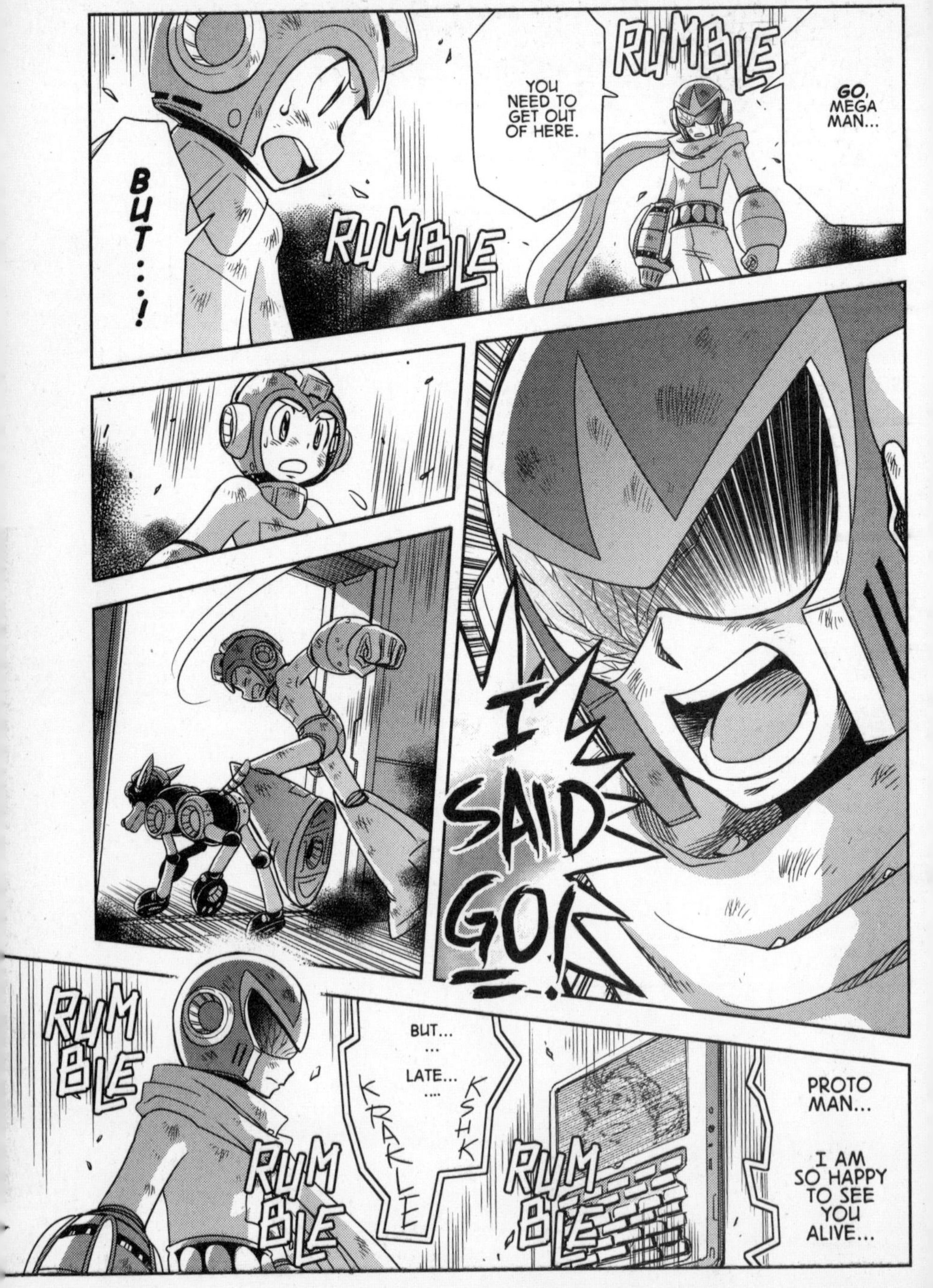
GO, MEGA MAN...
RUMBLE
YOU NEED TO GET OUT OF HERE.
BUT...!
RUMBLE
I SAID GO...!
PROTO MAN...
I AM SO HAPPY TO SEE YOU ALIVE...
RUM BLE
KSHK
BUT... ... LATE... ....
KRAKLE
RUM BLE
RUM BLE

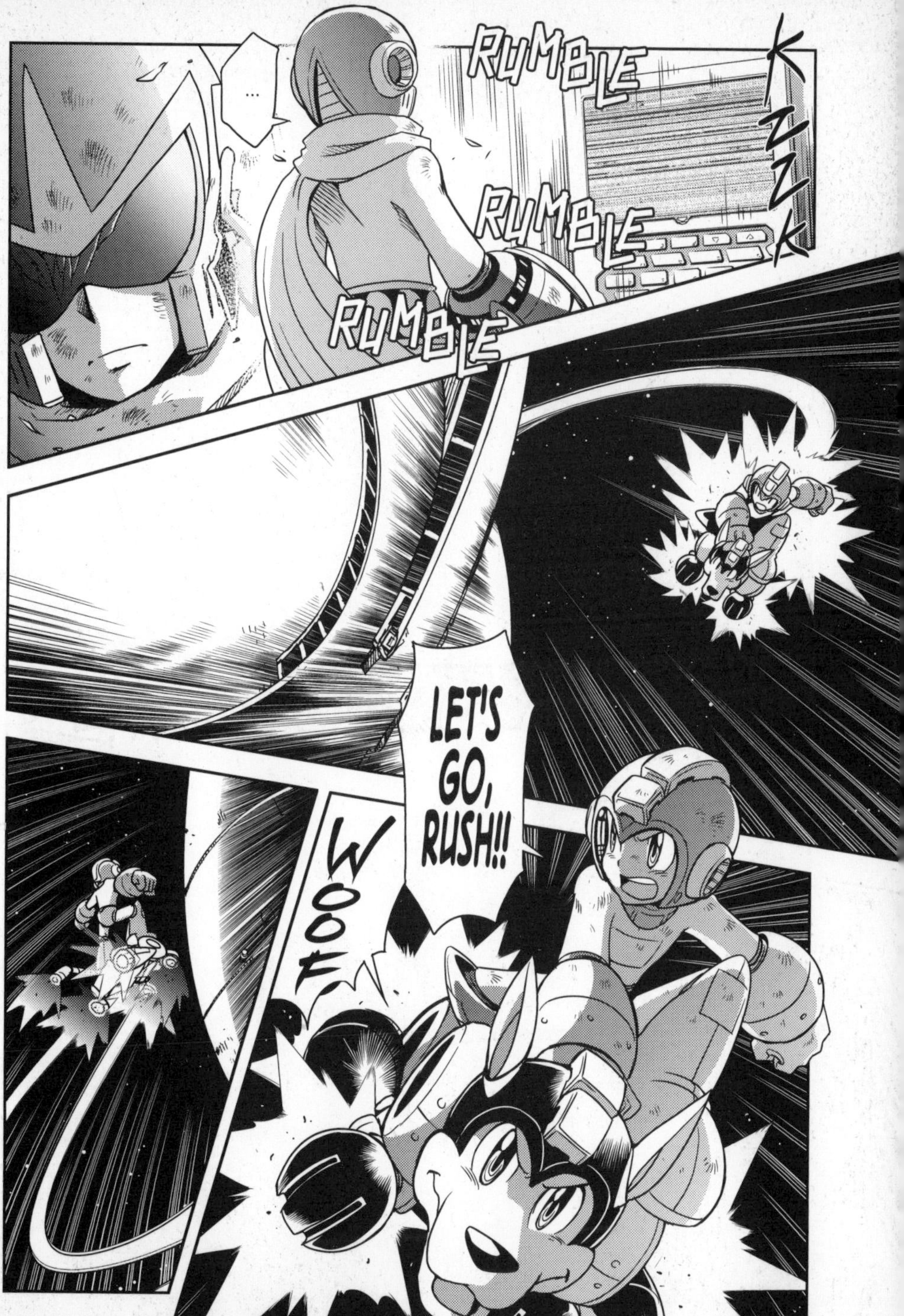
KZZK
RUMBLE
RUMBLE
RUMBLE
...
LET'S GO, RUSH!!
WOOF

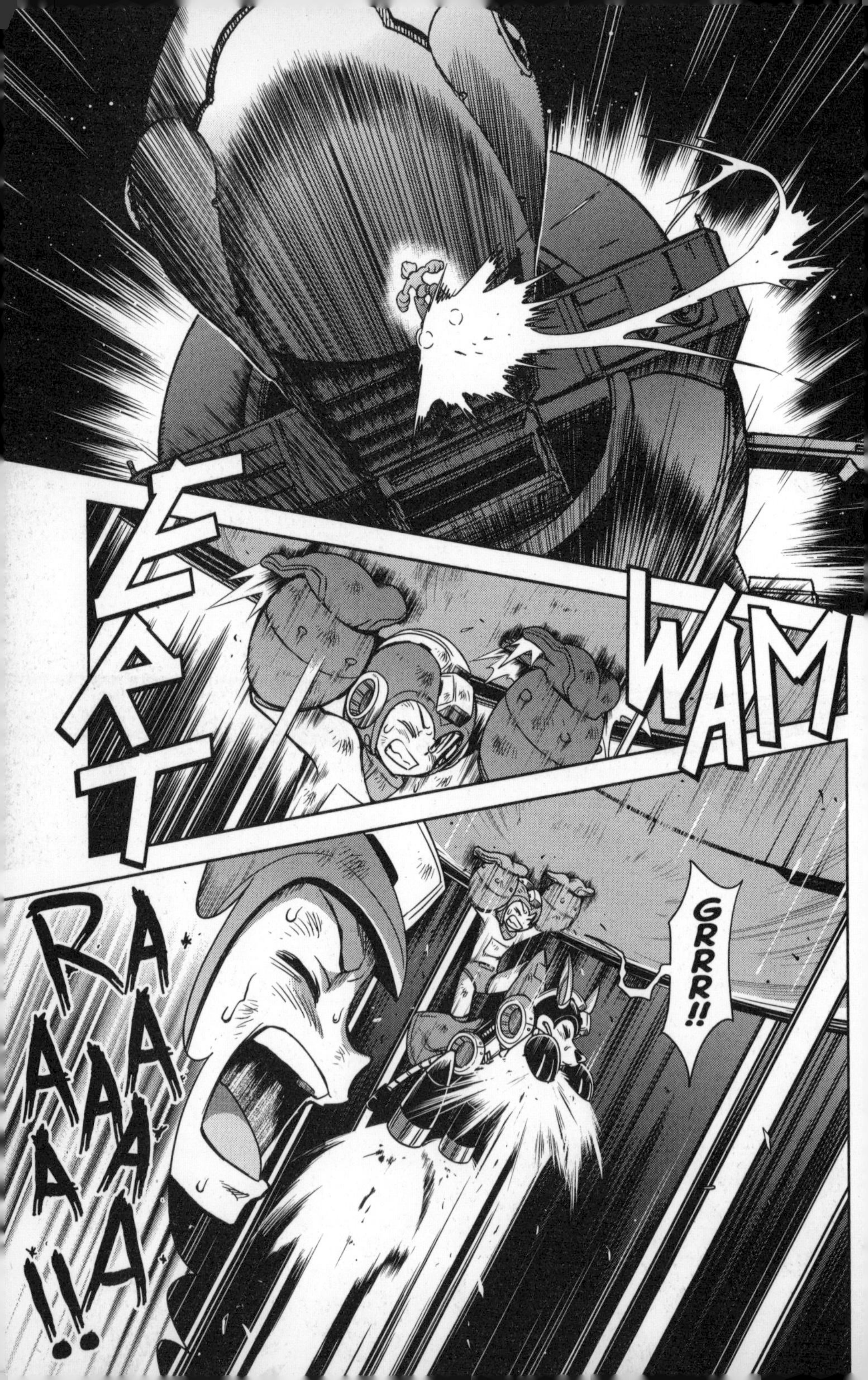
WAM
ZAT
GRRRR!!
RAAAAAAA!!

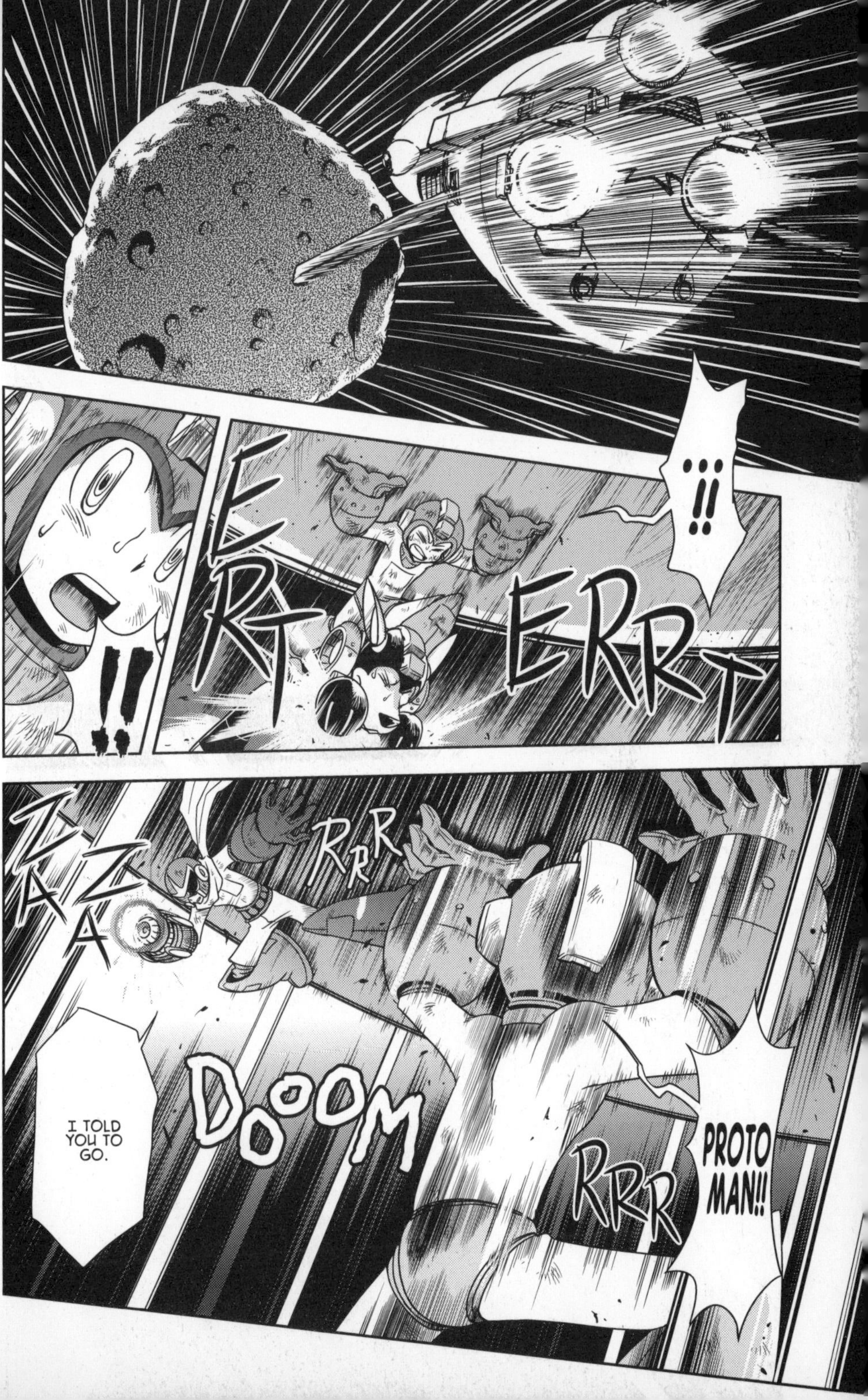

!!
ERRRT
ERRT
!!
RRRR
ZAZA
PROTO MAN!!
RRR
DOOOM
I TOLD YOU TO GO.

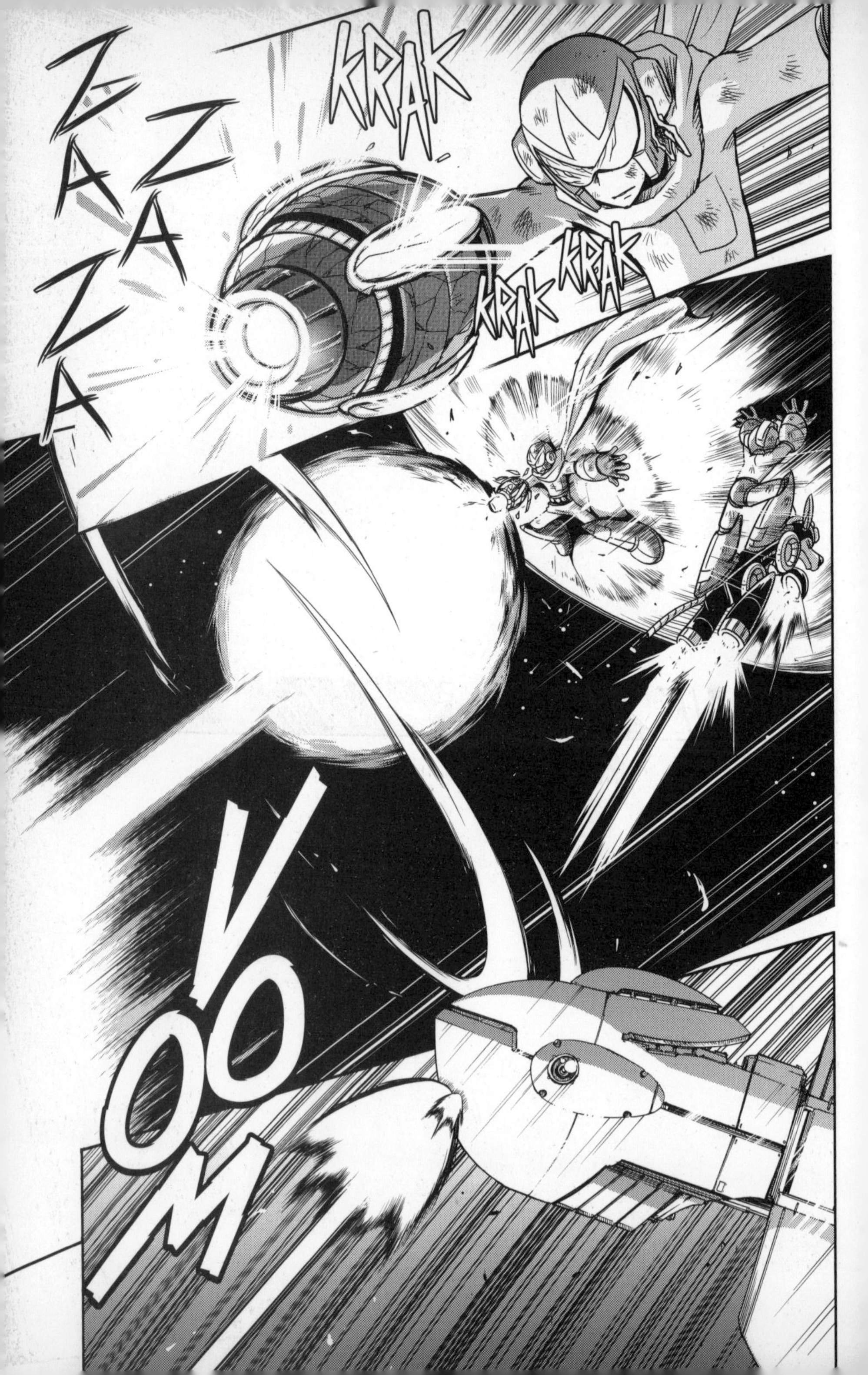
KRAK
ZAZAZA
KRAK KRAK
VOOM

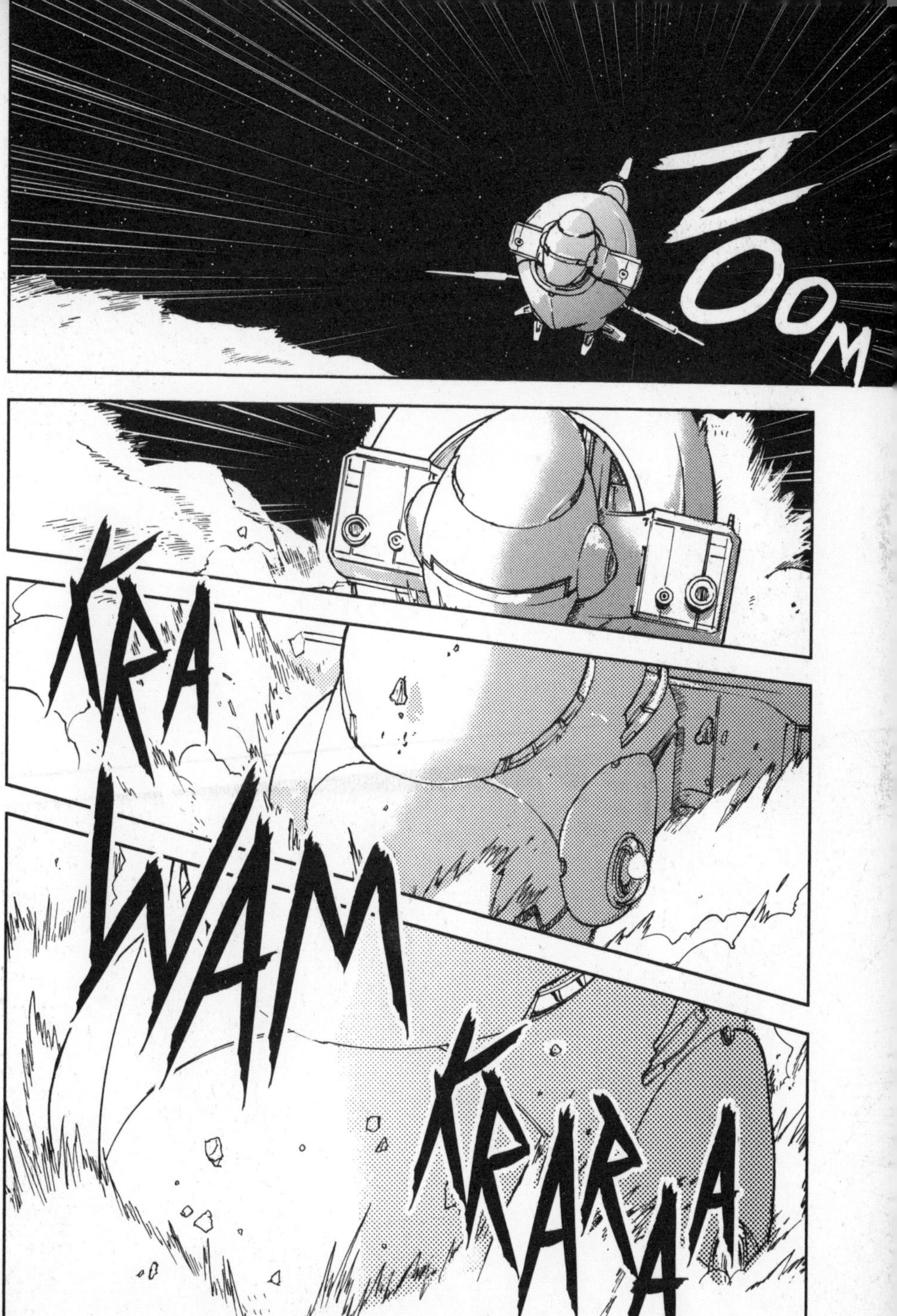
ZOOM
KRA
WAM
KRARAA

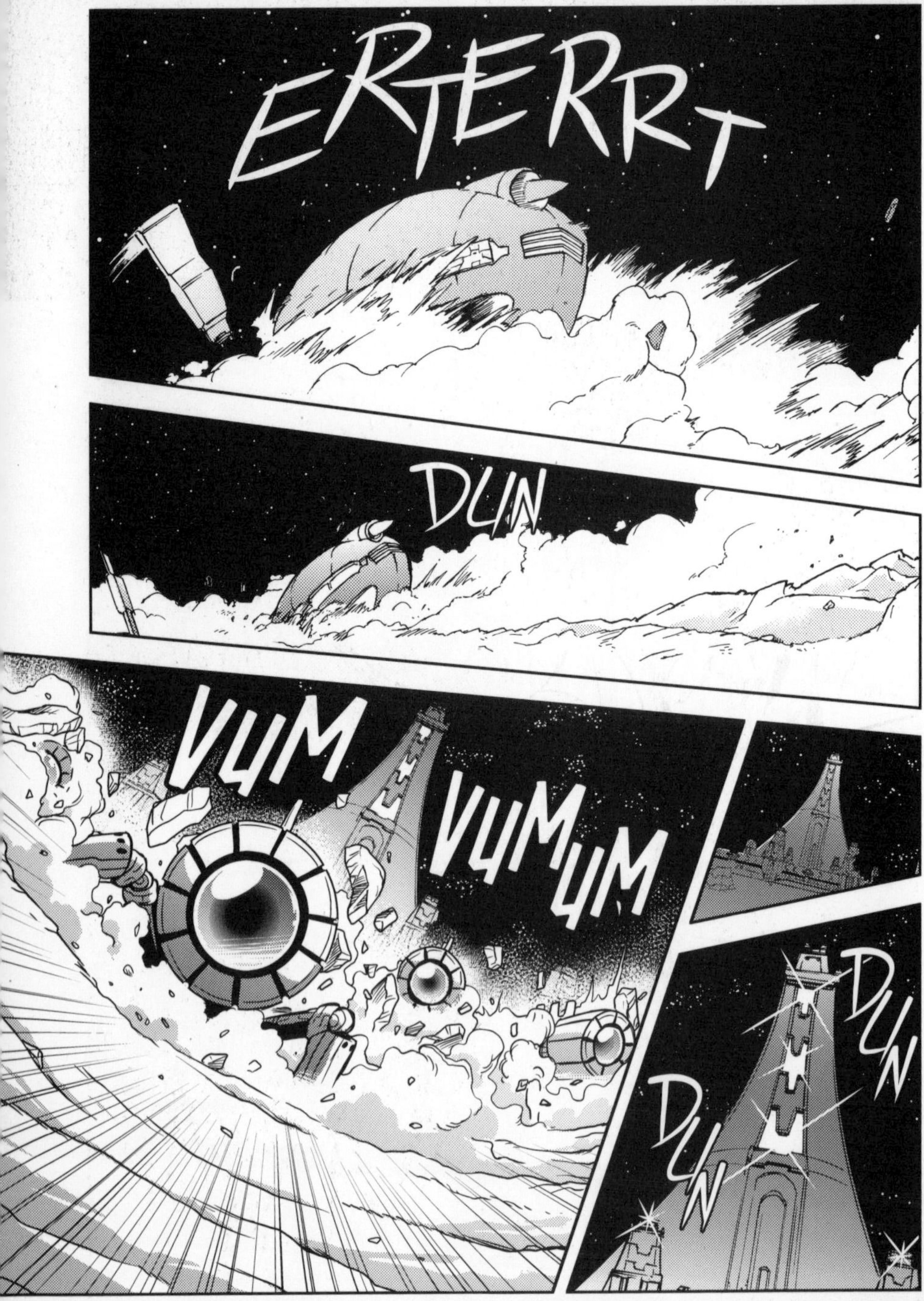
ERTERRT
DUN
DUN
DUN
VUM
VUMUM

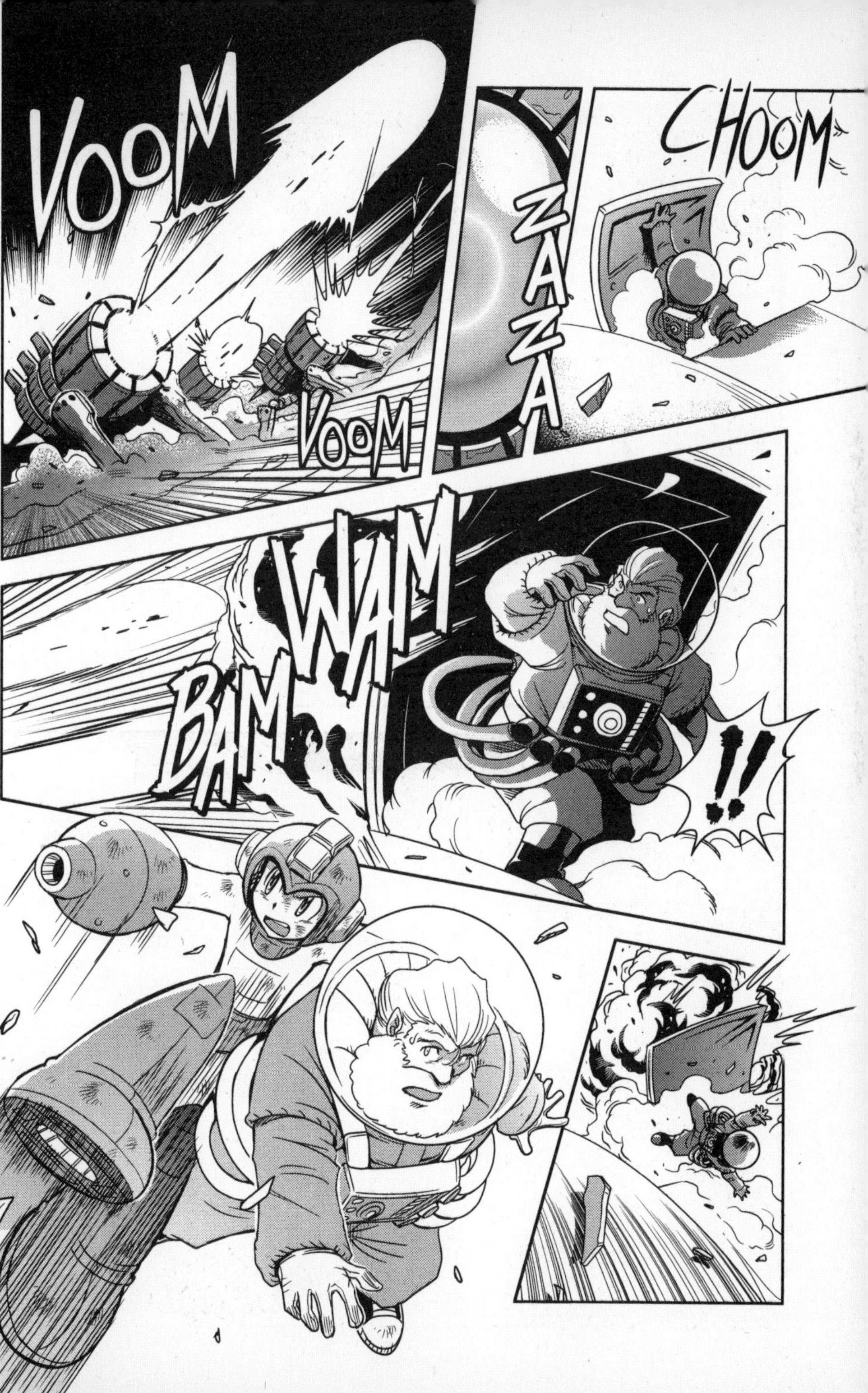
CHOOM
ZAZA
VOOM
VOOM
WAM
BAM
!!

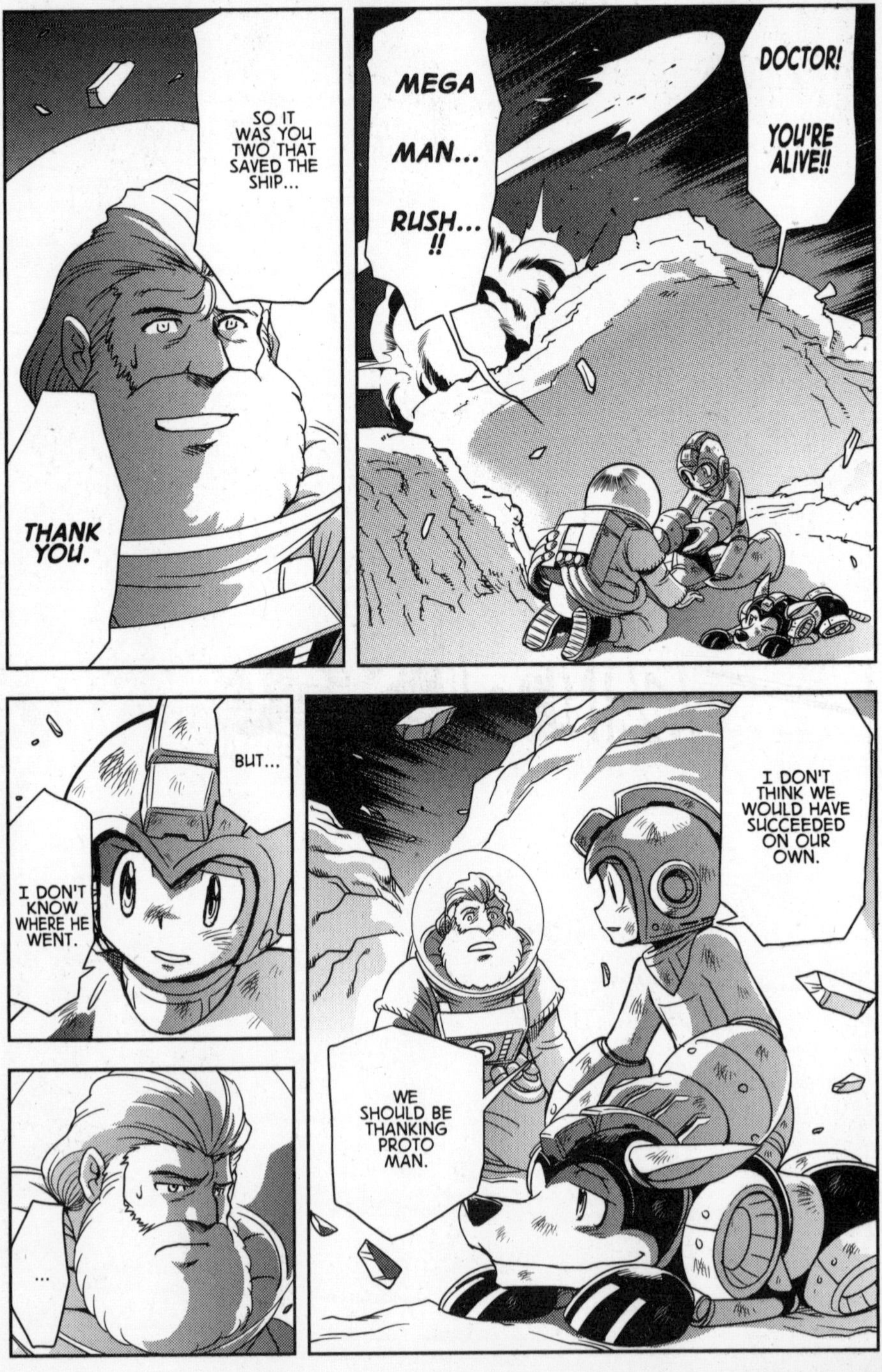
DOCTOR!
YOU'RE ALIVE!!
MEGA MAN...
RUSH... !!
SO IT WAS YOU TWO THAT SAVED THE SHIP...
THANK YOU.
I DON'T THINK WE WOULD HAVE SUCCEEDED ON OUR OWN.
WE SHOULD BE THANKING PROTO MAN.
BUT...
I DON'T KNOW WHERE HE WENT.
...

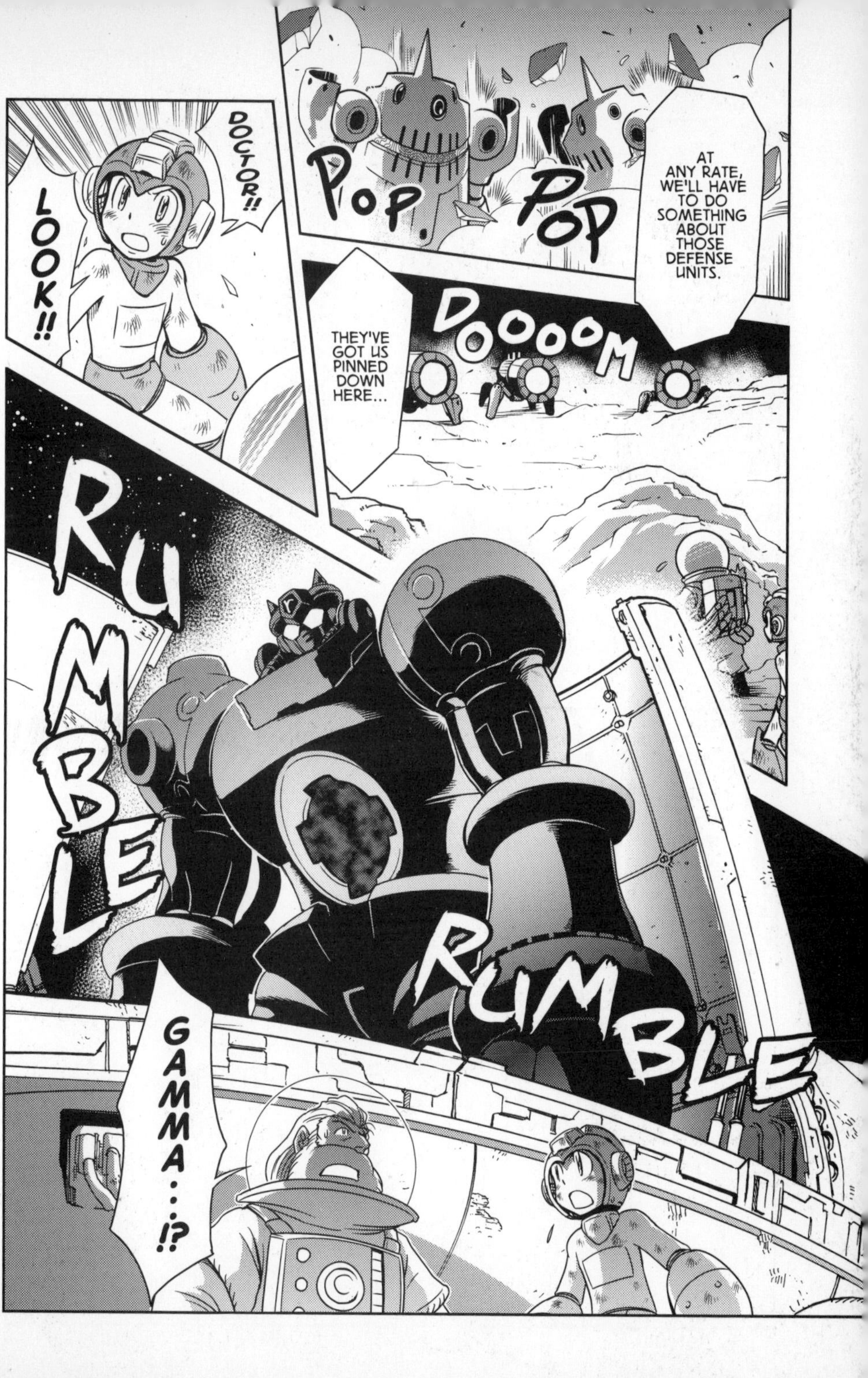

POP, POP
AT ANY RATE, WE'LL HAVE TO DO SOMETHING ABOUT THOSE DEFENSE UNITS.
DOOOOM
THEY'VE GOT US PINNED DOWN HERE...
DOCTOR!!
LOOK!!
RUMBLE
RUMBLE
GAMMA...!?

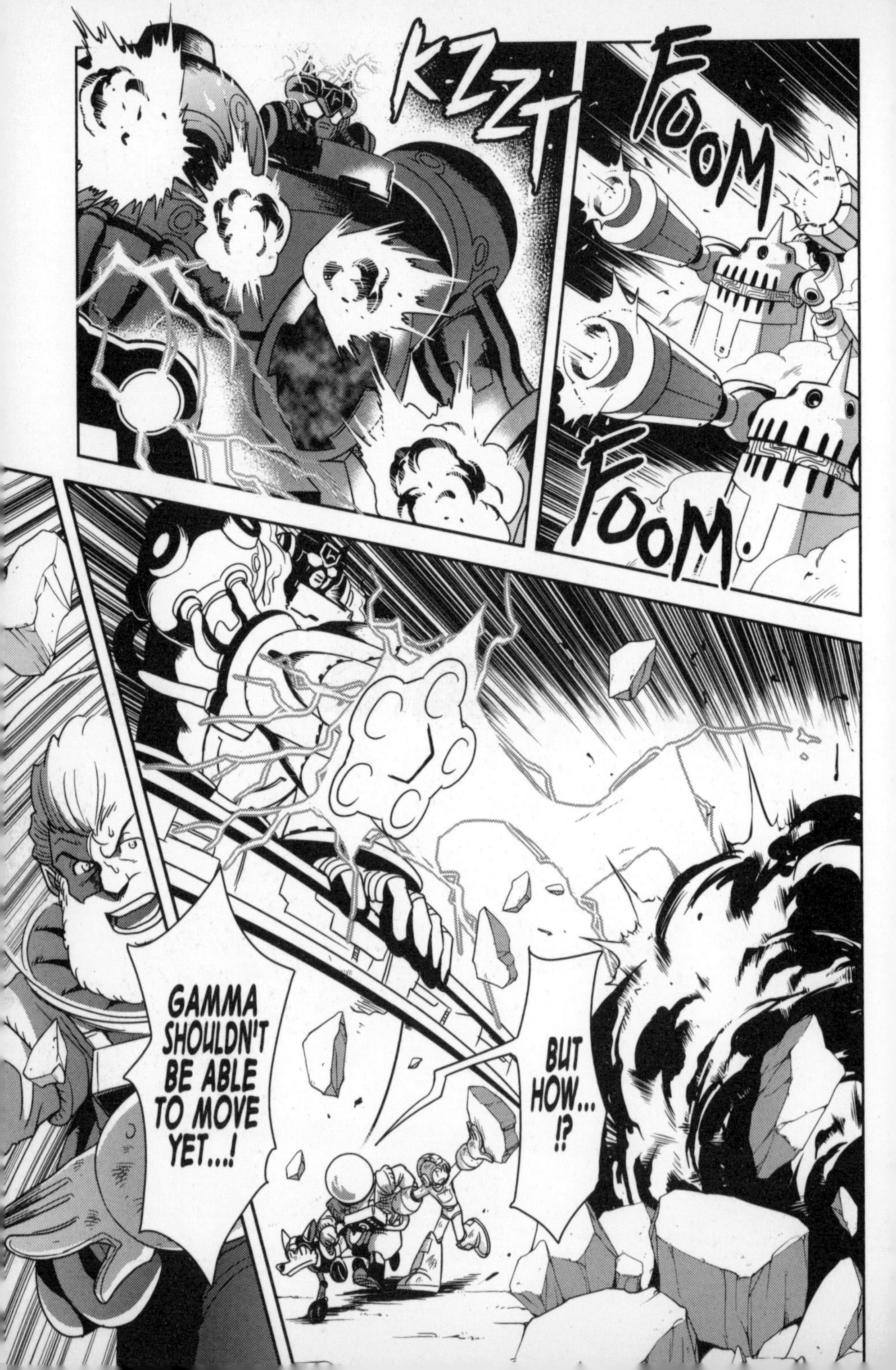
FOOM
FOOM
KZZT
BUT HOW... !?
GAMMA SHOULDN'T BE ABLE TO MOVE YET...!

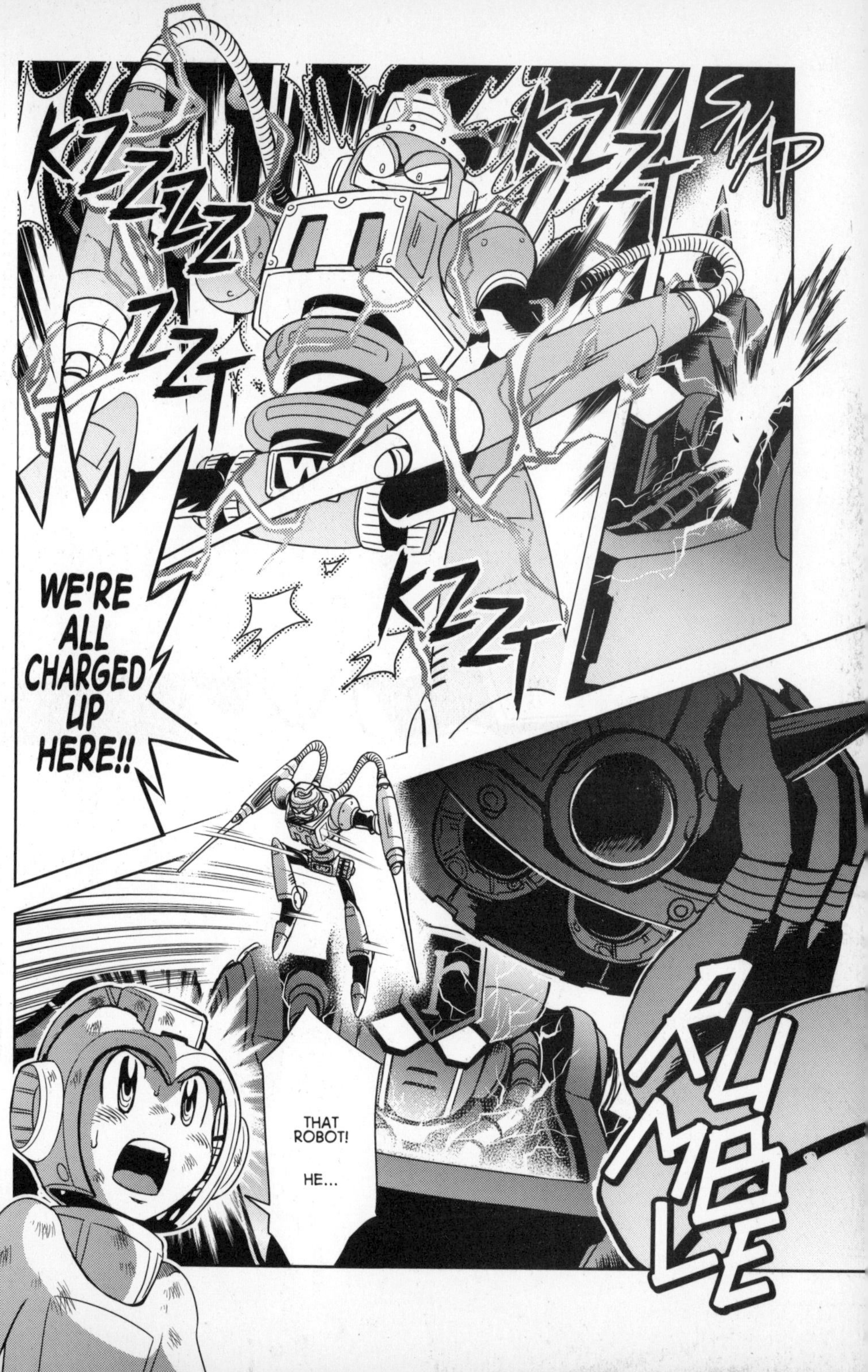
SNAP
KZZZT
KZZZZZ ZZT
WE'RE ALL CHARGED UP HERE!!
KZZZT
RUMBLE
THAT ROBOT!
HE...

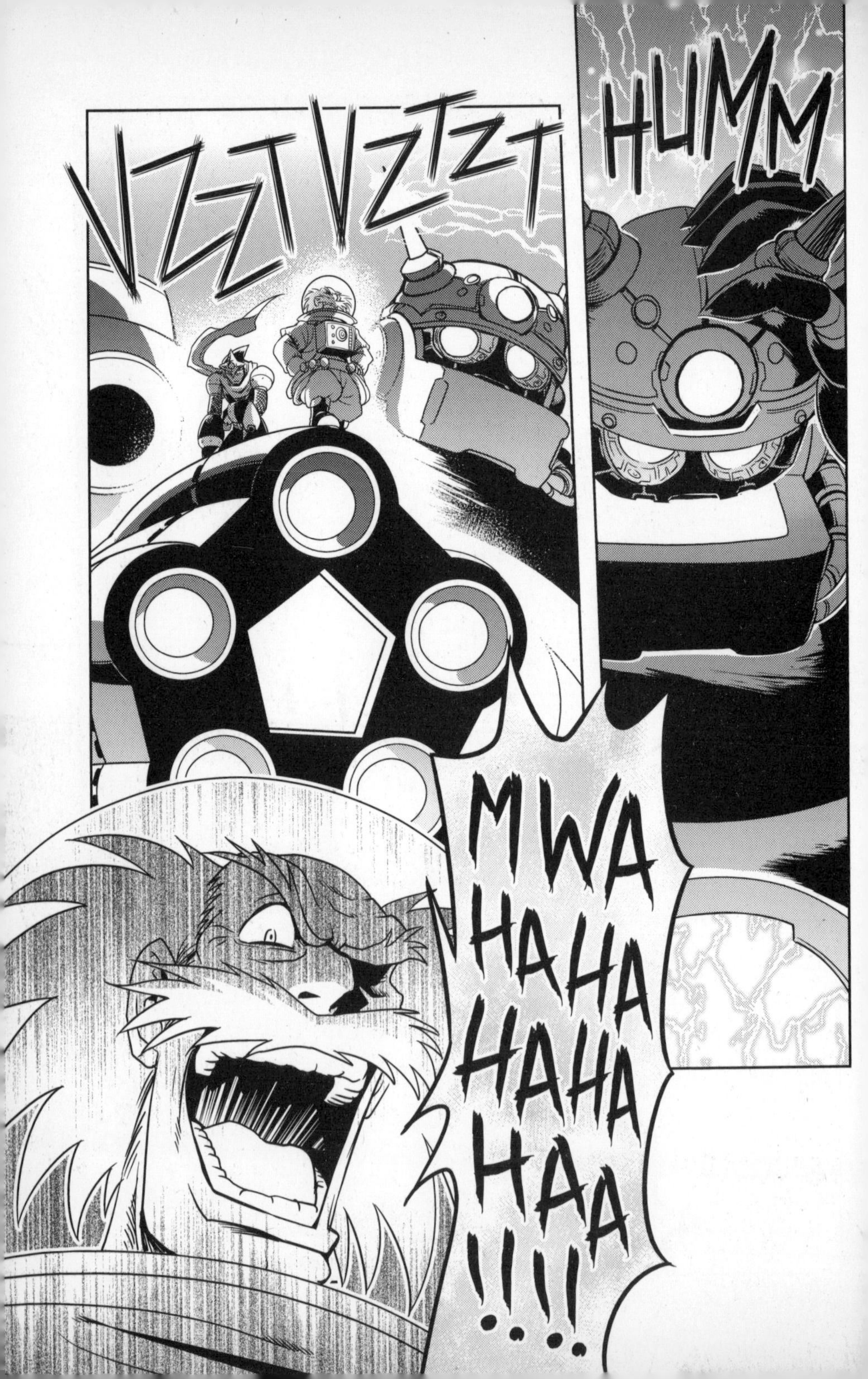
HUMM
VZZT VZTZT
MWA HAHA HAHA HAHA HAA !!!!

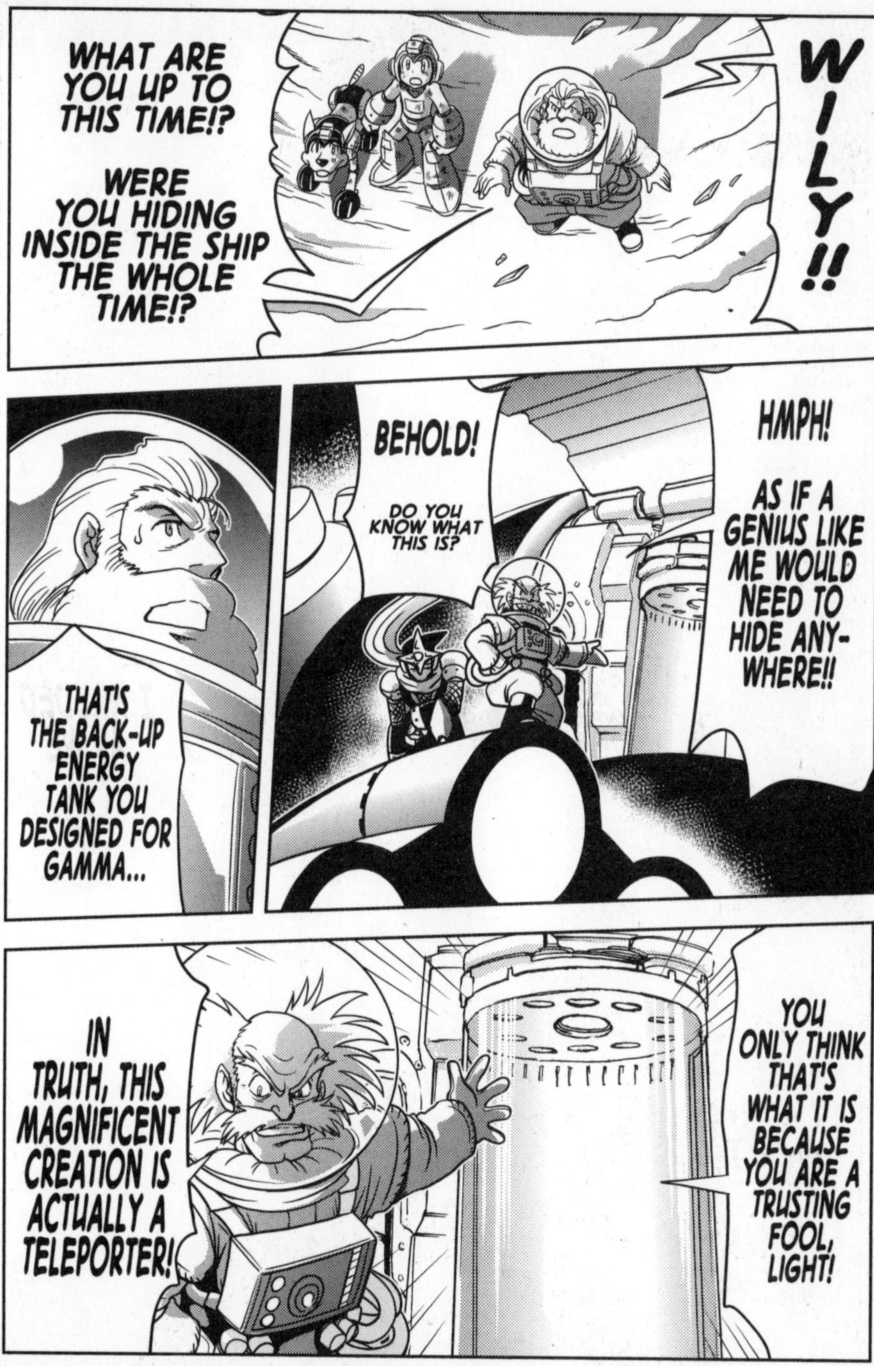
WILY!!
WHAT ARE YOU UP TO THIS TIME!?
WERE YOU HIDING INSIDE THE SHIP THE WHOLE TIME!?
HMPH!
AS IF A GENIUS LIKE ME WOULD NEED TO HIDE ANY-WHERE!!
BEHOLD!
DO YOU KNOW WHAT THIS IS?
THAT'S THE BACK-UP ENERGY TANK YOU DESIGNED FOR GAMMA...
YOU ONLY THINK THAT'S WHAT IT IS BECAUSE YOU ARE A TRUSTING FOOL, LIGHT!
IN TRUTH, THIS MAGNIFICENT CREATION IS ACTUALLY A TELEPORTER!

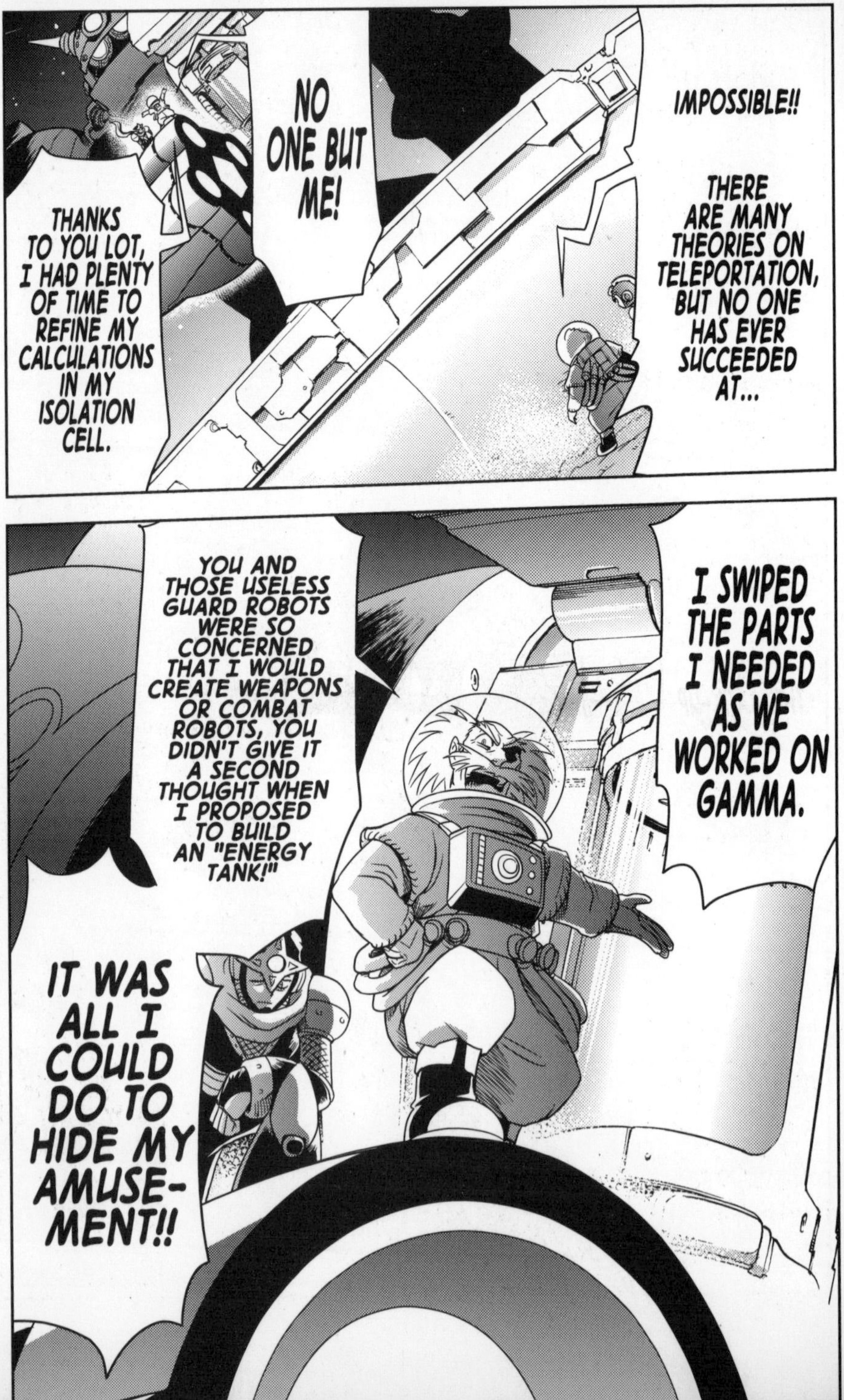
IMPOSSIBLE!!
THERE ARE MANY THEORIES ON TELEPORTATION, BUT NO ONE HAS EVER SUCCEEDED AT...
NO ONE BUT ME!
THANKS TO YOU LOT, I HAD PLENTY OF TIME TO REFINE MY CALCULATIONS IN MY ISOLATION CELL.
I SWIPED THE PARTS I NEEDED AS WE WORKED ON GAMMA.
YOU AND THOSE USELESS GUARD ROBOTS WERE SO CONCERNED THAT I WOULD CREATE WEAPONS OR COMBAT ROBOTS, YOU DIDN'T GIVE IT A SECOND THOUGHT WHEN I PROPOSED TO BUILD AN "ENERGY TANK!"
IT WAS ALL I COULD DO TO HIDE MY AMUSE-MENT!!

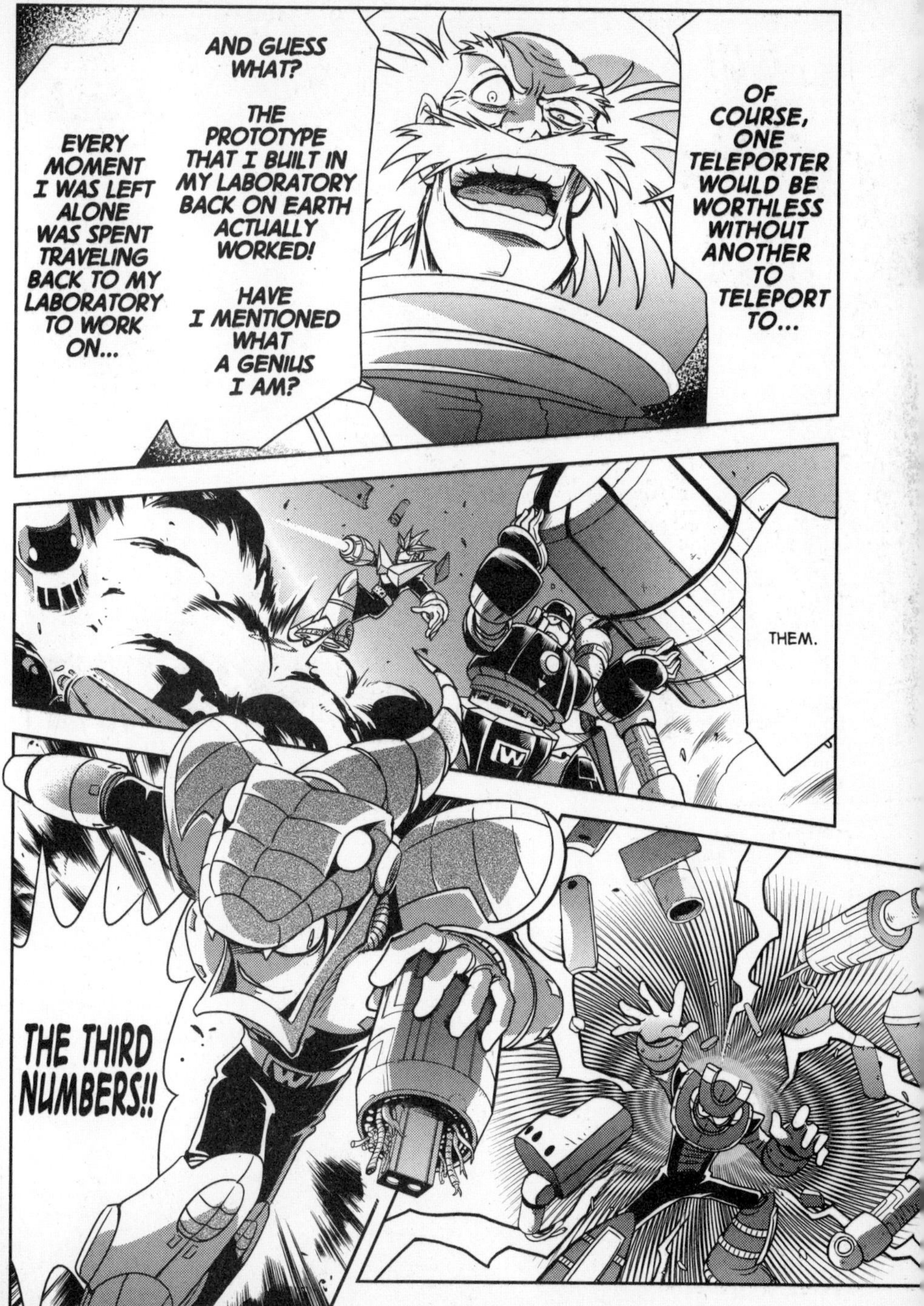
OF COURSE, ONE TELEPORTER WOULD BE WORTHLESS WITHOUT ANOTHER TO TELEPORT TO...
AND GUESS WHAT?
THE PROTOTYPE THAT I BUILT IN MY LABORATORY BACK ON EARTH ACTUALLY WORKED!
HAVE I MENTIONED WHAT A GENIUS I AM?
EVERY MOMENT I WAS LEFT ALONE WAS SPENT TRAVELING BACK TO MY LABORATORY TO WORK ON...
THEM.
THE THIRD NUMBERS!!

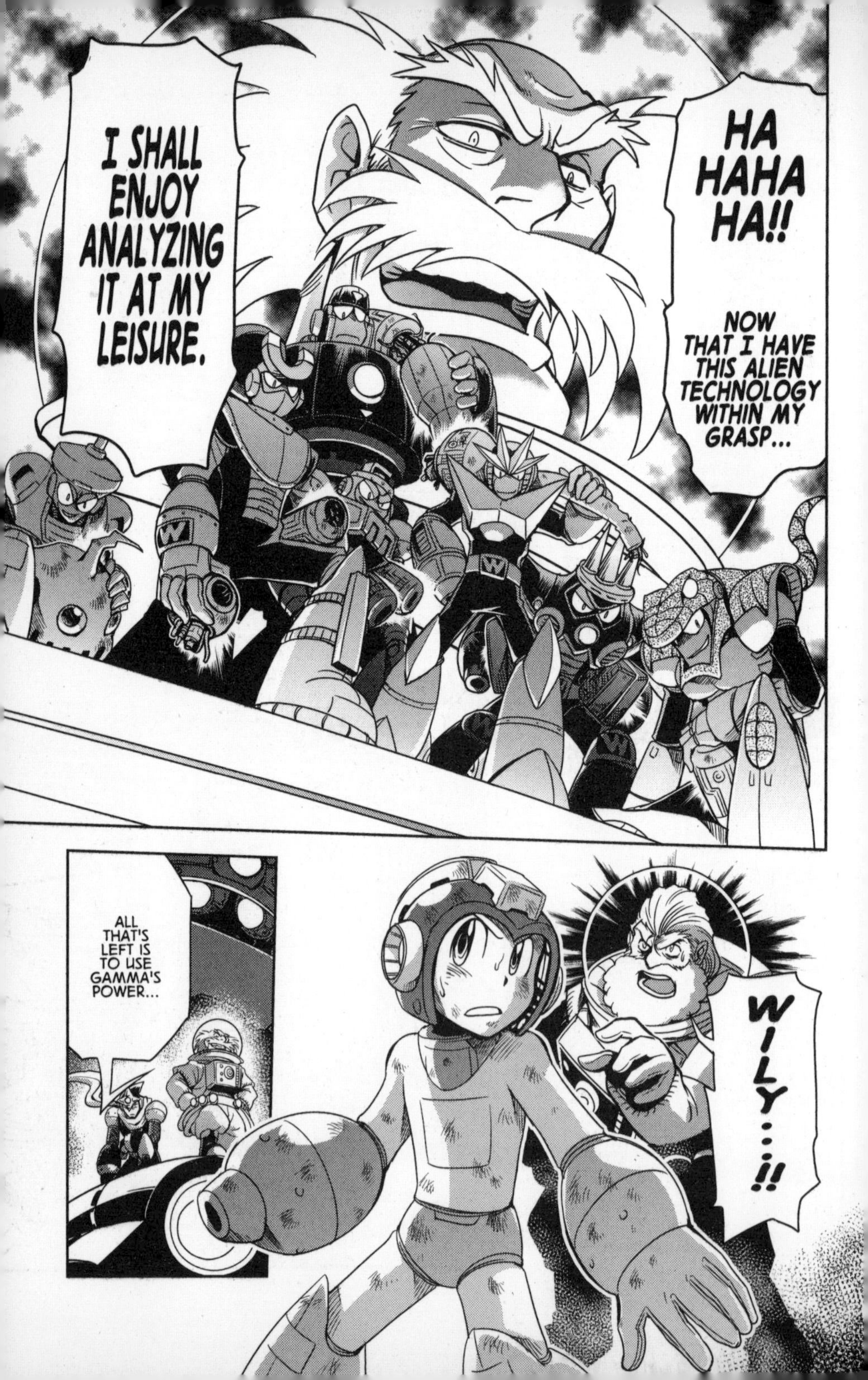
HA HAHAHA HA!!
NOW THAT I HAVE THIS ALIEN TECHNOLOGY WITHIN MY GRASP...
I SHALL ENJOY ANALYZING IT AT MY LEISURE.
WILY...!!
ALL THAT'S LEFT IS TO USE GAMMA'S POWER...

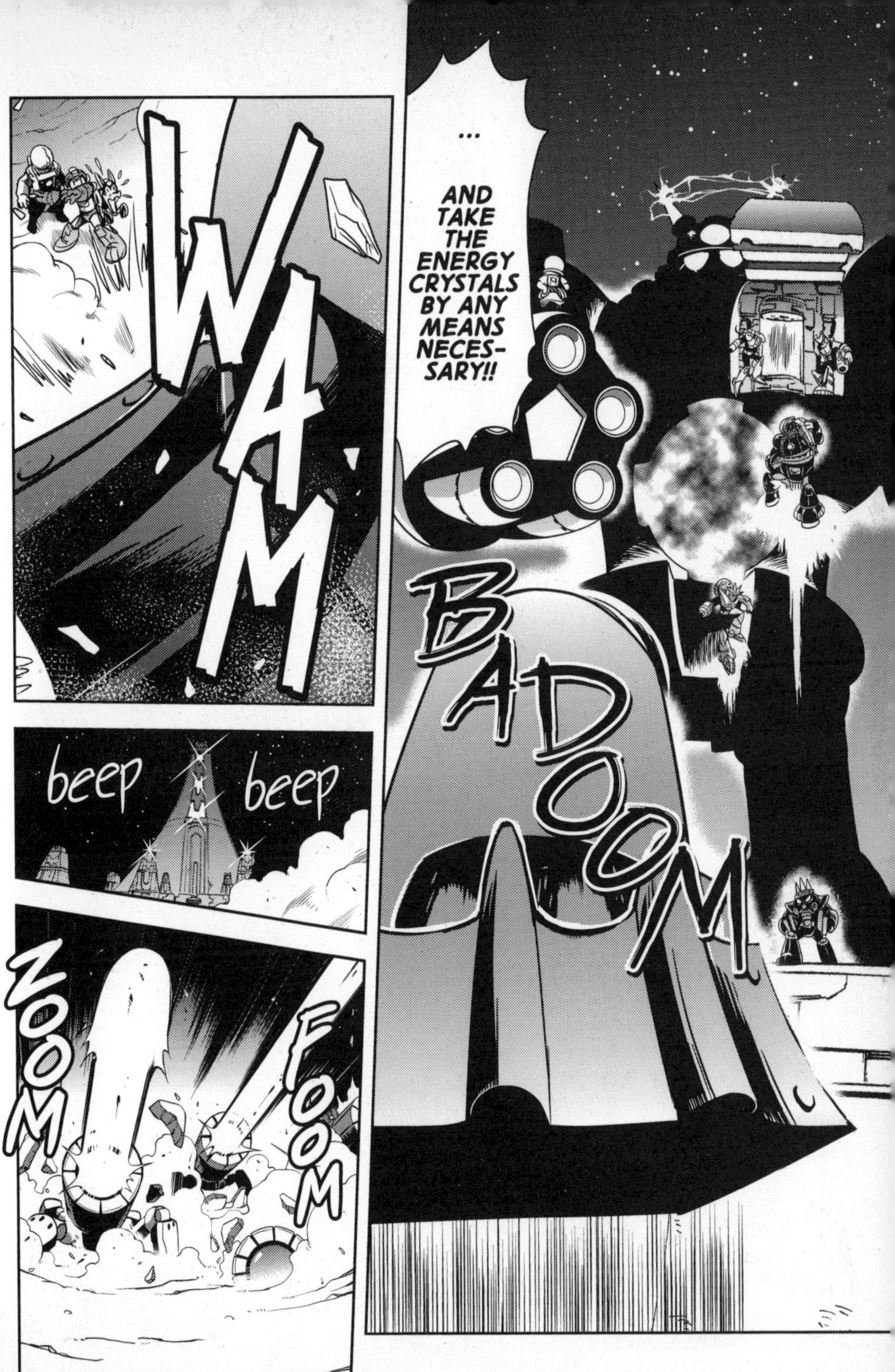
...
AND TAKE THE ENERGY CRYSTALS BY ANY MEANS NECES-SARY!!
BADOOM
WAM
beep beep
ZOOM
FOOM

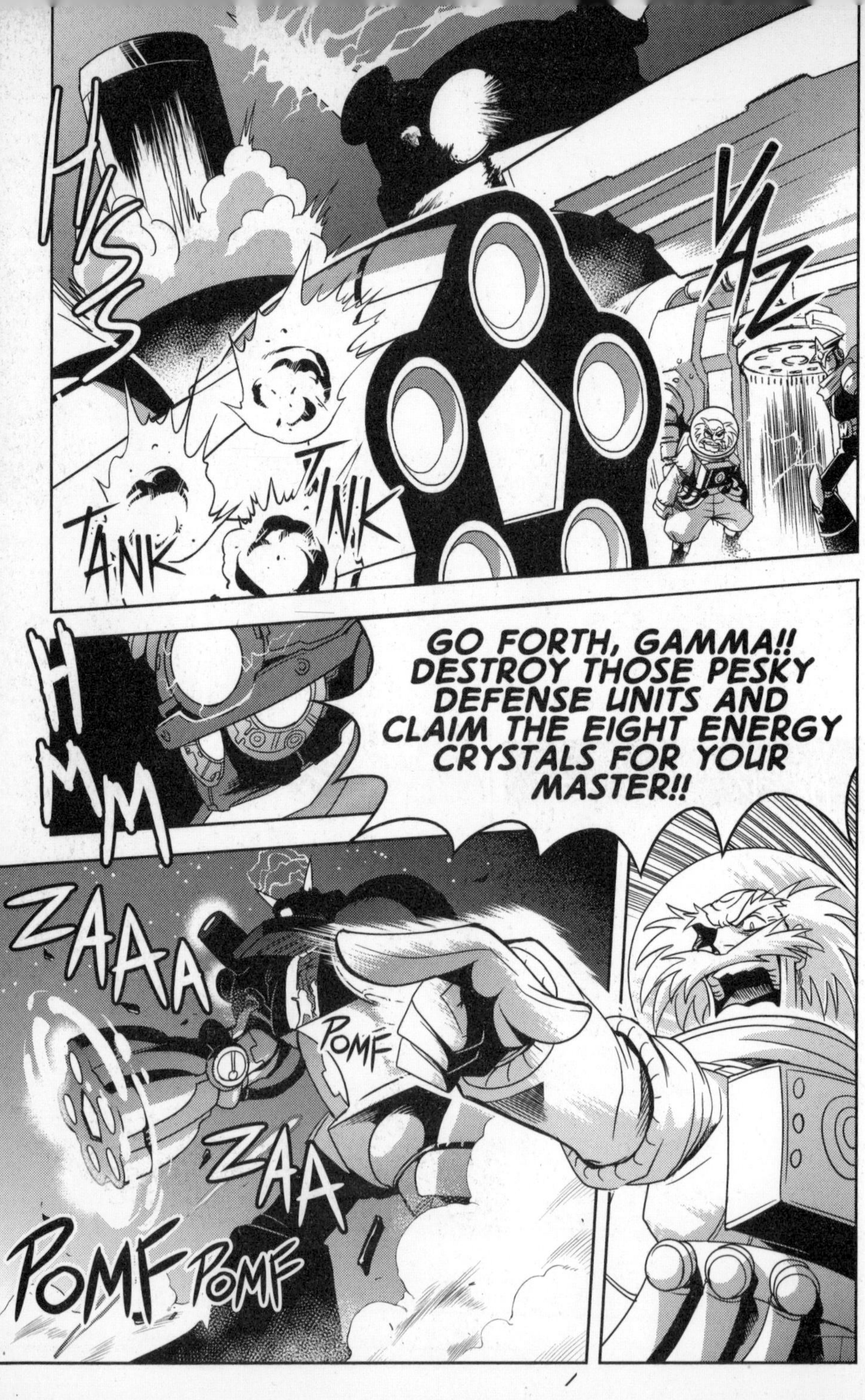
VAZ
HISS
TINK
TANK
HMM
GO FORTH, GAMMA!! DESTROY THOSE PESKY DEFENSE UNITS AND CLAIM THE EIGHT ENERGY CRYSTALS FOR YOUR MASTER!!
ZAAA
POMF
ZAA
POMF POMF

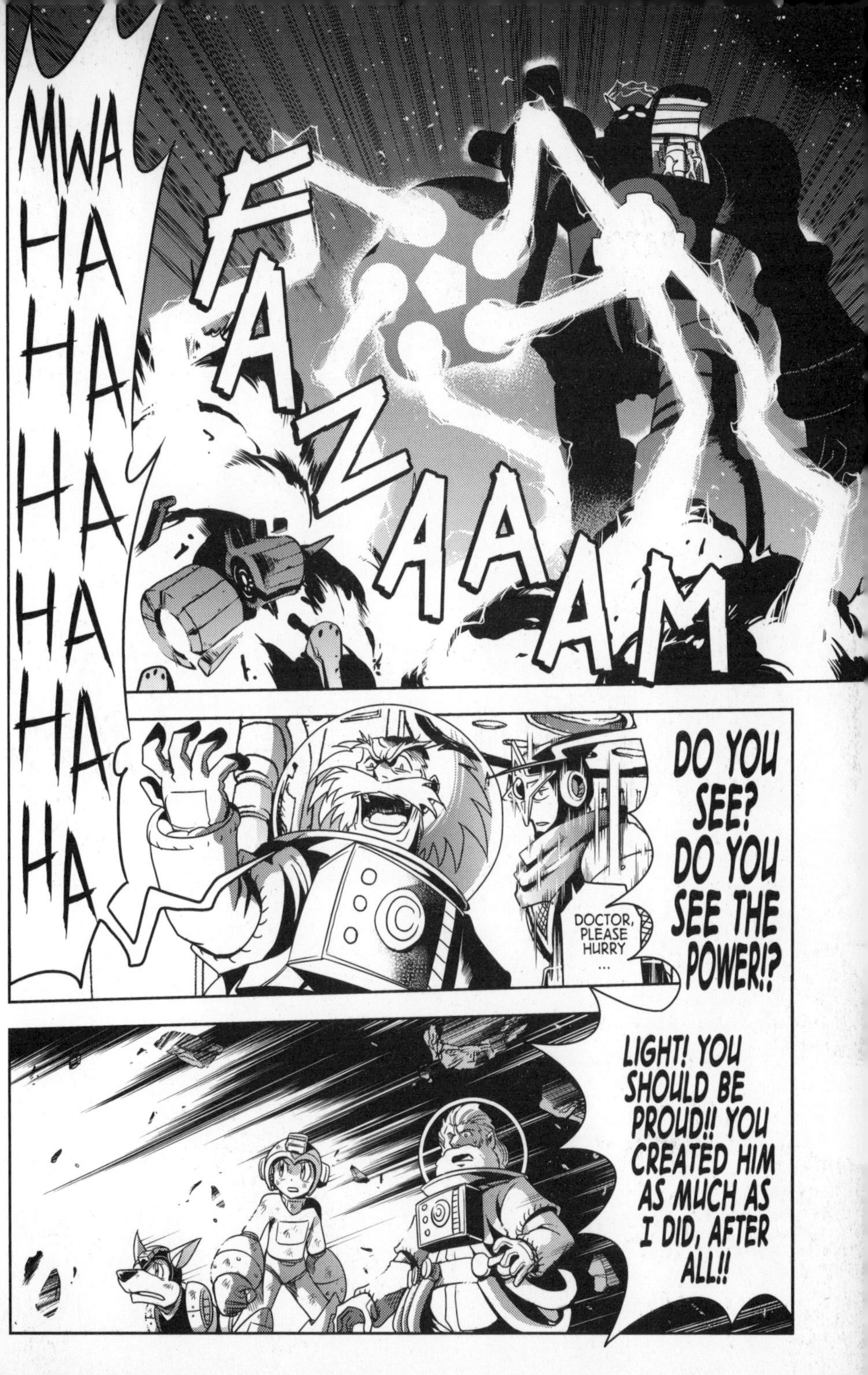
FAZAAAAM
MWA HA HA HA HA HA HA HA HA
DO YOU SEE? DO YOU SEE THE POWER!?
DOCTOR, PLEASE HURRY ...
LIGHT! YOU SHOULD BE PROUD!! YOU CREATED HIM AS MUCH AS I DID, AFTER ALL!!

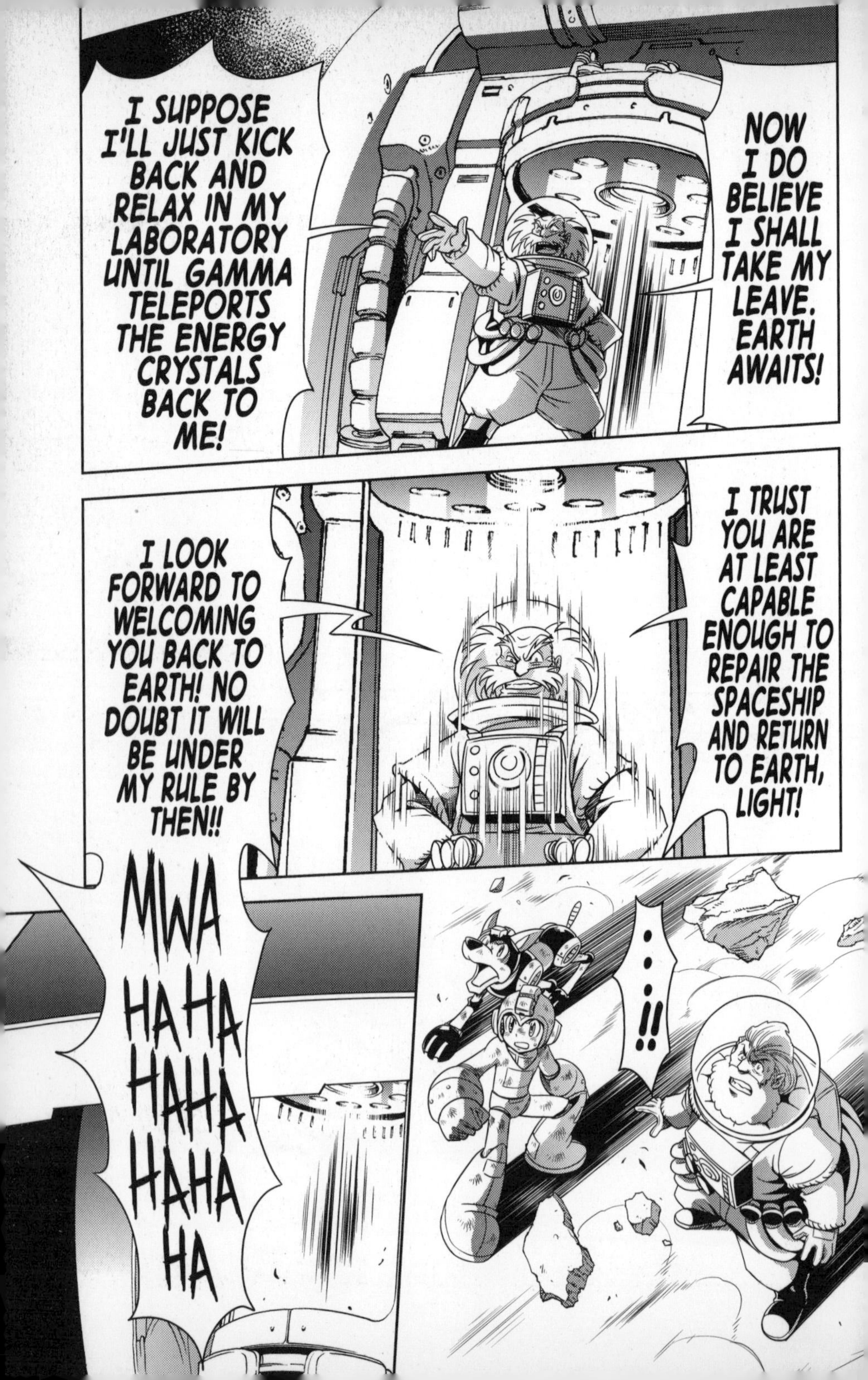
NOW I DO BELIEVE I SHALL TAKE MY LEAVE. EARTH AWAITS!
I SUPPOSE I'LL JUST KICK BACK AND RELAX IN MY LABORATORY UNTIL GAMMA TELEPORTS THE ENERGY CRYSTALS BACK TO ME!
I TRUST YOU ARE AT LEAST CAPABLE ENOUGH TO REPAIR THE SPACESHIP AND RETURN TO EARTH, LIGHT!
I LOOK FORWARD TO WELCOMING YOU BACK TO EARTH! NO DOUBT IT WILL BE UNDER MY RULE BY THEN!!
MWA HAHA HAHA HAHA HA
...!!

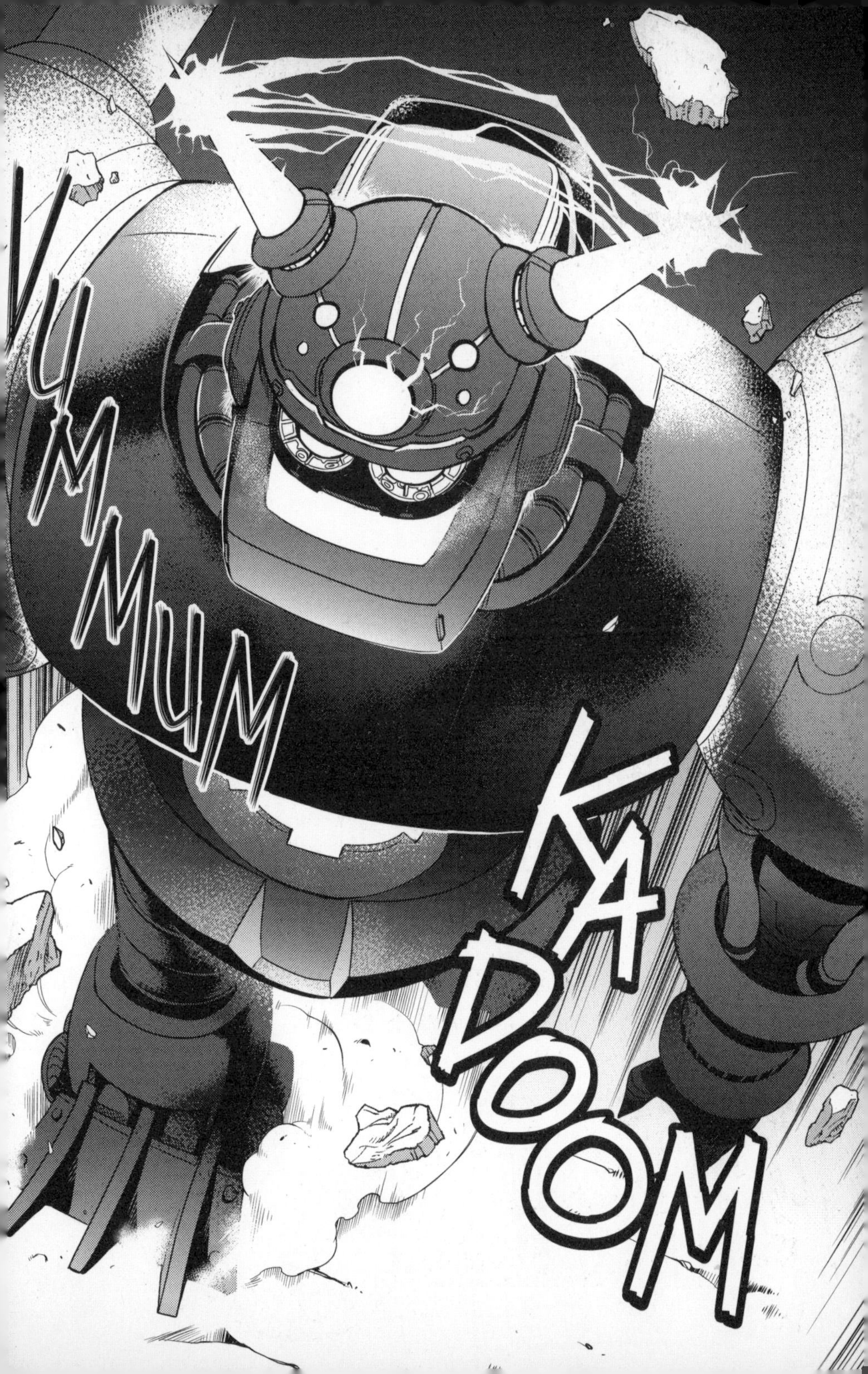
VUMMUMMUM
KADOOM

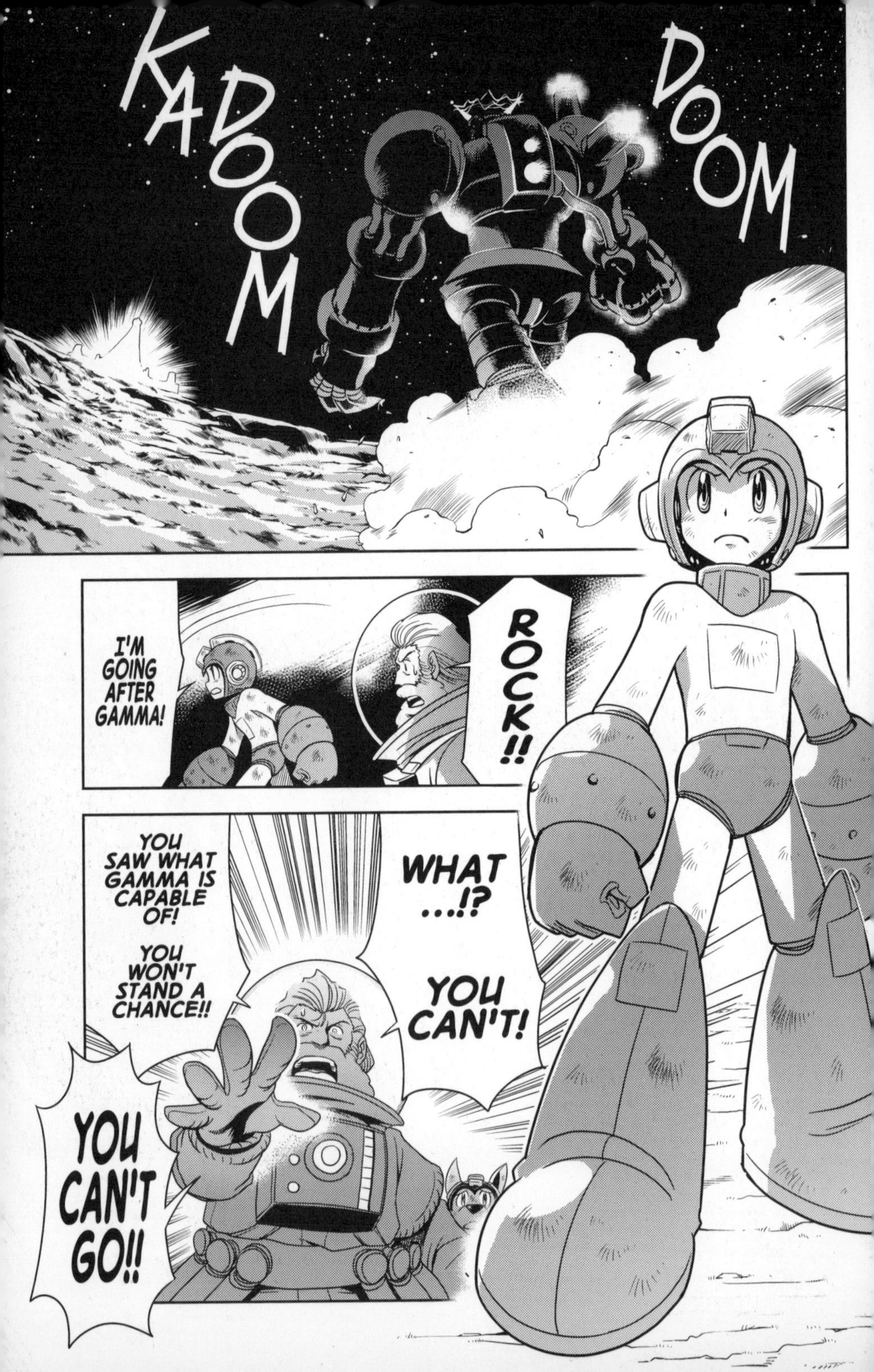
DOOM
KADOOM
ROCK!!
I'M GOING AFTER GAMMA!
WHAT ...!?
YOU CAN'T!
YOU SAW WHAT GAMMA IS CAPABLE OF!
YOU WON'T STAND A CHANCE!!
YOU CAN'T GO!!

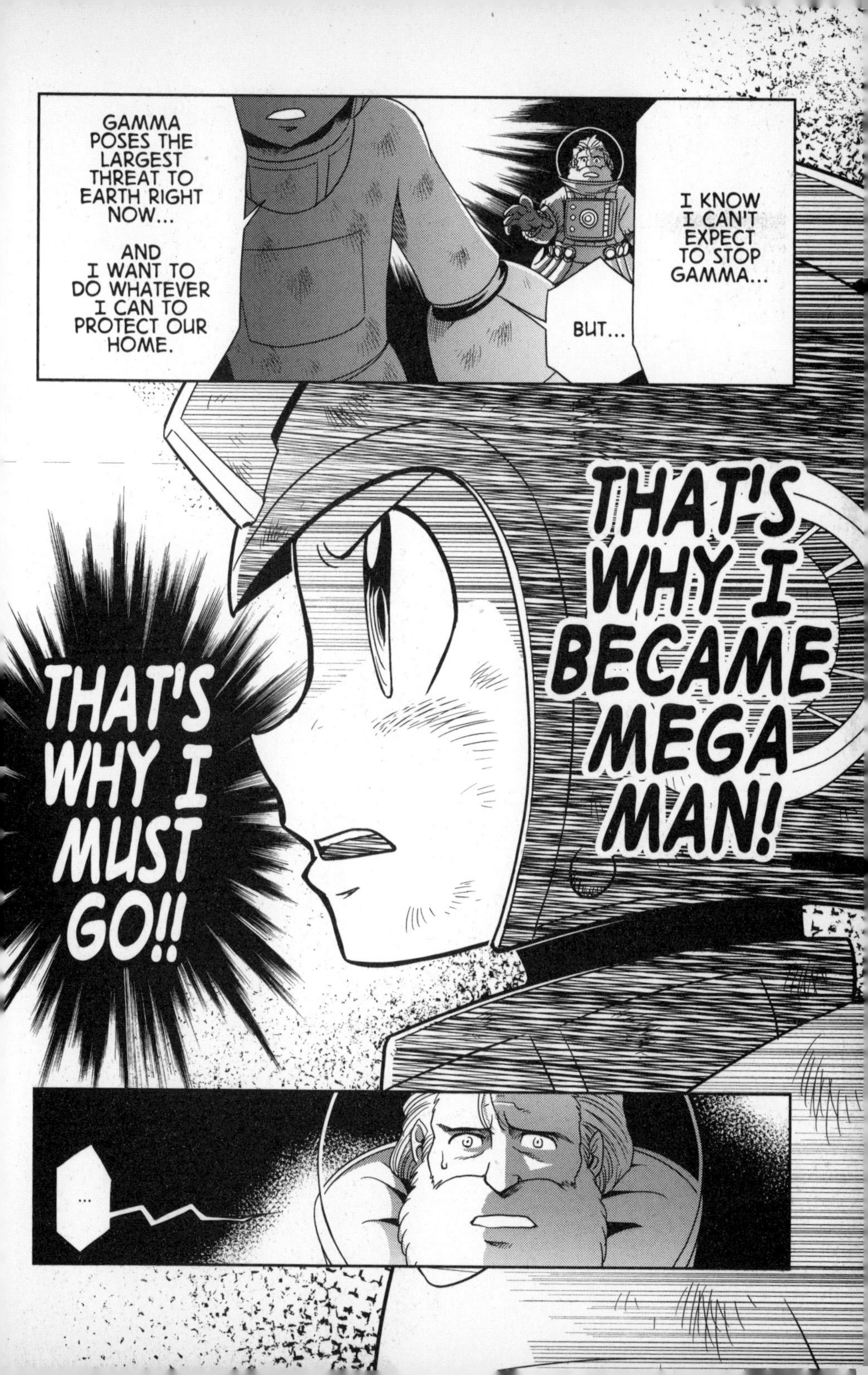
I KNOW I CAN'T EXPECT TO STOP GAMMA...
BUT...
GAMMA POSES THE LARGEST THREAT TO EARTH RIGHT NOW...
AND I WANT TO DO WHATEVER I CAN TO PROTECT OUR HOME.
THAT'S WHY I BECAME MEGA MAN!
THAT'S WHY I MUST GO!!
...

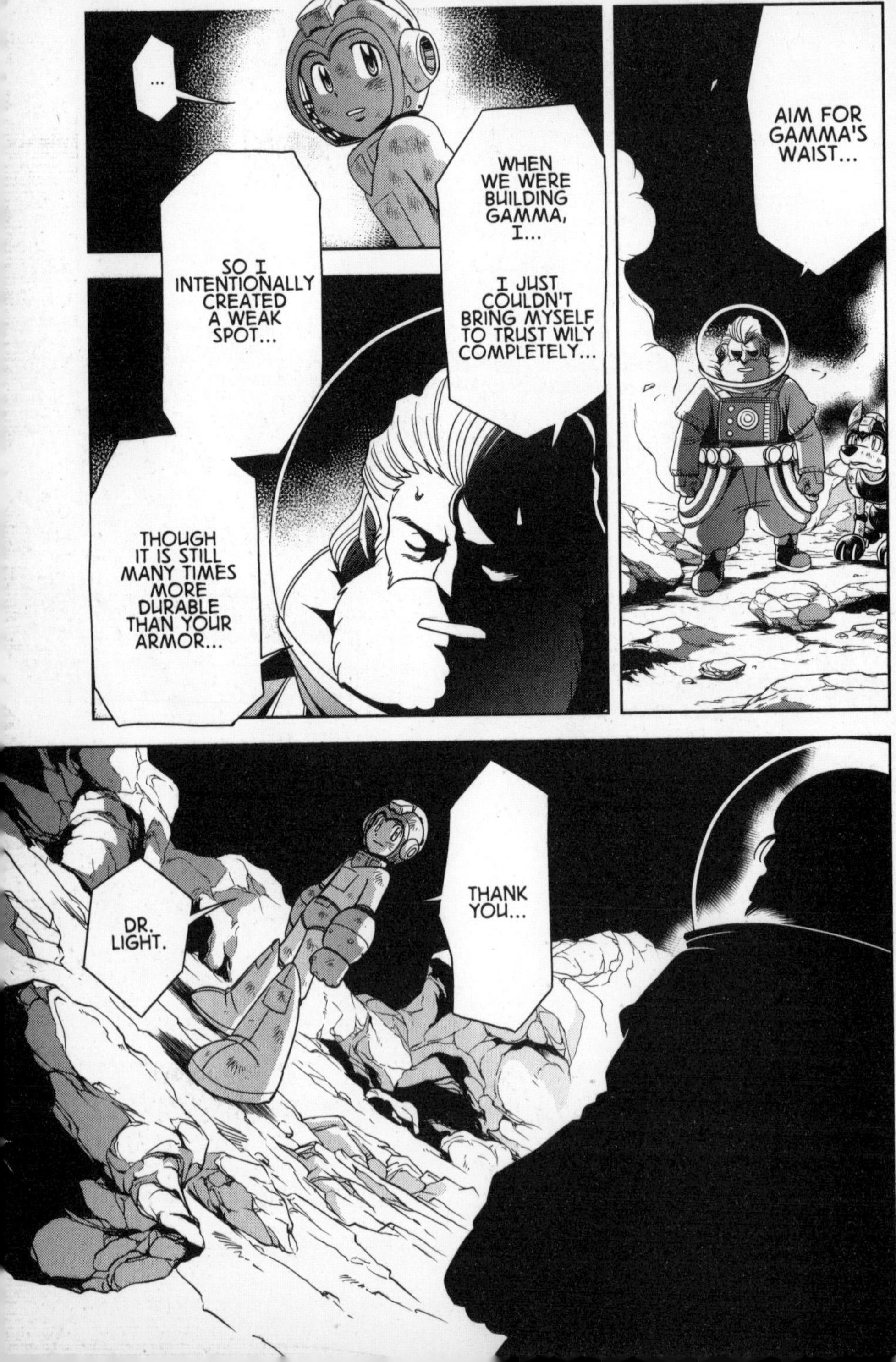
AIM FOR GAMMA'S WAIST...
...
WHEN WE WERE BUILDING GAMMA, I...
I JUST COULDN'T BRING MYSELF TO TRUST WILY COMPLETELY...
SO I INTENTIONALLY CREATED A WEAK SPOT...
THOUGH IT IS STILL MANY TIMES MORE DURABLE THAN YOUR ARMOR...
THANK YOU...
DR. LIGHT.

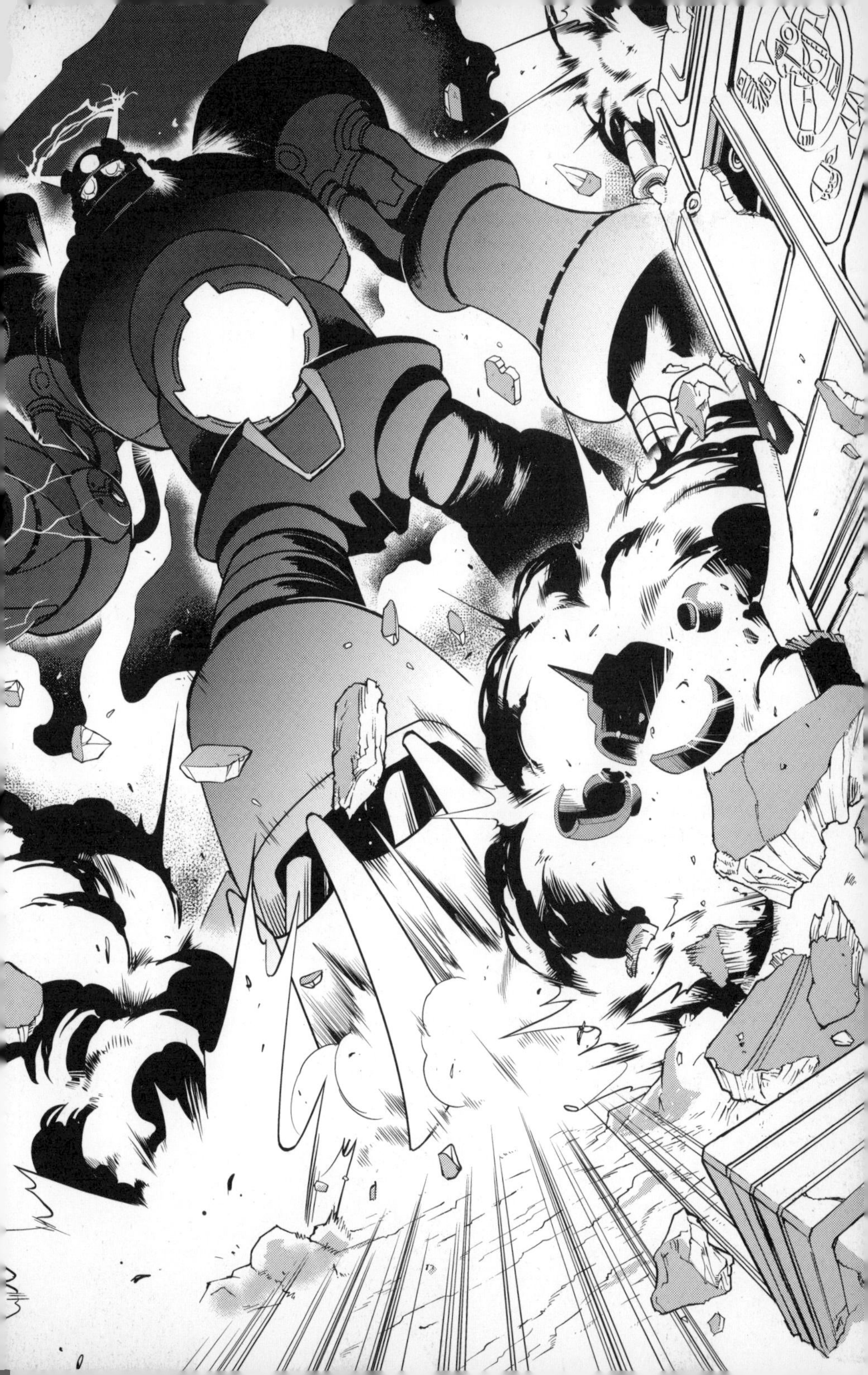

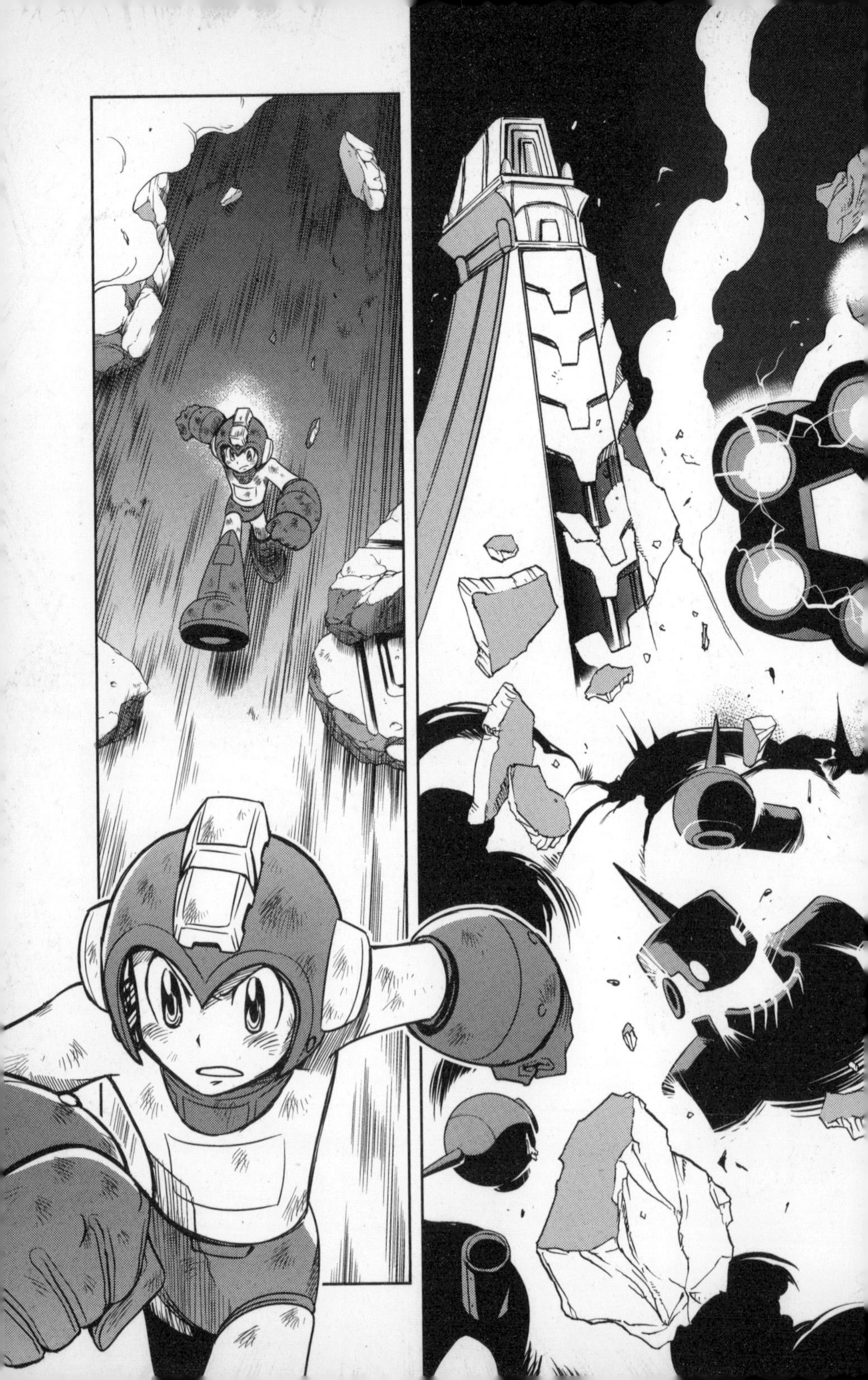

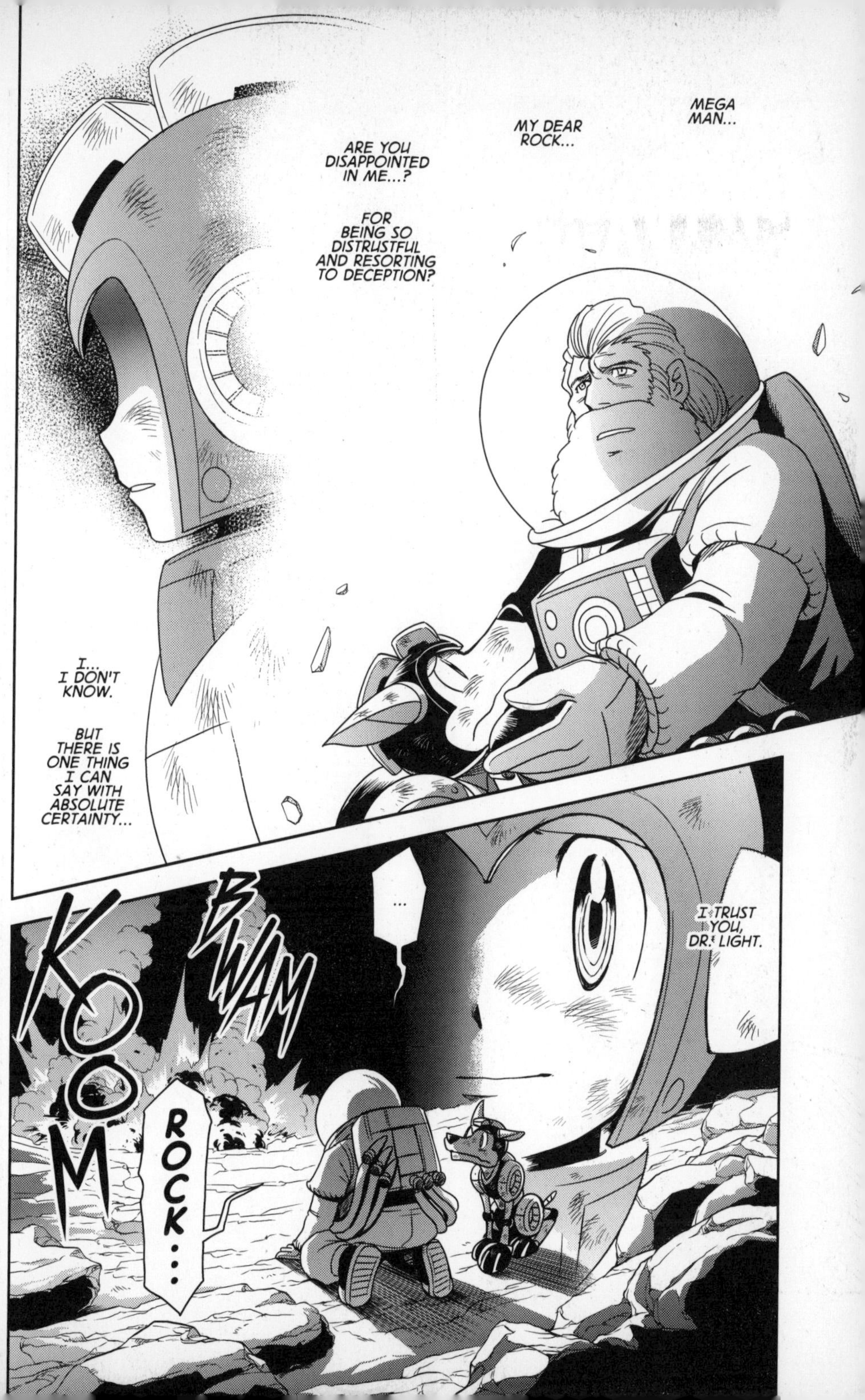
MEGA MAN...
MY DEAR ROCK...
ARE YOU DISAPPOINTED IN ME...?
FOR BEING SO DISTRUSTFUL AND RESORTING TO DECEPTION?
I... I DON'T KNOW.
BUT THERE IS ONE THING I CAN SAY WITH ABSOLUTE CERTAINTY...
I TRUST YOU, DR. LIGHT.
...
BWAM
KOOOM
ROCK...

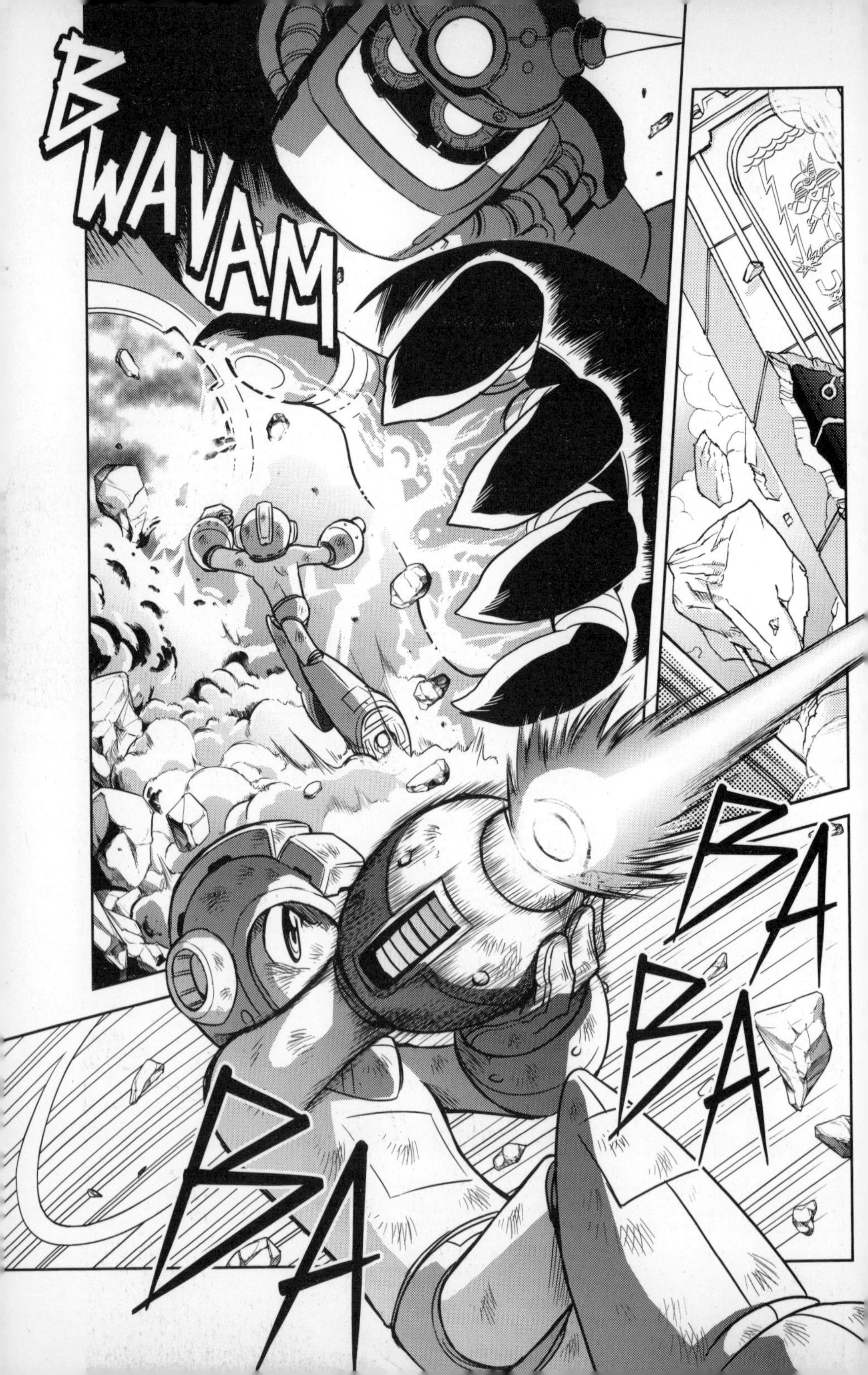
BWAVAM
BA BA
BA BA

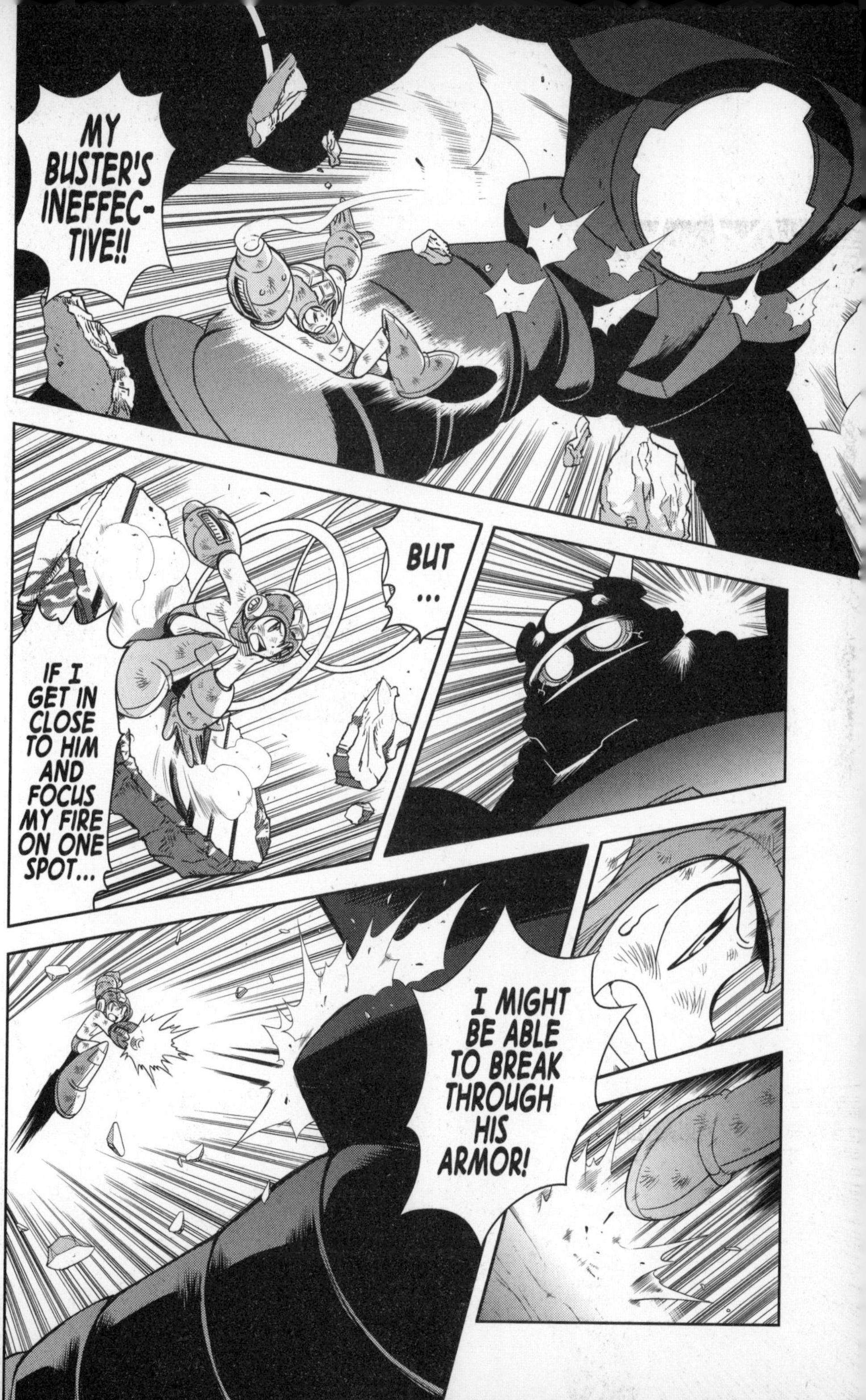
MY BUSTER'S INEFFEC-TIVE!!
BUT ...
IF I GET IN CLOSE TO HIM AND FOCUS MY FIRE ON ONE SPOT...
I MIGHT BE ABLE TO BREAK THROUGH HIS ARMOR!

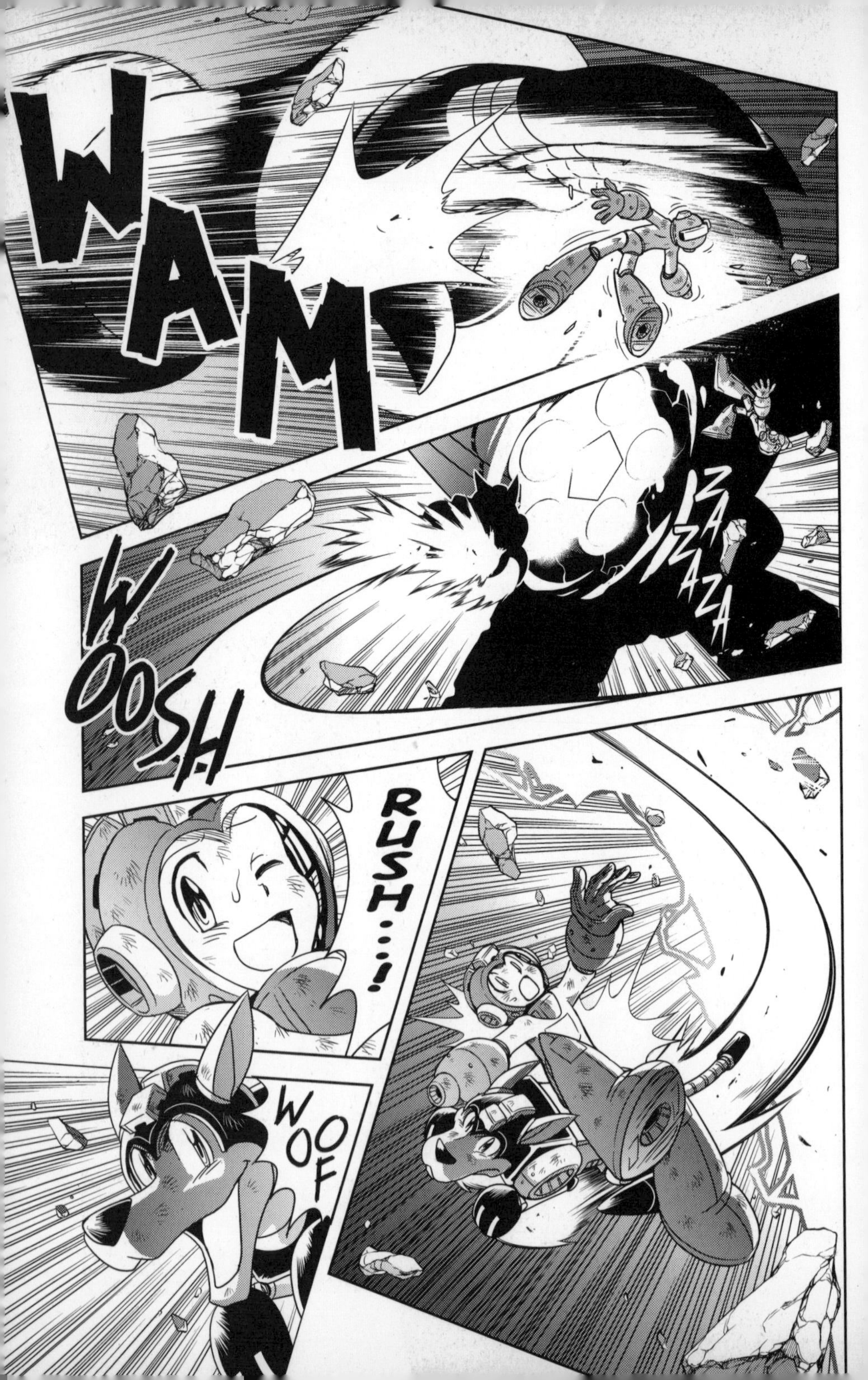
WAM
ZAZAZAZA
WOOSH
RUSH...!
WOOF

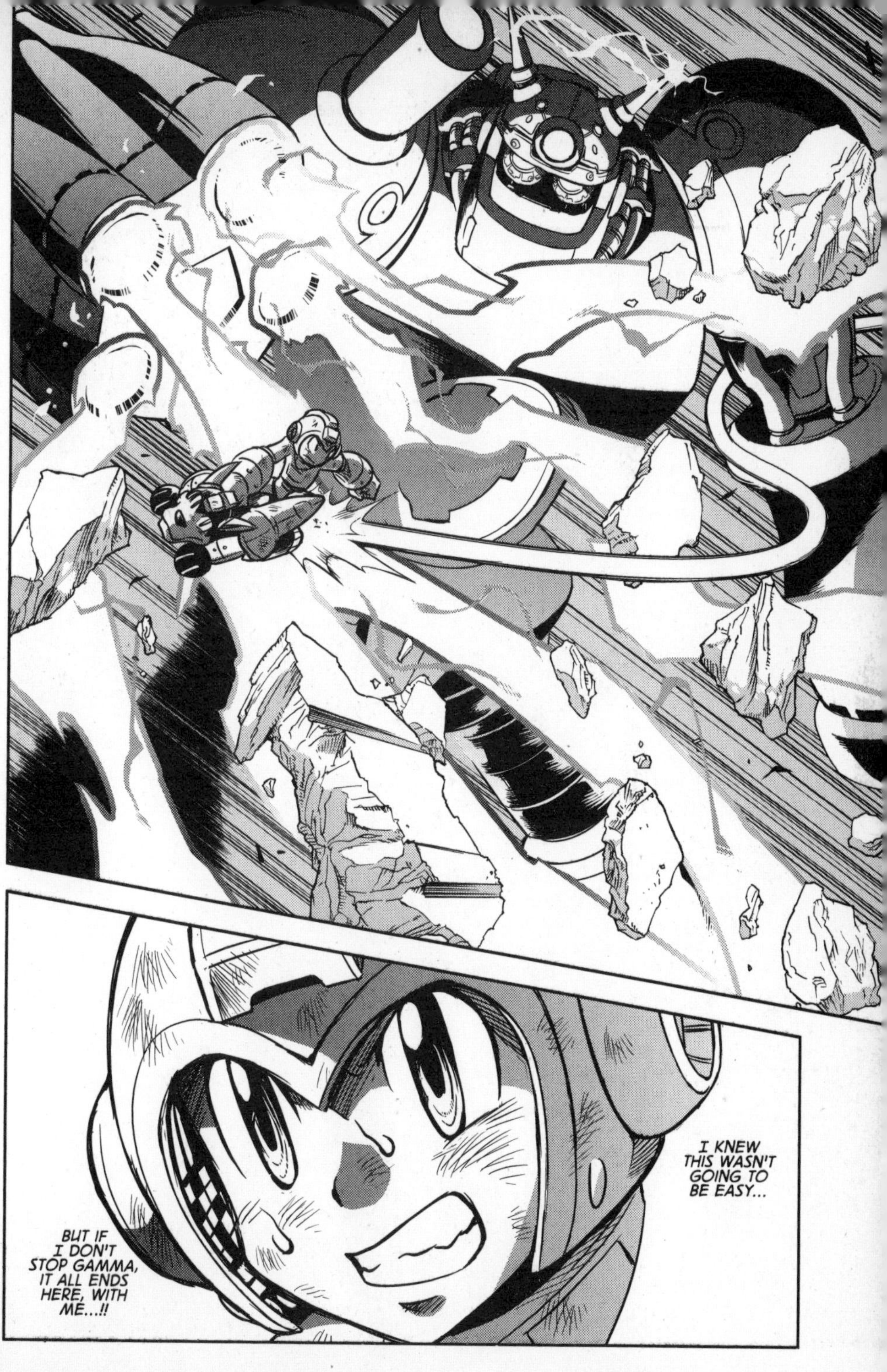
I KNEW THIS WASN'T GOING TO BE EASY...
BUT IF I DON'T STOP GAMMA, IT ALL ENDS HERE, WITH ME...!!

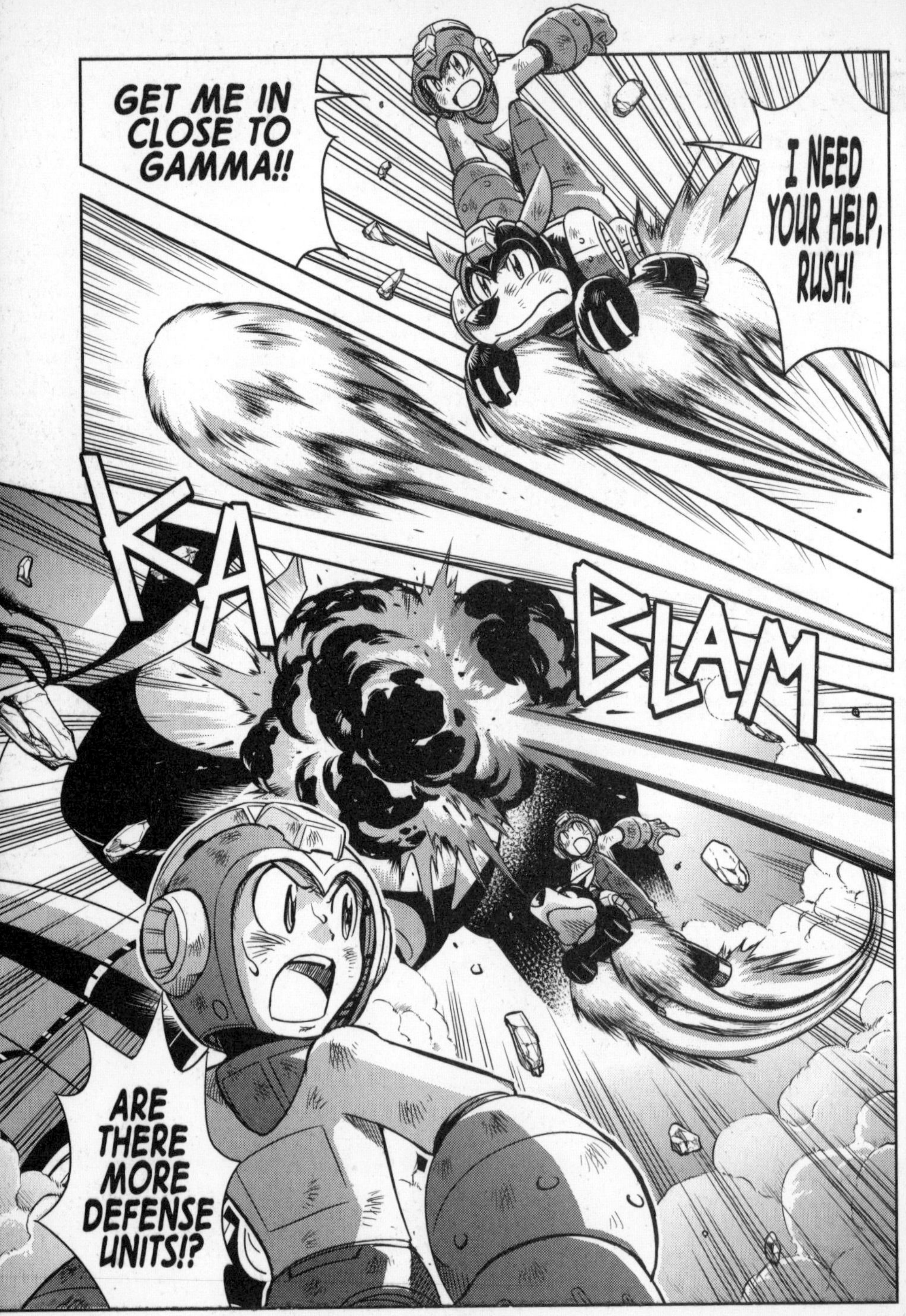
I NEED YOUR HELP, RUSH!
GET ME IN CLOSE TO GAMMA!!
KA BLAM
ARE THERE MORE DEFENSE UNITS!?

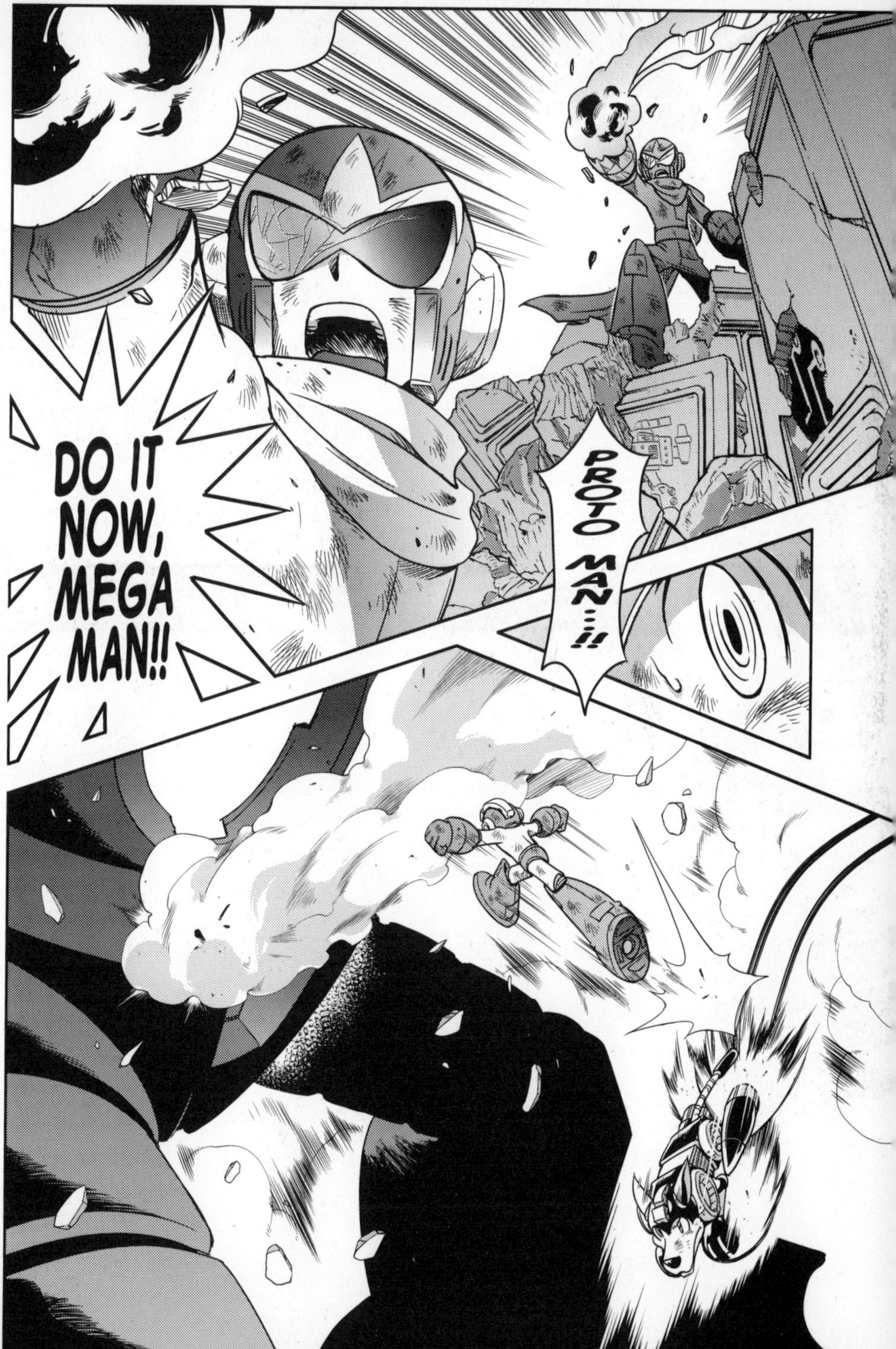
DO IT NOW, MEGA MAN!!
PROTO MAN...!!

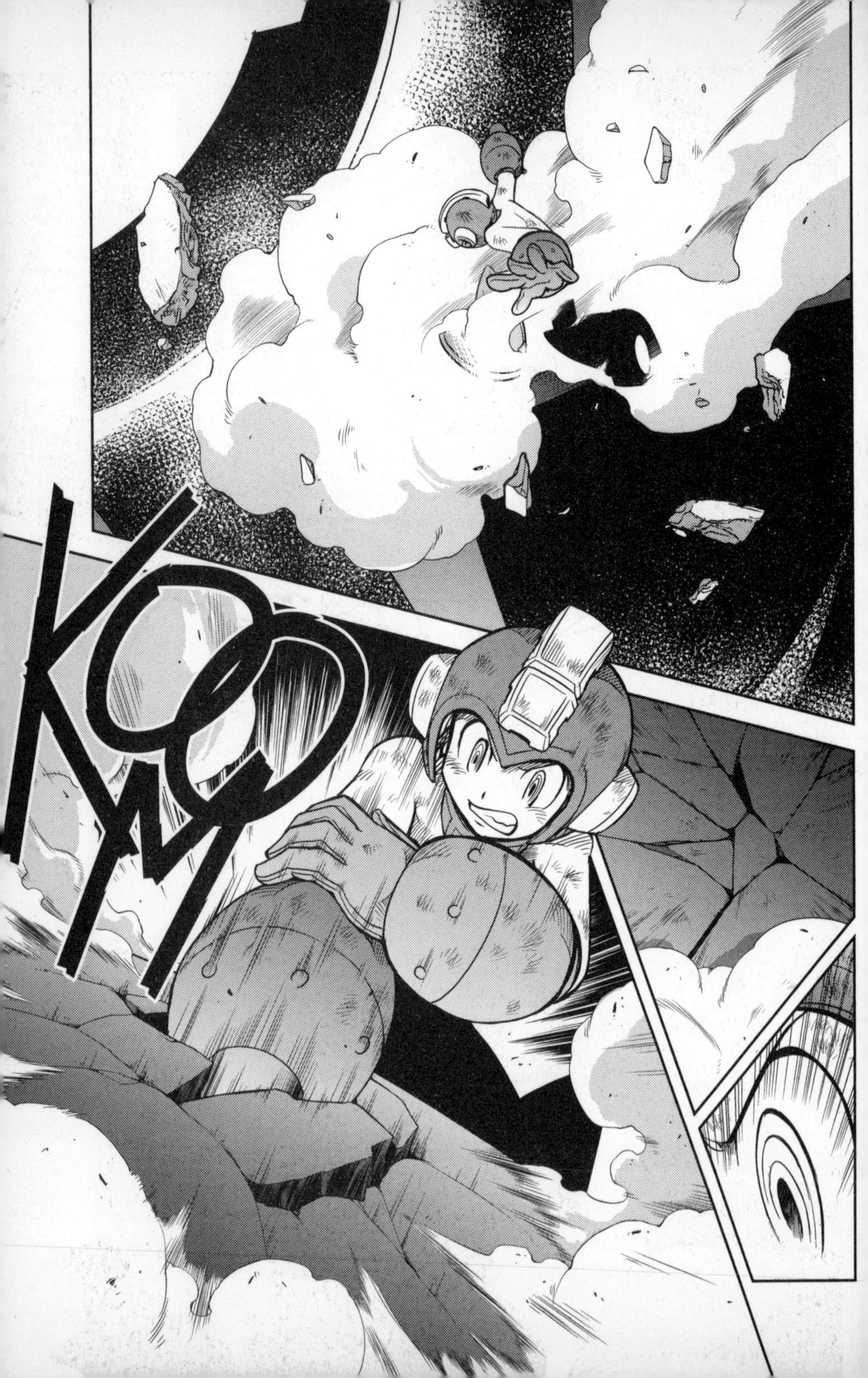
KOOM

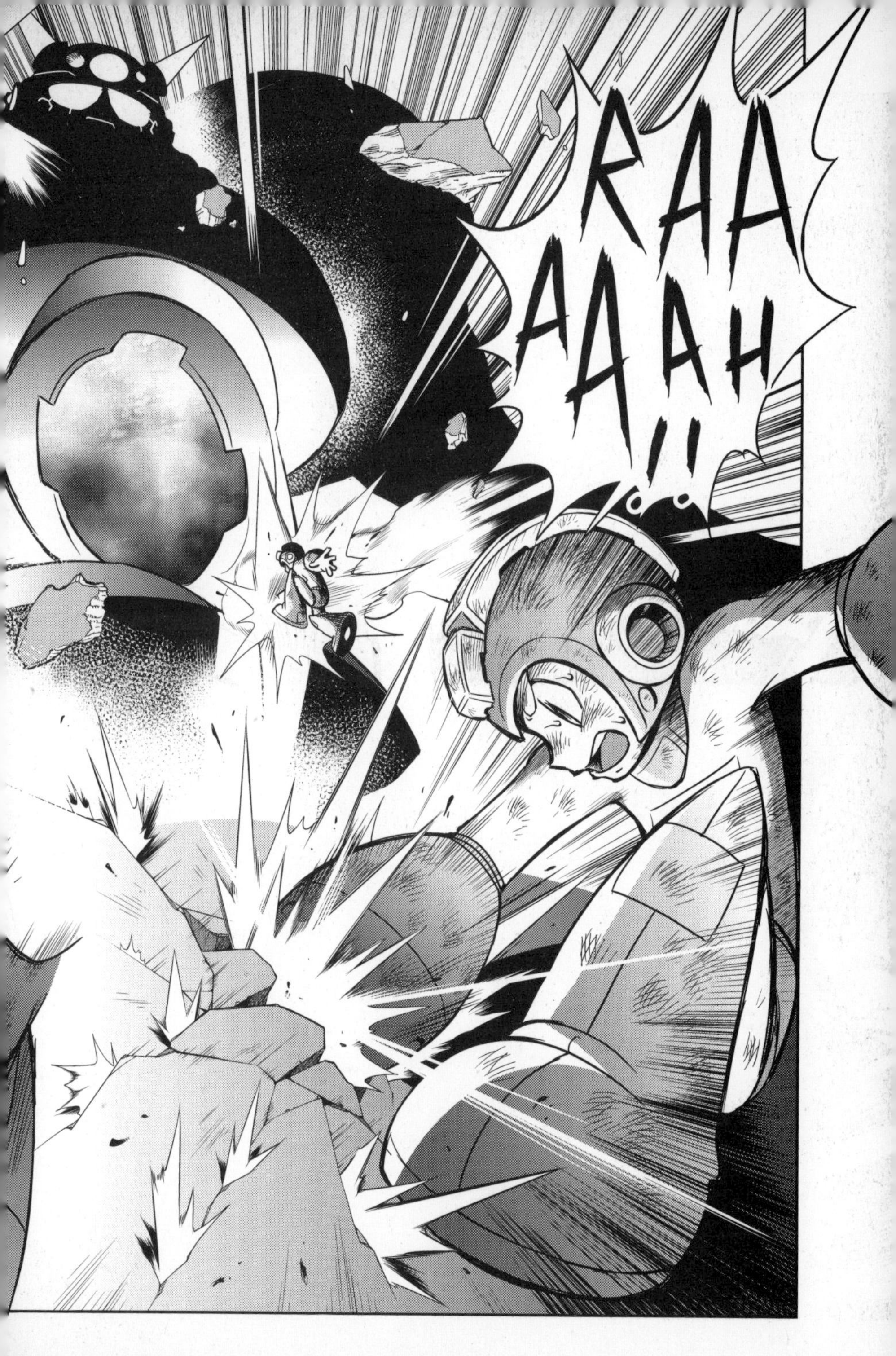
RAA AAAH !!

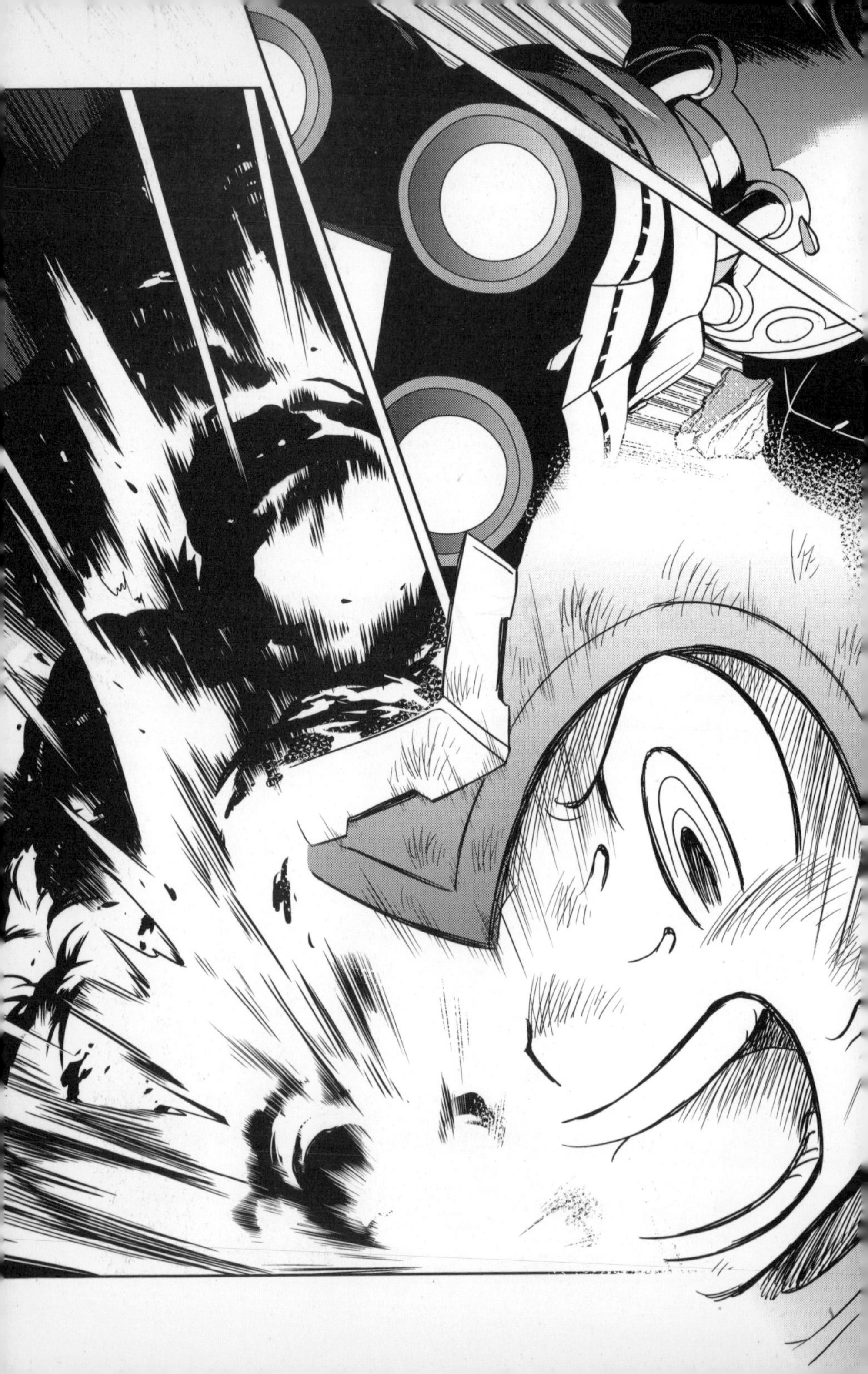

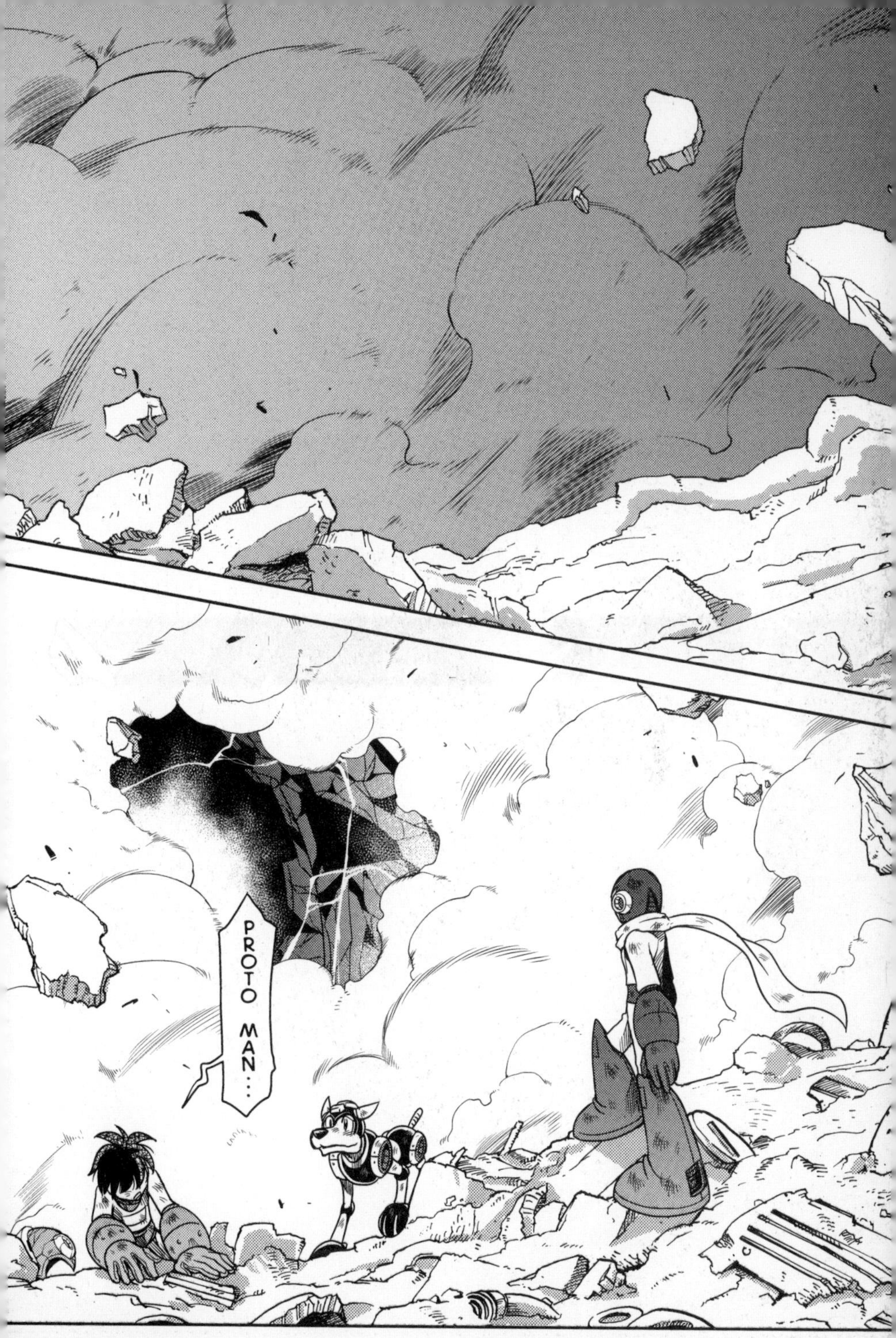
PROTO MAN...

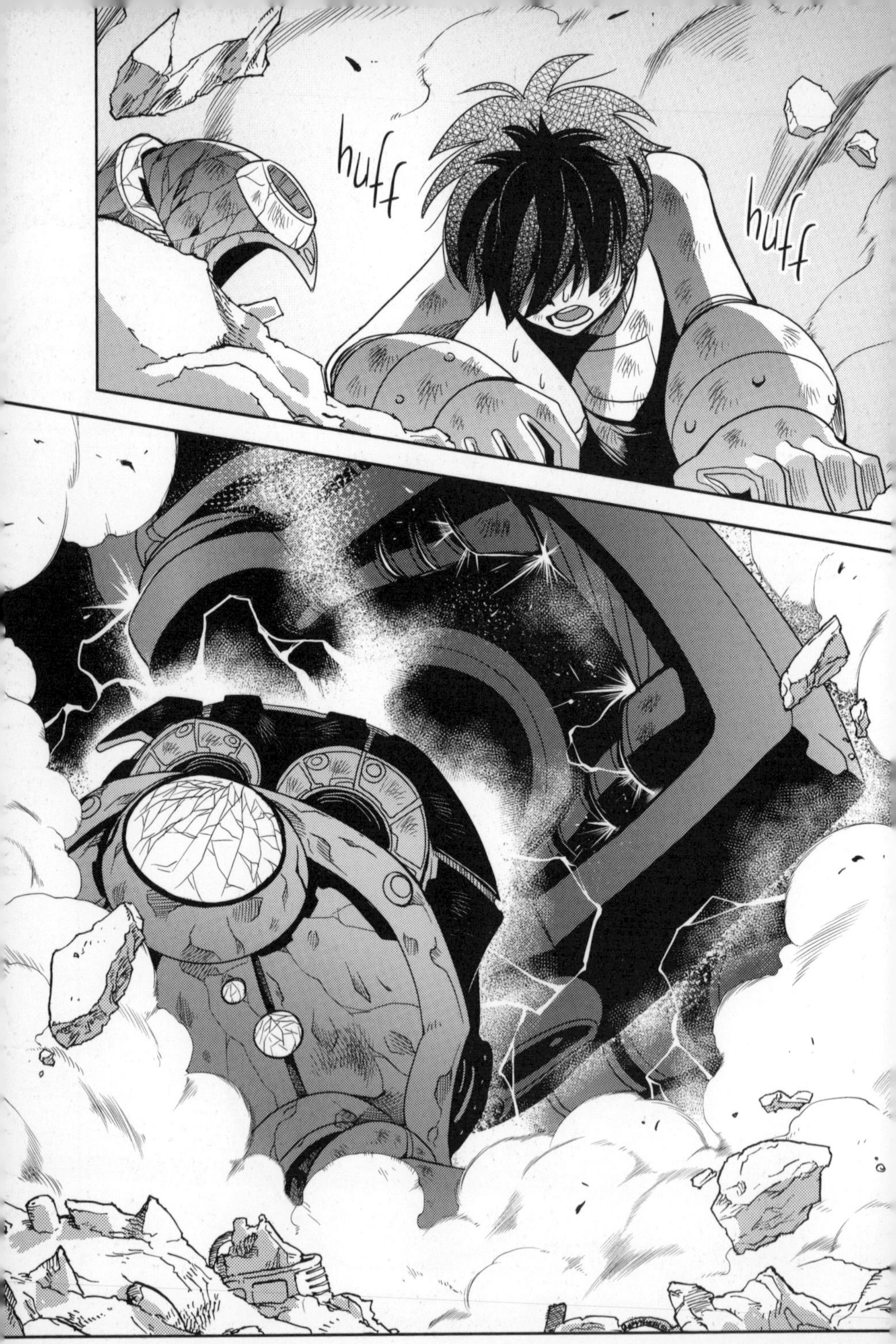
huff
huff

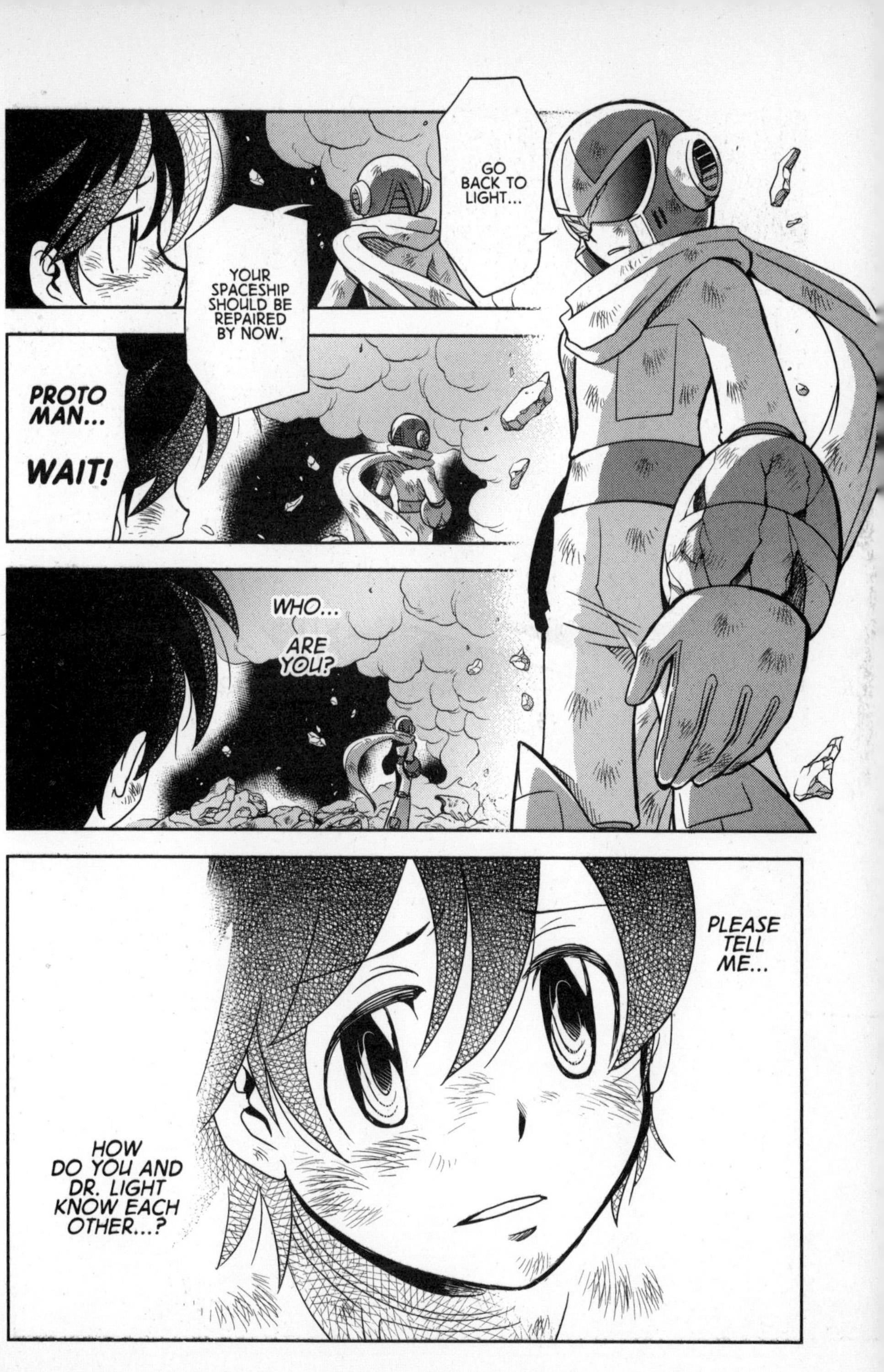
GO BACK TO LIGHT...
YOUR SPACESHIP SHOULD BE REPAIRED BY NOW.
PROTO MAN...
WAIT!
WHO... ARE YOU?
PLEASE TELL ME...
HOW DO YOU AND DR. LIGHT KNOW EACH OTHER...?

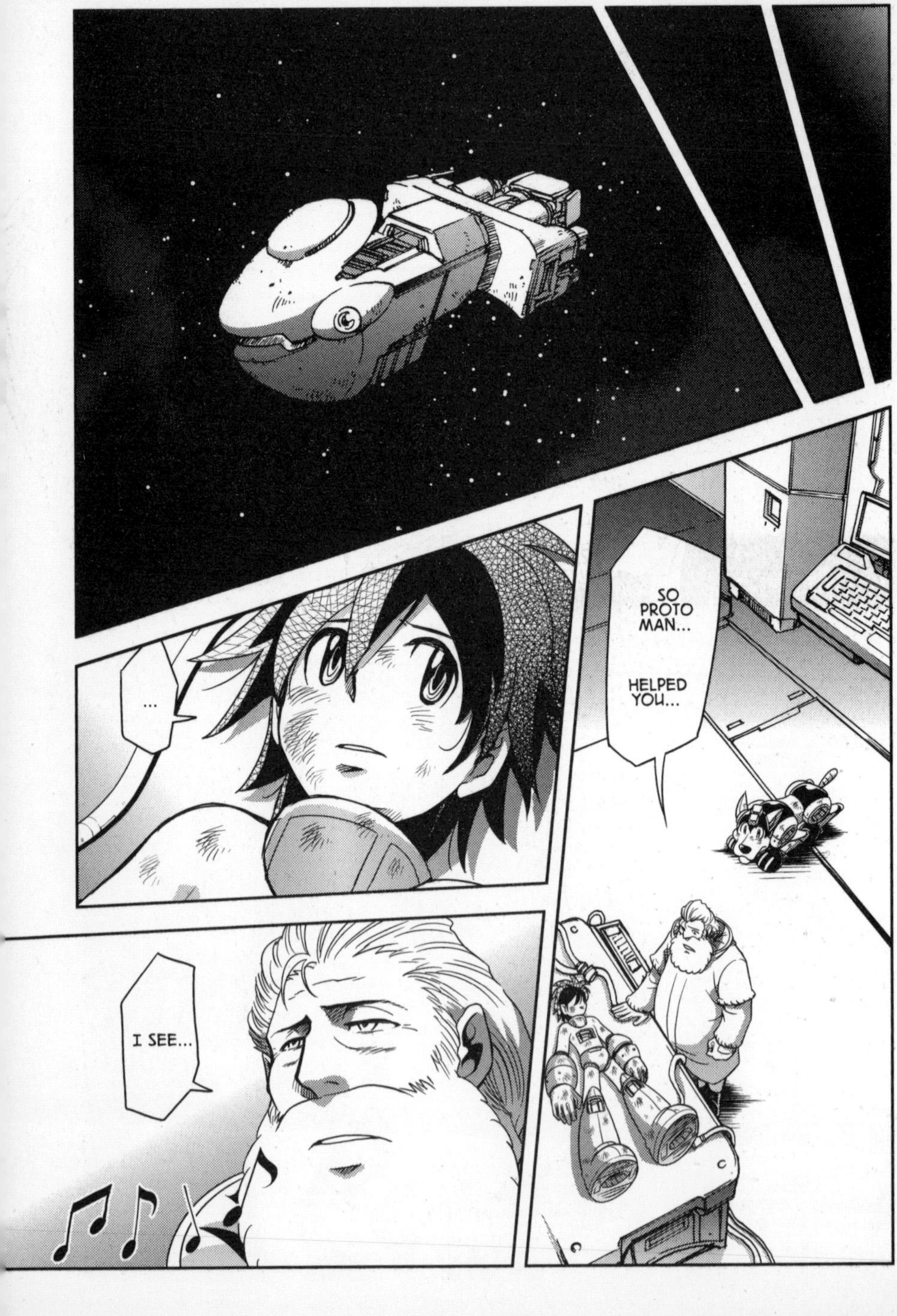
SO PROTO MAN...
HELPED YOU...
...
I SEE...

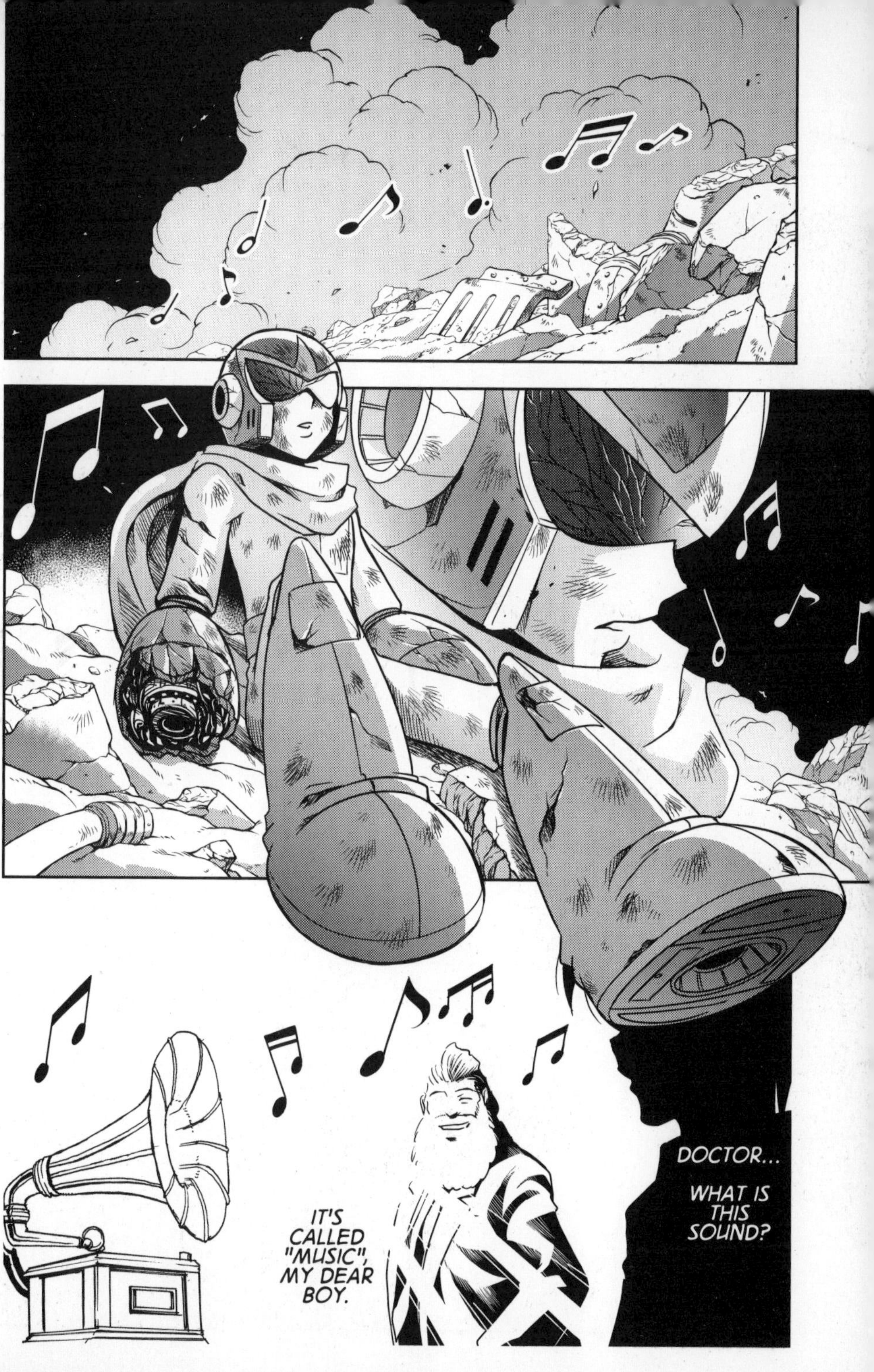
DOCTOR...
WHAT IS THIS SOUND?
IT'S CALLED "MUSIC", MY DEAR BOY.

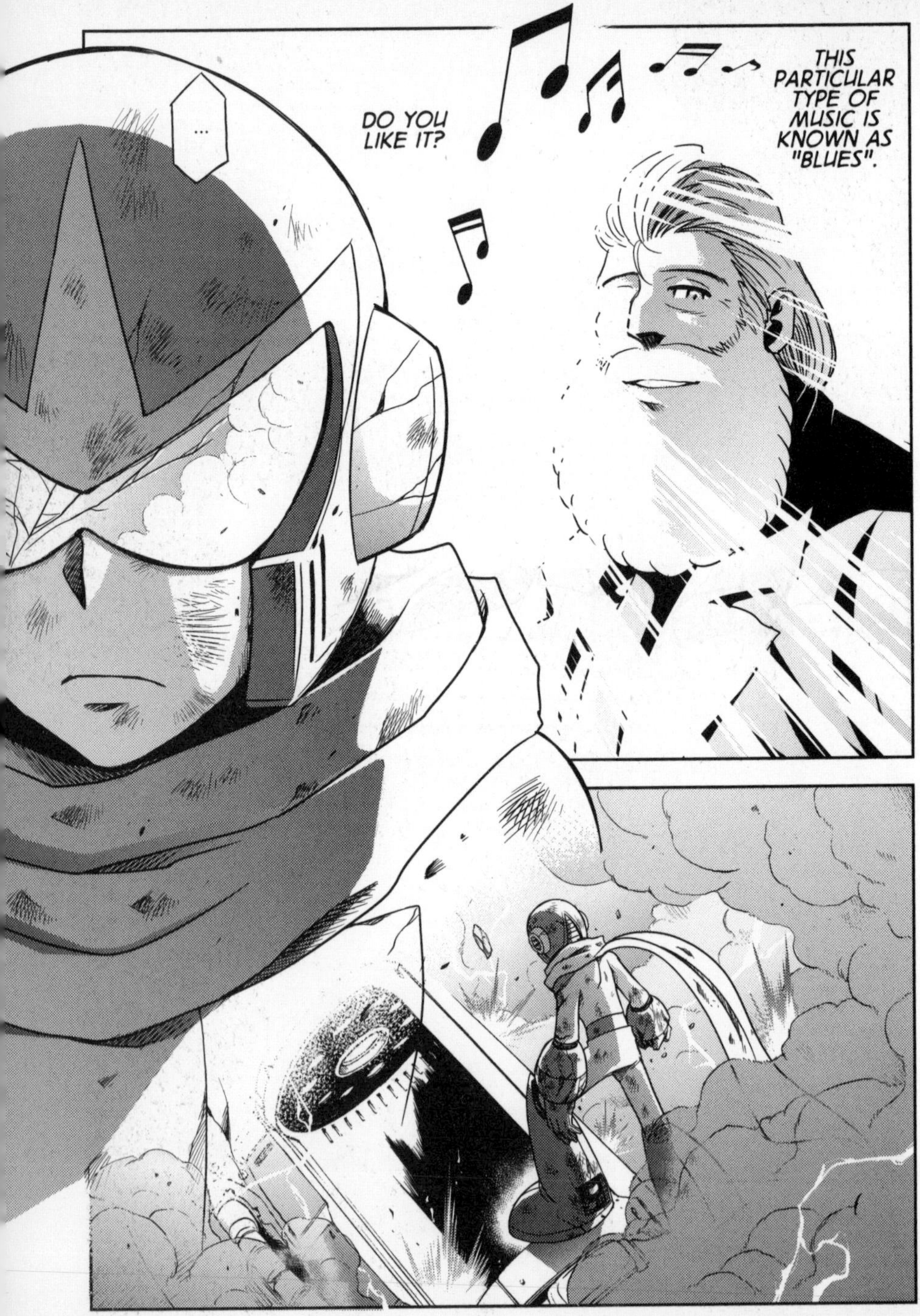
THIS PARTICULAR TYPE OF MUSIC IS KNOWN AS "BLUES".
DO YOU LIKE IT?
...

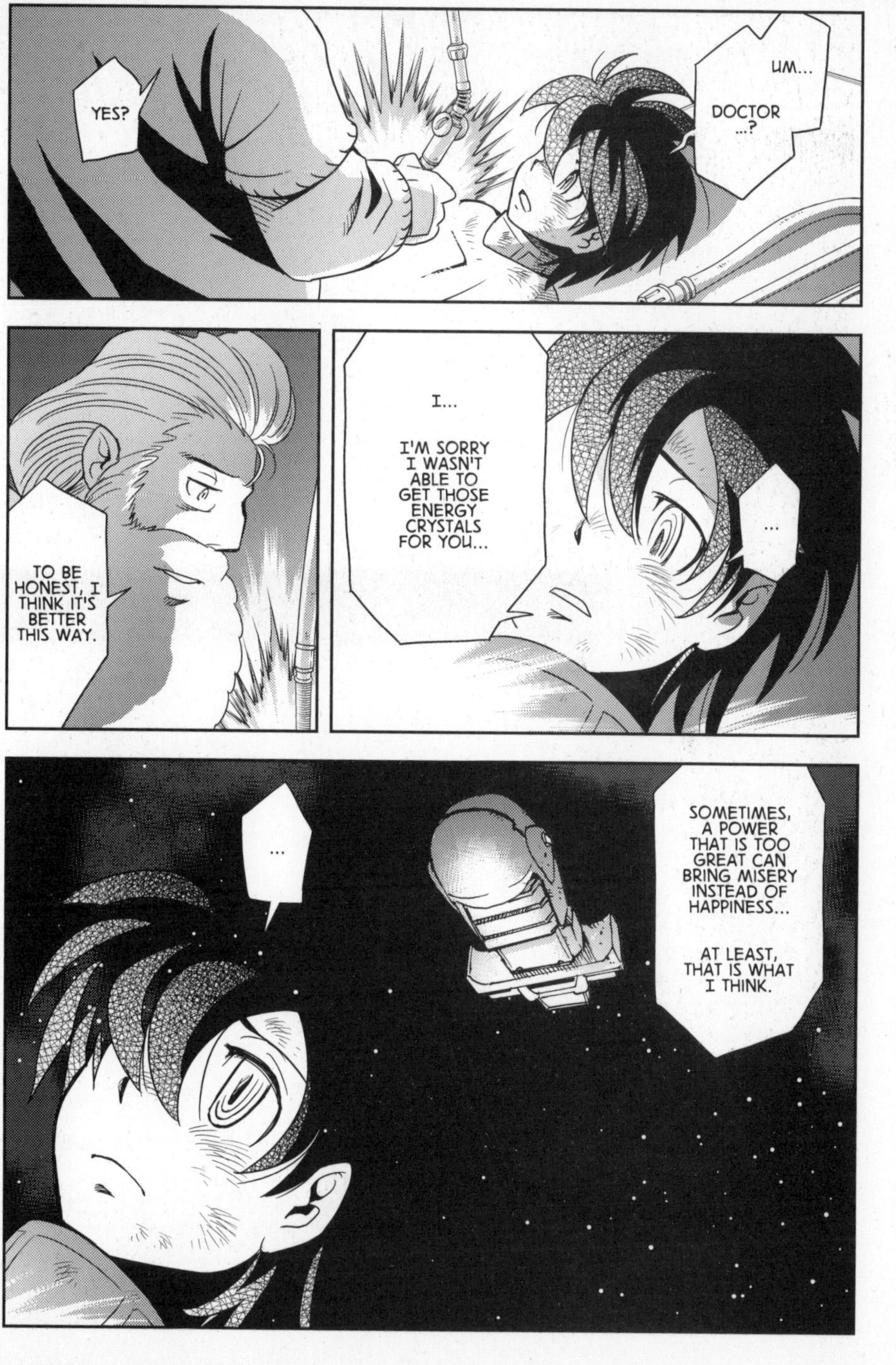
UM...
DOCTOR ...?
YES?
I...
I'M SORRY I WASN'T ABLE TO GET THOSE ENERGY CRYSTALS FOR YOU...
...
TO BE HONEST, I THINK IT'S BETTER THIS WAY.
SOMETIMES, A POWER THAT IS TOO GREAT CAN BRING MISERY INSTEAD OF HAPPINESS...
AT LEAST, THAT IS WHAT I THINK.
...

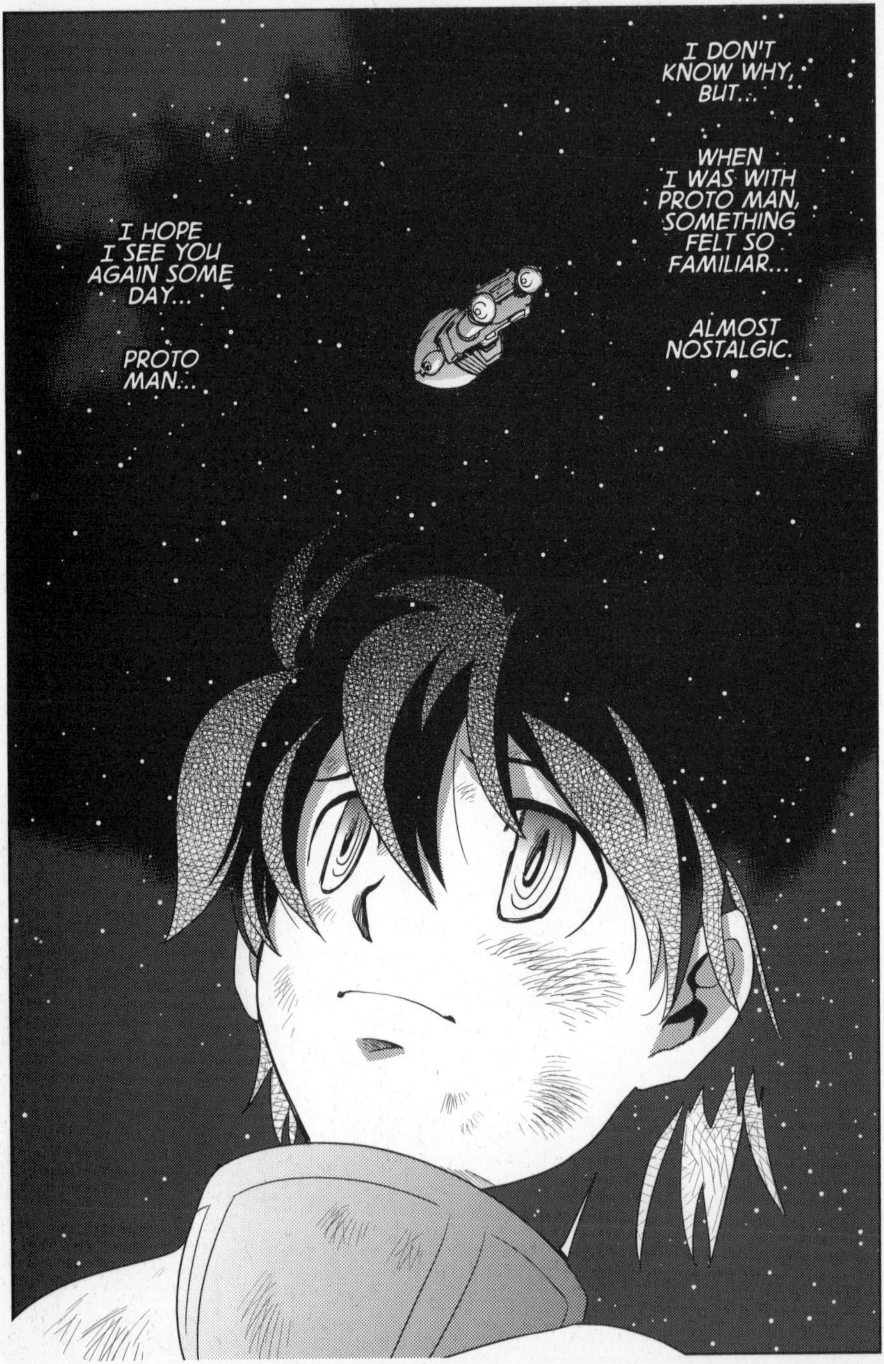
I DON'T KNOW WHY, BUT...
WHEN I WAS WITH PROTO MAN, SOMETHING FELT SO FAMILIAR...
ALMOST NOSTALGIC.
I HOPE I SEE YOU AGAIN SOME DAY...
PROTO MAN...

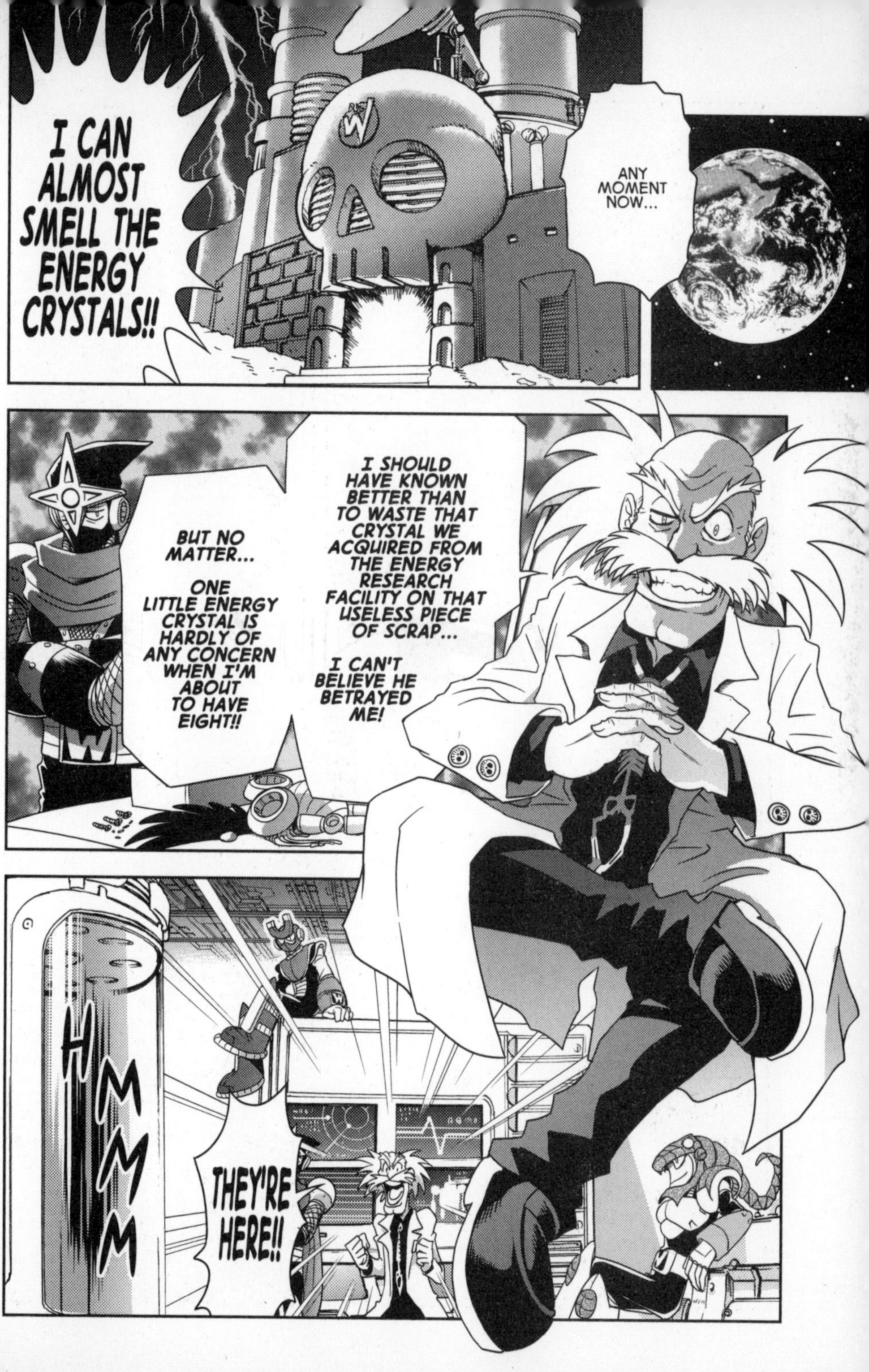
ANY MOMENT NOW...
I CAN ALMOST SMELL THE ENERGY CRYSTALS!!
I SHOULD HAVE KNOWN BETTER THAN TO WASTE THAT CRYSTAL WE ACQUIRED FROM THE ENERGY RESEARCH FACILITY ON THAT USELESS PIECE OF SCRAP...
I CAN'T BELIEVE HE BETRAYED ME!
BUT NO MATTER...
ONE LITTLE ENERGY CRYSTAL IS HARDLY OF ANY CONCERN WHEN I'M ABOUT TO HAVE EIGHT!!
THEY'RE HERE!!
HMMMM

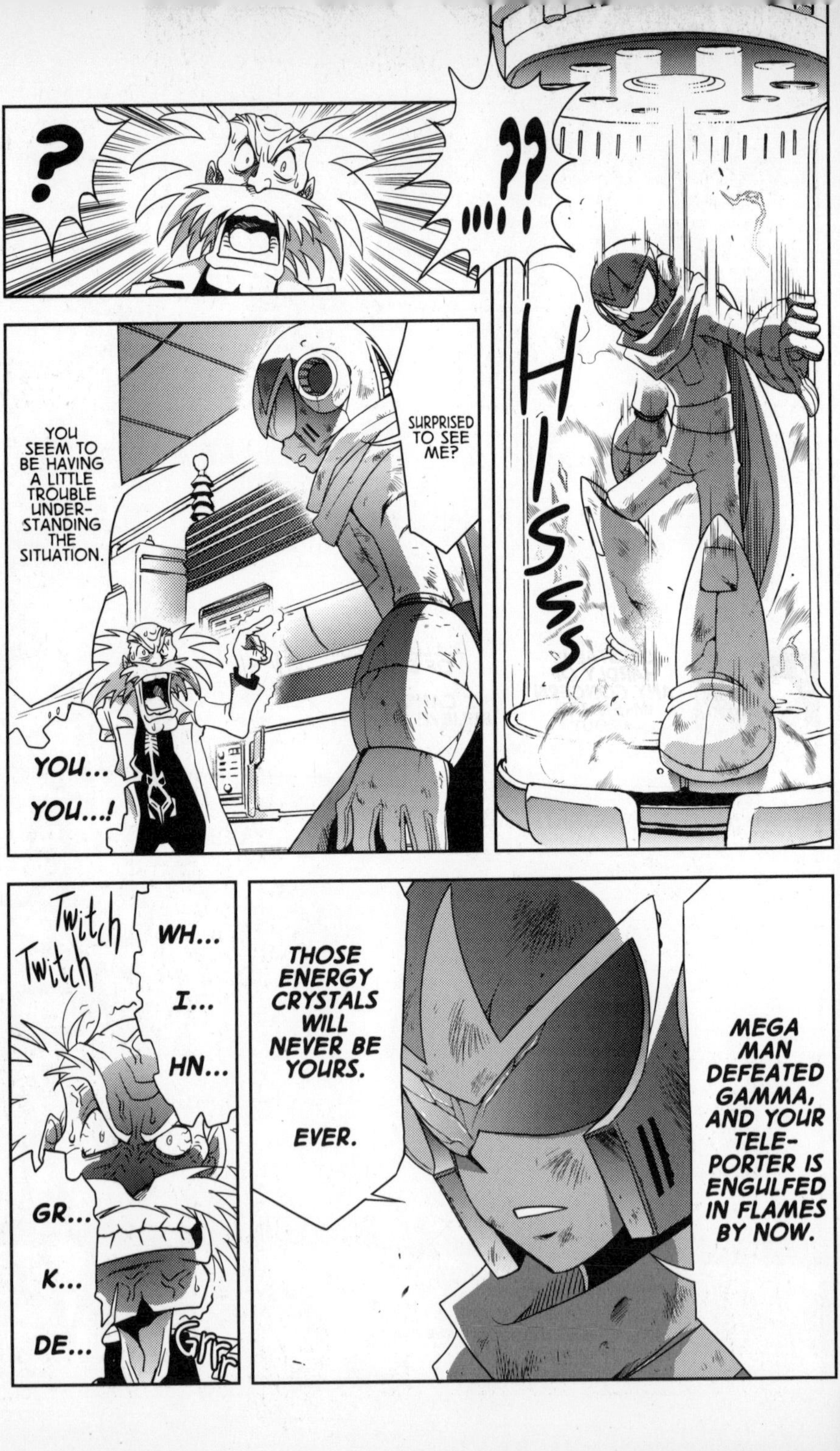
HISSS
??...!!
?
SURPRISED TO SEE ME?
YOU SEEM TO BE HAVING A LITTLE TROUBLE UNDER-STANDING THE SITUATION.
YOU... YOU...!
MEGA MAN DEFEATED GAMMA, AND YOUR TELE-PORTER IS ENGULFED IN FLAMES BY NOW.
THOSE ENERGY CRYSTALS WILL NEVER BE YOURS.
EVER.
WH...
I...
HN...
Twitch Twitch
GR...
K...
DE...
Grr

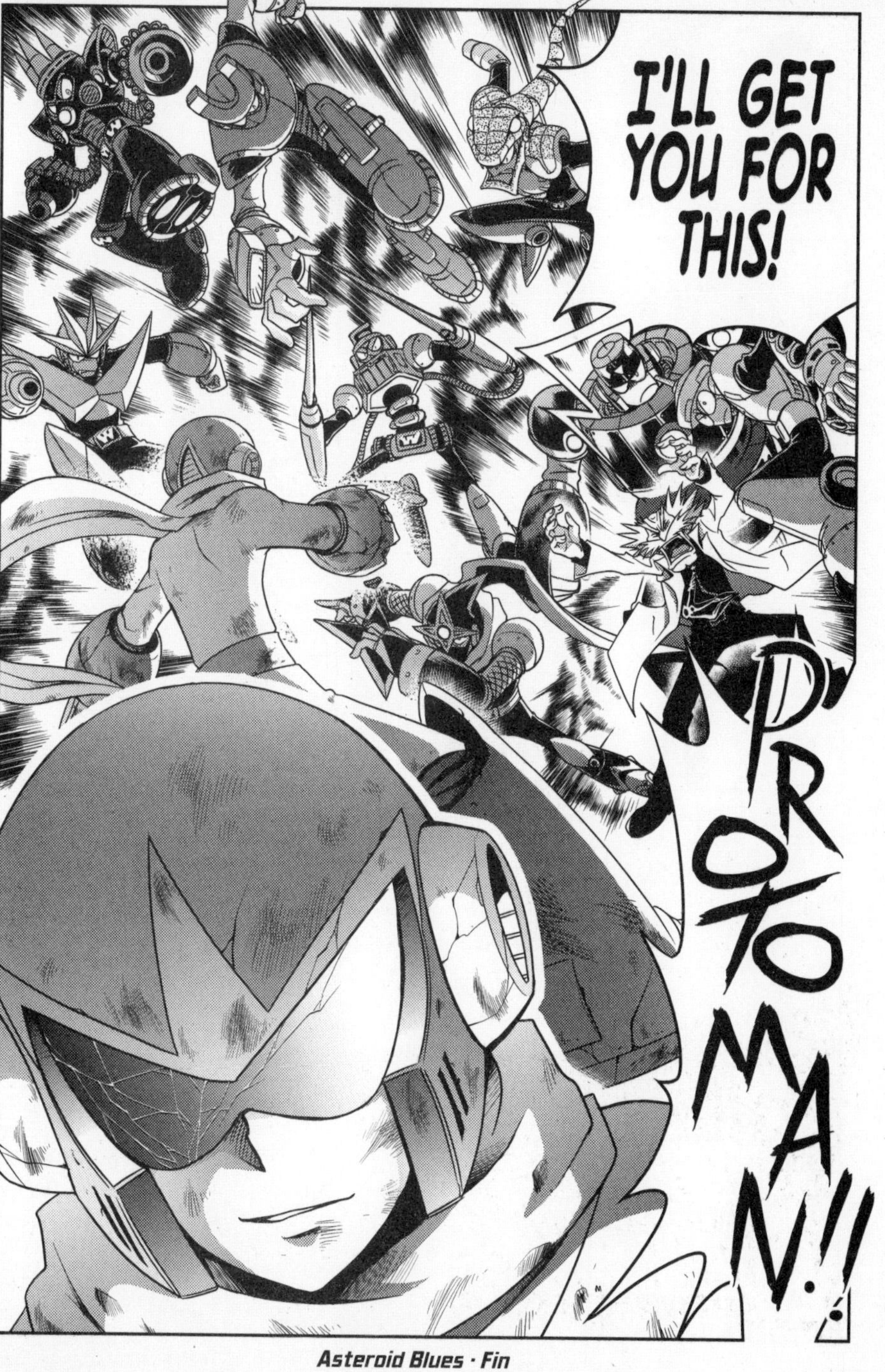
I'LL GET YOU FOR THIS!
PROTOMAN!!

Asteroid Blues · Fin

MEGAMAN GIGAMIX™

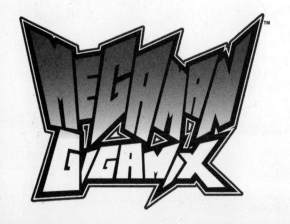

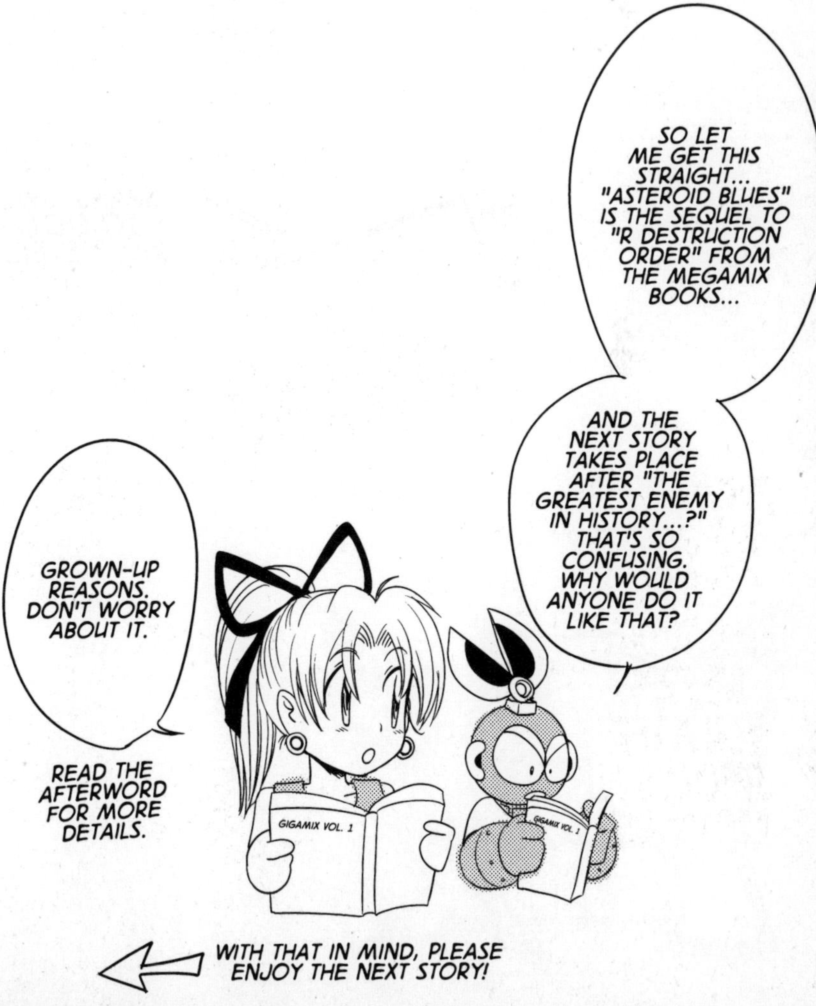
SO LET ME GET THIS STRAIGHT... "ASTEROID BLUES" IS THE SEQUEL TO "R DESTRUCTION ORDER" FROM THE MEGAMIX BOOKS...
AND THE NEXT STORY TAKES PLACE AFTER "THE GREATEST ENEMY IN HISTORY...?" THAT'S SO CONFUSING. WHY WOULD ANYONE DO IT LIKE THAT?
GROWN-UP REASONS. DON'T WORRY ABOUT IT.
READ THE AFTERWORD FOR MORE DETAILS.
GIGAMIX VOL. 1
GIGAMIX VOL. 1
WITH THAT IN MIND, PLEASE ENJOY THE NEXT STORY!

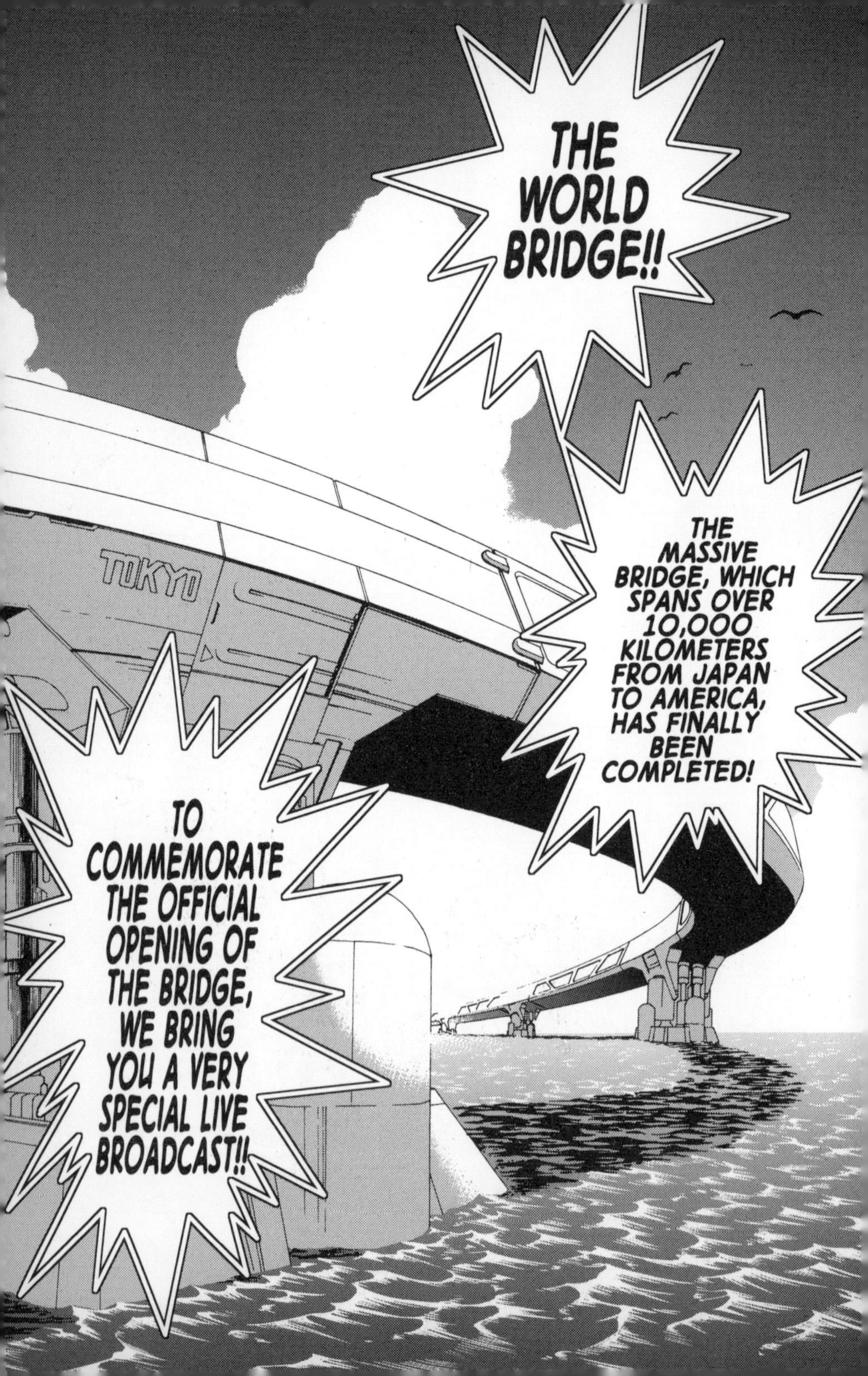
THE WORLD BRIDGE!!
THE MASSIVE BRIDGE, WHICH SPANS OVER 10,000 KILOMETERS FROM JAPAN TO AMERICA, HAS FINALLY BEEN COMPLETED!
TOKYO
TO COMMEMORATE THE OFFICIAL OPENING OF THE BRIDGE, WE BRING YOU A VERY SPECIAL LIVE BROADCAST!!

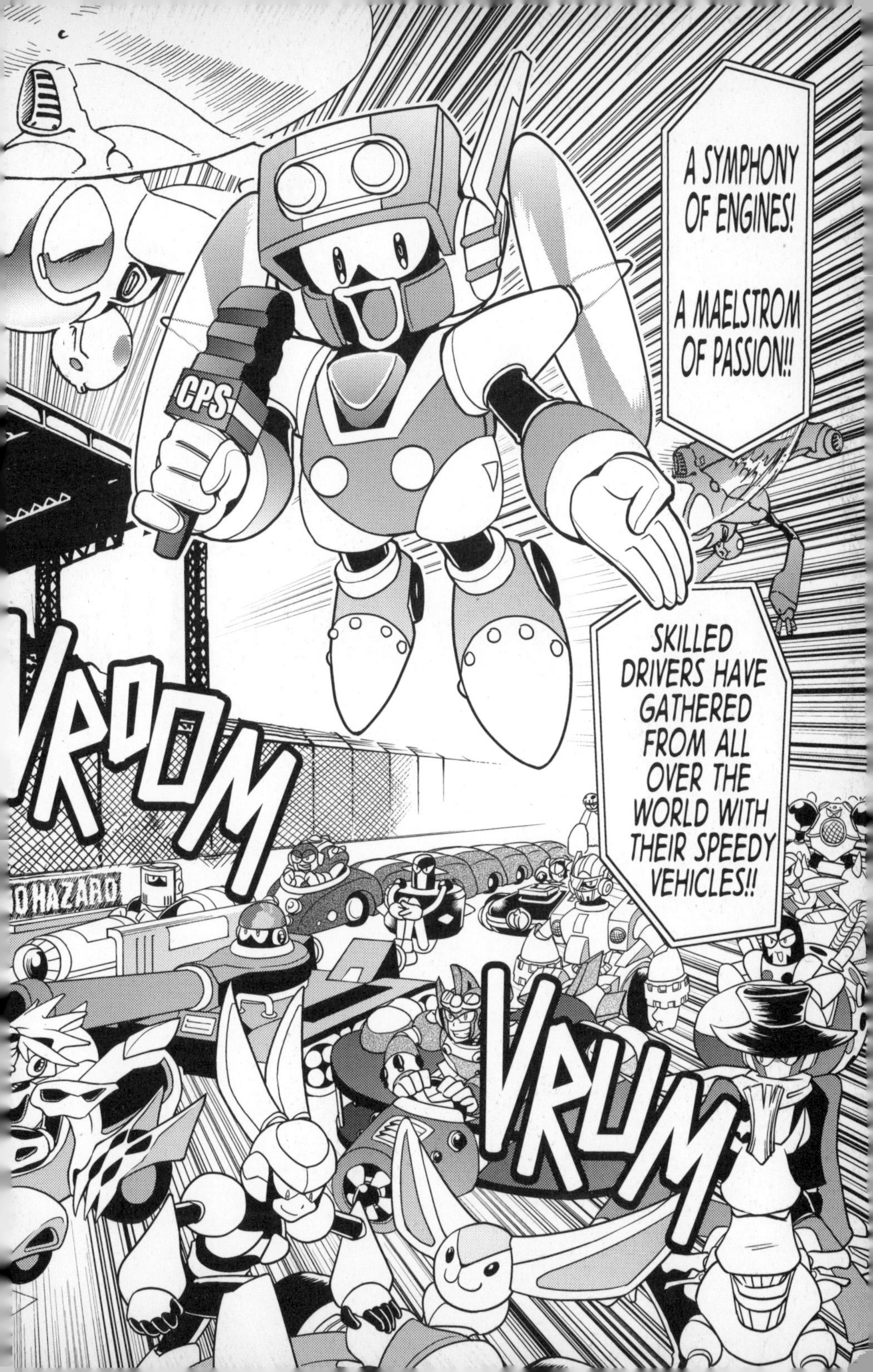
A SYMPHONY OF ENGINES!
A MAELSTROM OF PASSION!!
CPS
SKILLED DRIVERS HAVE GATHERED FROM ALL OVER THE WORLD WITH THEIR SPEEDY VEHICLES!!
VROOM
HAZARD
VRUM

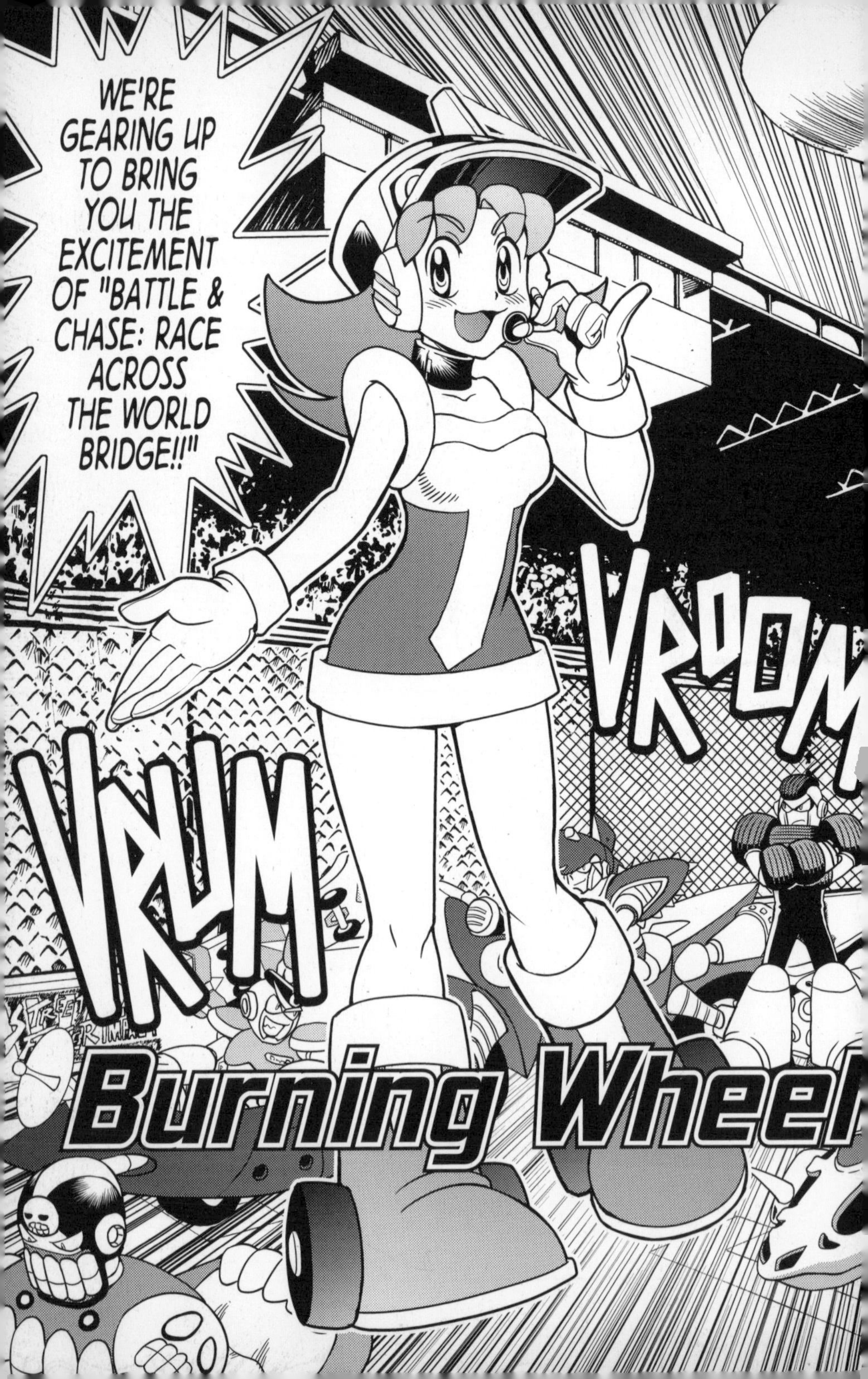
WE'RE GEARING UP TO BRING YOU THE EXCITEMENT OF "BATTLE & CHASE: RACE ACROSS THE WORLD BRIDGE!!"
VROOM
VRUM
Burning Wheel

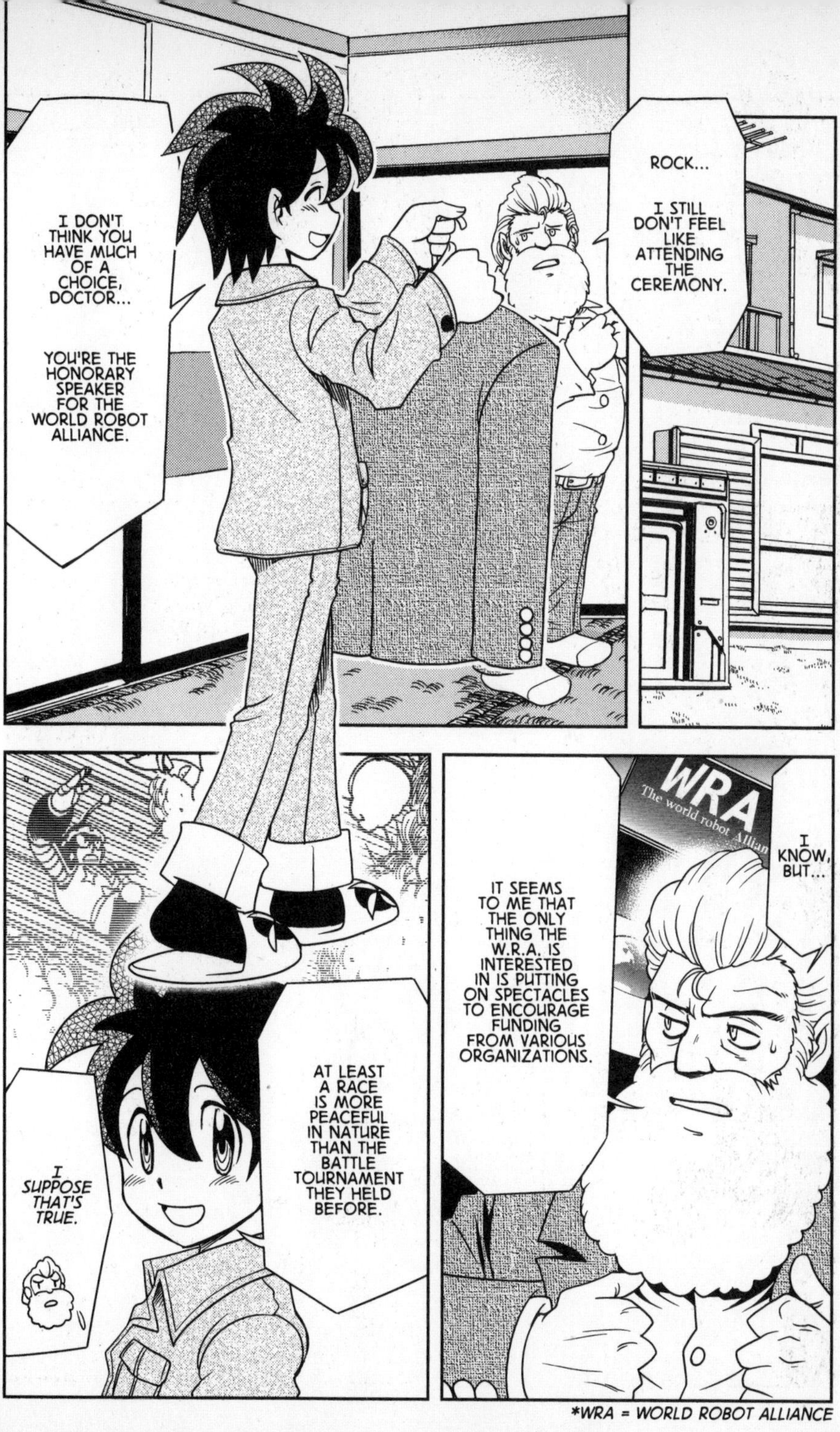
ROCK...
I STILL DON'T FEEL LIKE ATTENDING THE CEREMONY.
I DON'T THINK YOU HAVE MUCH OF A CHOICE, DOCTOR...
YOU'RE THE HONORARY SPEAKER FOR THE WORLD ROBOT ALLIANCE.
WRA
The world robot Allian
I KNOW, BUT...
IT SEEMS TO ME THAT THE ONLY THING THE W.R.A. IS INTERESTED IN IS PUTTING ON SPECTACLES TO ENCOURAGE FUNDING FROM VARIOUS ORGANIZATIONS.
AT LEAST A RACE IS MORE PEACEFUL IN NATURE THAN THE BATTLE TOURNAMENT THEY HELD BEFORE.
I SUPPOSE THAT'S TRUE.

*WRA = WORLD ROBOT ALLIANCE

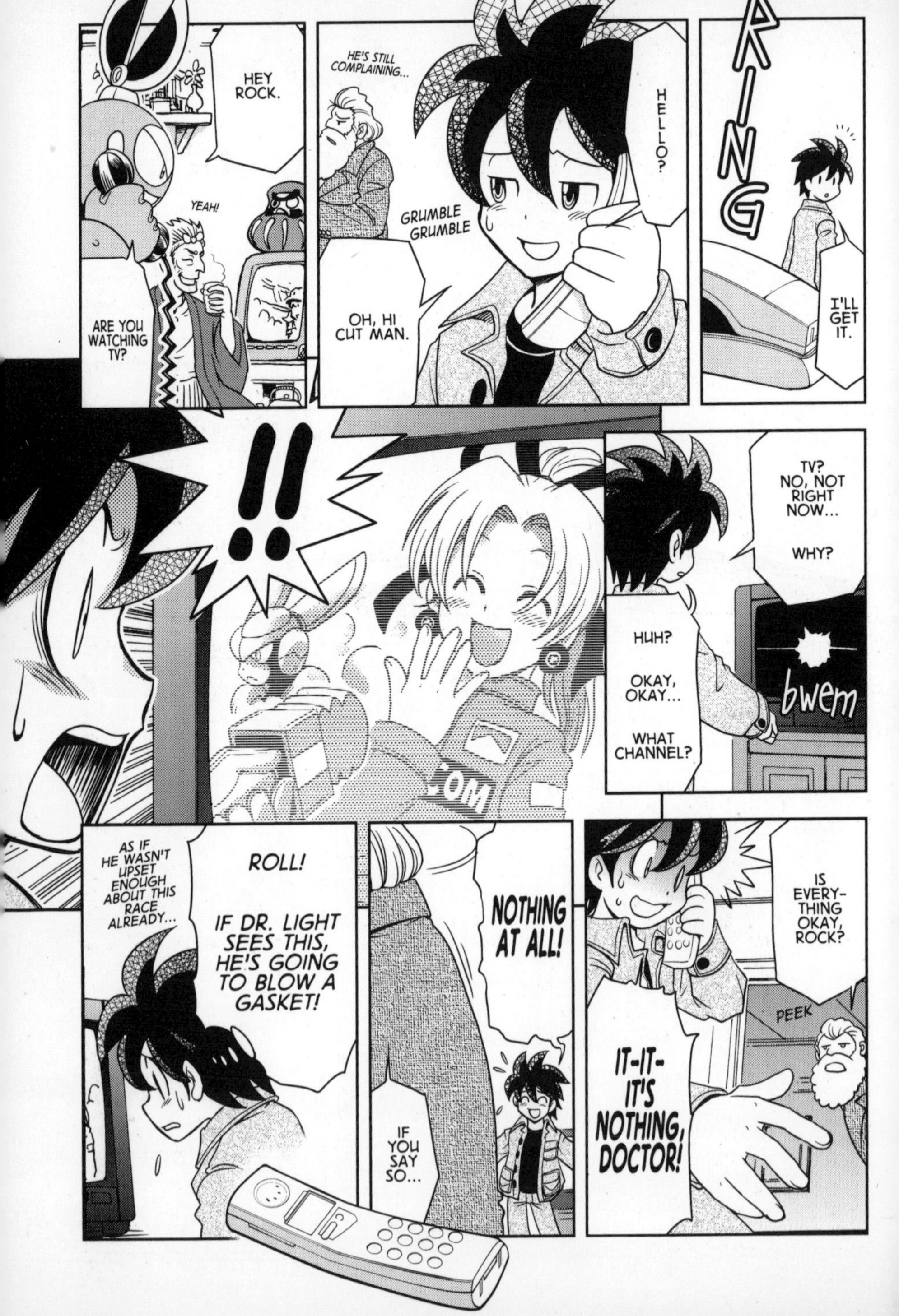
RING
I'LL GET IT.
HELLO?
HE'S STILL COMPLAINING...
GRUMBLE GRUMBLE
OH, HI CUT MAN.
HEY ROCK.
YEAH!
ARE YOU WATCHING TV?
TV? NO, NOT RIGHT NOW... WHY?
bwem
HUH? OKAY, OKAY... WHAT CHANNEL?
!!
COM
IS EVERY-THING OKAY, ROCK?
PEEK
IT-IT-IT'S NOTHING, DOCTOR!
NOTHING AT ALL!
IF YOU SAY SO...
ROLL!
IF DR. LIGHT SEES THIS, HE'S GOING TO BLOW A GASKET!
AS IF HE WASN'T UPSET ENOUGH ABOUT THIS RACE ALREADY...

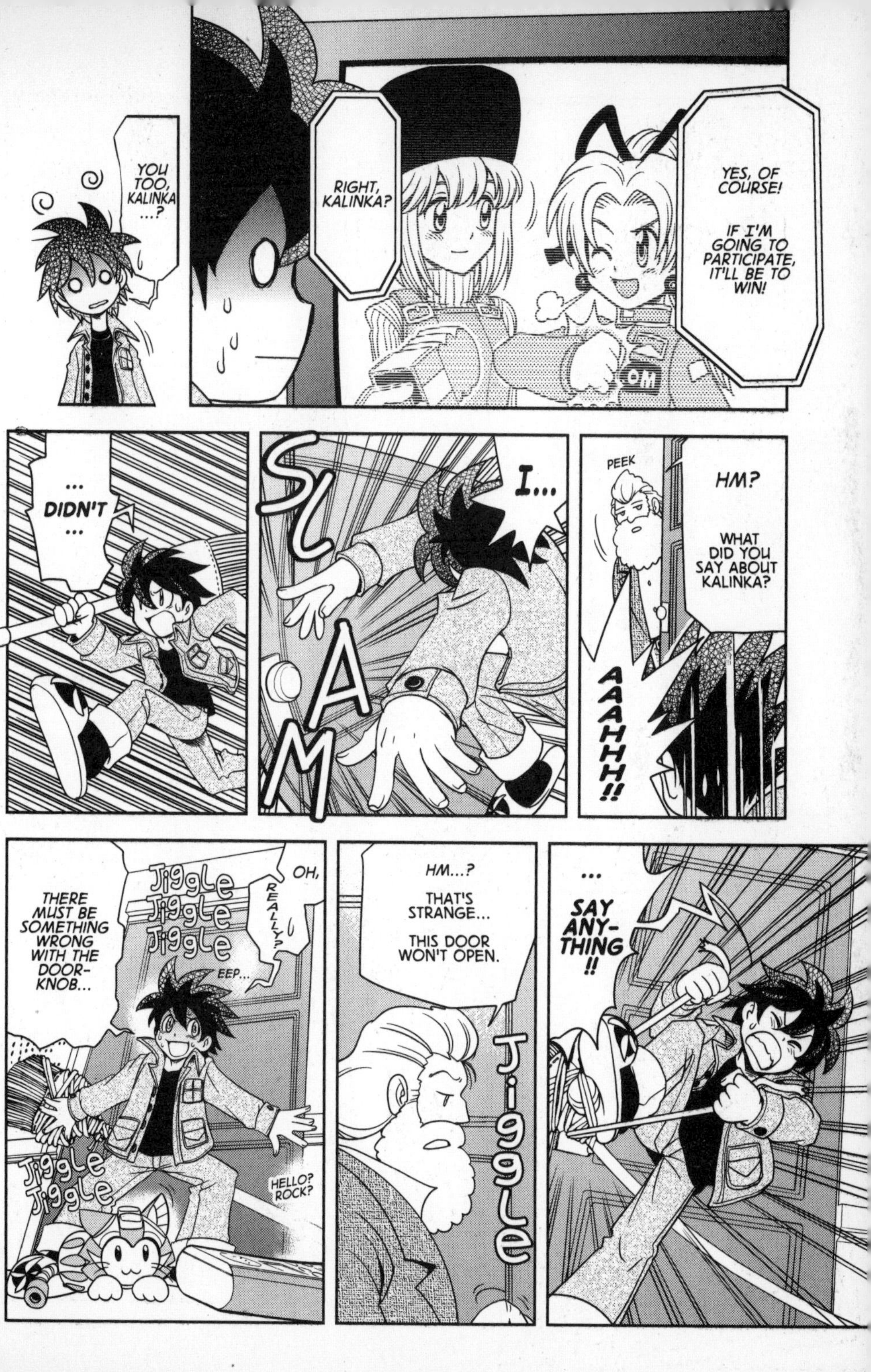
YES, OF COURSE!
IF I'M GOING TO PARTICIPATE, IT'LL BE TO WIN!
RIGHT, KALINKA?
YOU TOO, KALINKA ...?
PEEK
HM?
WHAT DID YOU SAY ABOUT KALINKA?
AAAHHH!!
I...
SLAM
... DIDN'T ...
... SAY ANY-THING!!
HM...?
THAT'S STRANGE...
THIS DOOR WON'T OPEN.
Jiggle
OH, REALLY?
Jiggle Jiggle Jiggle
THERE MUST BE SOMETHING WRONG WITH THE DOOR-KNOB...
EEP...
Jiggle Jiggle
HELLO? ROCK?

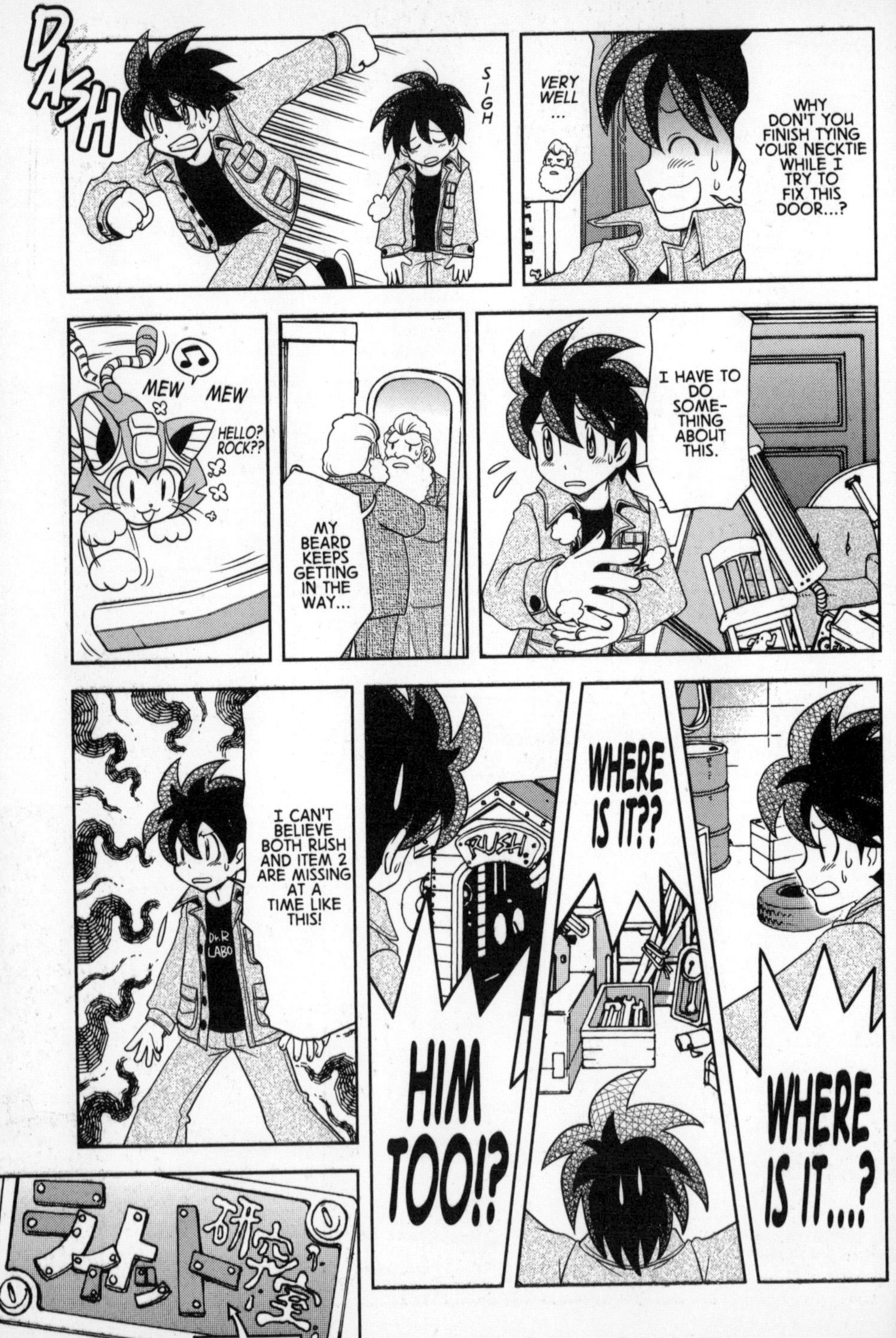
WHY DON'T YOU FINISH TYING YOUR NECKTIE WHILE I TRY TO FIX THIS DOOR...?
VERY WELL ...
SIGH
DASH
I HAVE TO DO SOME-THING ABOUT THIS.
MY BEARD KEEPS GETTING IN THE WAY...
MEW MEW
HELLO? ROCK??
WHERE IS IT...?
WHERE IS IT??
HIM TOO!?
RUSH
I CAN'T BELIEVE BOTH RUSH AND ITEM 2 ARE MISSING AT A TIME LIKE THIS!
Dr. R LABO
AUTO'S LABORATORY

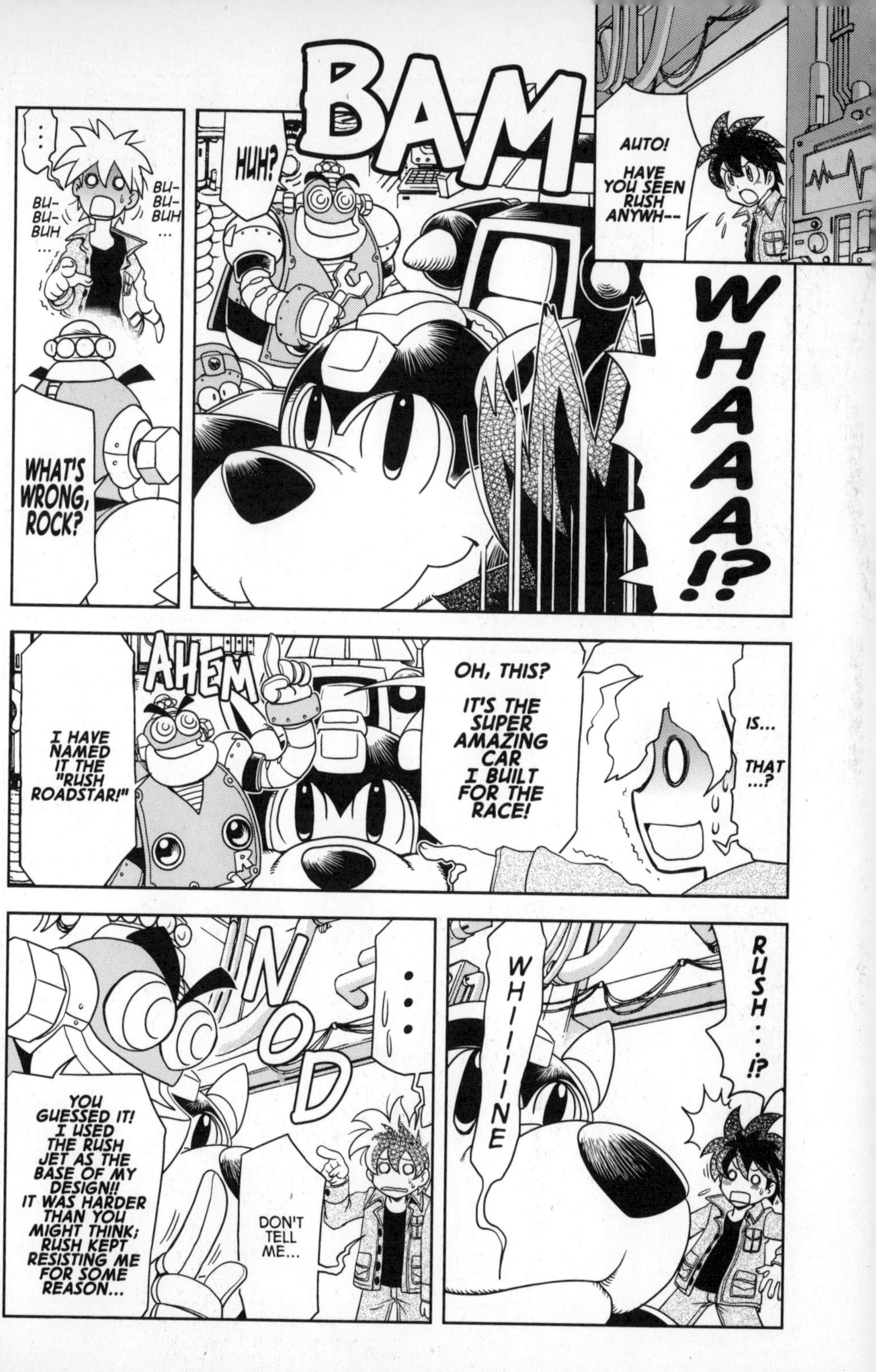
AUTO!
HAVE YOU SEEN RUSH ANYWH--
BAM
WHAAAA!?
HUH?
...
BU-BU-BUH...
BU-BU-BUH...
WHAT'S WRONG, ROCK?
IS... THAT...?
OH, THIS? IT'S THE SUPER AMAZING CAR I BUILT FOR THE RACE!
AHEM
I HAVE NAMED IT THE "RUSH ROADSTAR!"
RUSH...!?
WHIIIINE
...
NOD
DON'T TELL ME...
YOU GUESSED IT! I USED THE RUSH JET AS THE BASE OF MY DESIGN!! IT WAS HARDER THAN YOU MIGHT THINK; RUSH KEPT RESISTING ME FOR SOME REASON...

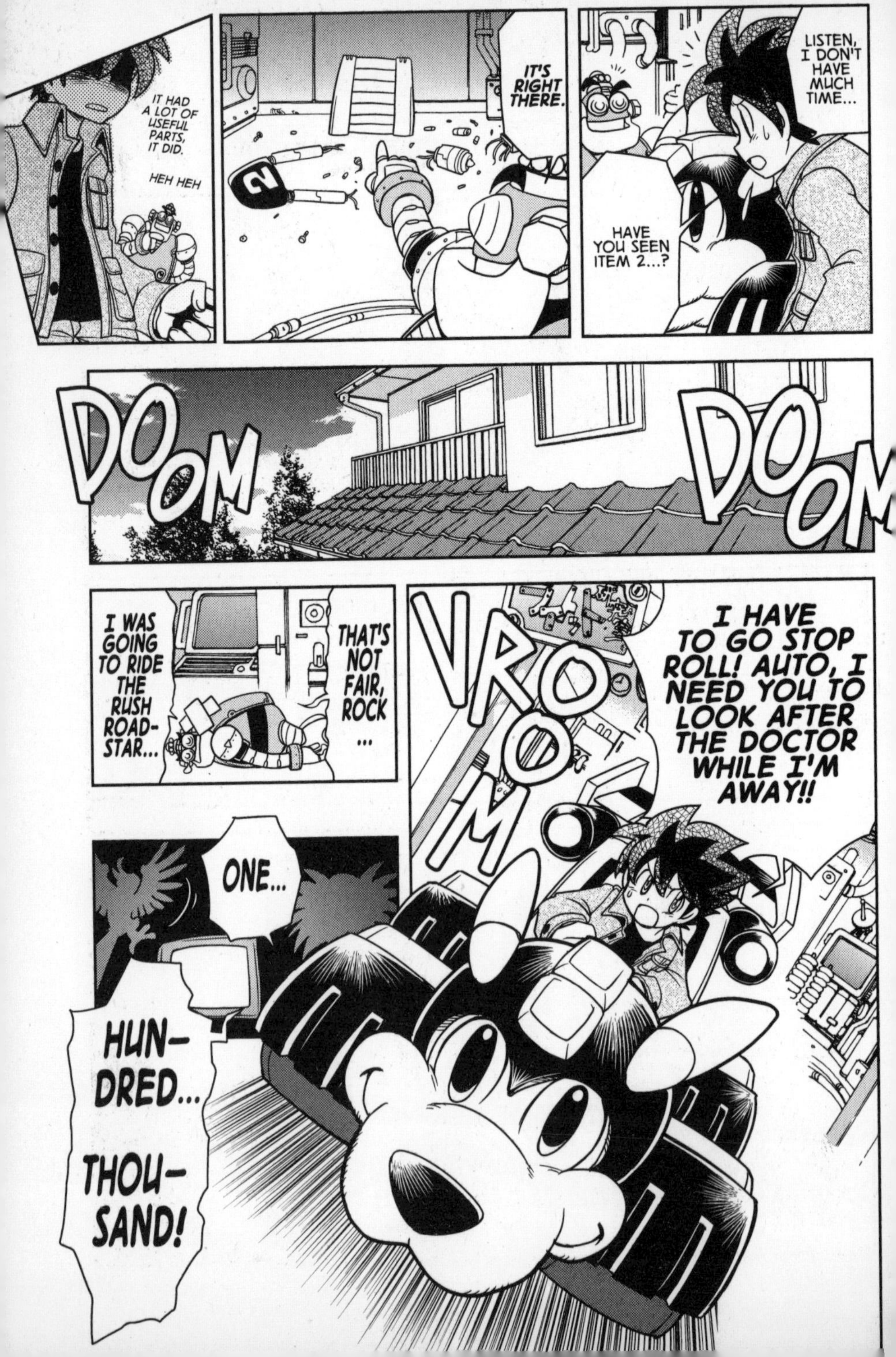
LISTEN, I DON'T HAVE MUCH TIME...
HAVE YOU SEEN ITEM 2...?
IT'S RIGHT THERE.
IT HAD A LOT OF USEFUL PARTS, IT DID.
HEH HEH
DOOM
DOOM
I HAVE TO GO STOP ROLL! AUTO, I NEED YOU TO LOOK AFTER THE DOCTOR WHILE I'M AWAY!!
VROOOM
THAT'S NOT FAIR, ROCK...
I WAS GOING TO RIDE THE RUSH ROAD-STAR...
ONE...
HUN-DRED... THOU-SAND!

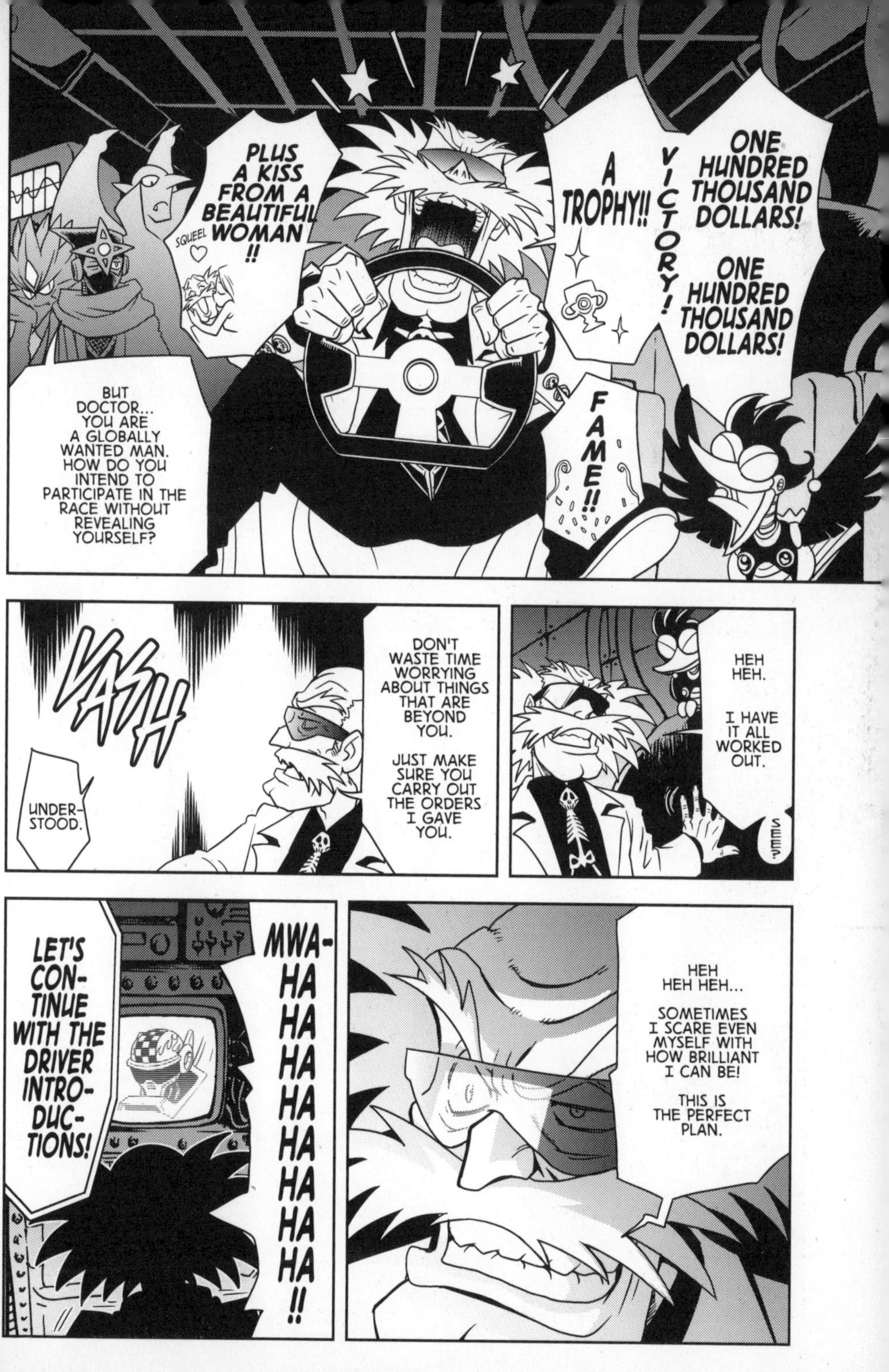
ONE HUNDRED THOUSAND DOLLARS!
ONE HUNDRED THOUSAND DOLLARS!
VICTORY!
A TROPHY!!
FAME!!
PLUS A KISS FROM A BEAUTIFUL WOMAN!!
SQUEEL ♡
BUT DOCTOR... YOU ARE A GLOBALLY WANTED MAN. HOW DO YOU INTEND TO PARTICIPATE IN THE RACE WITHOUT REVEALING YOURSELF?
HEH HEH.
I HAVE IT ALL WORKED OUT.
SEE?
DON'T WASTE TIME WORRYING ABOUT THINGS THAT ARE BEYOND YOU.
JUST MAKE SURE YOU CARRY OUT THE ORDERS I GAVE YOU.
VASH
UNDER-STOOD.
HEH HEH HEH...
SOMETIMES I SCARE EVEN MYSELF WITH HOW BRILLIANT I CAN BE!
THIS IS THE PERFECT PLAN.
MWA-HA HA HA HA HA HA HA HA HA HA HA HA!!
LET'S CON-TINUE WITH THE DRIVER INTRO-DUC-TIONS!

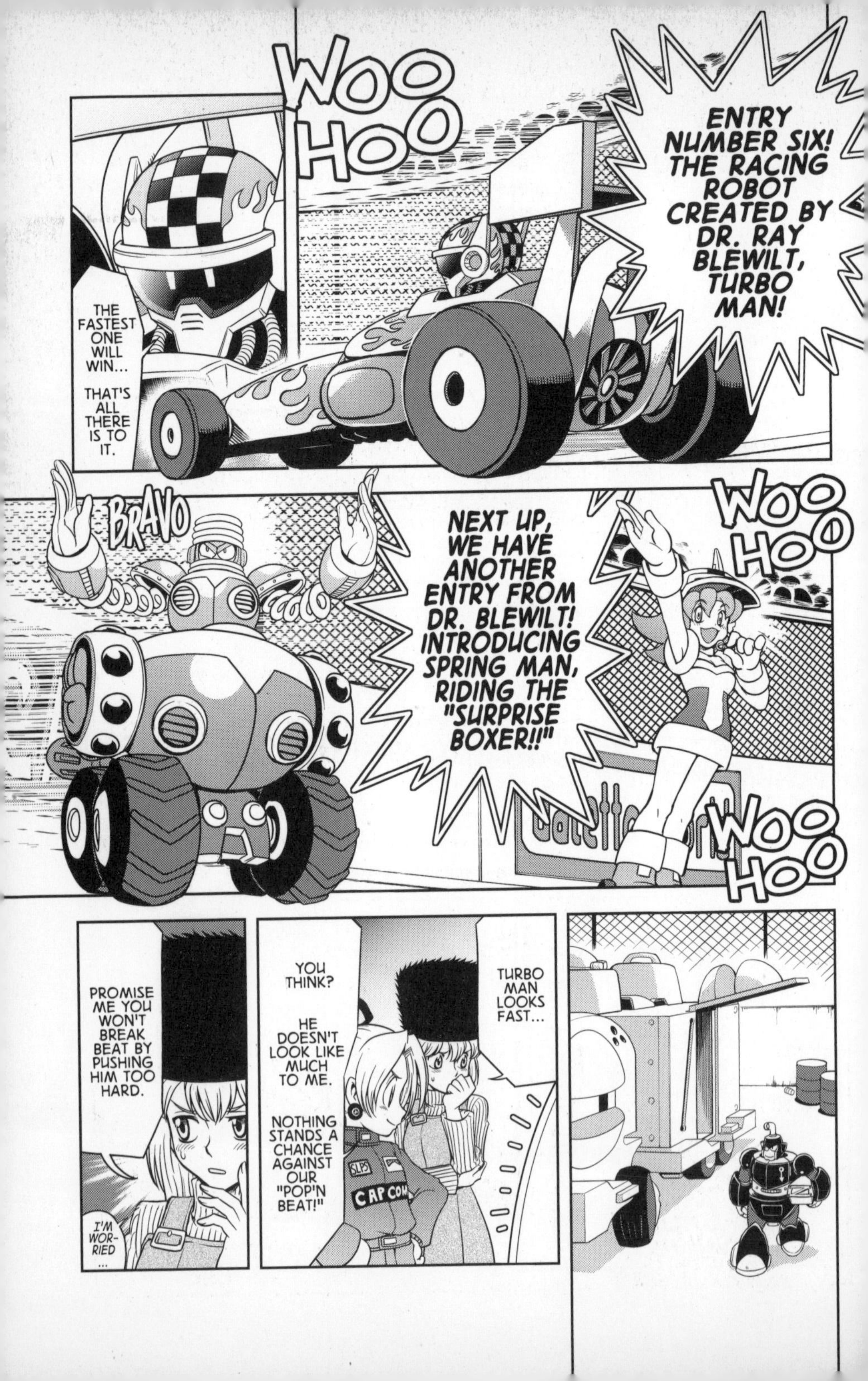
WOO HOO
ENTRY NUMBER SIX! THE RACING ROBOT CREATED BY DR. RAY BLEWILT, TURBO MAN!
THE FASTEST ONE WILL WIN...
THAT'S ALL THERE IS TO IT.
WOO HOO
NEXT UP, WE HAVE ANOTHER ENTRY FROM DR. BLEWILT! INTRODUCING SPRING MAN, RIDING THE "SURPRISE BOXER!!"
WOO HOO
BRAVO
TURBO MAN LOOKS FAST...
YOU THINK?
HE DOESN'T LOOK LIKE MUCH TO ME.
NOTHING STANDS A CHANCE AGAINST OUR "POP'N BEAT!"
CAPCOM
PROMISE ME YOU WON'T BREAK BEAT BY PUSHING HIM TOO HARD.
I'M WORRIED...

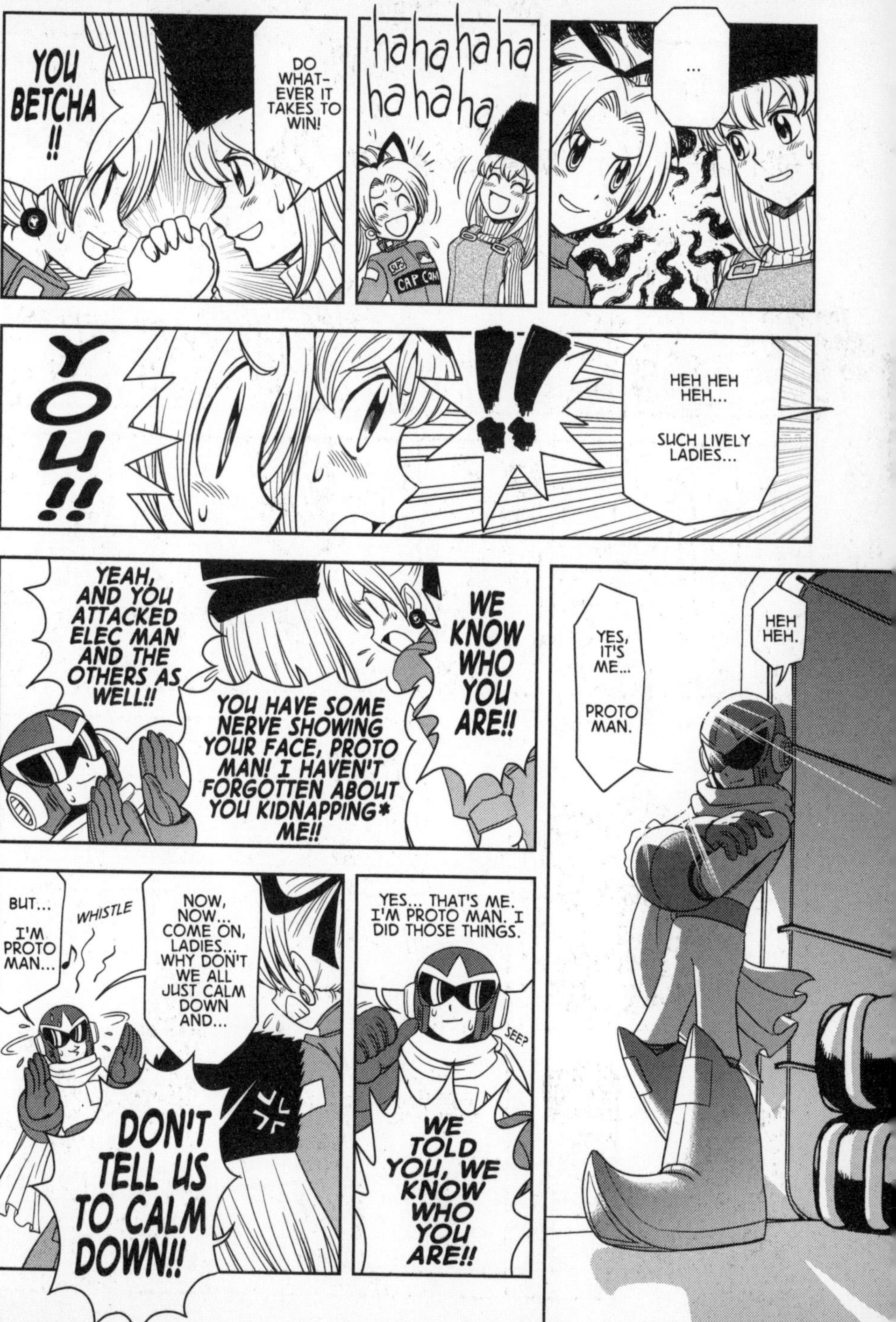
...
ha ha ha ha
ha ha ha
DO WHAT-EVER IT TAKES TO WIN!
YOU BETCHA!!
HEH HEH HEH...
SUCH LIVELY LADIES...
!!
YOU!!
HEH HEH.
YES, IT'S ME...
PROTO MAN.
WE KNOW WHO YOU ARE!!
YOU HAVE SOME NERVE SHOWING YOUR FACE, PROTO MAN! I HAVEN'T FORGOTTEN ABOUT YOU KIDNAPPING* ME!!
YEAH, AND YOU ATTACKED ELEC MAN AND THE OTHERS AS WELL!!
YES... THAT'S ME. I'M PROTO MAN. I DID THOSE THINGS.
SEE?
WE TOLD YOU, WE KNOW WHO YOU ARE!!
NOW, NOW... COME ON, LADIES... WHY DON'T WE ALL JUST CALM DOWN AND...
WHISTLE
BUT... I'M PROTO MAN...
DON'T TELL US TO CALM DOWN!!

*SEE "THE GREATEST ENEMY IN HISTORY" IN "MEGA MAN MEGAMIX VOL. 3" FOR DETAILS.

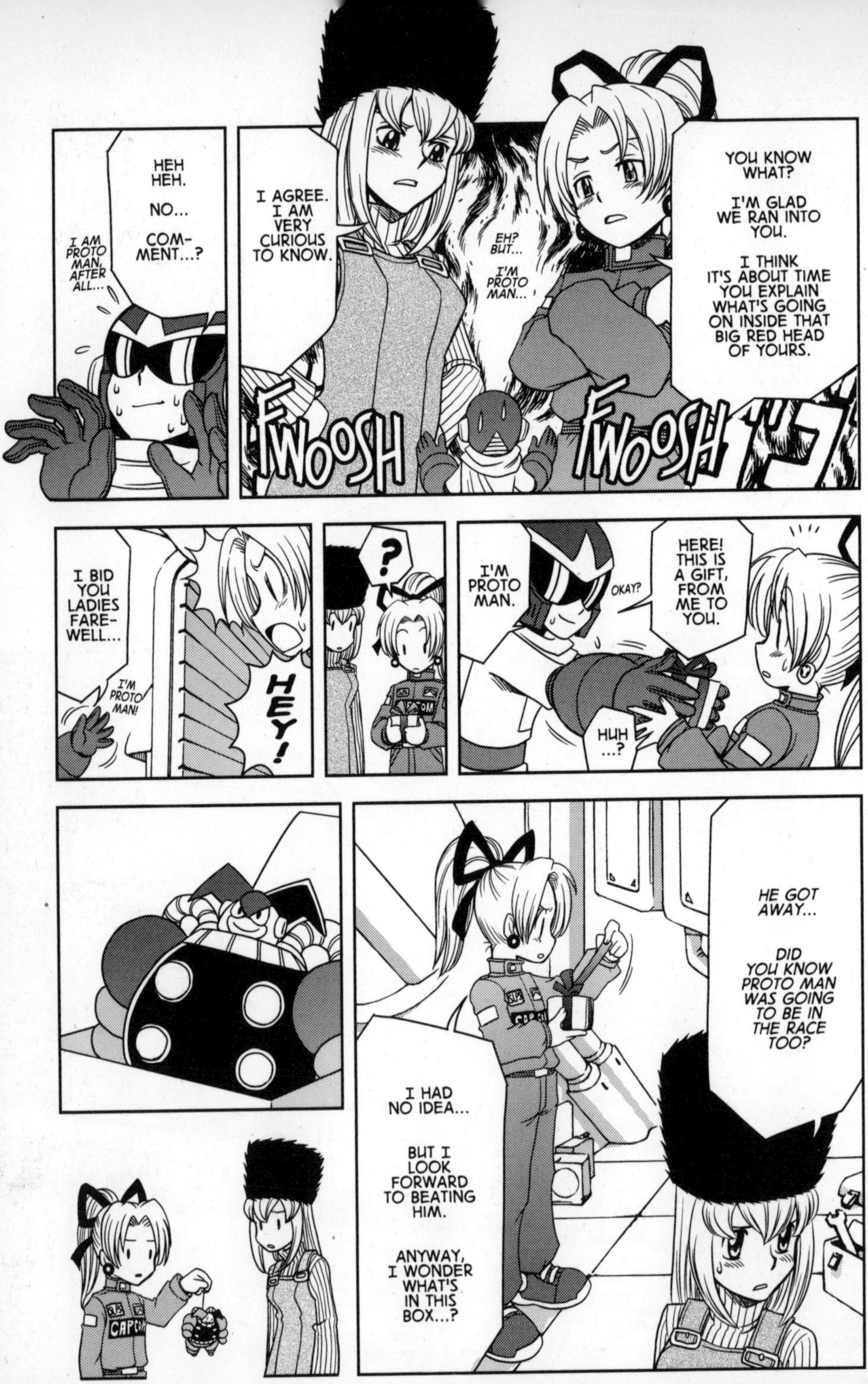
YOU KNOW WHAT?
I'M GLAD WE RAN INTO YOU.
I THINK IT'S ABOUT TIME YOU EXPLAIN WHAT'S GOING ON INSIDE THAT BIG RED HEAD OF YOURS.
EH? BUT... I'M PROTO MAN...
I AGREE. I AM VERY CURIOUS TO KNOW.
FWOOSH
FWOOSH
HEH HEH.
NO... COM-MENT...?
I AM PROTO MAN, AFTER ALL...
HERE! THIS IS A GIFT, FROM ME TO YOU.
I'M PROTO MAN.
OKAY?
HUH ...?
?
I BID YOU LADIES FARE-WELL...
I'M PROTO MAN!
HEY!
HE GOT AWAY...
DID YOU KNOW PROTO MAN WAS GOING TO BE IN THE RACE TOO?
I HAD NO IDEA...
BUT I LOOK FORWARD TO BEATING HIM.
ANYWAY, I WONDER WHAT'S IN THIS BOX...?

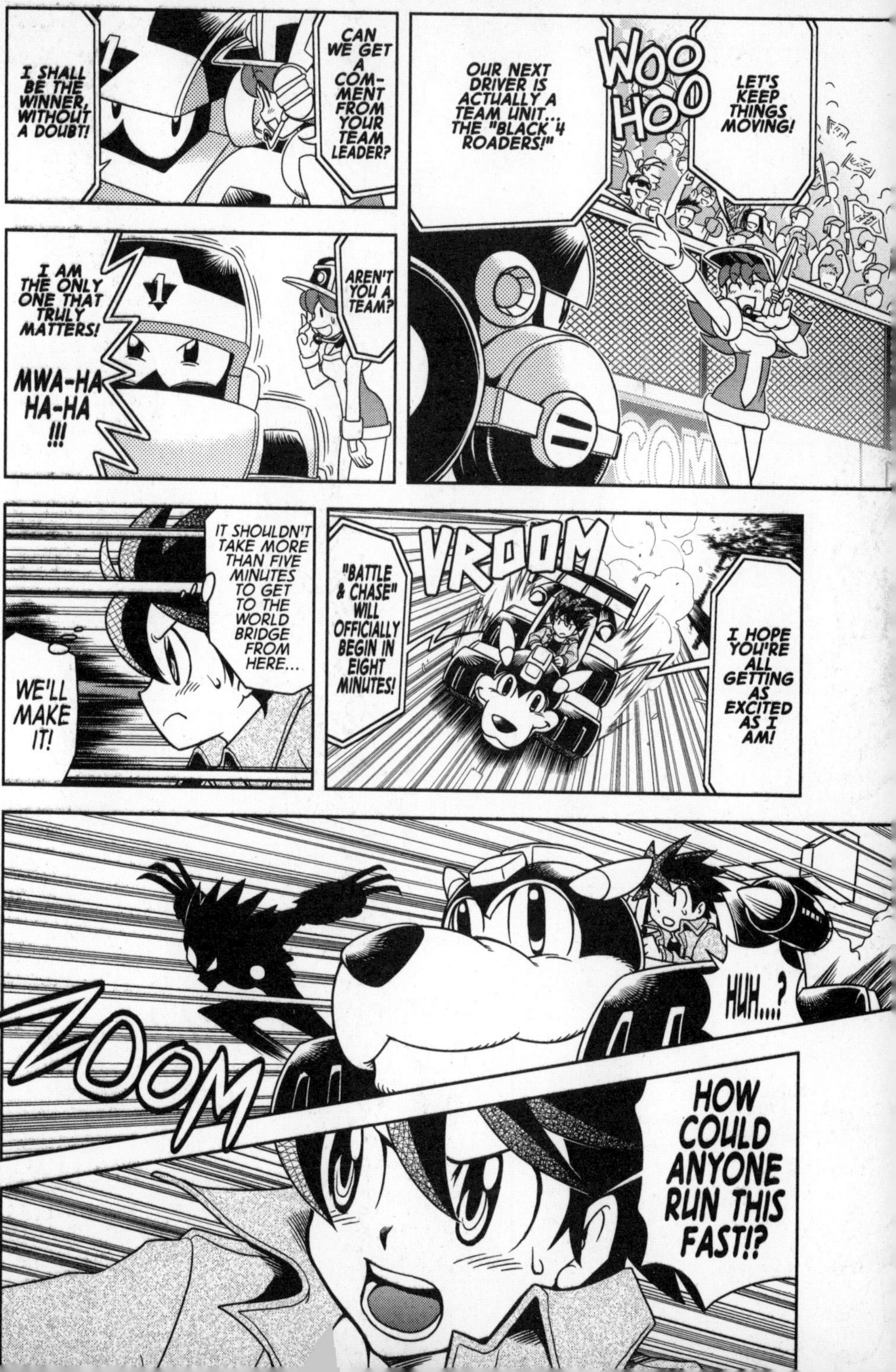
LET'S KEEP THINGS MOVING!
WOO HOO
OUR NEXT DRIVER IS ACTUALLY A TEAM UNIT... THE "BLACK 4 ROADERS!"
CAN WE GET A COM-MENT FROM YOUR TEAM LEADER?
I SHALL BE THE WINNER, WITHOUT A DOUBT!
AREN'T YOU A TEAM?
I AM THE ONLY ONE THAT TRULY MATTERS!
MWA-HA HA-HA !!!
I HOPE YOU'RE ALL GETTING AS EXCITED AS I AM!
VROOM
"BATTLE & CHASE" WILL OFFICIALLY BEGIN IN EIGHT MINUTES!
IT SHOULDN'T TAKE MORE THAN FIVE MINUTES TO GET TO THE WORLD BRIDGE FROM HERE...
WE'LL MAKE IT!
HUH...?
ZOOM
HOW COULD ANYONE RUN THIS FAST!?

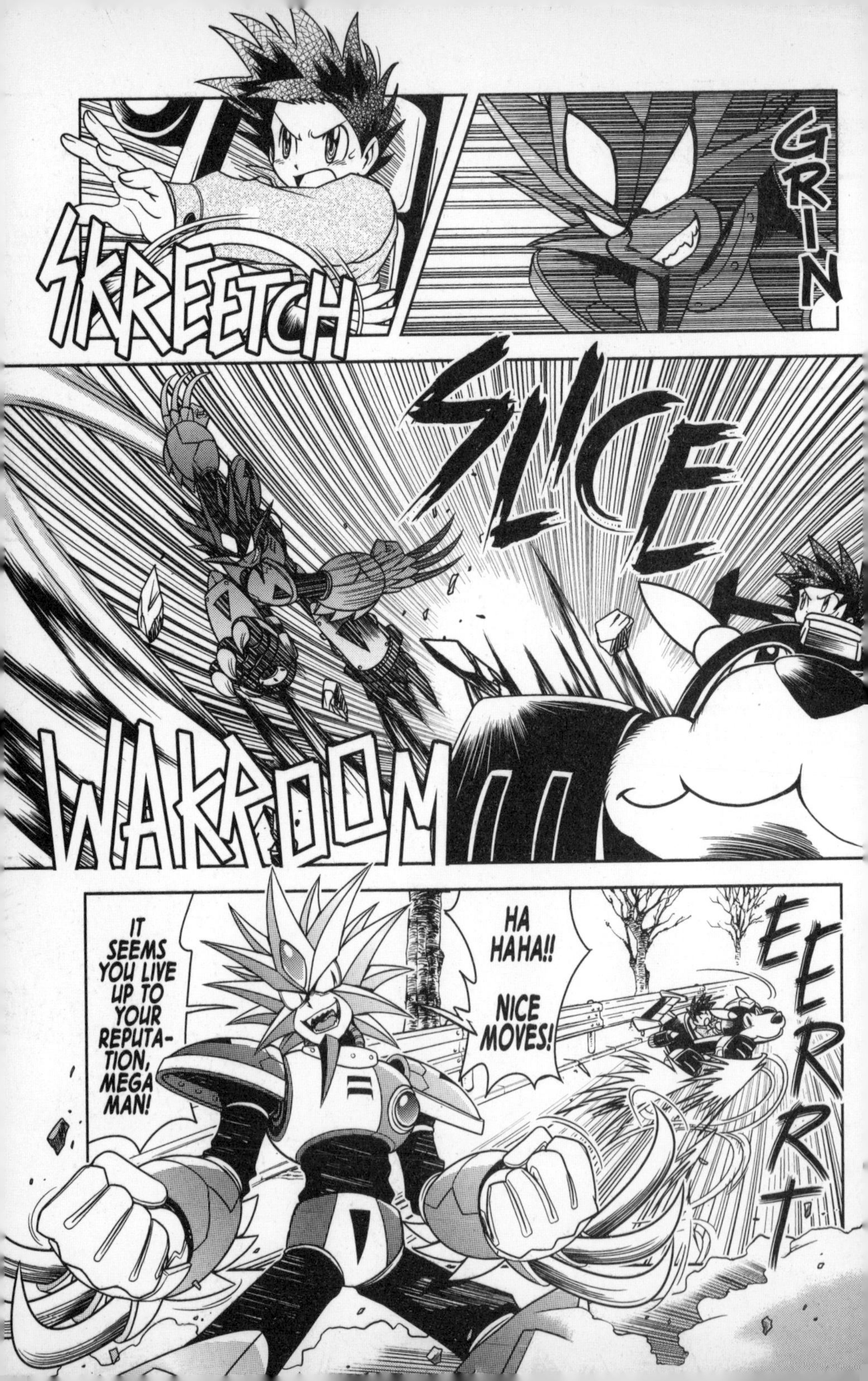
GRIN
SKREETCH
SLICE
WAKROOM
EEERRRT
HA HAHA!!
NICE MOVES!
IT SEEMS YOU LIVE UP TO YOUR REPUTATION, MEGA MAN!

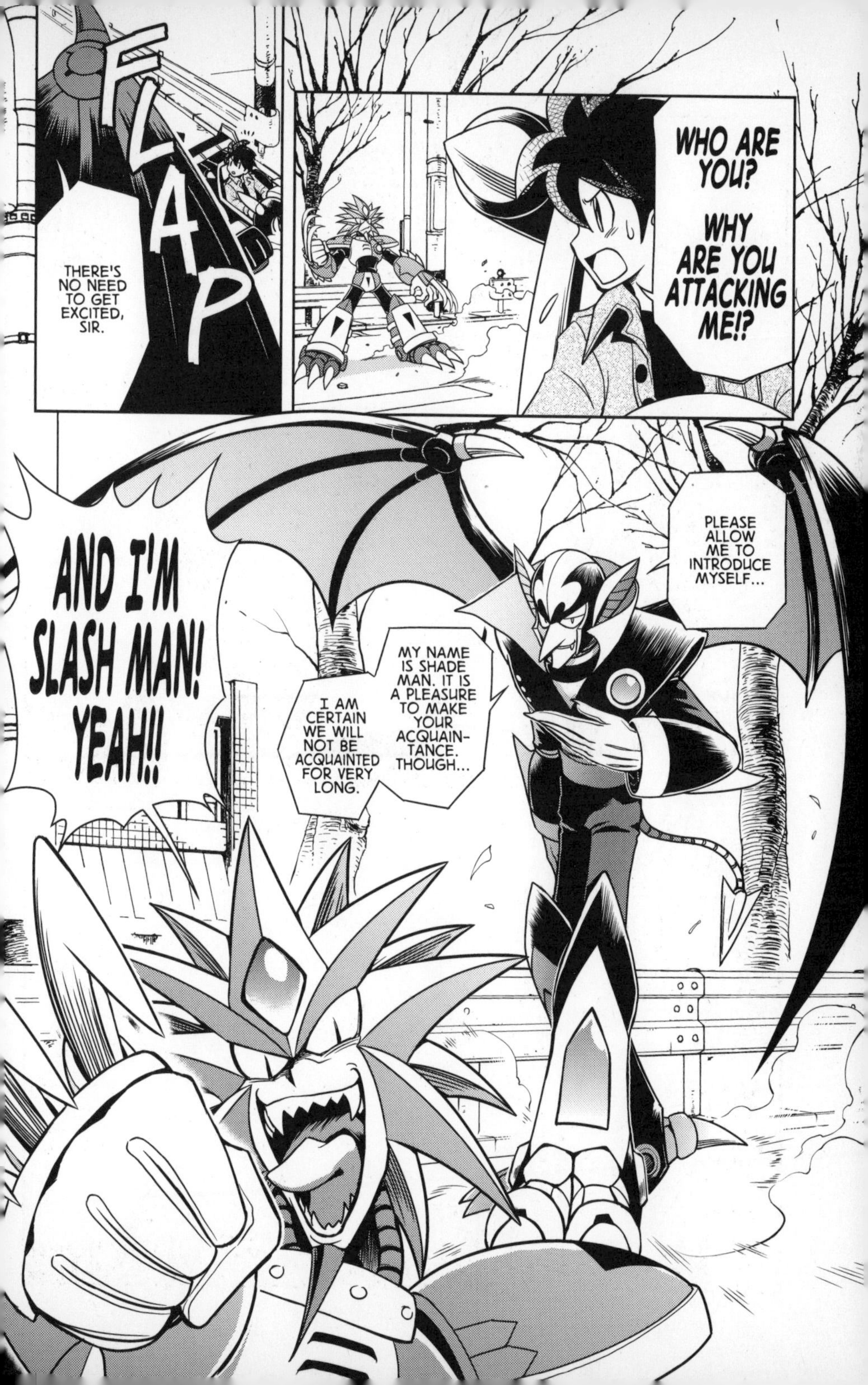
WHO ARE YOU?
WHY ARE YOU ATTACKING ME!?
FLAP
THERE'S NO NEED TO GET EXCITED, SIR.
PLEASE ALLOW ME TO INTRODUCE MYSELF...
MY NAME IS SHADE MAN. IT IS A PLEASURE TO MAKE YOUR ACQUAIN- TANCE. THOUGH...
I AM CERTAIN WE WILL NOT BE ACQUAINTED FOR VERY LONG.
AND I'M SLASH MAN! YEAH!!

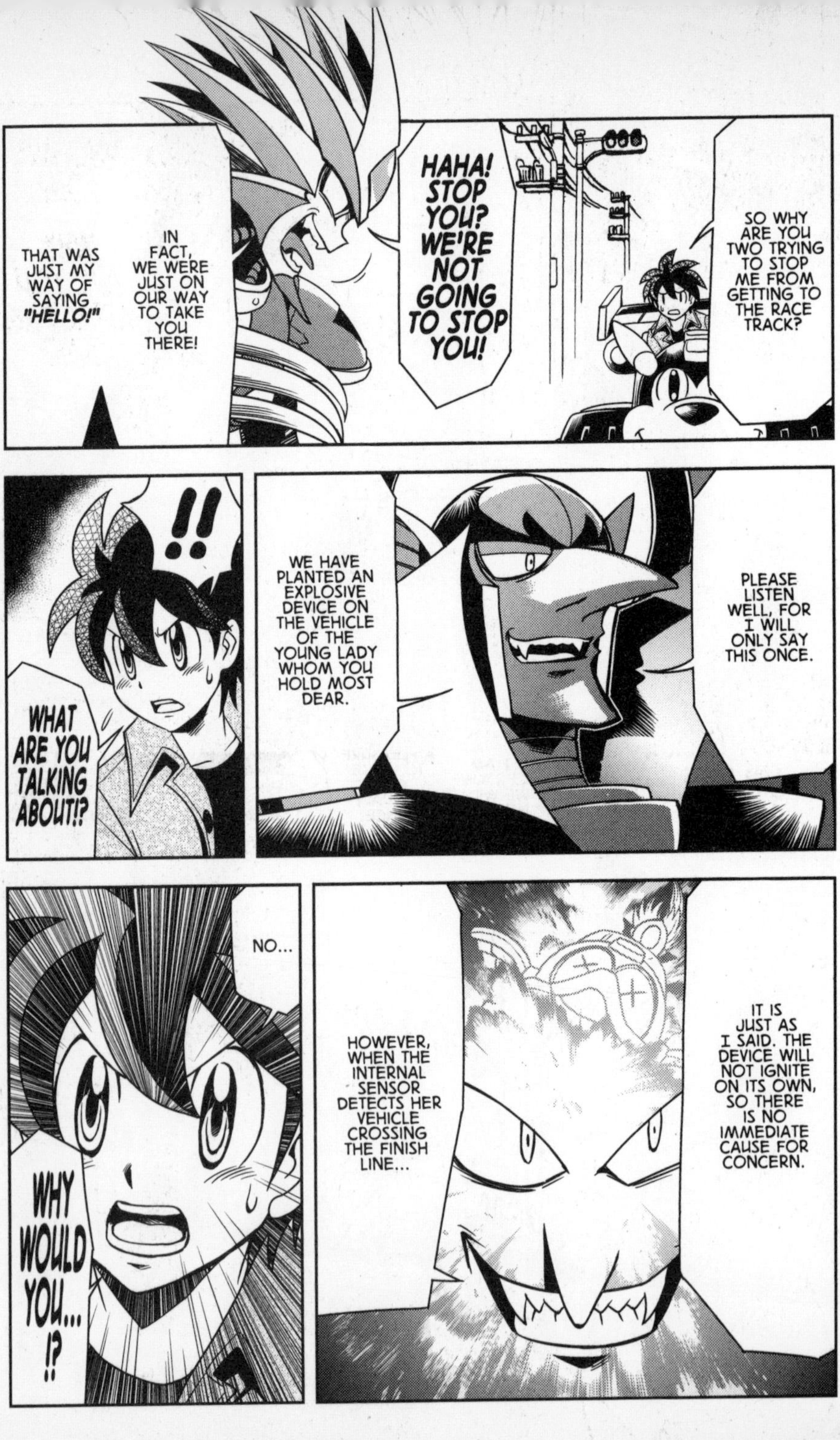
SO WHY ARE YOU TWO TRYING TO STOP ME FROM GETTING TO THE RACE TRACK?
HAHA! STOP YOU? WE'RE NOT GOING TO STOP YOU!
IN FACT, WE WERE JUST ON OUR WAY TO TAKE YOU THERE!
THAT WAS JUST MY WAY OF SAYING "HELLO!"
PLEASE LISTEN WELL, FOR I WILL ONLY SAY THIS ONCE.
WE HAVE PLANTED AN EXPLOSIVE DEVICE ON THE VEHICLE OF THE YOUNG LADY WHOM YOU HOLD MOST DEAR.
!!
WHAT ARE YOU TALKING ABOUT!?
IT IS JUST AS I SAID. THE DEVICE WILL NOT IGNITE ON ITS OWN, SO THERE IS NO IMMEDIATE CAUSE FOR CONCERN.
HOWEVER, WHEN THE INTERNAL SENSOR DETECTS HER VEHICLE CROSSING THE FINISH LINE...
NO...
WHY WOULD YOU...!?

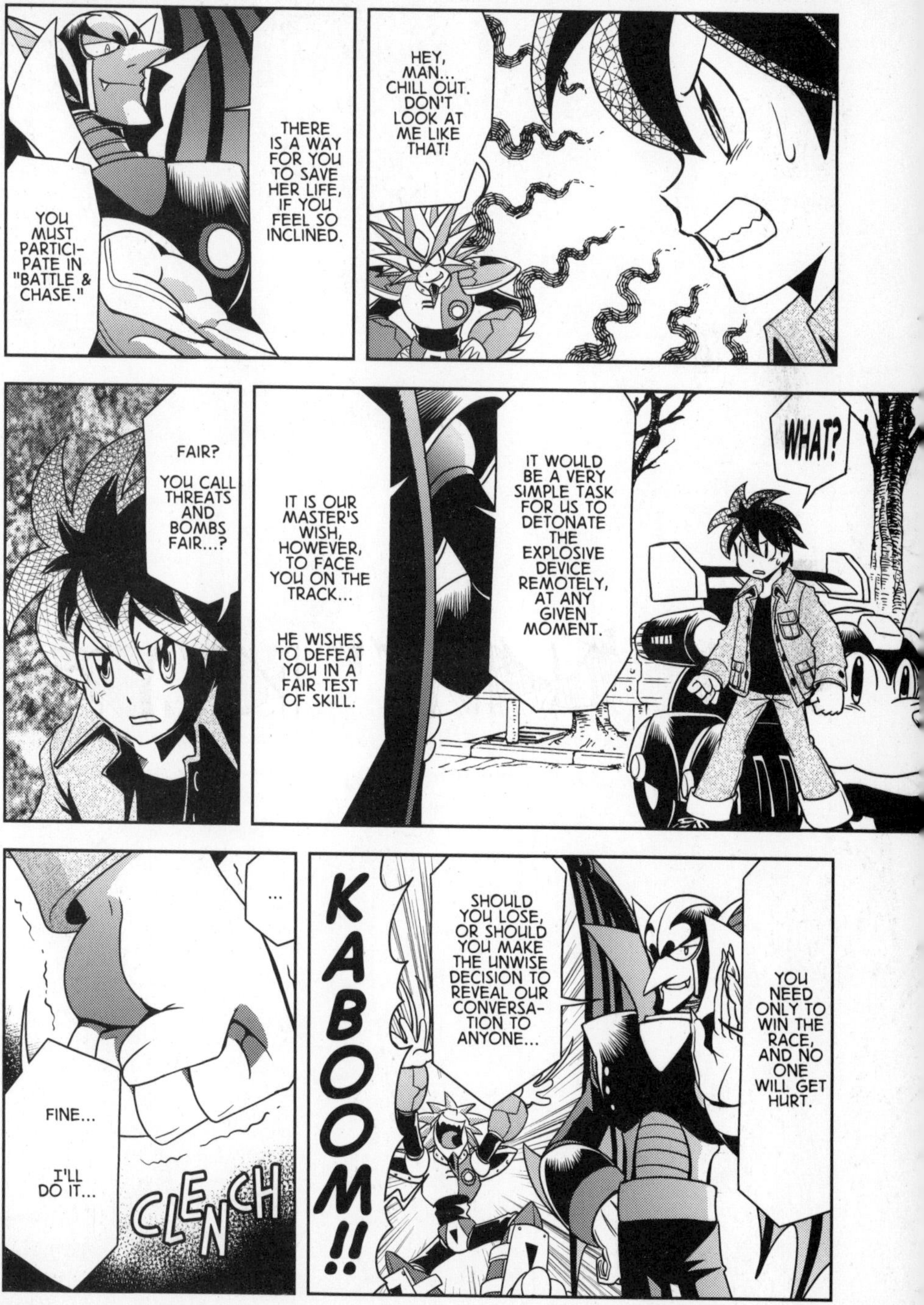
HEY, MAN... CHILL OUT. DON'T LOOK AT ME LIKE THAT!
THERE IS A WAY FOR YOU TO SAVE HER LIFE, IF YOU FEEL SO INCLINED.
YOU MUST PARTICIPATE IN "BATTLE & CHASE."
WHAT?
IT WOULD BE A VERY SIMPLE TASK FOR US TO DETONATE THE EXPLOSIVE DEVICE REMOTELY, AT ANY GIVEN MOMENT.
IT IS OUR MASTER'S WISH, HOWEVER, TO FACE YOU ON THE TRACK...
HE WISHES TO DEFEAT YOU IN A FAIR TEST OF SKILL.
FAIR?
YOU CALL THREATS AND BOMBS FAIR...?
YOU NEED ONLY TO WIN THE RACE, AND NO ONE WILL GET HURT.
SHOULD YOU LOSE, OR SHOULD YOU MAKE THE UNWISE DECISION TO REVEAL OUR CONVERSATION TO ANYONE...
KABOOOM!!
...
FINE...
I'LL DO IT...
CLENCH

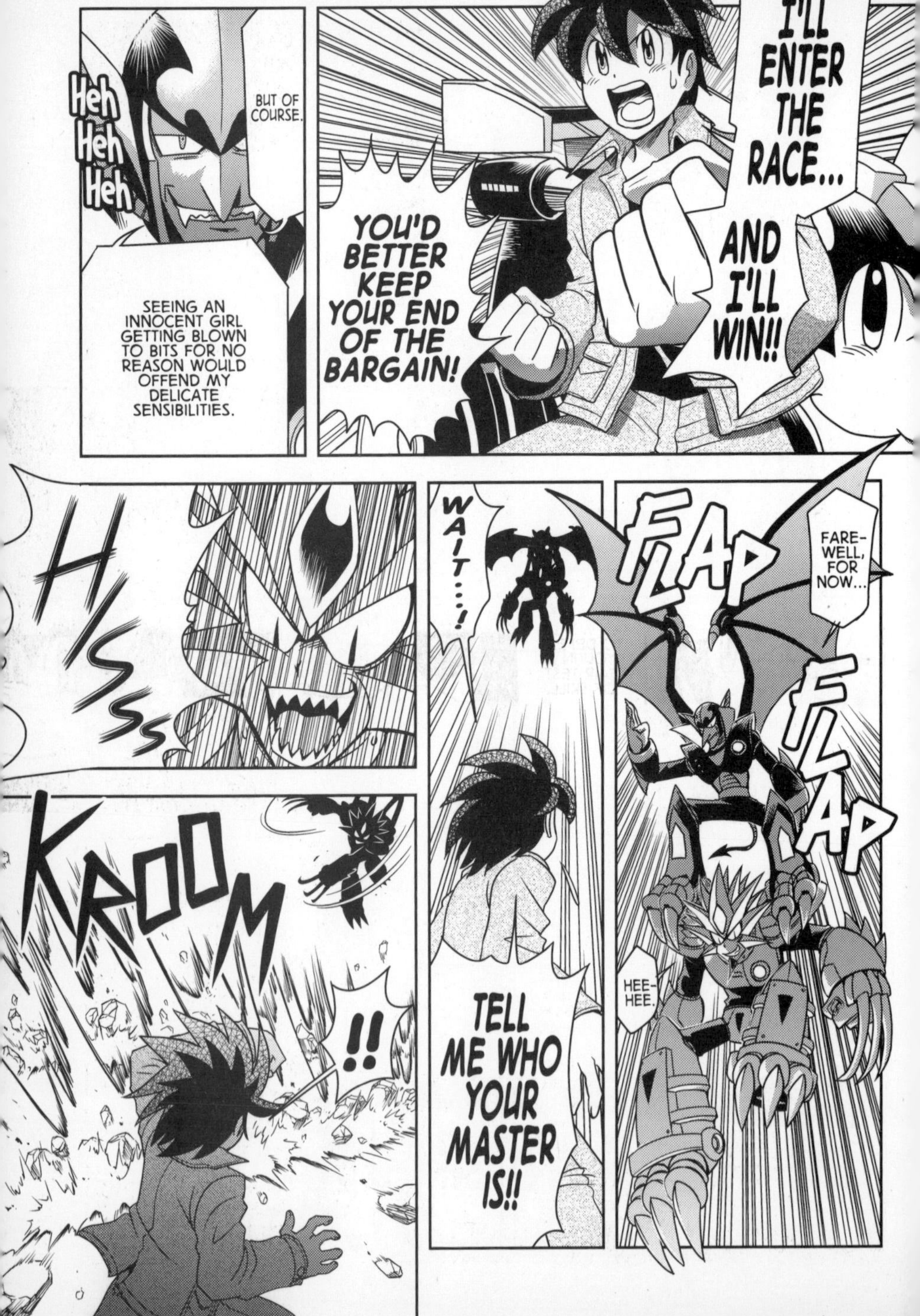
I'LL ENTER THE RACE...
AND I'LL WIN!!
YOU'D BETTER KEEP YOUR END OF THE BARGAIN!
Heh Heh Heh
BUT OF COURSE.
SEEING AN INNOCENT GIRL GETTING BLOWN TO BITS FOR NO REASON WOULD OFFEND MY DELICATE SENSIBILITIES.
FAREWELL, FOR NOW...
FLAP
FLAP
HEE-HEE.
WAIT...!
TELL ME WHO YOUR MASTER IS!!
HISSS
KROOM
!!

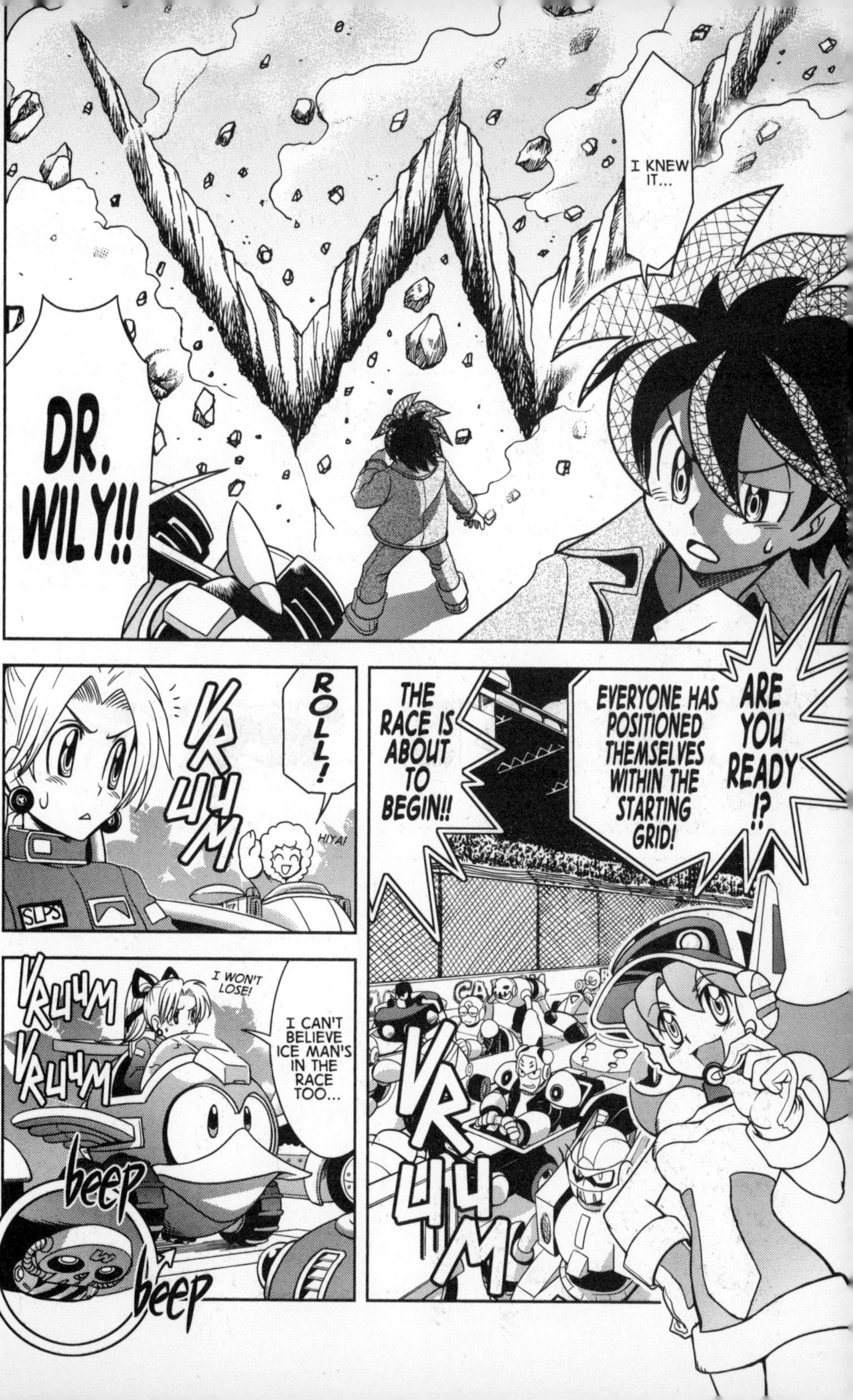
I KNEW IT...
DR. WILY!!
ARE YOU READY!?
EVERYONE HAS POSITIONED THEMSELVES WITHIN THE STARTING GRID!
THE RACE IS ABOUT TO BEGIN!!
VRUUM
ROLL!
HIYA!
VRUUM
SLPS
I WON'T LOSE!
I CAN'T BELIEVE ICE MAN'S IN THE RACE TOO...
VRUUM
VRUUM
beep
beep

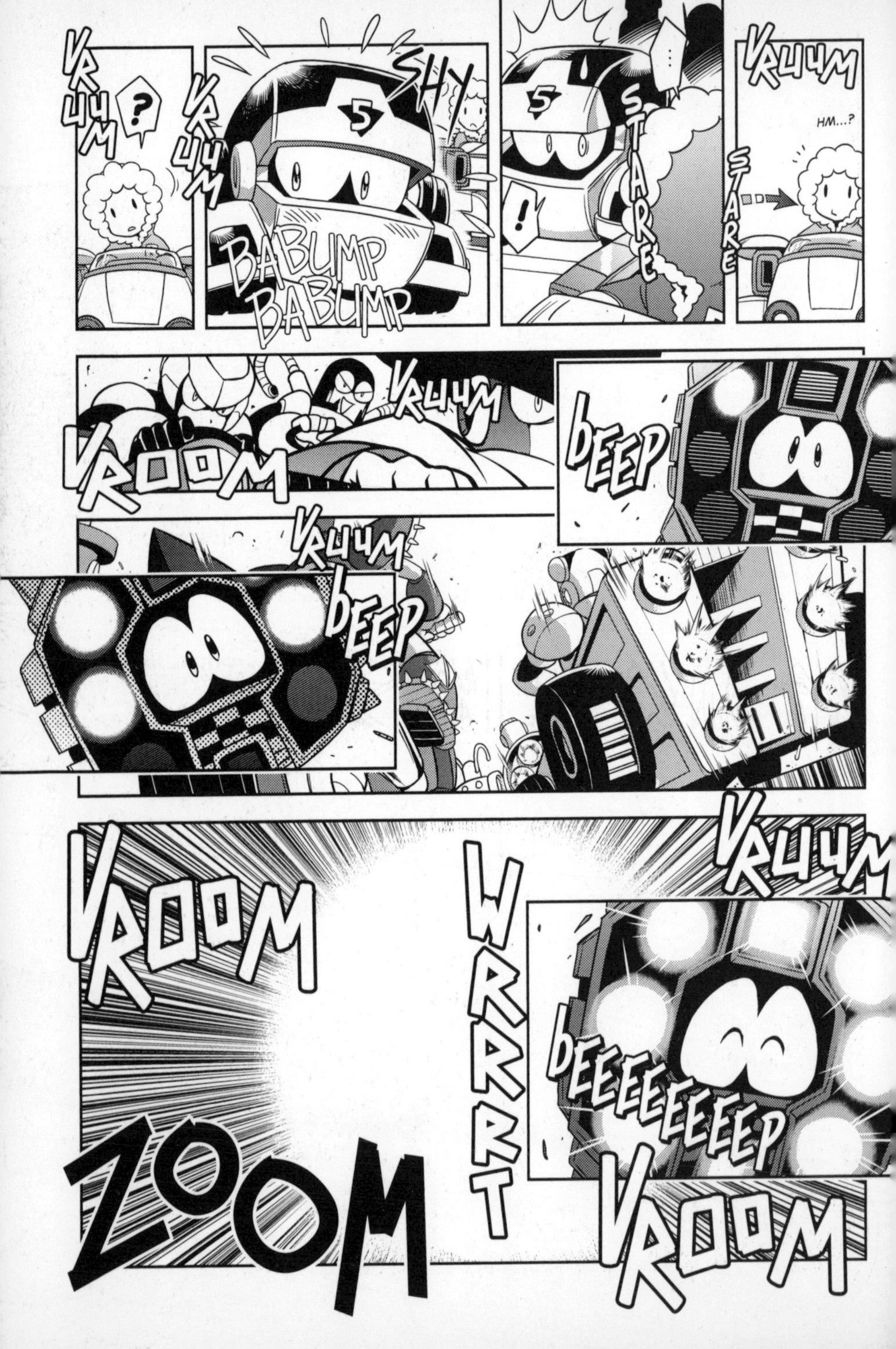
VRUUM
HM...?
STARE
STARE
!
SHY
VRUUM
BABUMP BABUMP
VRUUM
?
BEEP
VRUUM
VROOM
VRUUM
BEEP
VRUUM
BEEEEEEEEEP
WRRRT
VROOM
VROOM
ZOOM

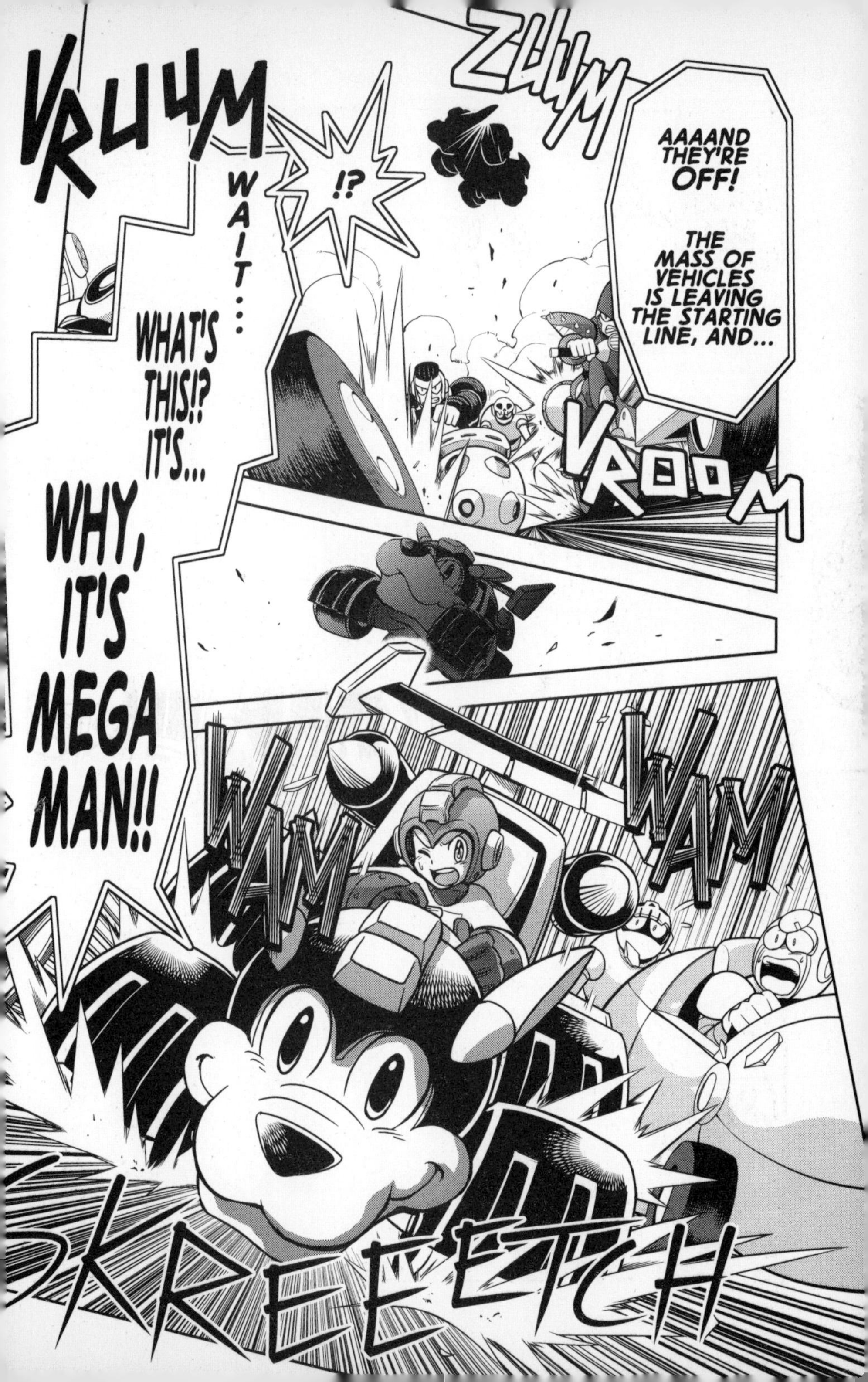
AAAAND THEY'RE OFF!
THE MASS OF VEHICLES IS LEAVING THE STARTING LINE, AND...
ZUUM
VROOM
!?
WAIT...
VRUUM
WHAT'S THIS!? IT'S...
WHY, IT'S MEGA MAN!!
WAM
WAM
SKREEETCH

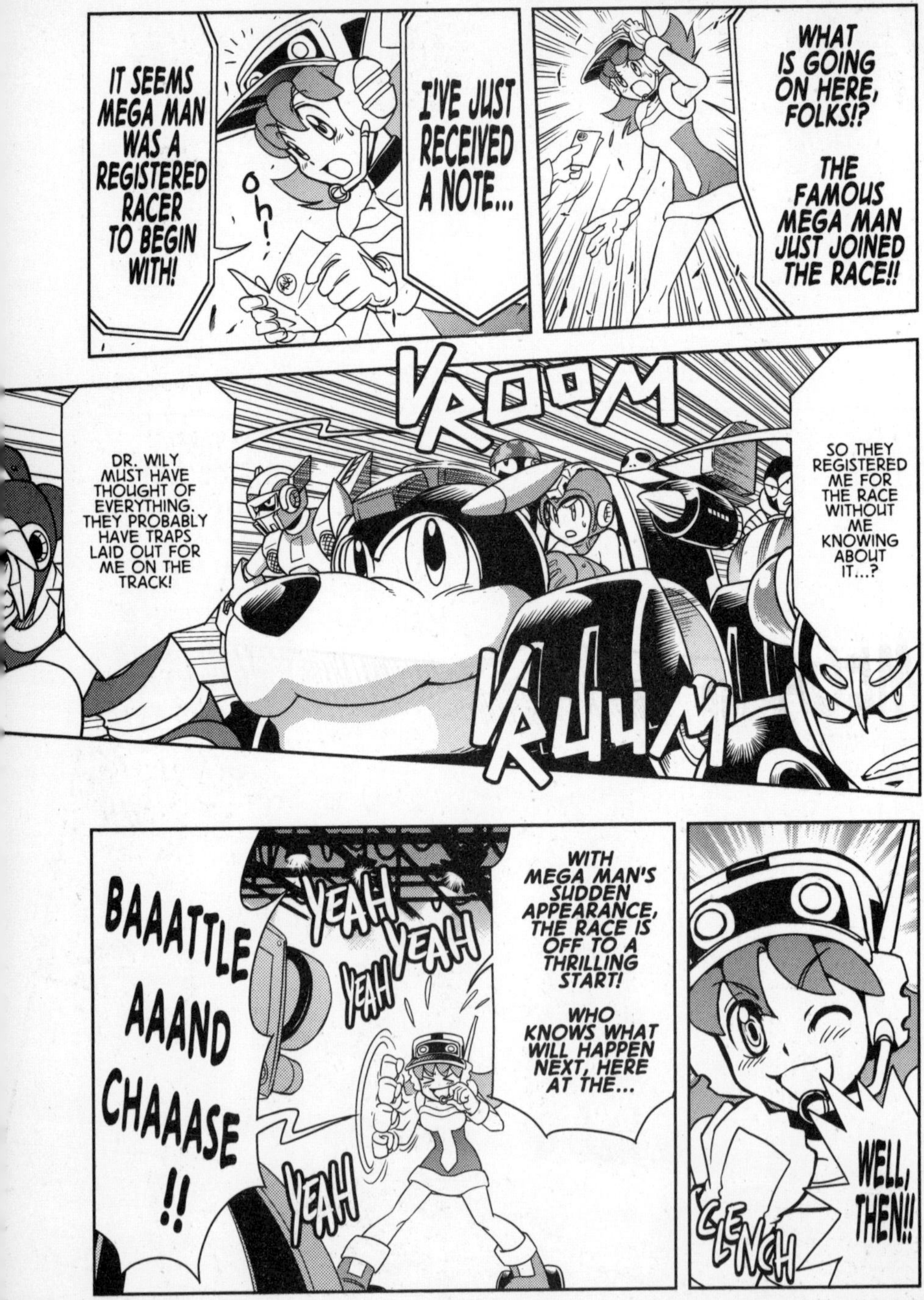
WHAT IS GOING ON HERE, FOLKS!?
THE FAMOUS MEGA MAN JUST JOINED THE RACE!!
I'VE JUST RECEIVED A NOTE...
Oh!
IT SEEMS MEGA MAN WAS A REGISTERED RACER TO BEGIN WITH!
VROOM
SO THEY REGISTERED ME FOR THE RACE WITHOUT ME KNOWING ABOUT IT...?
DR. WILY MUST HAVE THOUGHT OF EVERYTHING. THEY PROBABLY HAVE TRAPS LAID OUT FOR ME ON THE TRACK!
VRUUM
WELL, THEN!!
CLENCH
WITH MEGA MAN'S SUDDEN APPEARANCE, THE RACE IS OFF TO A THRILLING START!
WHO KNOWS WHAT WILL HAPPEN NEXT, HERE AT THE...
YEAH
YEAH
YEAH
YEAH
BAAATTLE AAAND CHAAASE !!

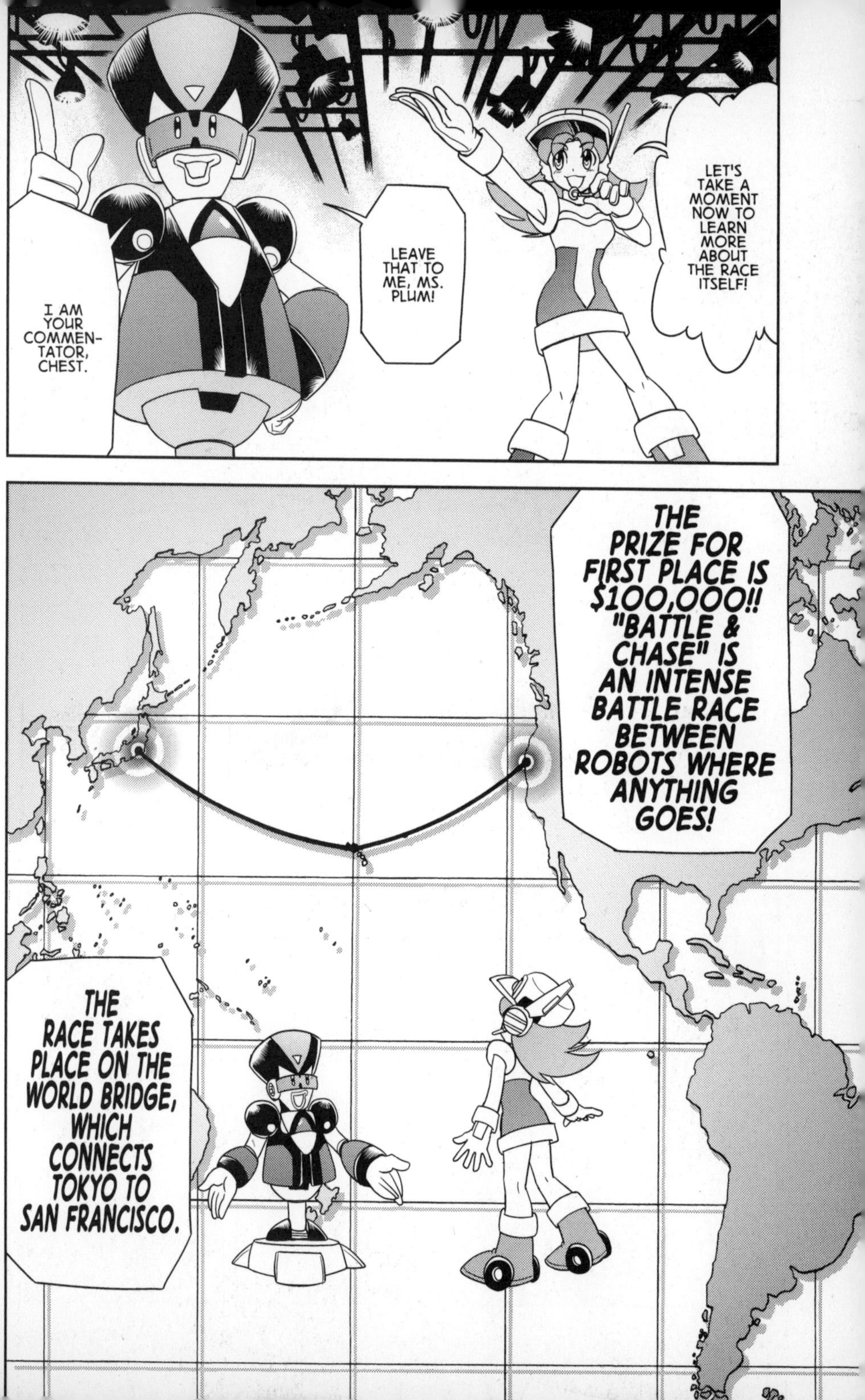
LET'S TAKE A MOMENT NOW TO LEARN MORE ABOUT THE RACE ITSELF!
LEAVE THAT TO ME, MS. PLUM!
I AM YOUR COMMENTATOR, CHEST.
THE PRIZE FOR FIRST PLACE IS $100,000!! "BATTLE & CHASE" IS AN INTENSE BATTLE RACE BETWEEN ROBOTS WHERE ANYTHING GOES!
THE RACE TAKES PLACE ON THE WORLD BRIDGE, WHICH CONNECTS TOKYO TO SAN FRANCISCO.

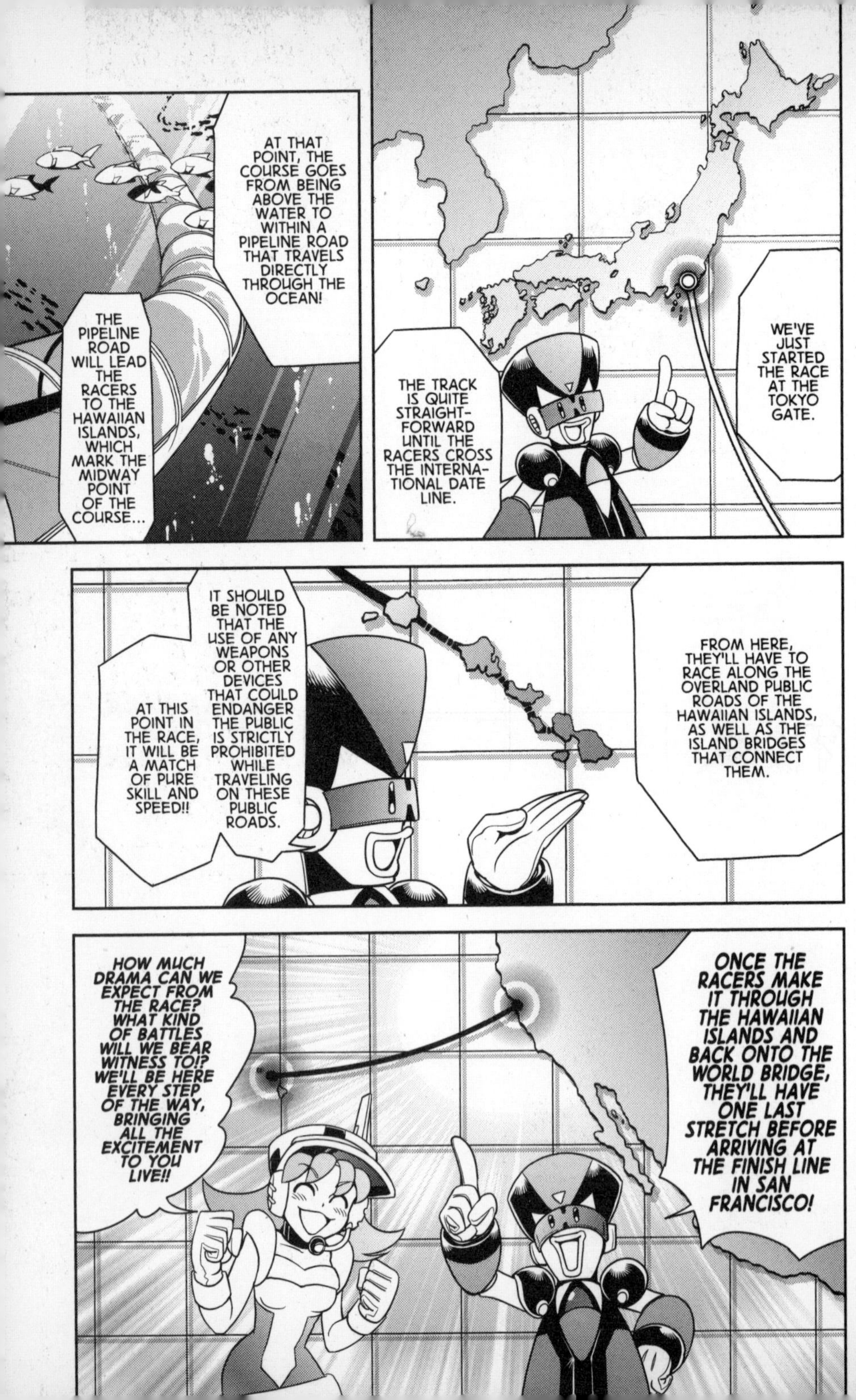
WE'VE JUST STARTED THE RACE AT THE TOKYO GATE.
THE TRACK IS QUITE STRAIGHTFORWARD UNTIL THE RACERS CROSS THE INTERNATIONAL DATE LINE.
AT THAT POINT, THE COURSE GOES FROM BEING ABOVE THE WATER TO WITHIN A PIPELINE ROAD THAT TRAVELS DIRECTLY THROUGH THE OCEAN!
THE PIPELINE ROAD WILL LEAD THE RACERS TO THE HAWAIIAN ISLANDS, WHICH MARK THE MIDWAY POINT OF THE COURSE...
FROM HERE, THEY'LL HAVE TO RACE ALONG THE OVERLAND PUBLIC ROADS OF THE HAWAIIAN ISLANDS, AS WELL AS THE ISLAND BRIDGES THAT CONNECT THEM.
IT SHOULD BE NOTED THAT THE USE OF ANY WEAPONS OR OTHER DEVICES THAT COULD ENDANGER THE PUBLIC IS STRICTLY PROHIBITED WHILE TRAVELING ON THESE PUBLIC ROADS.
AT THIS POINT IN THE RACE, IT WILL BE A MATCH OF PURE SKILL AND SPEED!!
ONCE THE RACERS MAKE IT THROUGH THE HAWAIIAN ISLANDS AND BACK ONTO THE WORLD BRIDGE, THEY'LL HAVE ONE LAST STRETCH BEFORE ARRIVING AT THE FINISH LINE IN SAN FRANCISCO!
HOW MUCH DRAMA CAN WE EXPECT FROM THE RACE? WHAT KIND OF BATTLES WILL WE BEAR WITNESS TO!? WE'LL BE HERE EVERY STEP OF THE WAY, BRINGING ALL THE EXCITEMENT TO YOU LIVE!!

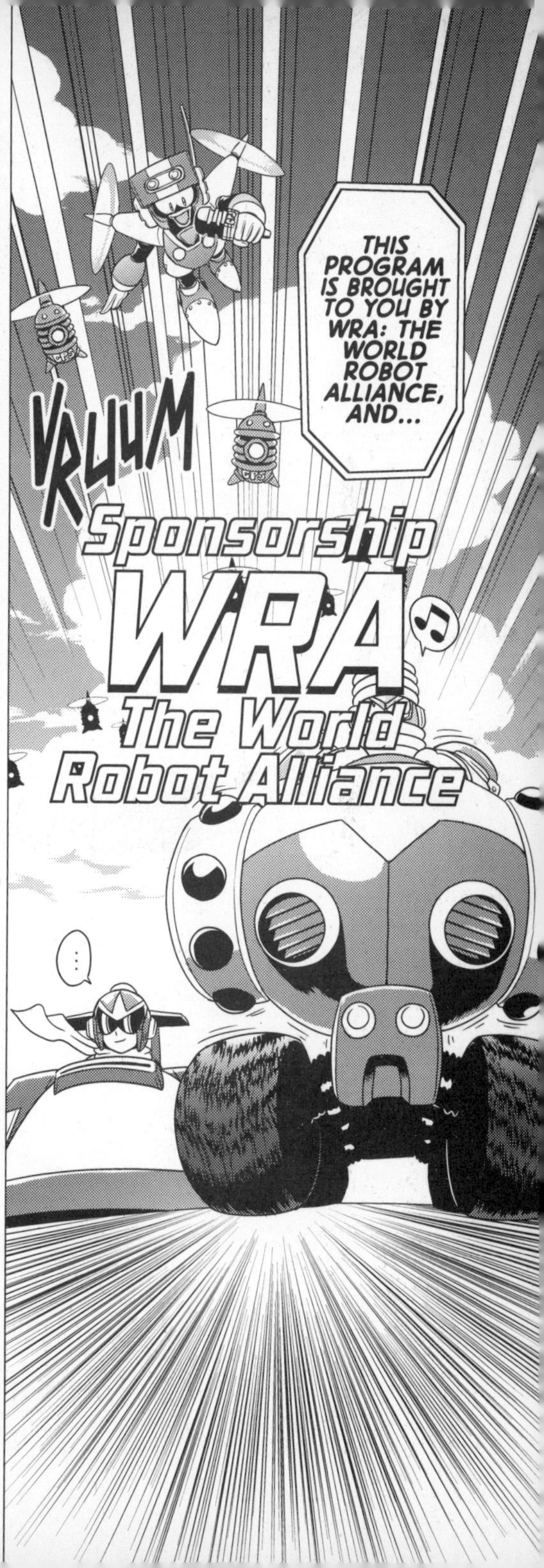
THIS PROGRAM IS BROUGHT TO YOU BY WRA: THE WORLD ROBOT ALLIANCE, AND...
VRUUM
Sponsorship
WRA
The World Robot Alliance
...

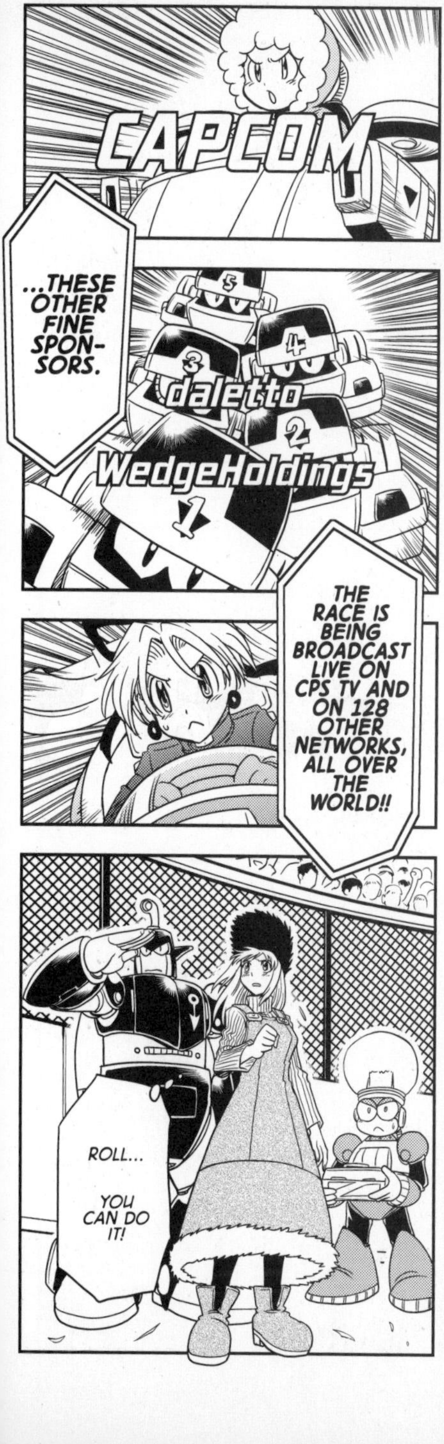
CAPCOM
...THESE OTHER FINE SPON-SORS.
daletto
WedgeHoldings
THE RACE IS BEING BROADCAST LIVE ON CPS TV AND ON 128 OTHER NETWORKS, ALL OVER THE WORLD!!
ROLL...
YOU CAN DO IT!

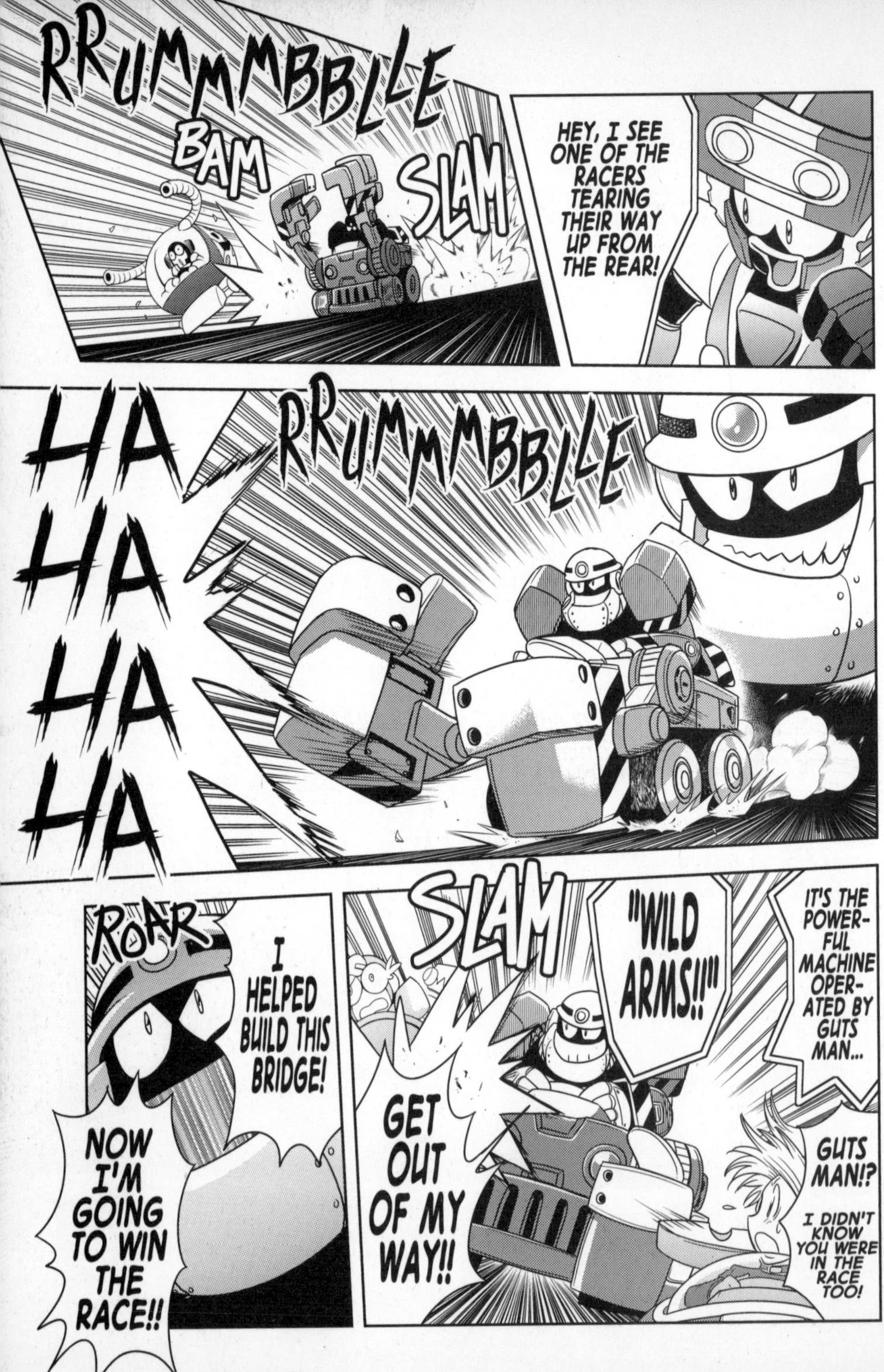
HEY, I SEE ONE OF THE RACERS TEARING THEIR WAY UP FROM THE REAR!
RRUMMMBBLLE
SLAM
BAM
RRUMMMBBLLE
HA HA HA HA
IT'S THE POWER-FUL MACHINE OPER-ATED BY GUTS MAN...
"WILD ARMS!!"
SLAM
GUTS MAN!?
I DIDN'T KNOW YOU WERE IN THE RACE TOO!
GET OUT OF MY WAY!!
ROAR
I HELPED BUILD THIS BRIDGE!
NOW I'M GOING TO WIN THE RACE!!

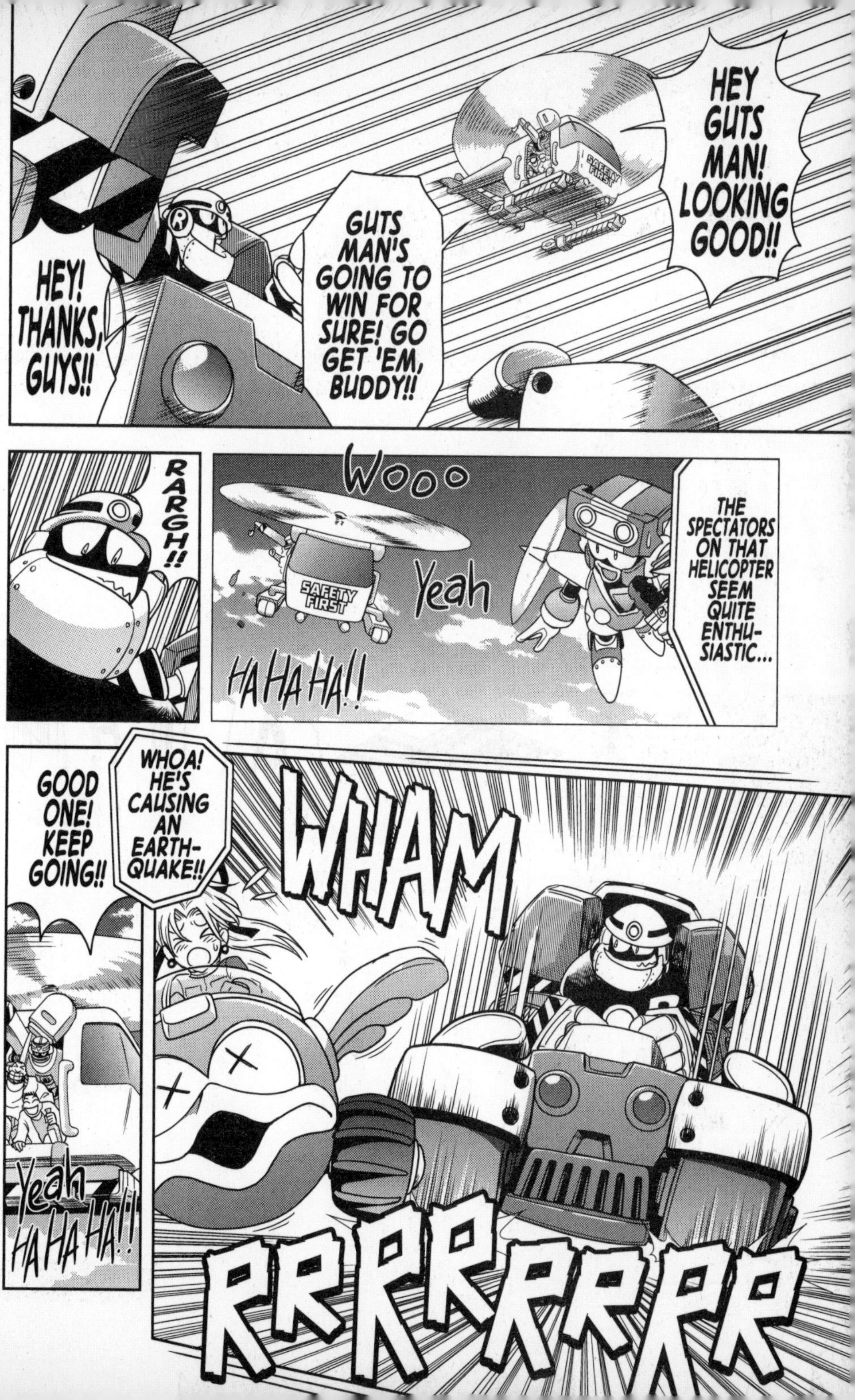
HEY GUTS MAN! LOOKING GOOD!!
GUTS MAN'S GOING TO WIN FOR SURE! GO GET 'EM, BUDDY!!
HEY! THANKS, GUYS!!
THE SPECTATORS ON THAT HELICOPTER SEEM QUITE ENTHUSIASTIC...
WOOO
Yeah
HA HA HA!!
SAFETY FIRST
RARGH!!
WHAM
RRRRRRRR
WHOA! HE'S CAUSING AN EARTHQUAKE!!
GOOD ONE! KEEP GOING!!
Yeah
HA HA HA!!

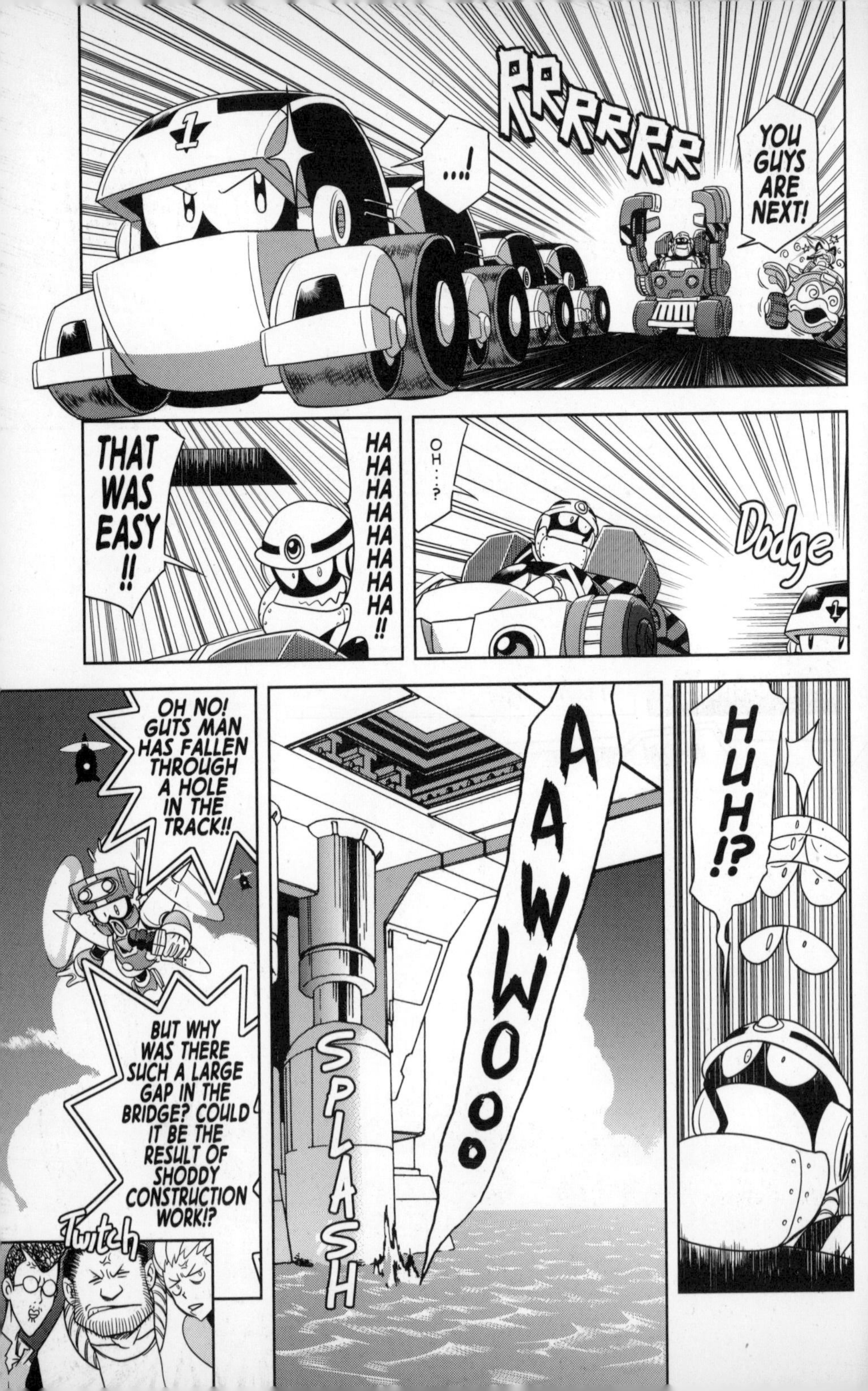

YOU GUYS ARE NEXT!
RRRRRR
...!
OH...?
Dodge
HAHAHAHAHAHAHAHAHAHA!!
THAT WAS EASY!!
HUH!?
AAWWOOOO
SPLASH
OH NO! GUTS MAN HAS FALLEN THROUGH A HOLE IN THE TRACK!!
BUT WHY WAS THERE SUCH A LARGE GAP IN THE BRIDGE? COULD IT BE THE RESULT OF SHODDY CONSTRUCTION WORK!?
Twitch

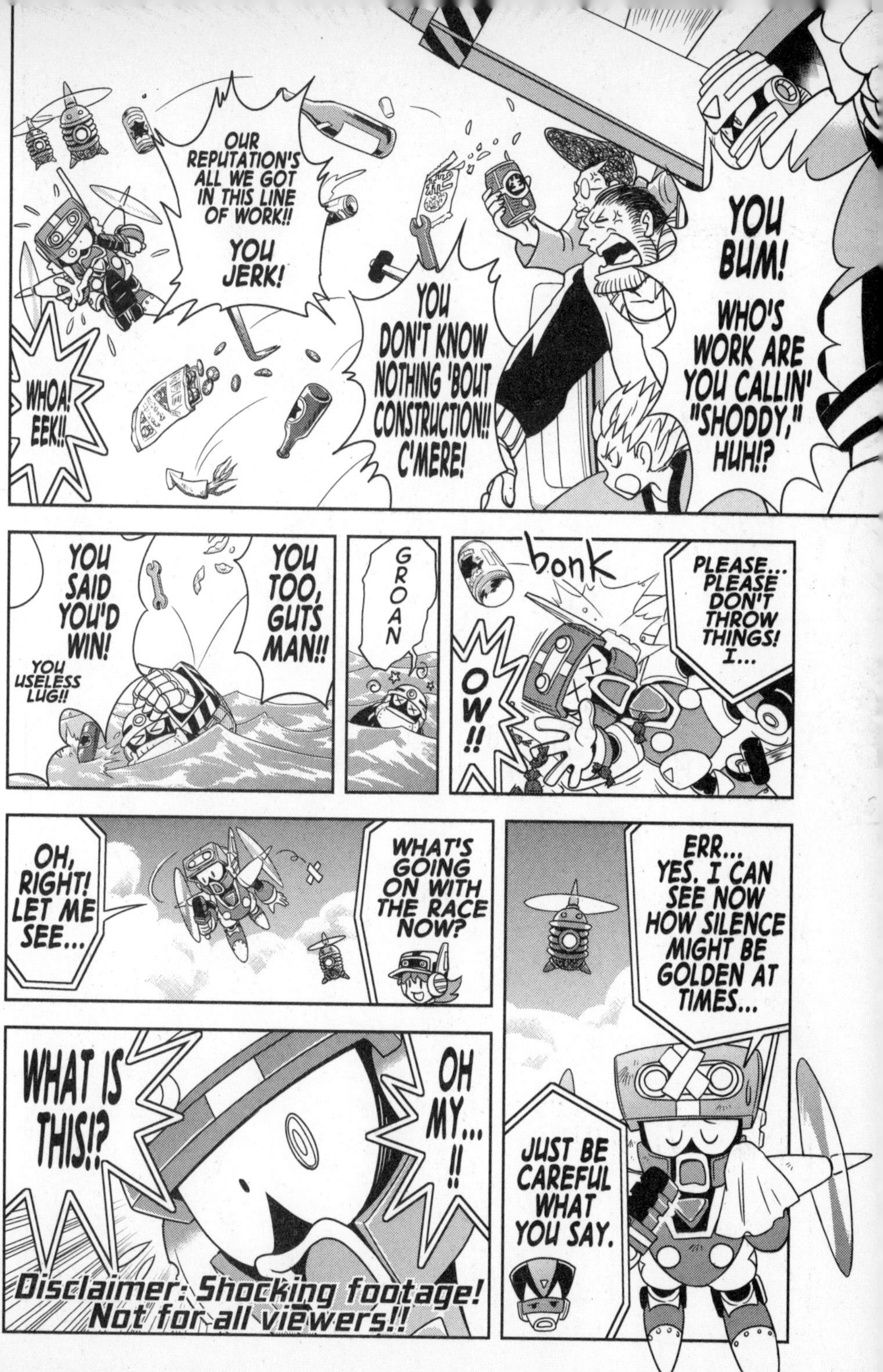
YOU BUM! WHO'S WORK ARE YOU CALLIN' "SHODDY," HUH!?
YOU DON'T KNOW NOTHING 'BOUT CONSTRUCTION!! C'MERE!
OUR REPUTATION'S ALL WE GOT IN THIS LINE OF WORK!! YOU JERK!
WHOA! EEK!!
bonk
PLEASE... PLEASE DON'T THROW THINGS! I...
OW!!
GROAN
YOU TOO, GUTS MAN!!
YOU SAID YOU'D WIN!
YOU USELESS LUG!!
ERR... YES. I CAN SEE NOW HOW SILENCE MIGHT BE GOLDEN AT TIMES...
JUST BE CAREFUL WHAT YOU SAY.
WHAT'S GOING ON WITH THE RACE NOW?
OH, RIGHT! LET ME SEE...
OH MY...!!
WHAT IS THIS!?
Disclaimer: Shocking footage! Not for all viewers!!

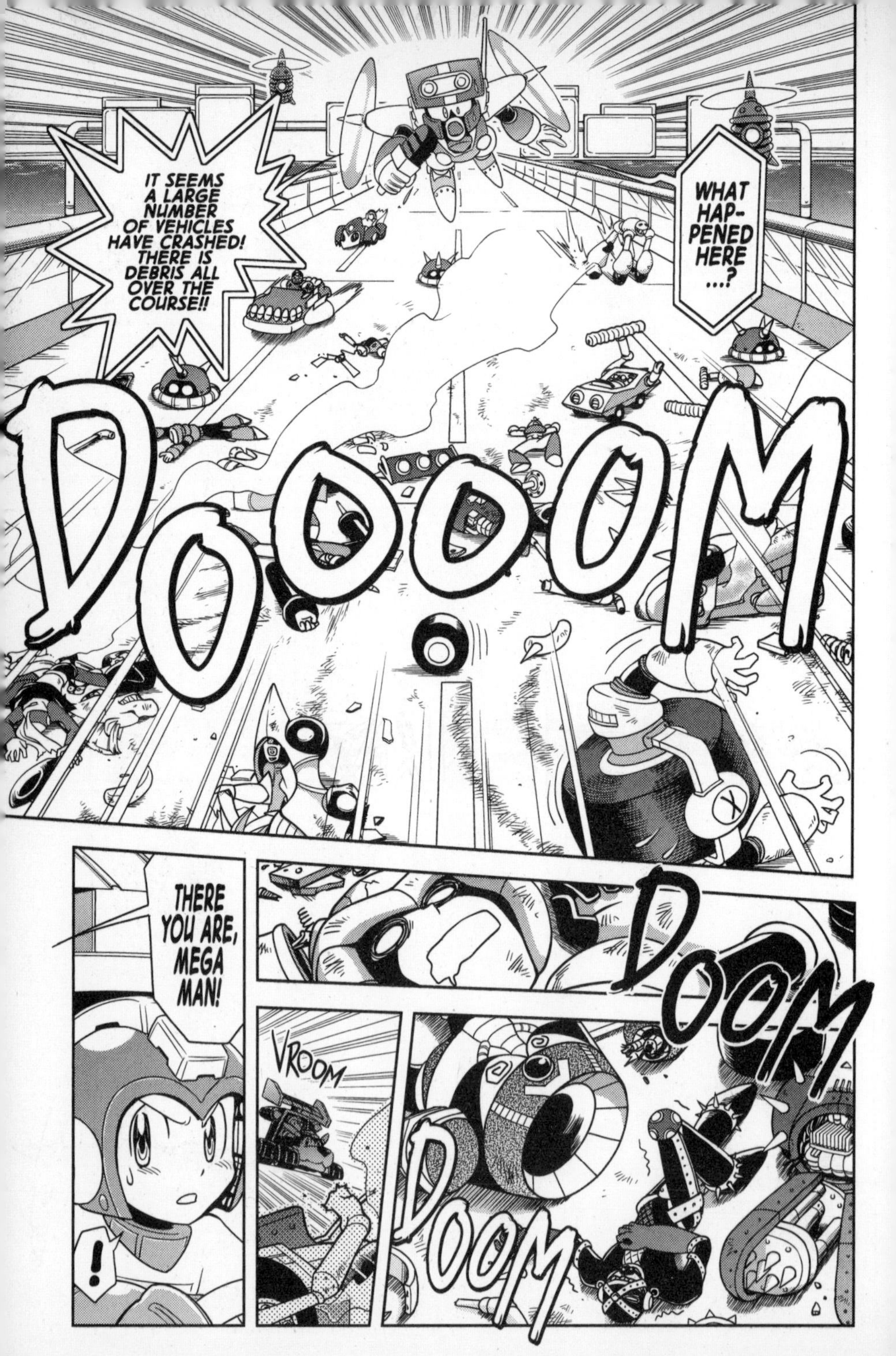
WHAT HAP-PENED HERE ...?
IT SEEMS A LARGE NUMBER OF VEHICLES HAVE CRASHED! THERE IS DEBRIS ALL OVER THE COURSE!!
DOOOOM
DOOM
DOOM
VROOM
THERE YOU ARE, MEGA MAN!
!

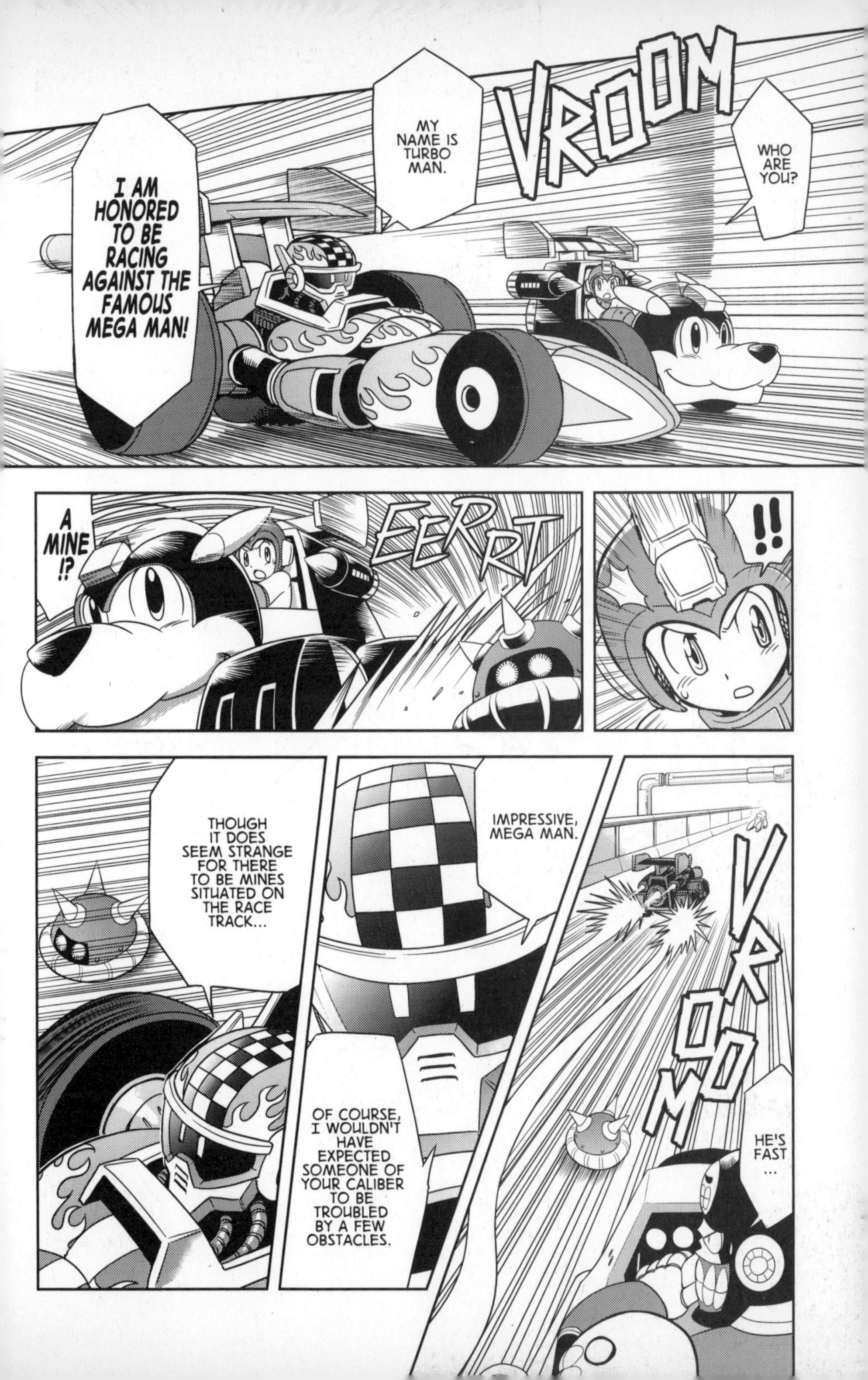
WHO ARE YOU?
VROOM
MY NAME IS TURBO MAN.
I AM HONORED TO BE RACING AGAINST THE FAMOUS MEGA MAN!
!!
EERRT
A MINE !?
VROOOM
HE'S FAST ...
IMPRESSIVE, MEGA MAN.
OF COURSE, I WOULDN'T HAVE EXPECTED SOMEONE OF YOUR CALIBER TO BE TROUBLED BY A FEW OBSTACLES.
THOUGH IT DOES SEEM STRANGE FOR THERE TO BE MINES SITUATED ON THE RACE TRACK...

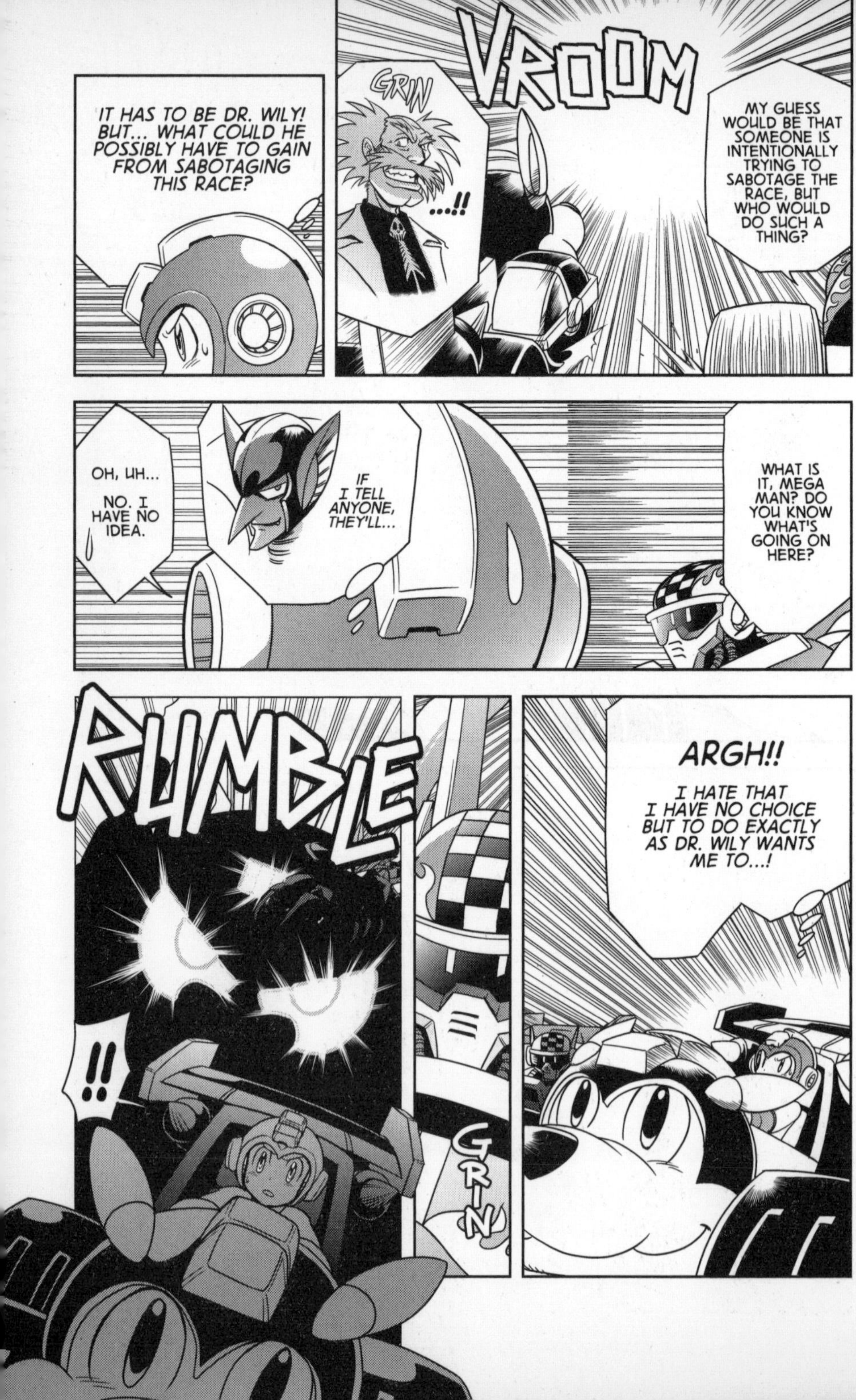
VROOM
MY GUESS WOULD BE THAT SOMEONE IS INTENTIONALLY TRYING TO SABOTAGE THE RACE, BUT WHO WOULD DO SUCH A THING?
GRIN
...!!
IT HAS TO BE DR. WILY! BUT... WHAT COULD HE POSSIBLY HAVE TO GAIN FROM SABOTAGING THIS RACE?
WHAT IS IT, MEGA MAN? DO YOU KNOW WHAT'S GOING ON HERE?
IF I TELL ANYONE, THEY'LL...
OH, UH...
NO. I HAVE NO IDEA.
ARGH!!
I HATE THAT I HAVE NO CHOICE BUT TO DO EXACTLY AS DR. WILY WANTS ME TO...!
GRIN
RUMBLE
!!

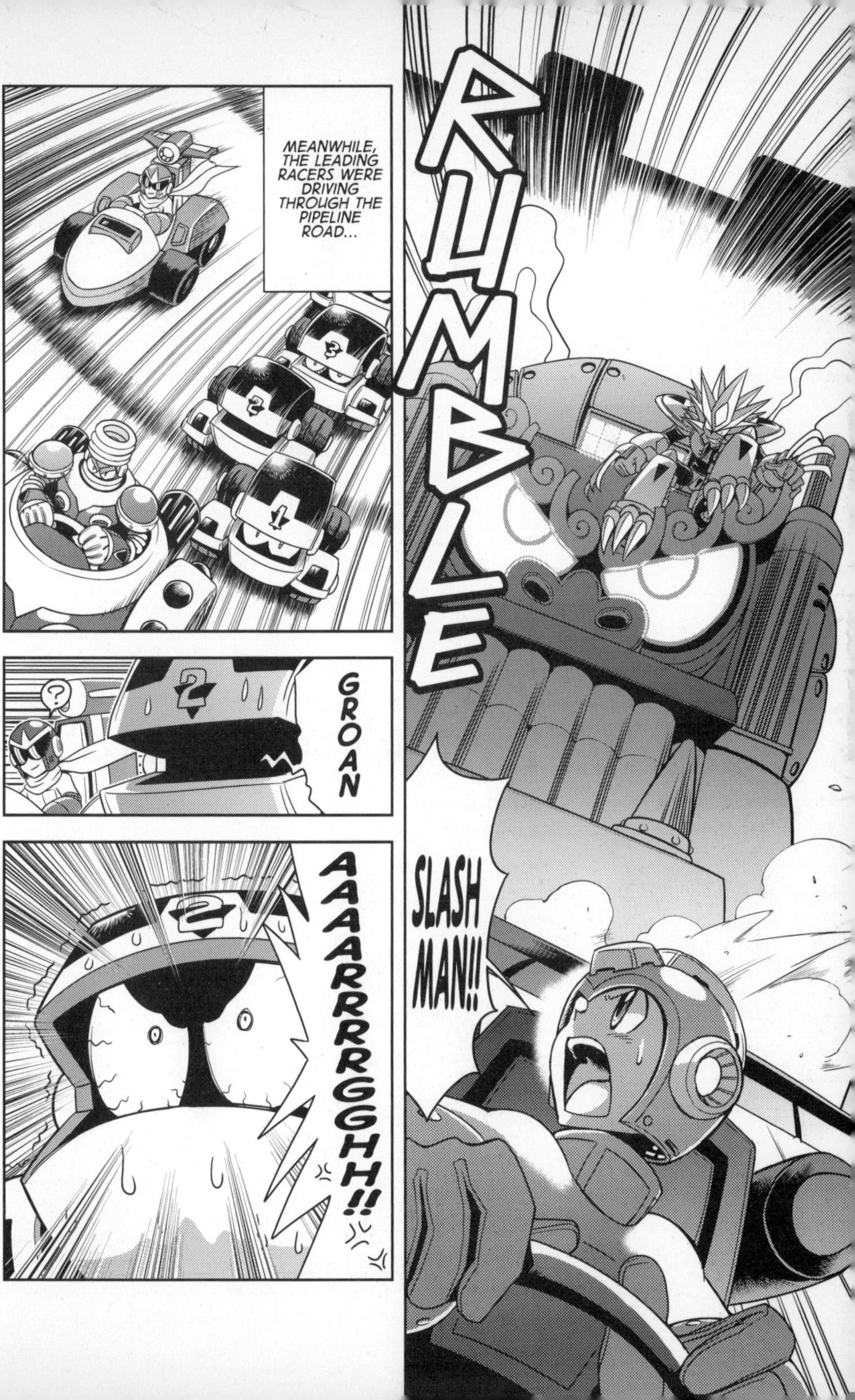
RUMBLE
SLASH MAN!!
MEANWHILE, THE LEADING RACERS WERE DRIVING THROUGH THE PIPELINE ROAD...
?
GROAN
AAAARRRRGGHH!!

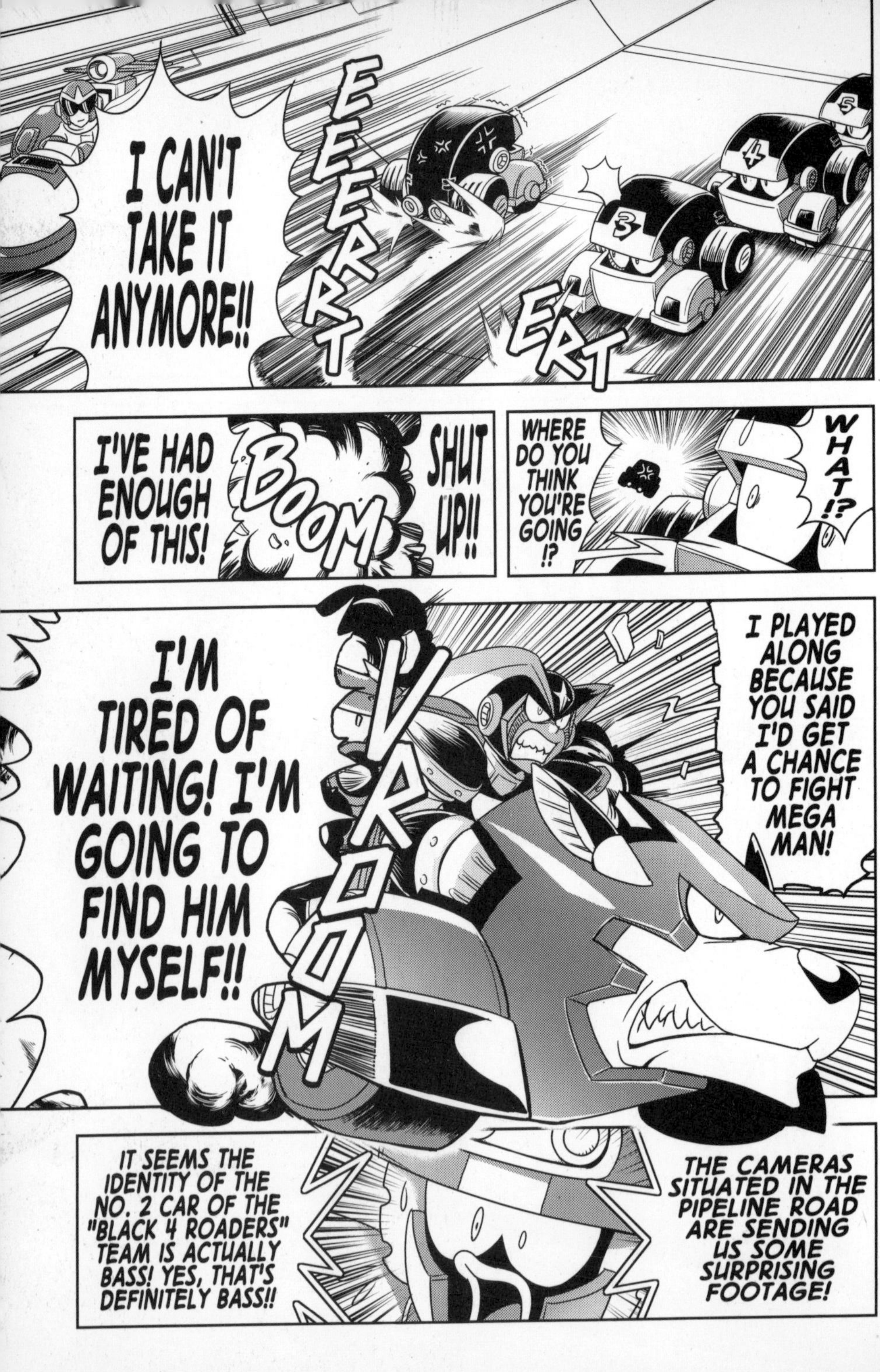
EEERRT
ERT
I CAN'T TAKE IT ANYMORE!!
WHAT!?
WHERE DO YOU THINK YOU'RE GOING!?
SHUT UP!!
BOOM
I'VE HAD ENOUGH OF THIS!
I PLAYED ALONG BECAUSE YOU SAID I'D GET A CHANCE TO FIGHT MEGA MAN!
VROOOM
I'M TIRED OF WAITING! I'M GOING TO FIND HIM MYSELF!!
THE CAMERAS SITUATED IN THE PIPELINE ROAD ARE SENDING US SOME SURPRISING FOOTAGE!
IT SEEMS THE IDENTITY OF THE NO. 2 CAR OF THE "BLACK 4 ROADERS" TEAM IS ACTUALLY BASS! YES, THAT'S DEFINITELY BASS!!

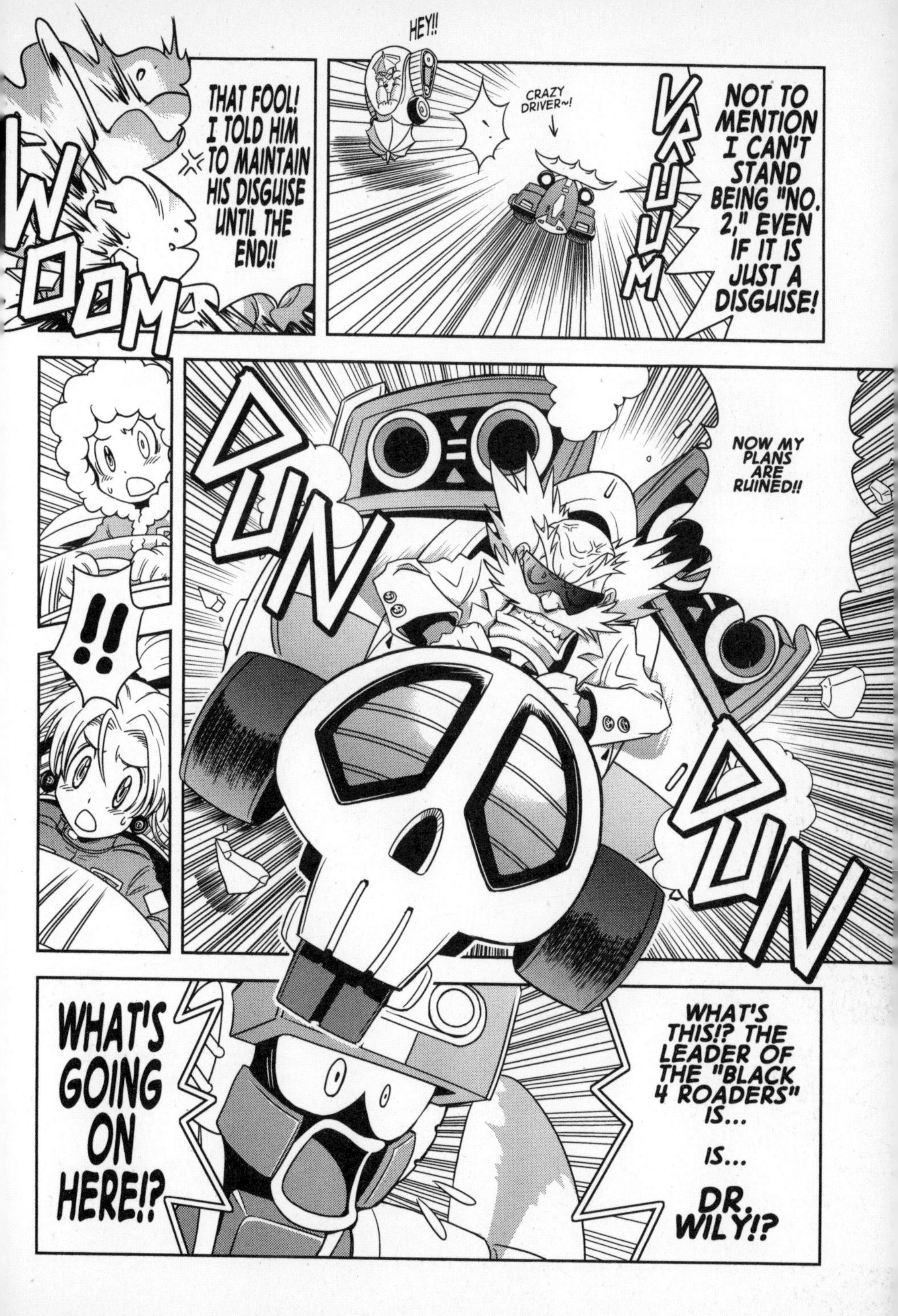
NOT TO MENTION I CAN'T STAND BEING "NO. 2," EVEN IF IT IS JUST A DISGUISE!
VRUUM
HEY!!
CRAZY DRIVER~!
THAT FOOL! I TOLD HIM TO MAINTAIN HIS DISGUISE UNTIL THE END!!
W-OOM
NOW MY PLANS ARE RUINED!!
DUN DUN
DUN DUN
!!
WHAT'S THIS!? THE LEADER OF THE "BLACK 4 ROADERS" IS...
IS...
DR. WILY!?
WHAT'S GOING ON HERE!?

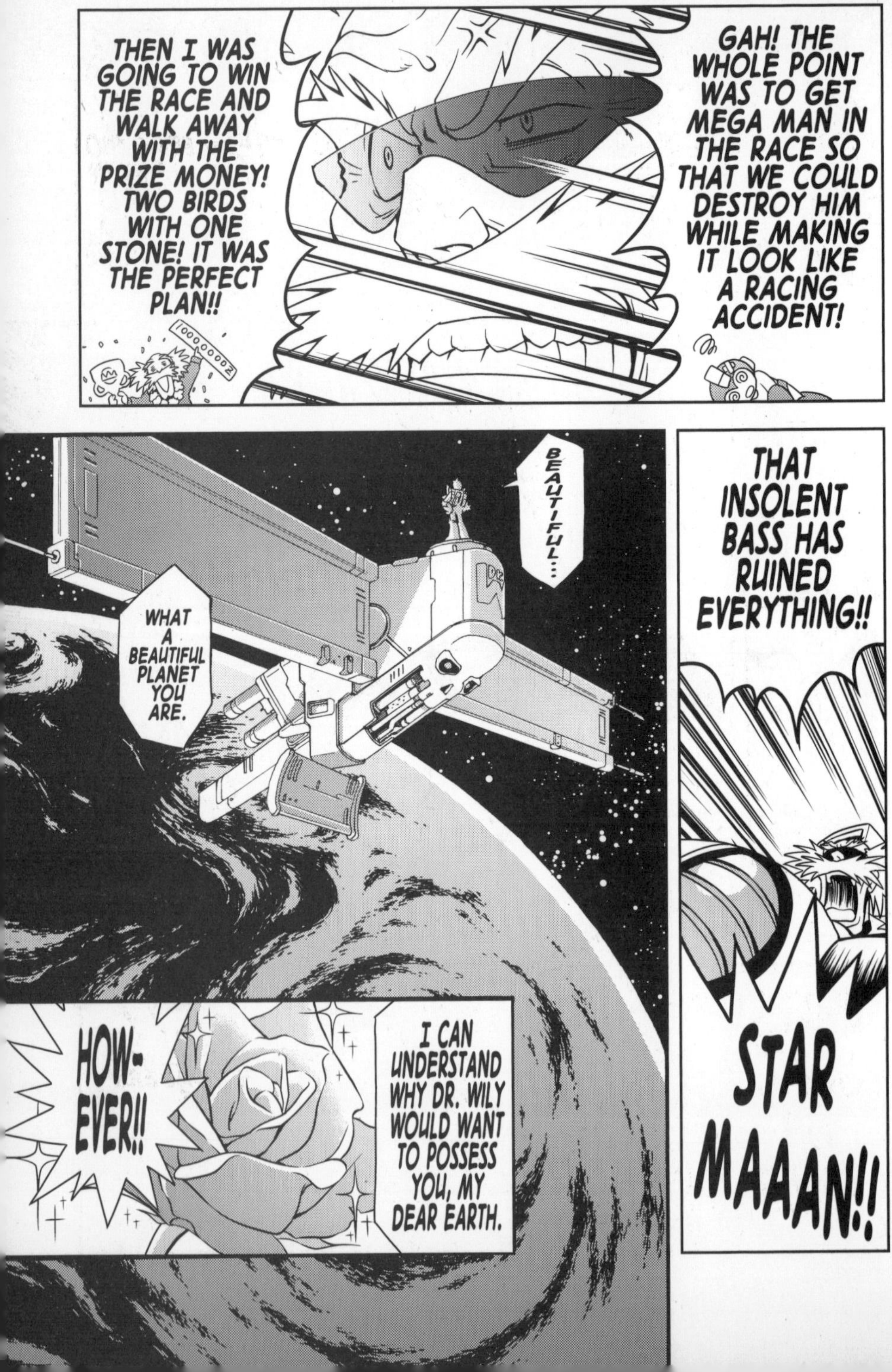
GAH! THE WHOLE POINT WAS TO GET MEGA MAN IN THE RACE SO THAT WE COULD DESTROY HIM WHILE MAKING IT LOOK LIKE A RACING ACCIDENT!
THEN I WAS GOING TO WIN THE RACE AND WALK AWAY WITH THE PRIZE MONEY! TWO BIRDS WITH ONE STONE! IT WAS THE PERFECT PLAN!!
THAT INSOLENT BASS HAS RUINED EVERYTHING!!
STAR MAAAN!!
BEAUTIFUL...
WHAT A BEAUTIFUL PLANET YOU ARE.
I CAN UNDERSTAND WHY DR. WILY WOULD WANT TO POSSESS YOU, MY DEAR EARTH.
HOW-EVER!!

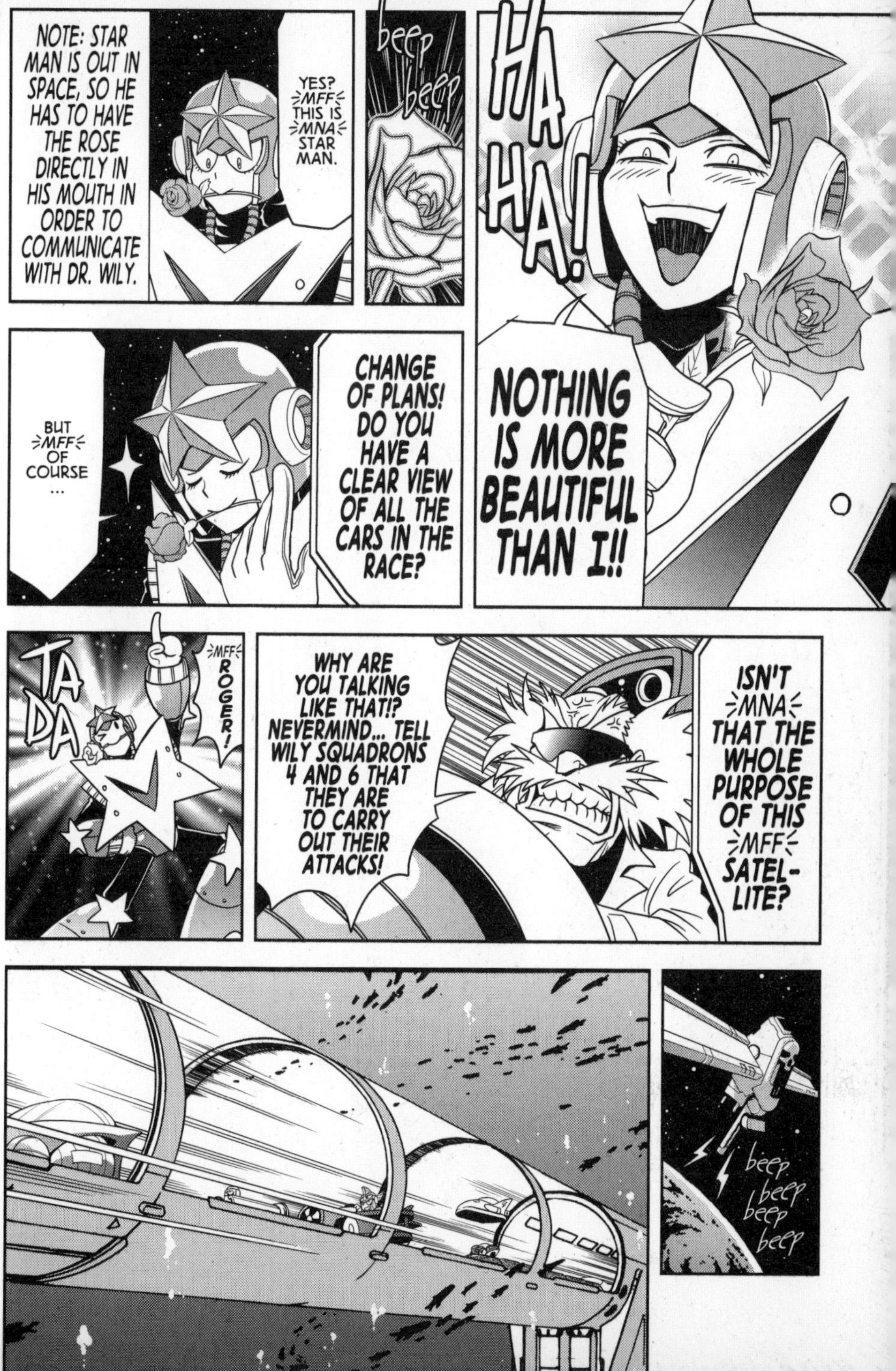
HA HA!
NOTHING IS MORE BEAUTIFUL THAN I!!
beep beep
YES? MFF THIS IS MNA STAR MAN.
NOTE: STAR MAN IS OUT IN SPACE, SO HE HAS TO HAVE THE ROSE DIRECTLY IN HIS MOUTH IN ORDER TO COMMUNICATE WITH DR. WILY.
CHANGE OF PLANS! DO YOU HAVE A CLEAR VIEW OF ALL THE CARS IN THE RACE?
BUT MFF OF COURSE ...
ISN'T MNA THAT THE WHOLE PURPOSE OF THIS MFF SATEL-LITE?
WHY ARE YOU TALKING LIKE THAT!? NEVERMIND... TELL WILY SQUADRONS 4 AND 6 THAT THEY ARE TO CARRY OUT THEIR ATTACKS!
MFF ROGER!
TA DA
beep beep beep beep

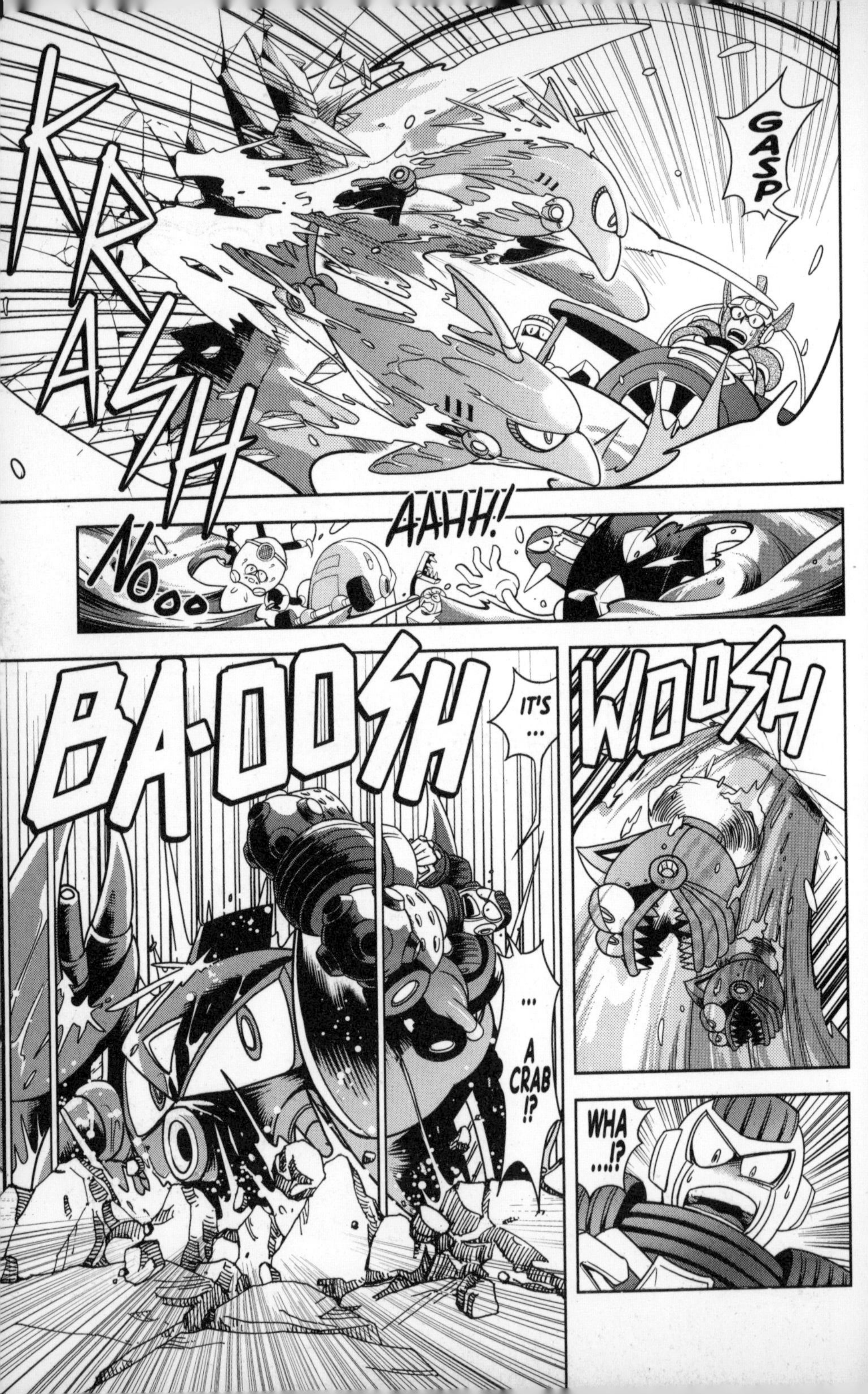
GASP
KRASH
AAHH!
NOOO
WOOSH
WHA ...!?
BA-OOSH
IT'S ...
... A CRAB !?

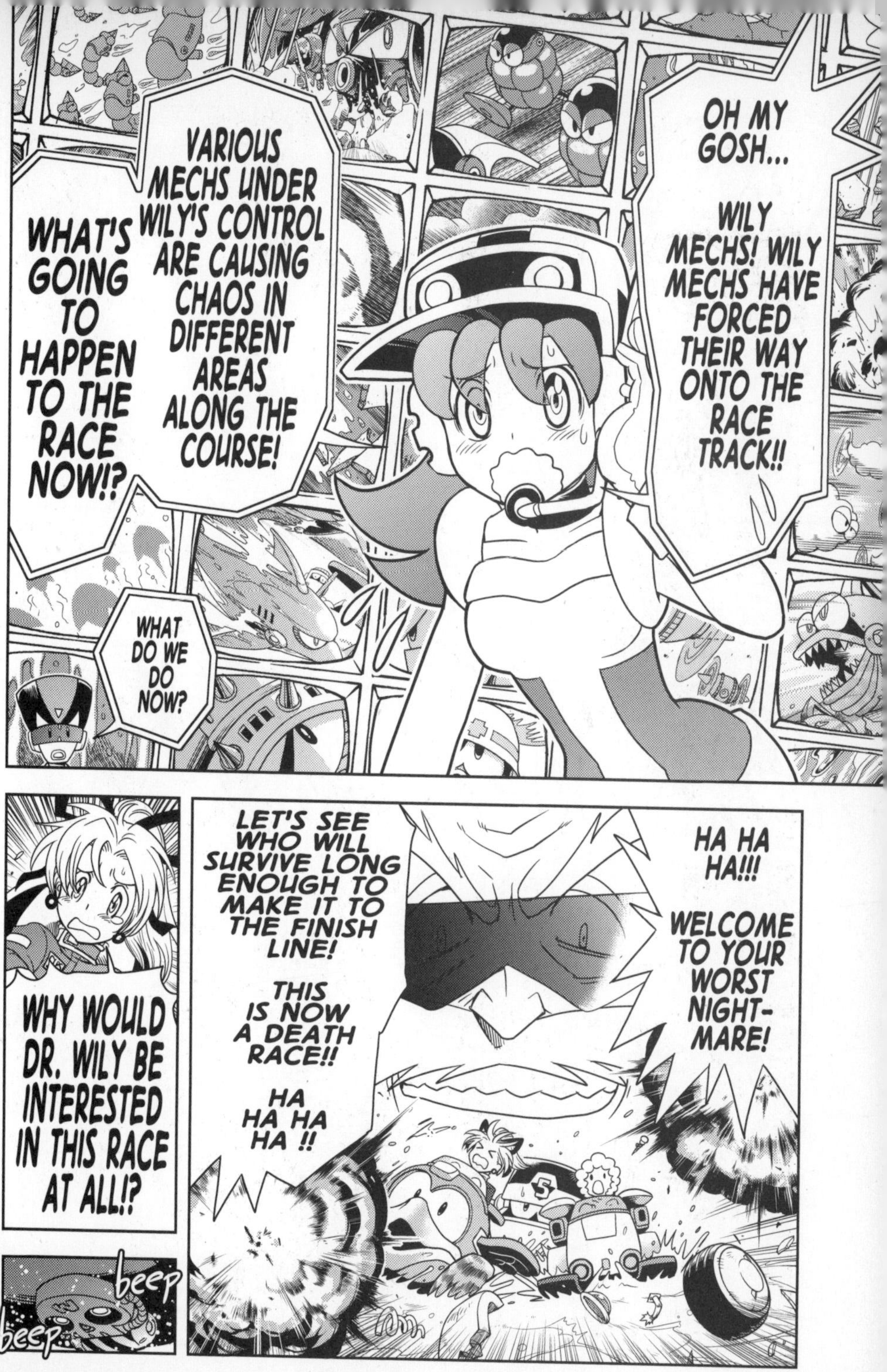
OH MY GOSH...
WILY MECHS! WILY MECHS HAVE FORCED THEIR WAY ONTO THE RACE TRACK!!
VARIOUS MECHS UNDER WILY'S CONTROL ARE CAUSING CHAOS IN DIFFERENT AREAS ALONG THE COURSE!
WHAT'S GOING TO HAPPEN TO THE RACE NOW!?
WHAT DO WE DO NOW?
HA HA HA!!!
WELCOME TO YOUR WORST NIGHT-MARE!
LET'S SEE WHO WILL SURVIVE LONG ENOUGH TO MAKE IT TO THE FINISH LINE!
THIS IS NOW A DEATH RACE!!
HA HA HA HA !!
WHY WOULD DR. WILY BE INTERESTED IN THIS RACE AT ALL!?
beep
beep

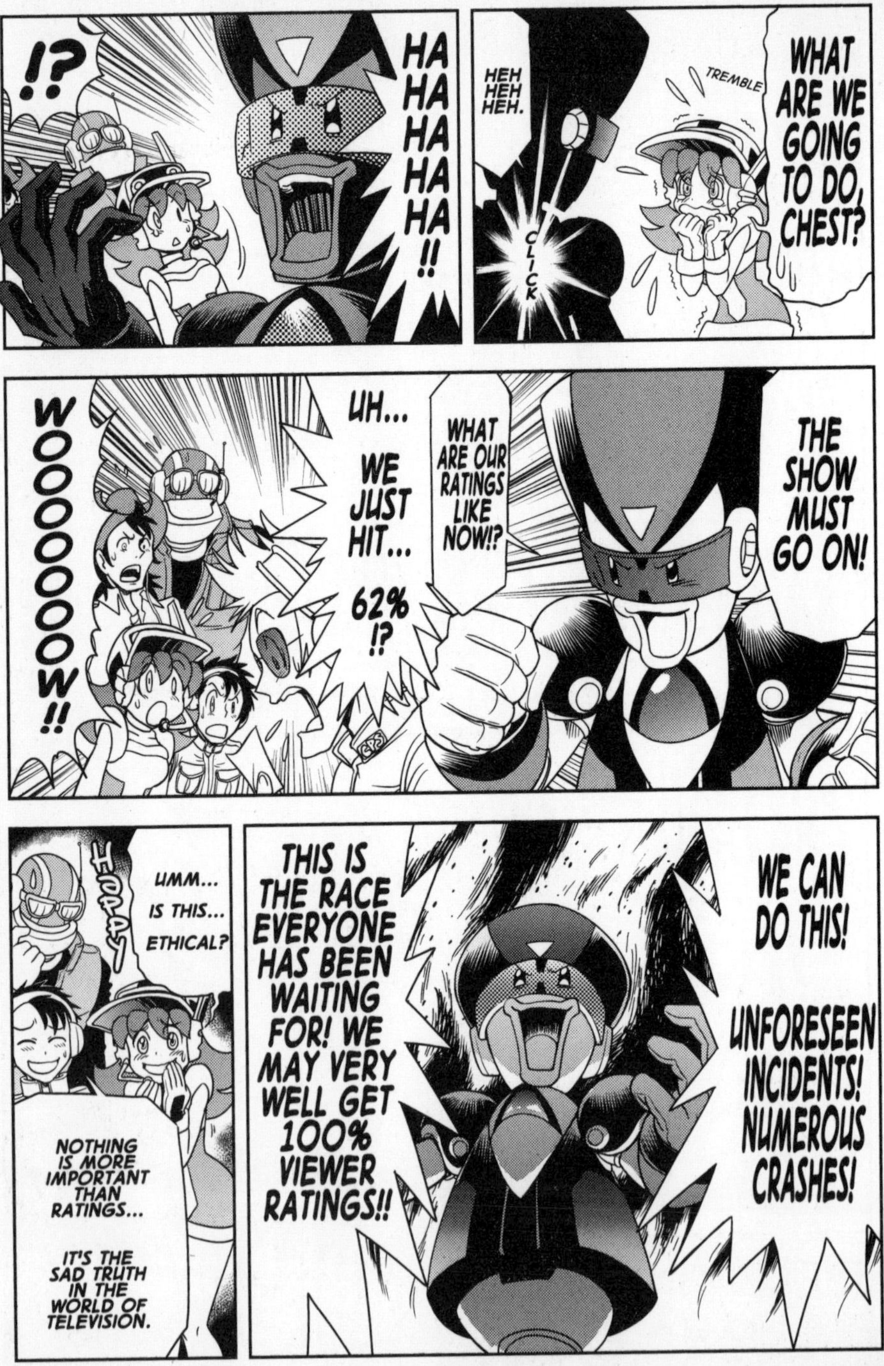
WHAT ARE WE GOING TO DO, CHEST?
TREMBLE
HEH HEH HEH.
CLICK
HA HA HA HA HA!!
!?
THE SHOW MUST GO ON!
WHAT ARE OUR RATINGS LIKE NOW!?
UH... WE JUST HIT... 62% !?
WOOOOOOOOW!!
WE CAN DO THIS! UNFORESEEN INCIDENTS! NUMEROUS CRASHES!
THIS IS THE RACE EVERYONE HAS BEEN WAITING FOR! WE MAY VERY WELL GET 100% VIEWER RATINGS!!
HOORAY
UMM... IS THIS... ETHICAL?
NOTHING IS MORE IMPORTANT THAN RATINGS...
IT'S THE SAD TRUTH IN THE WORLD OF TELEVISION.

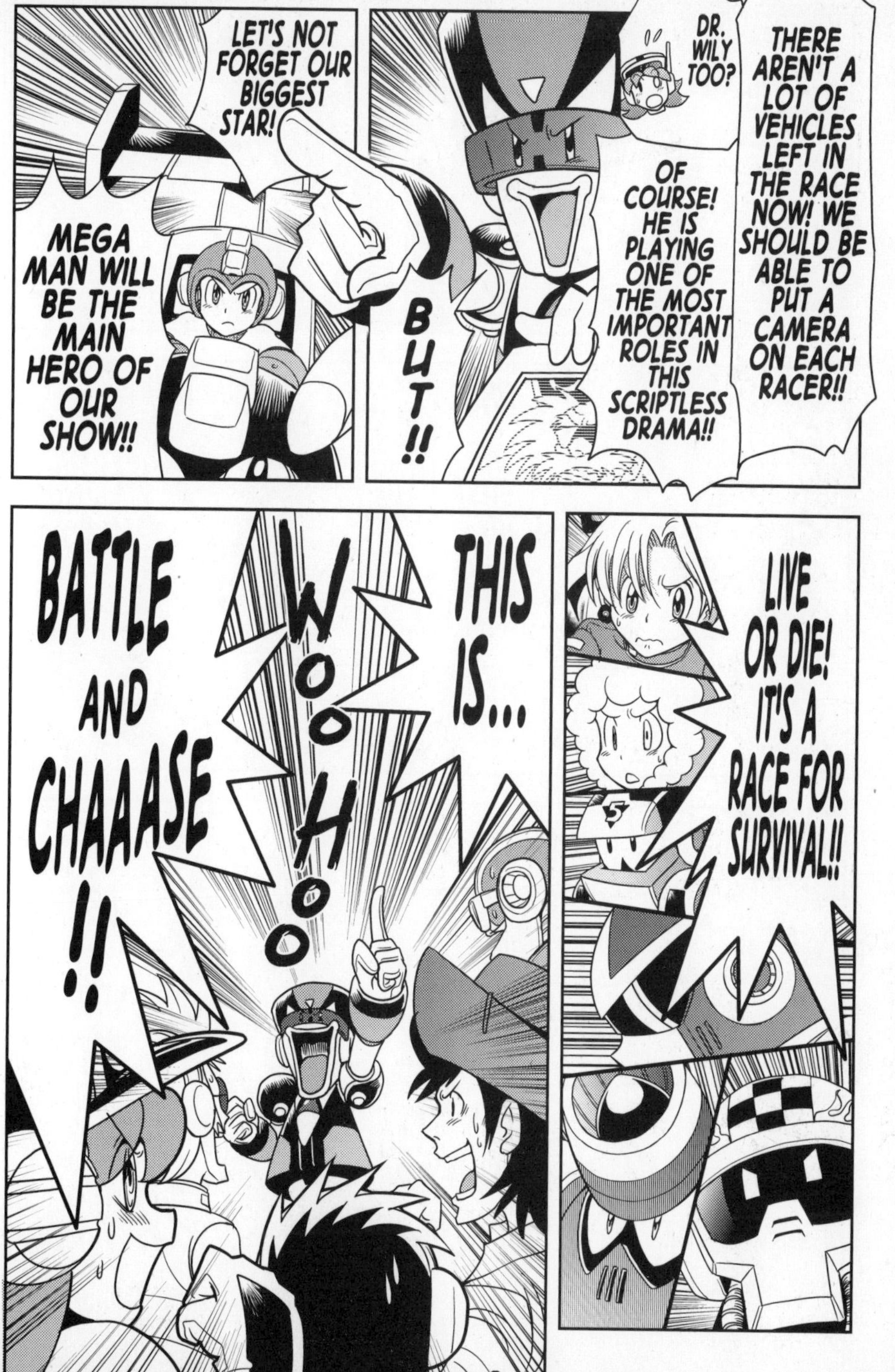
THERE AREN'T A LOT OF VEHICLES LEFT IN THE RACE NOW! WE SHOULD BE ABLE TO PUT A CAMERA ON EACH RACER!!
DR. WILY TOO?
OF COURSE! HE IS PLAYING ONE OF THE MOST IMPORTANT ROLES IN THIS SCRIPTLESS DRAMA!!
BUT!!
LET'S NOT FORGET OUR BIGGEST STAR!
MEGA MAN WILL BE THE MAIN HERO OF OUR SHOW!!
LIVE OR DIE! IT'S A RACE FOR SURVIVAL!!
THIS IS...
WOOHOOO
BATTLE AND CHAAASE!!

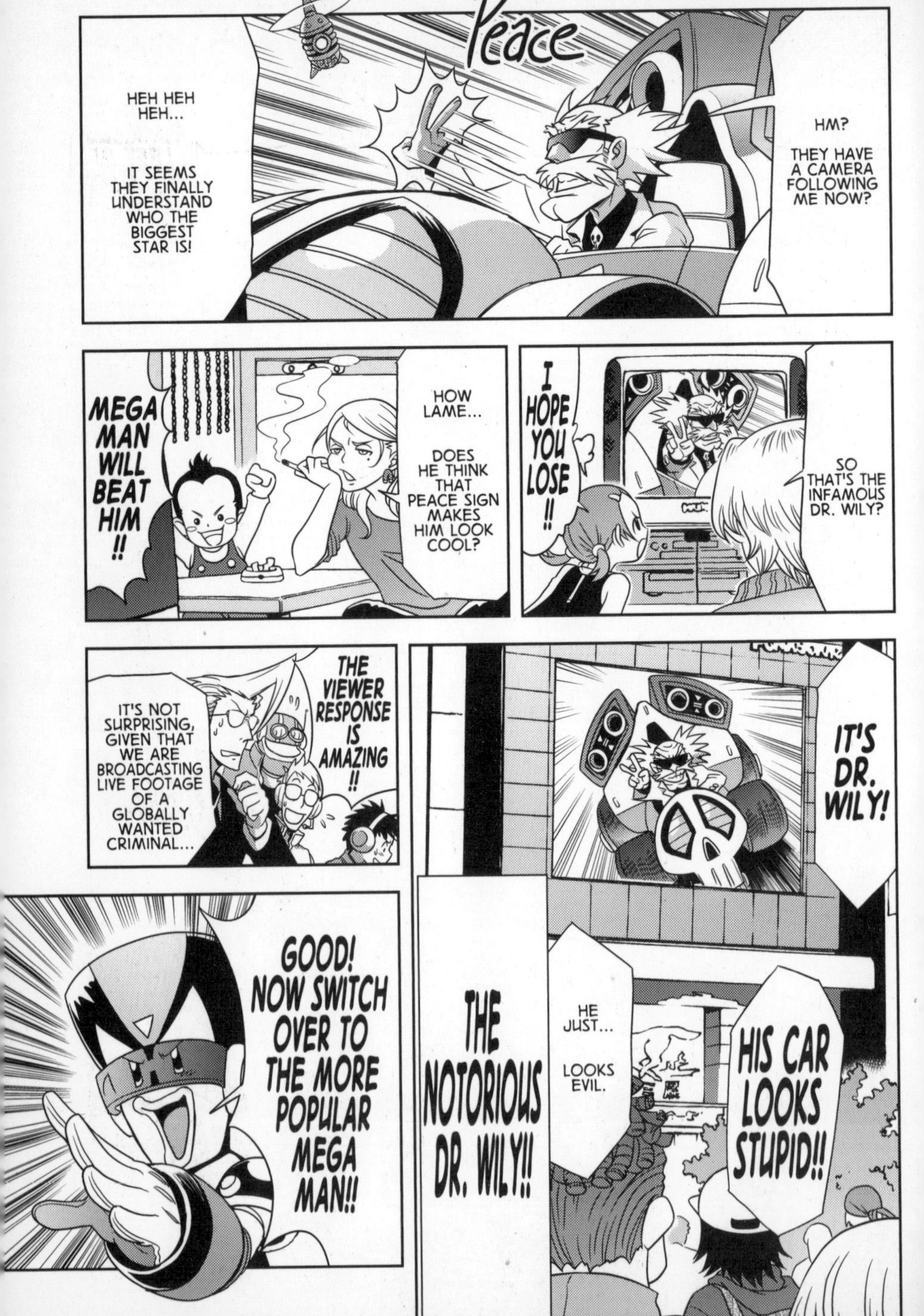
HM? THEY HAVE A CAMERA FOLLOWING ME NOW?
Peace
HEH HEH HEH... IT SEEMS THEY FINALLY UNDERSTAND WHO THE BIGGEST STAR IS!
SO THAT'S THE INFAMOUS DR. WILY?
I HOPE YOU LOSE!!
HOW LAME... DOES HE THINK THAT PEACE SIGN MAKES HIM LOOK COOL?
MEGA MAN WILL BEAT HIM!!
IT'S DR. WILY!
HIS CAR LOOKS STUPID!!
HE JUST... LOOKS EVIL.
THE NOTORIOUS DR. WILY!!
THE VIEWER RESPONSE IS AMAZING!!
IT'S NOT SURPRISING, GIVEN THAT WE ARE BROADCASTING LIVE FOOTAGE OF A GLOBALLY WANTED CRIMINAL...
GOOD! NOW SWITCH OVER TO THE MORE POPULAR MEGA MAN!!

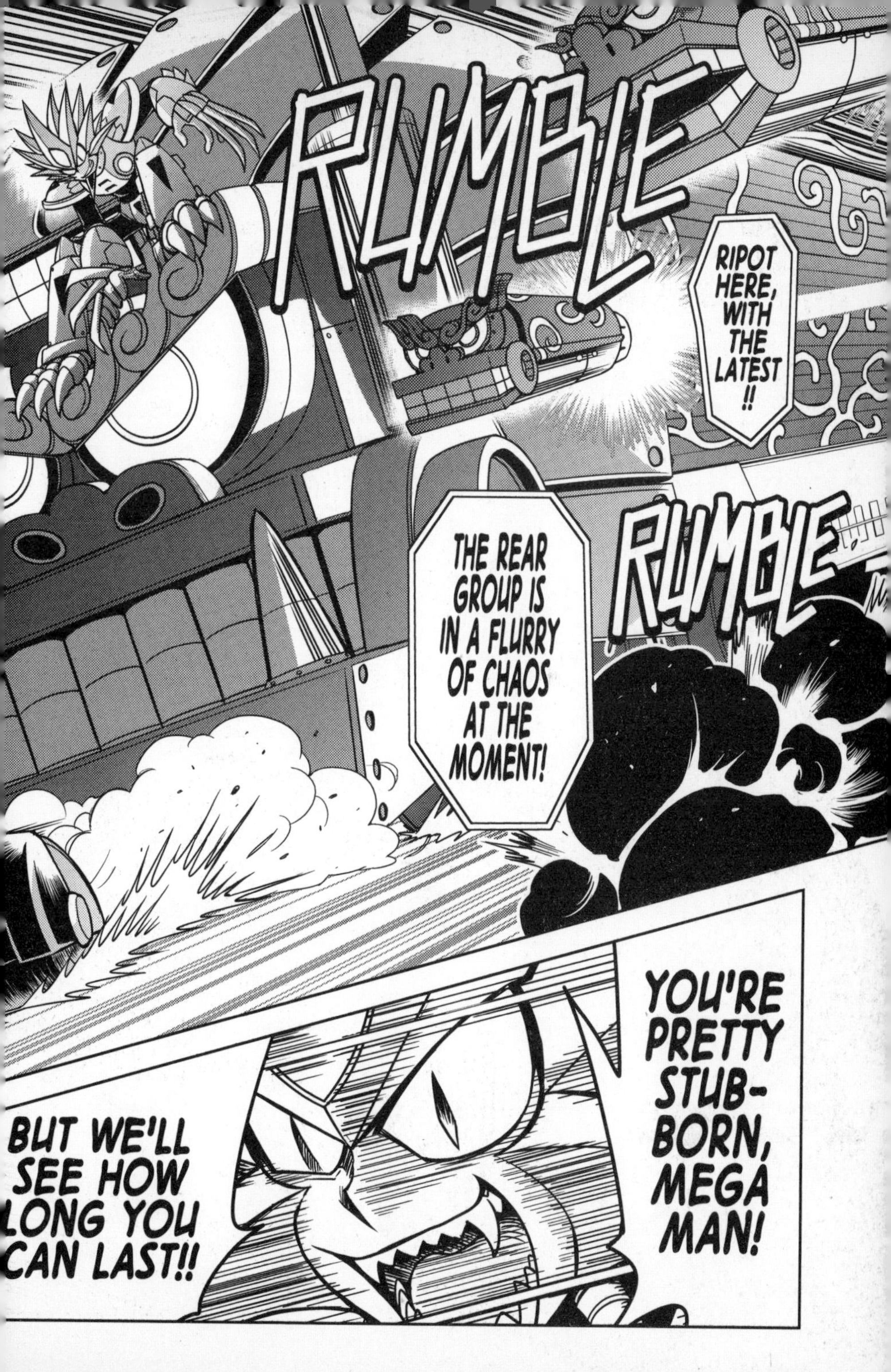
RUMBLE
RIPOT HERE, WITH THE LATEST!!
RUMBLE
THE REAR GROUP IS IN A FLURRY OF CHAOS AT THE MOMENT!
YOU'RE PRETTY STUB-BORN, MEGA MAN!
BUT WE'LL SEE HOW LONG YOU CAN LAST!!

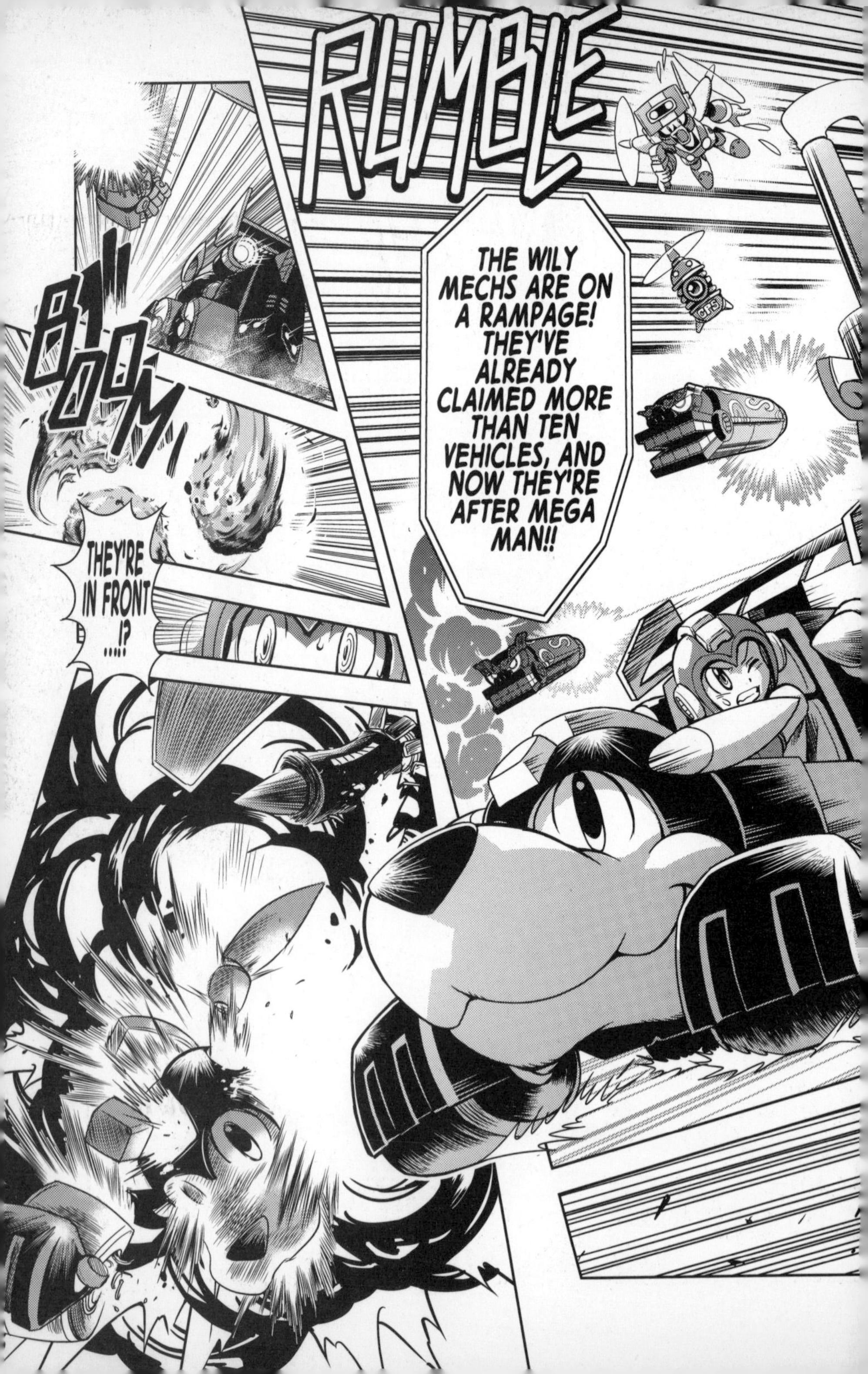
RUMBLE
THE WILY MECHS ARE ON A RAMPAGE! THEY'VE ALREADY CLAIMED MORE THAN TEN VEHICLES, AND NOW THEY'RE AFTER MEGA MAN!!
BOOM
THEY'RE IN FRONT ...!?

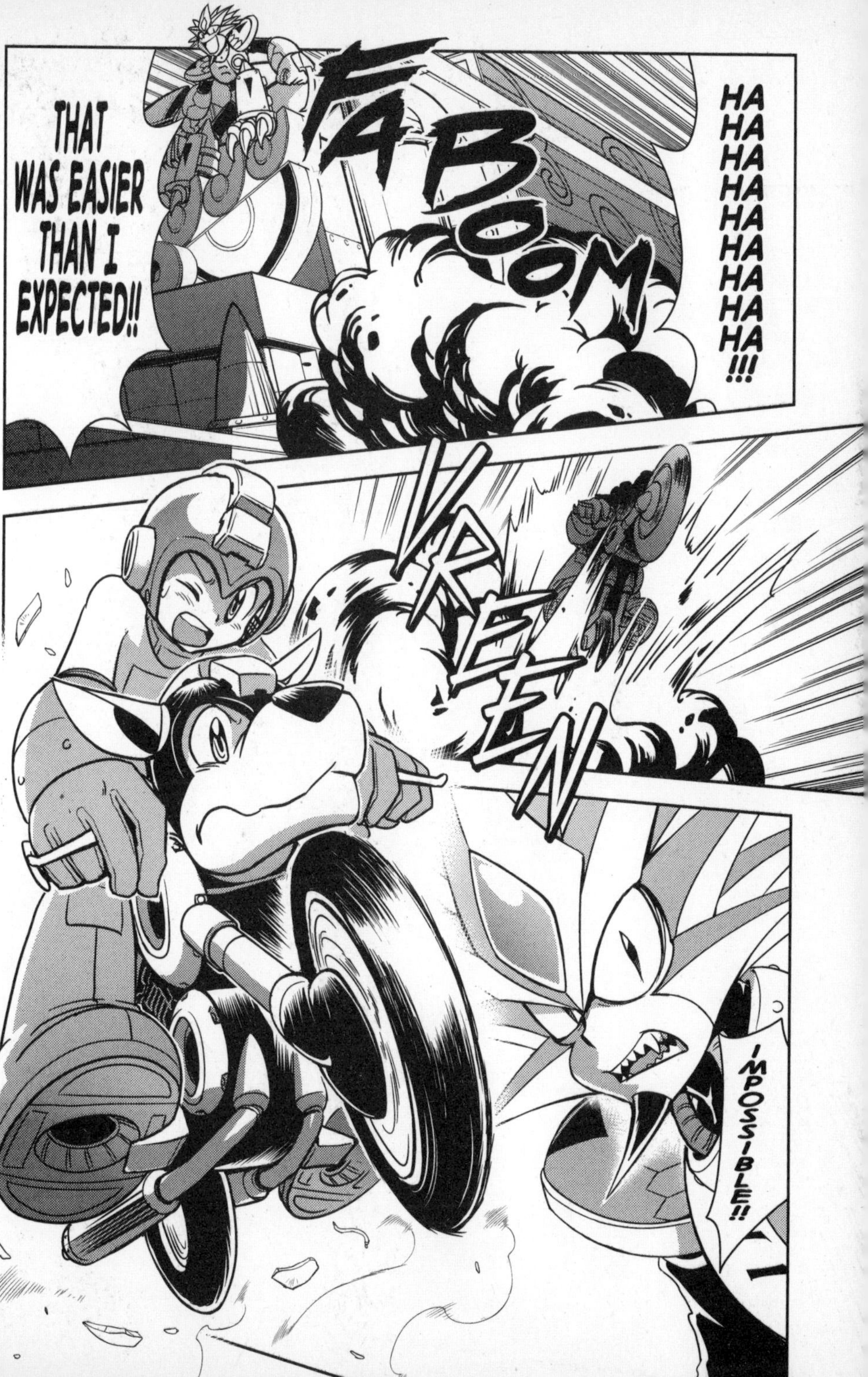
HAHAHAHAHAHAHAHAHA!!!
FABOOM
THAT WAS EASIER THAN I EXPECTED!!
VREEEN
IMPOSSIBLE!!

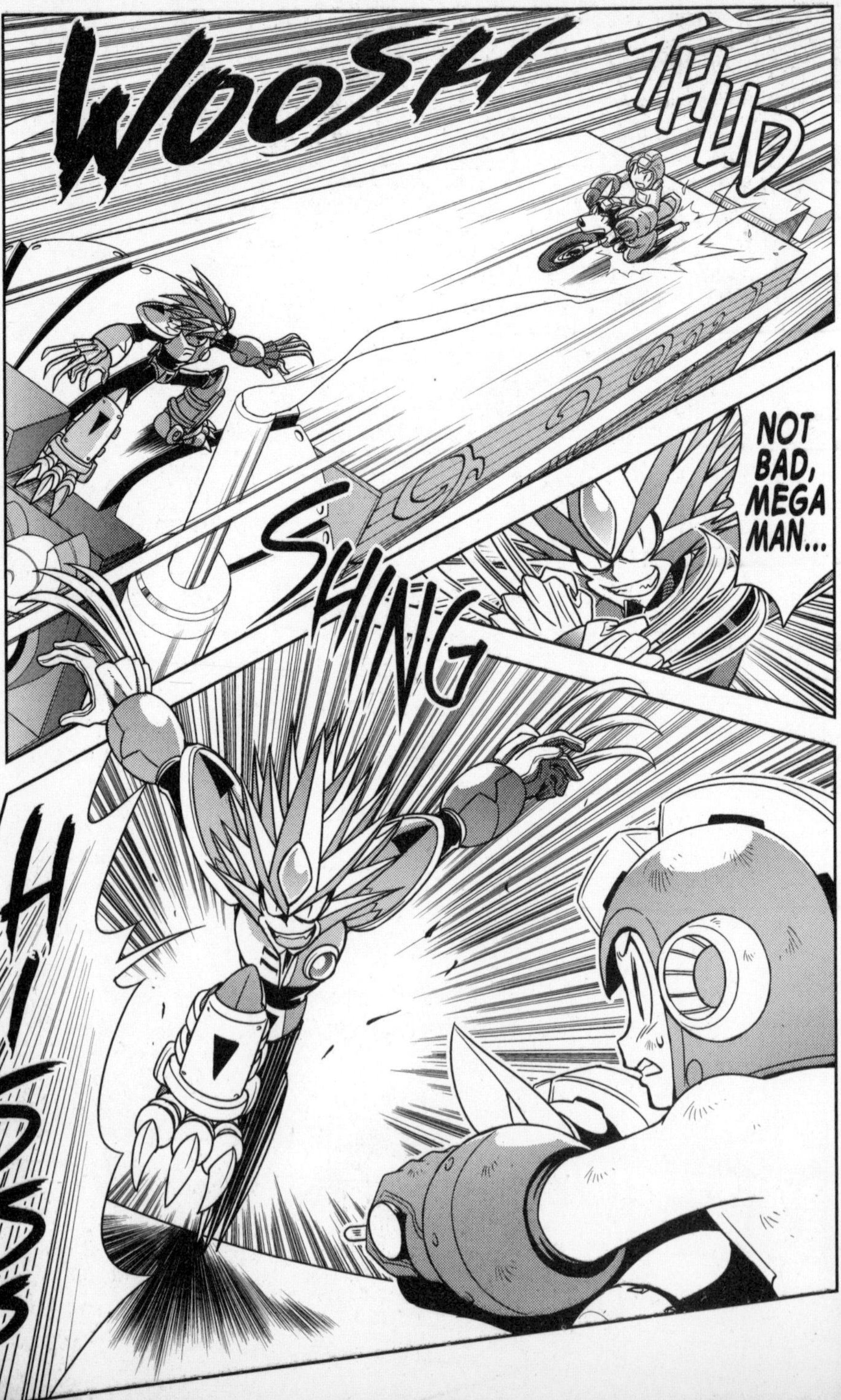
THUD
WOOSH
NOT BAD, MEGA MAN...
SHING
HISSS

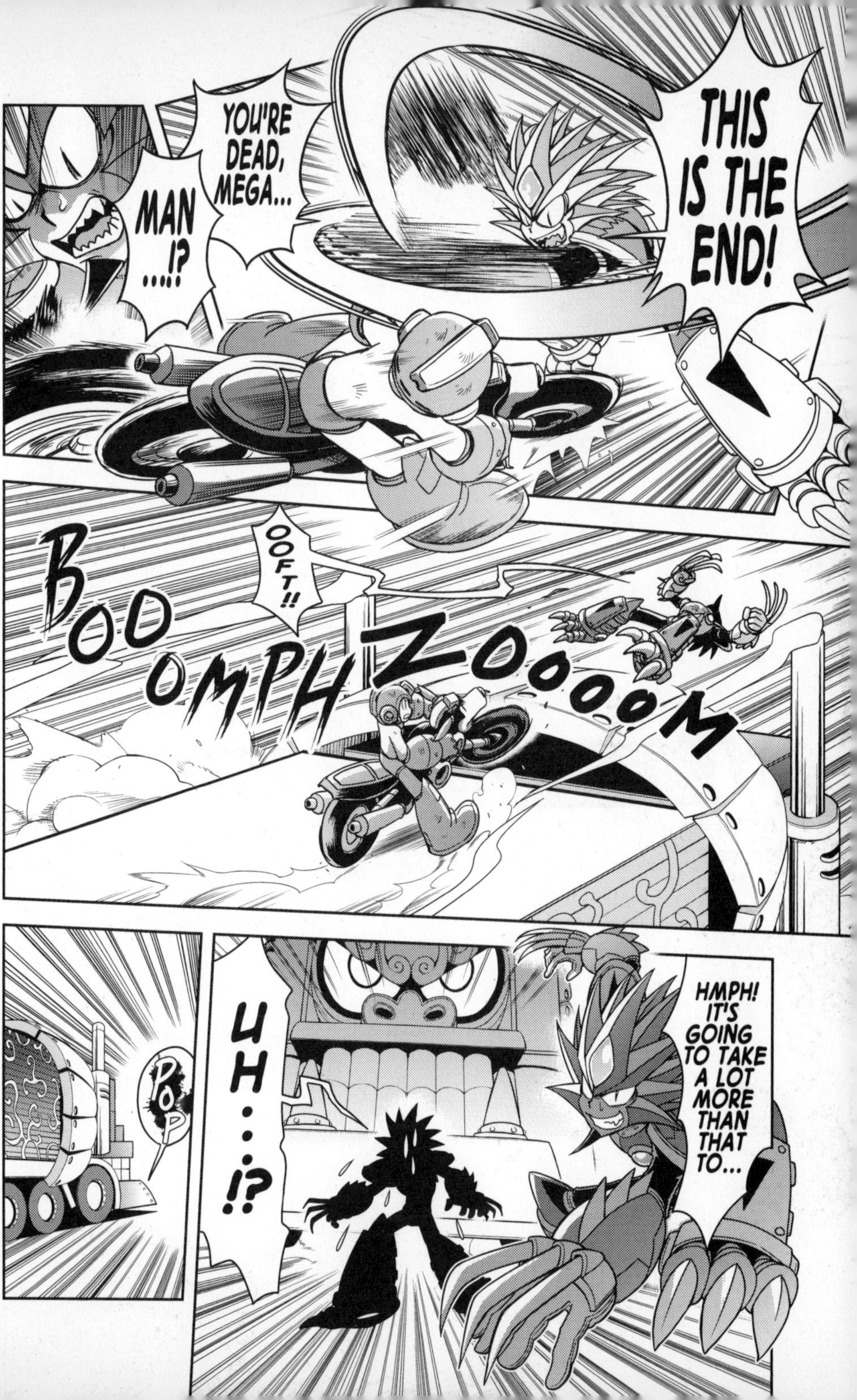
THIS IS THE END!
YOU'RE DEAD, MEGA...
MAN ....!?
OOFT!!
BOOOMPH
ZOOOOOM
HMPH! IT'S GOING TO TAKE A LOT MORE THAN THAT TO...
UH...!?
POP

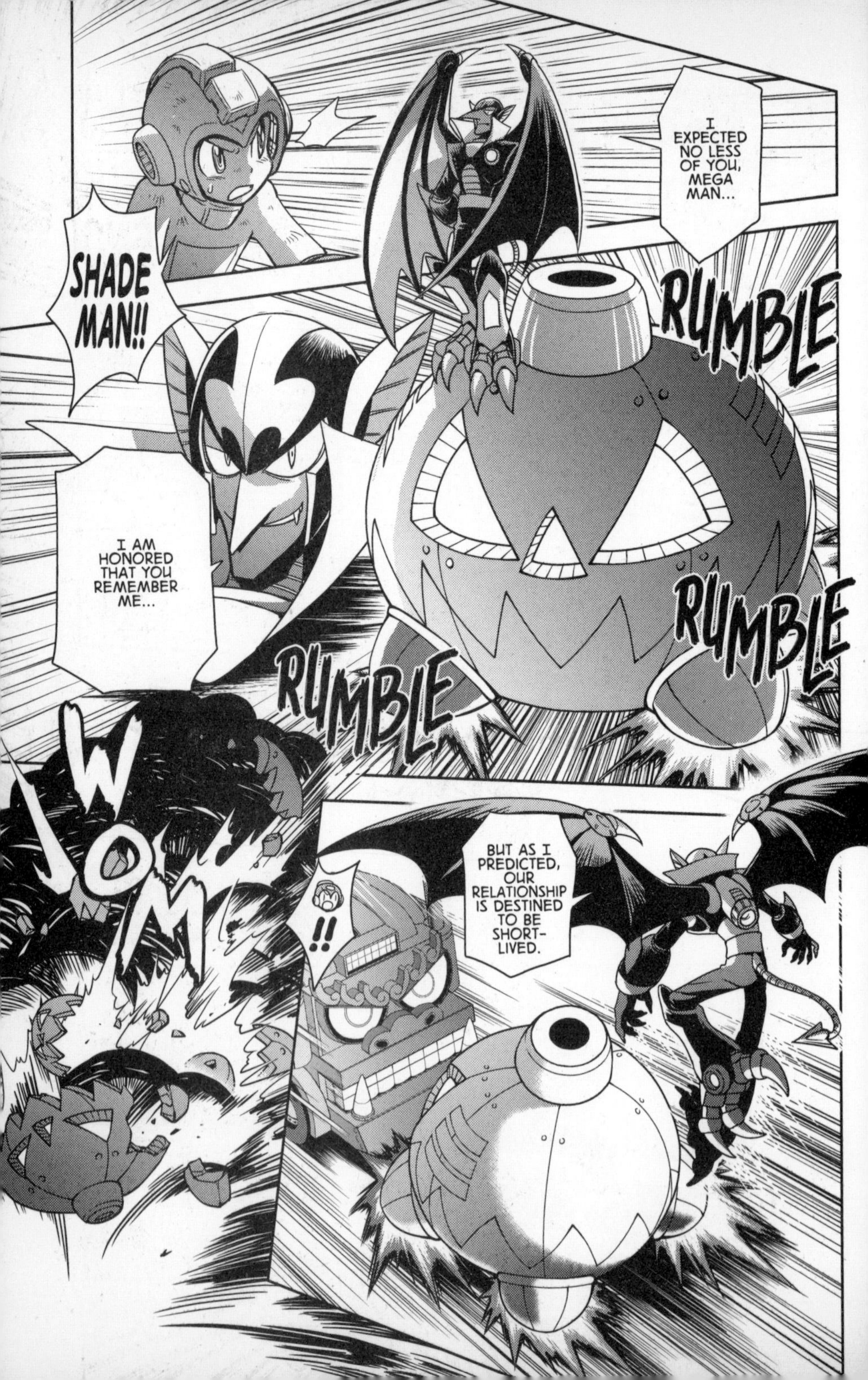
I EXPECTED NO LESS OF YOU, MEGA MAN...
SHADE MAN!!
RUMBLE
I AM HONORED THAT YOU REMEMBER ME...
RUMBLE
RUMBLE
BUT AS I PREDICTED, OUR RELATIONSHIP IS DESTINED TO BE SHORT-LIVED.
!!
WOM

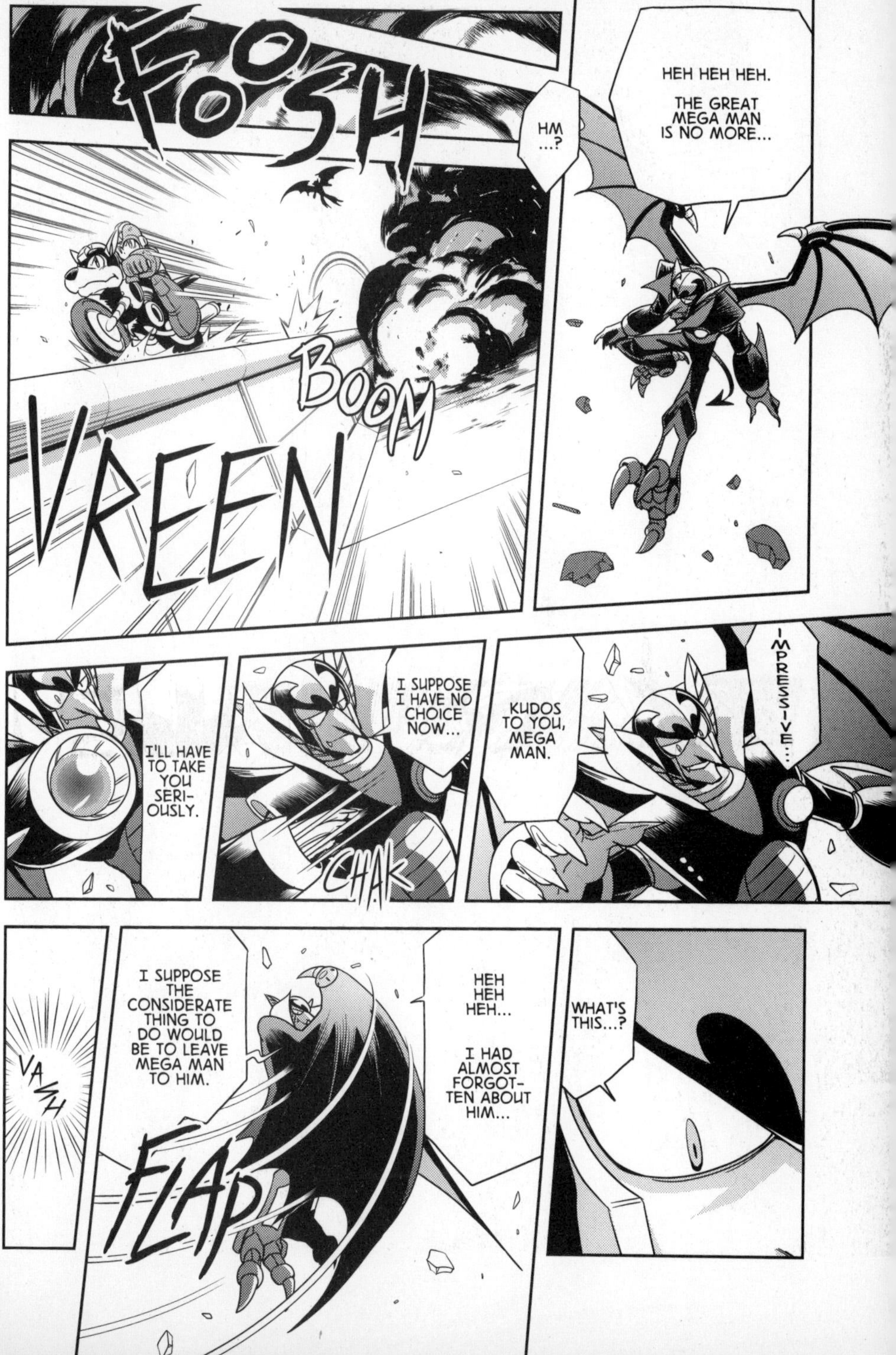
HEH HEH HEH.
THE GREAT MEGA MAN IS NO MORE...
HM ...?
FOOSH
BOOM
VREEN
IMPRESSIVE...
KUDOS TO YOU, MEGA MAN.
I SUPPOSE I HAVE NO CHOICE NOW...
CHAK
I'LL HAVE TO TAKE YOU SERI-OUSLY.
WHAT'S THIS...?
HEH HEH HEH...
I HAD ALMOST FORGOT-TEN ABOUT HIM...
I SUPPOSE THE CONSIDERATE THING TO DO WOULD BE TO LEAVE MEGA MAN TO HIM.
FLAP
VASH

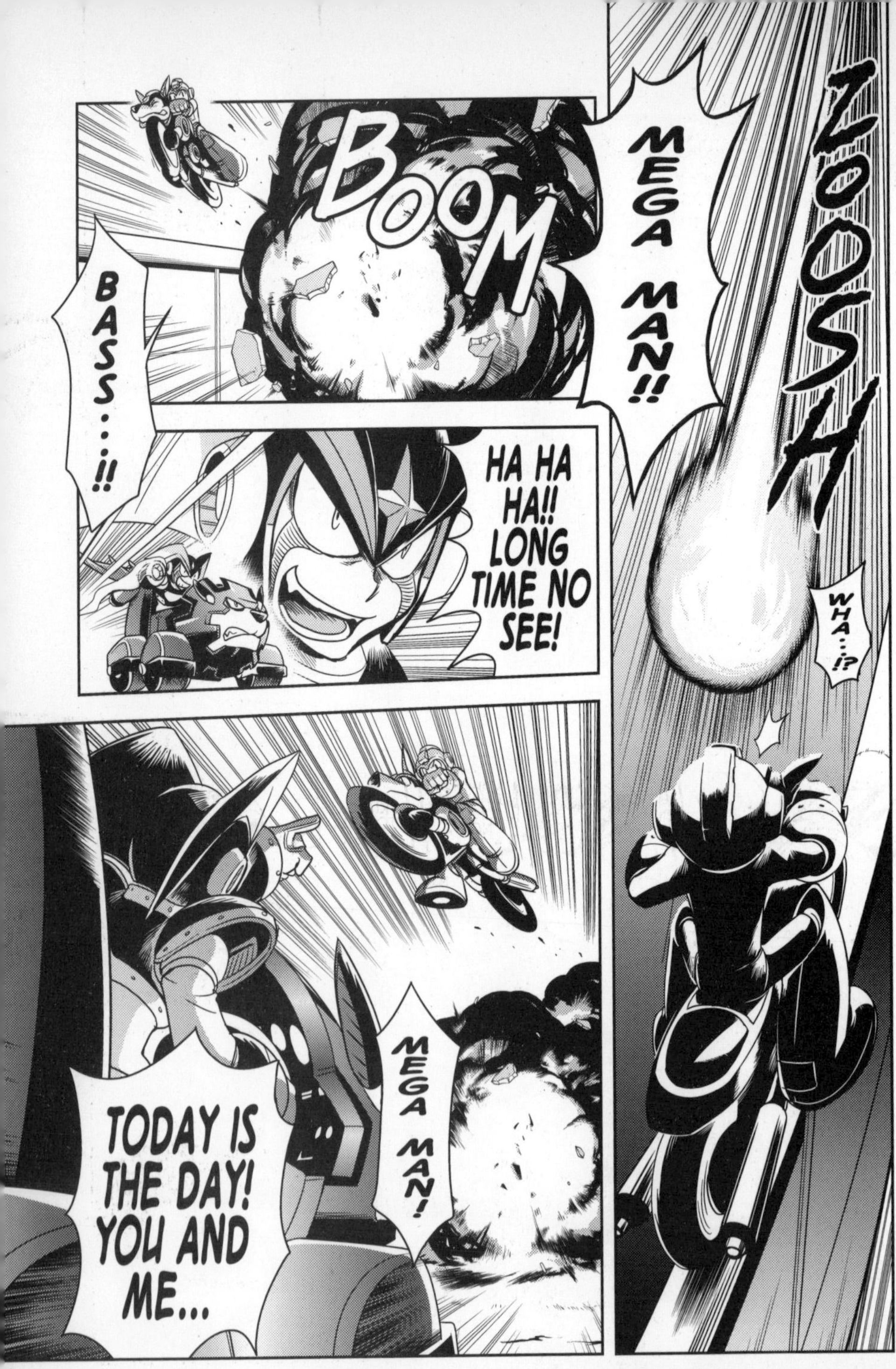
ZOOSH
MEGA MAN!!
WHA...!?
BOOM
BASS...!!
HA HA HA!! LONG TIME NO SEE!
MEGA MAN!
TODAY IS THE DAY! YOU AND ME...

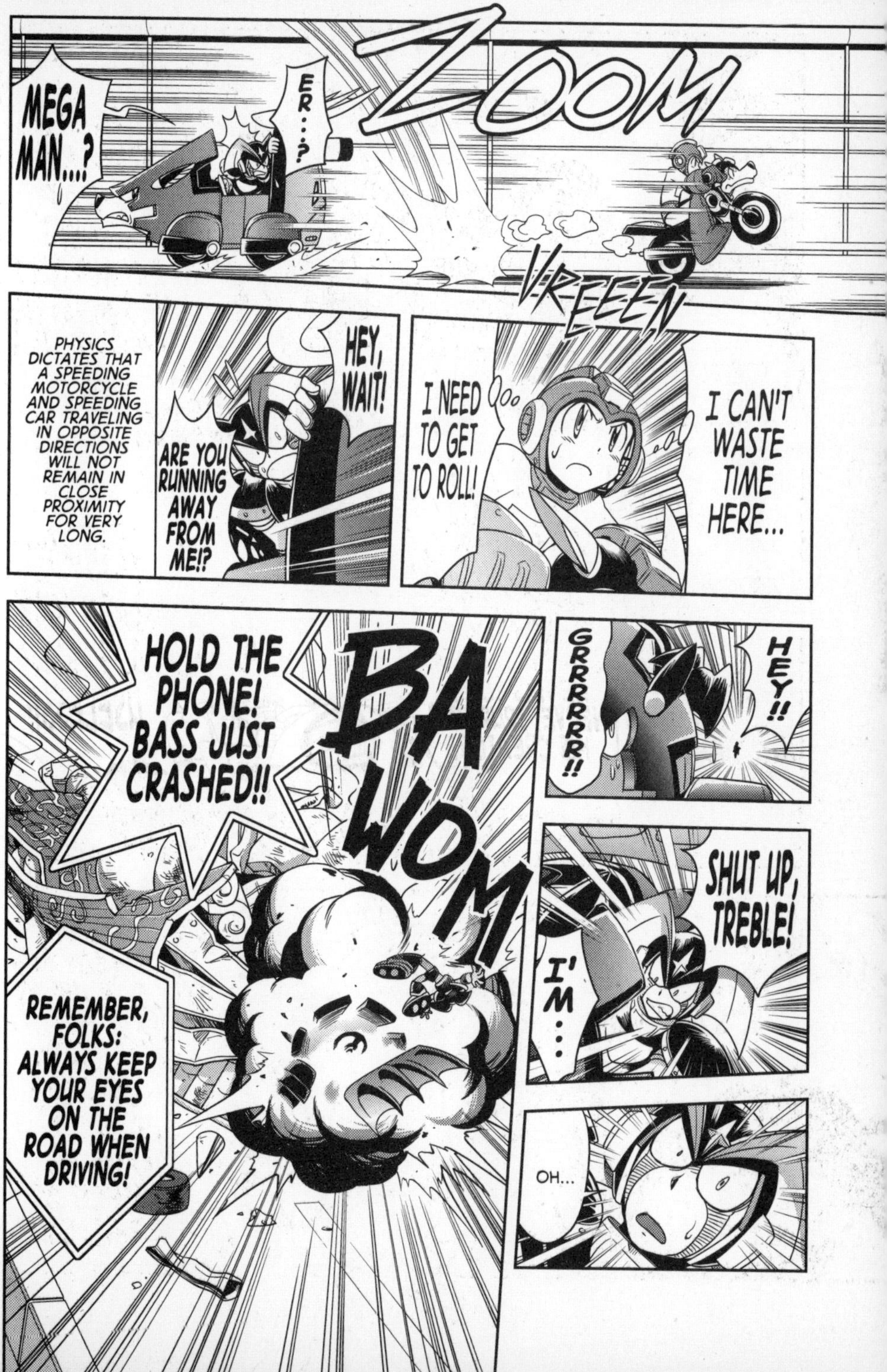
ZOOM
ER...?
MEGA MAN...?
VREEEN
I CAN'T WASTE TIME HERE...
I NEED TO GET TO ROLL!
HEY, WAIT!
ARE YOU RUNNING AWAY FROM ME!?
PHYSICS DICTATES THAT A SPEEDING MOTORCYCLE AND SPEEDING CAR TRAVELING IN OPPOSITE DIRECTIONS WILL NOT REMAIN IN CLOSE PROXIMITY FOR VERY LONG.
HEY!!
GRRRRRR!!
SHUT UP, TREBLE!
I'M...
OH...
BA WOM
HOLD THE PHONE! BASS JUST CRASHED!!
REMEMBER, FOLKS: ALWAYS KEEP YOUR EYES ON THE ROAD WHEN DRIVING!

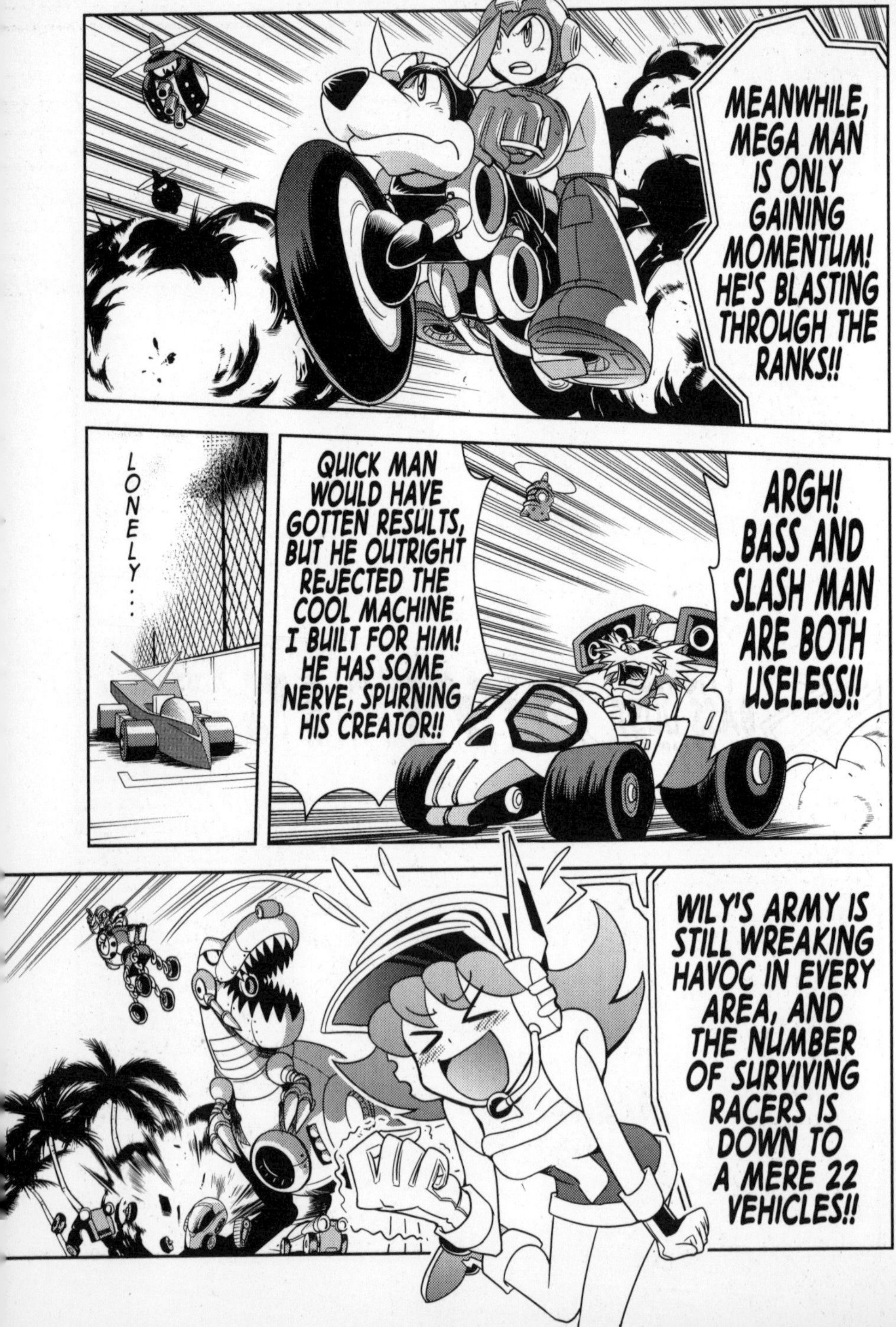
MEANWHILE, MEGA MAN IS ONLY GAINING MOMENTUM! HE'S BLASTING THROUGH THE RANKS!!
ARGH! BASS AND SLASH MAN ARE BOTH USELESS!!
QUICK MAN WOULD HAVE GOTTEN RESULTS, BUT HE OUTRIGHT REJECTED THE COOL MACHINE I BUILT FOR HIM! HE HAS SOME NERVE, SPURNING HIS CREATOR!!
LONELY...
WILY'S ARMY IS STILL WREAKING HAVOC IN EVERY AREA, AND THE NUMBER OF SURVIVING RACERS IS DOWN TO A MERE 22 VEHICLES!!

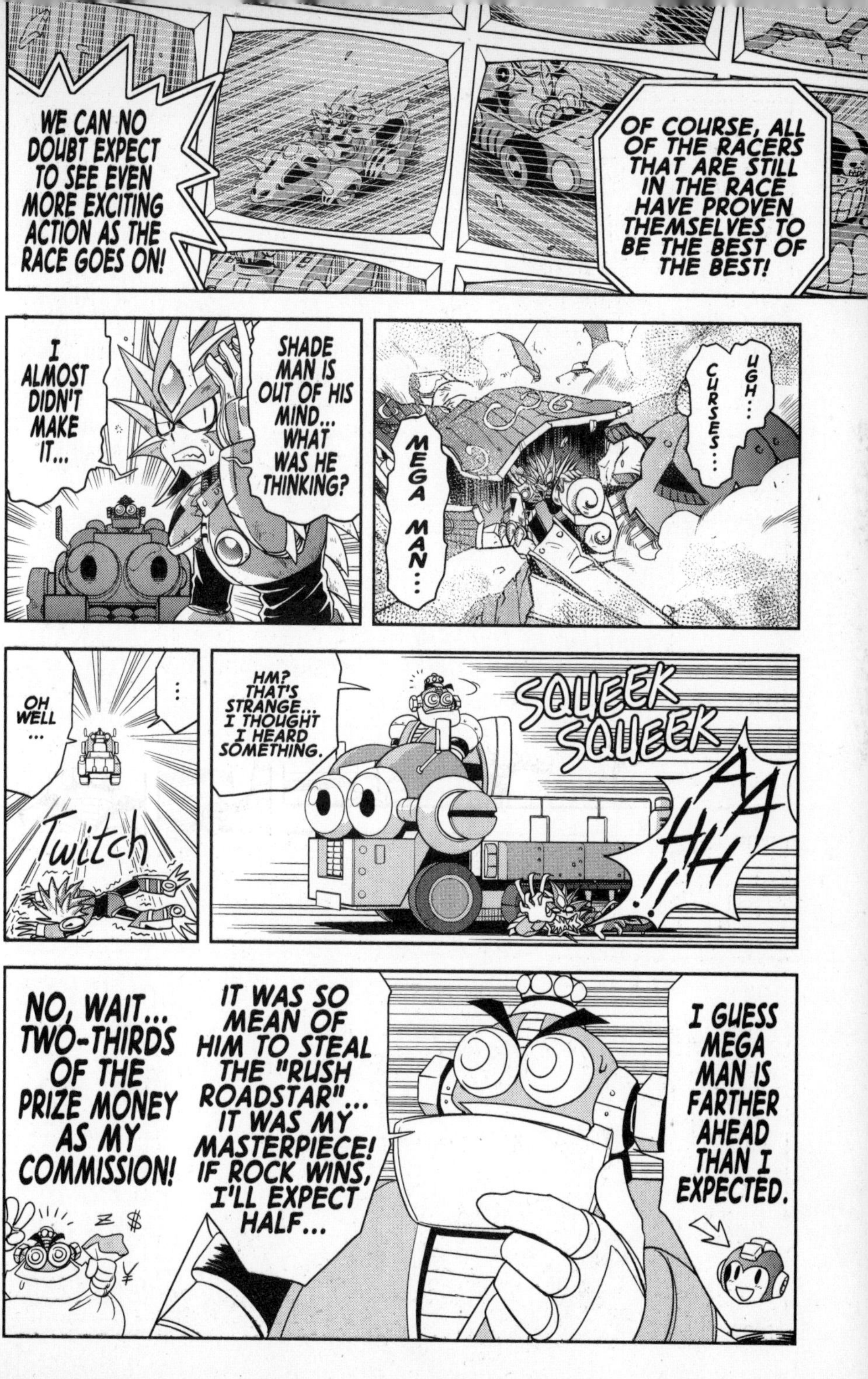
OF COURSE, ALL OF THE RACERS THAT ARE STILL IN THE RACE HAVE PROVEN THEMSELVES TO BE THE BEST OF THE BEST!
WE CAN NO DOUBT EXPECT TO SEE EVEN MORE EXCITING ACTION AS THE RACE GOES ON!
UGH... CURSES...
MEGA MAN...
SHADE MAN IS OUT OF HIS MIND... WHAT WAS HE THINKING?
I ALMOST DIDN'T MAKE IT...
SQUEEK SQUEEK
AAHH!!
HM? THAT'S STRANGE... I THOUGHT I HEARD SOMETHING.
...
OH WELL ...
Twitch
I GUESS MEGA MAN IS FARTHER AHEAD THAN I EXPECTED.
IT WAS SO MEAN OF HIM TO STEAL THE "RUSH ROADSTAR"... IT WAS MY MASTERPIECE! IF ROCK WINS, I'LL EXPECT HALF...
NO, WAIT... TWO-THIRDS OF THE PRIZE MONEY AS MY COMMISSION!

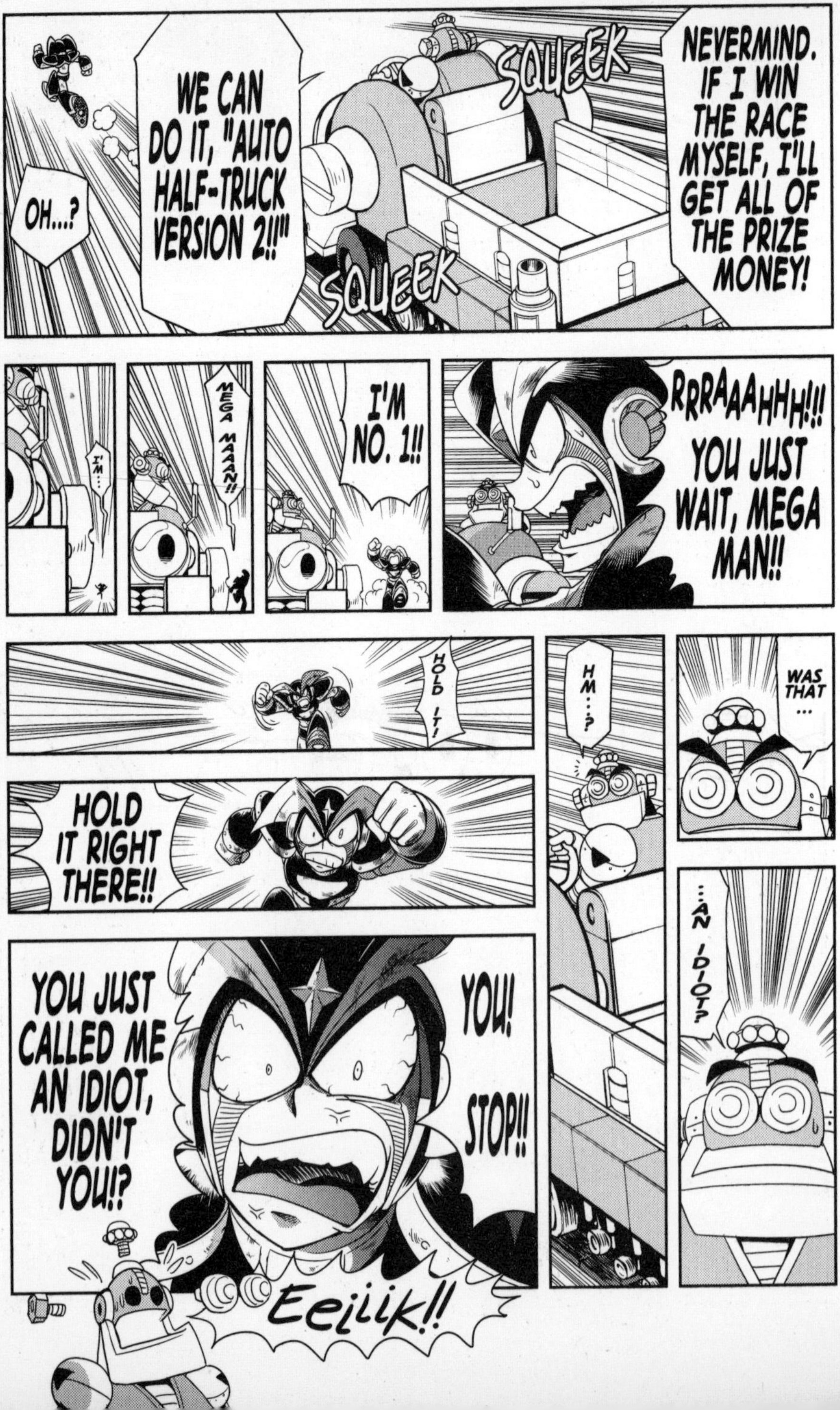
NEVERMIND. IF I WIN THE RACE MYSELF, I'LL GET ALL OF THE PRIZE MONEY!
SQUEEK
WE CAN DO IT, "AUTO HALF-TRUCK VERSION 2!!"
SQUEEK
OH...?
RRRAAAHHH!!! YOU JUST WAIT, MEGA MAN!!
I'M NO. 1!!
MEGA MAAAN!!
I'M...
WAS THAT...
...AN IDIOT?
HM...?
HOLD IT!
HOLD IT RIGHT THERE!!
YOU! STOP!!
YOU JUST CALLED ME AN IDIOT, DIDN'T YOU!?
Eeiiik!!

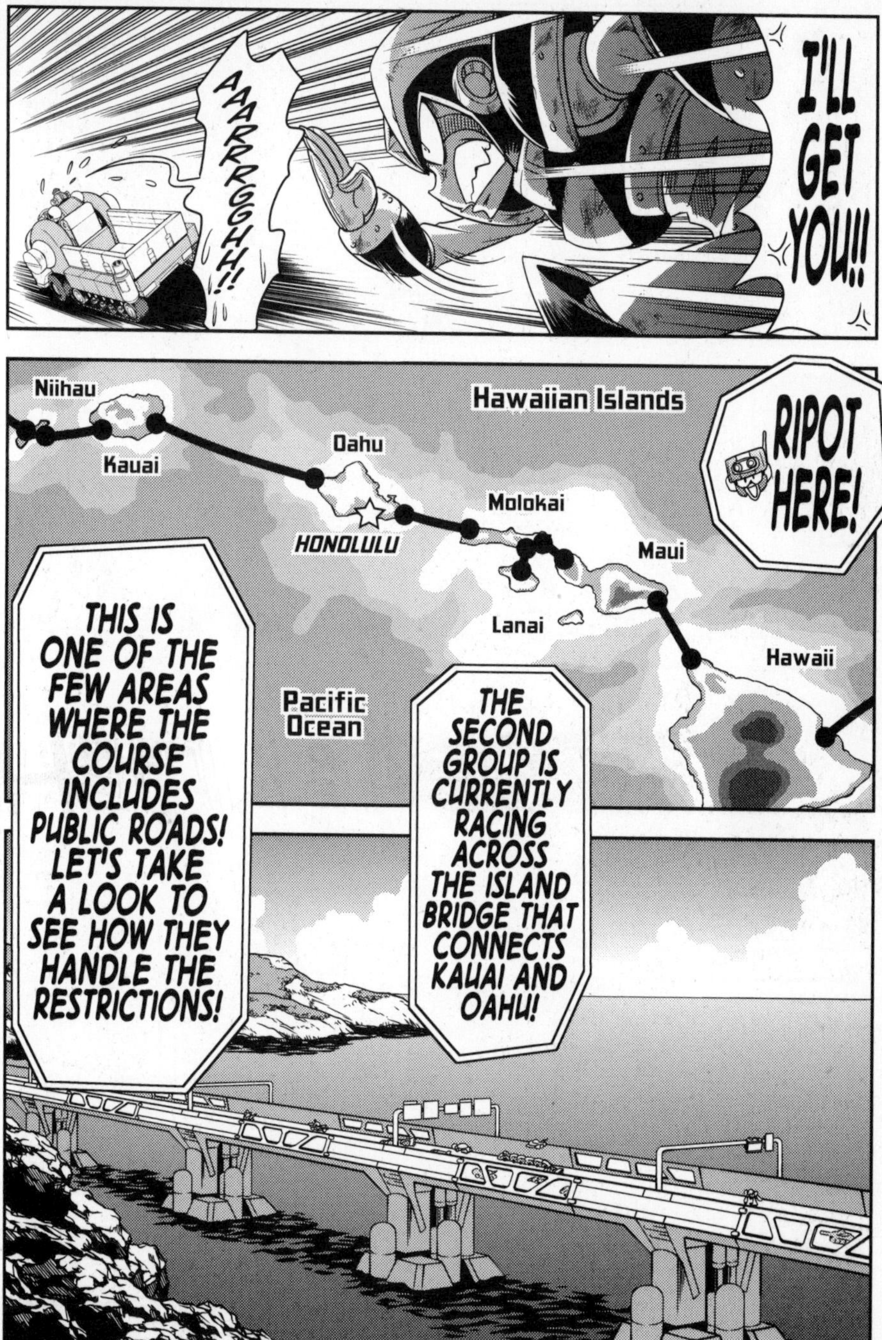

I'LL GET YOU!!
AAARRRGGHH!!
RIPOT HERE!
Hawaiian Islands
Niihau
Kauai
Oahu
HONOLULU
Molokai
Maui
Lanai
Hawaii
Pacific Ocean
THE SECOND GROUP IS CURRENTLY RACING ACROSS THE ISLAND BRIDGE THAT CONNECTS KAUAI AND OAHU!
THIS IS ONE OF THE FEW AREAS WHERE THE COURSE INCLUDES PUBLIC ROADS! LET'S TAKE A LOOK TO SEE HOW THEY HANDLE THE RESTRICTIONS!

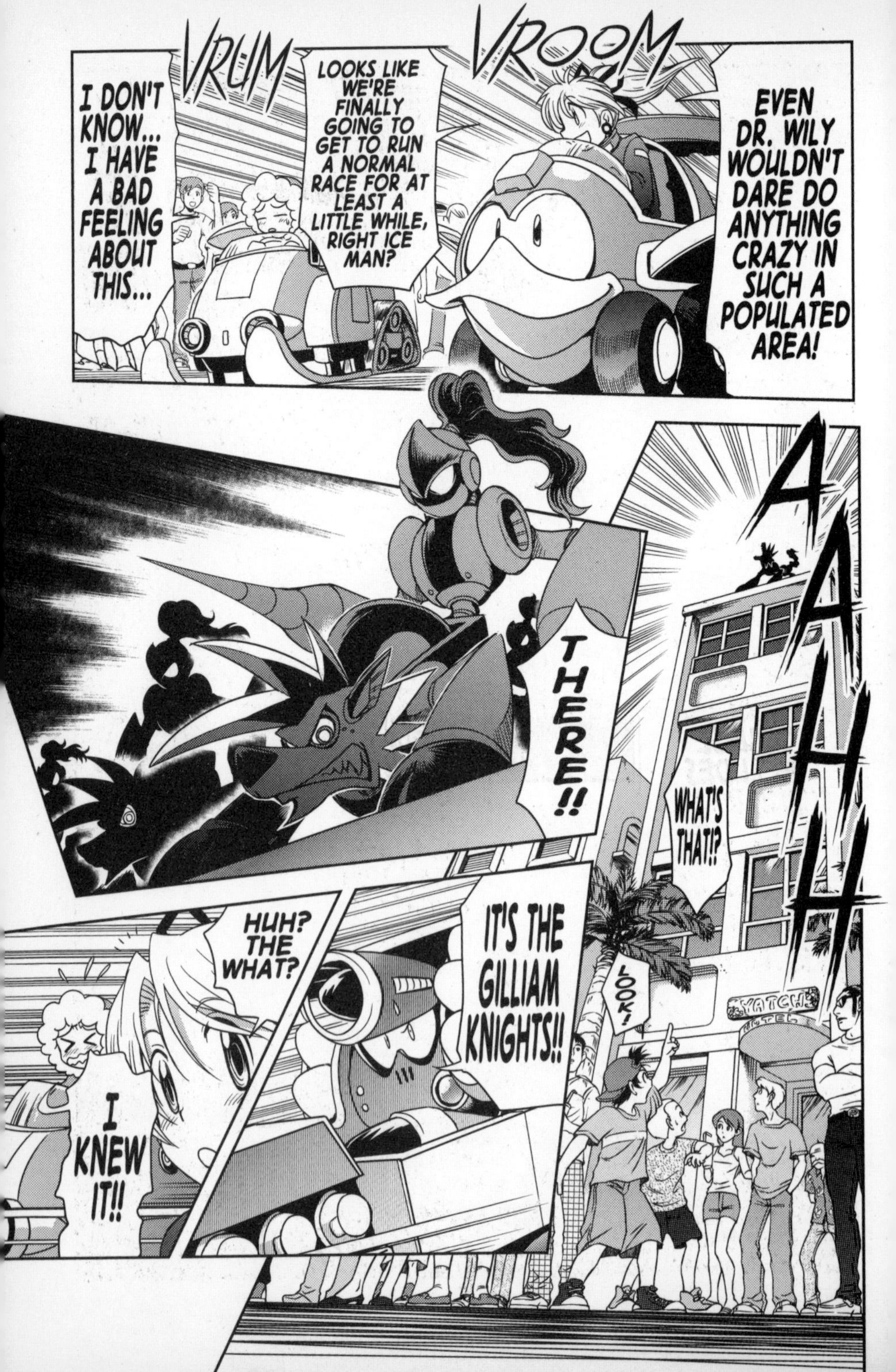
VROOM
EVEN DR. WILY WOULDN'T DARE DO ANYTHING CRAZY IN SUCH A POPULATED AREA!
LOOKS LIKE WE'RE FINALLY GOING TO GET TO RUN A NORMAL RACE FOR AT LEAST A LITTLE WHILE, RIGHT ICE MAN?
VRUM
I DON'T KNOW... I HAVE A BAD FEELING ABOUT THIS...
AAHH
WHAT'S THAT!?
LOOK!
YATCH HOTEL
THERE!!
IT'S THE GILLIAM KNIGHTS!!
HUH? THE WHAT?
I KNEW IT!!

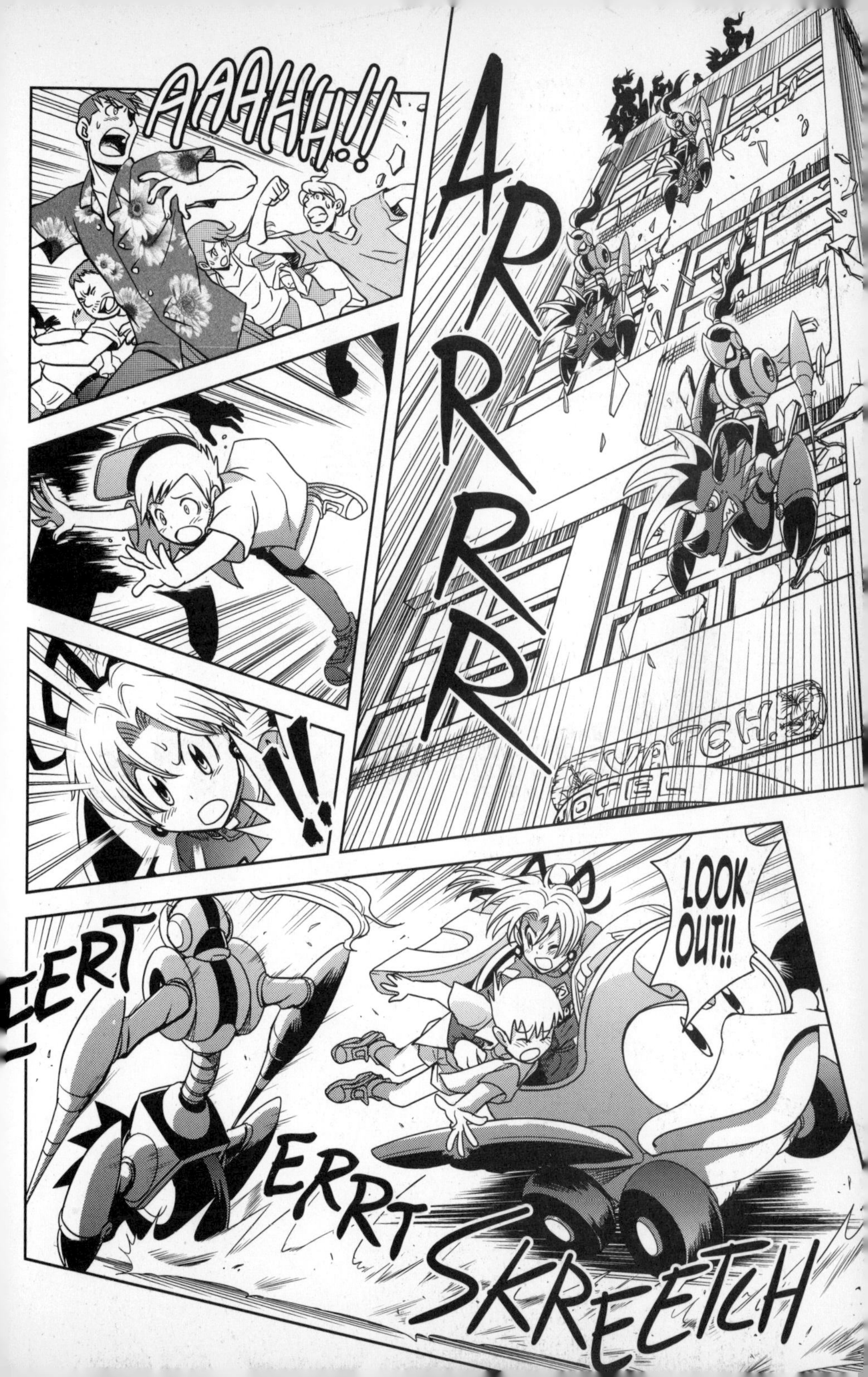

ARRRR
AAAHHH!!
!!
LOOK OUT!!
SKREETCH
ERRRT
EERT

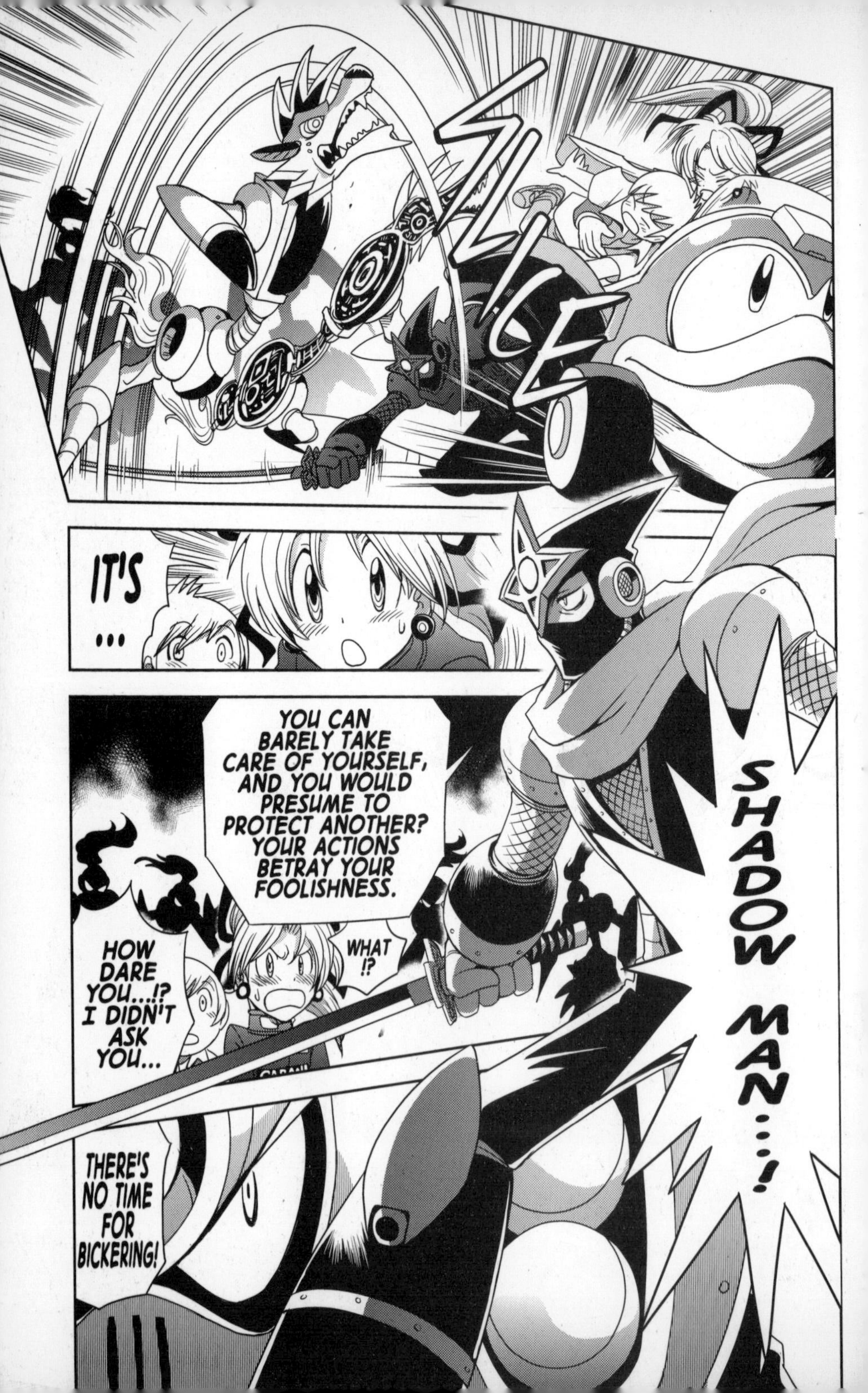
SLICE
IT'S ...
SHADOW MAN...!
YOU CAN BARELY TAKE CARE OF YOURSELF, AND YOU WOULD PRESUME TO PROTECT ANOTHER? YOUR ACTIONS BETRAY YOUR FOOLISHNESS.
WHAT !?
HOW DARE YOU...!? I DIDN'T ASK YOU...
THERE'S NO TIME FOR BICKERING!

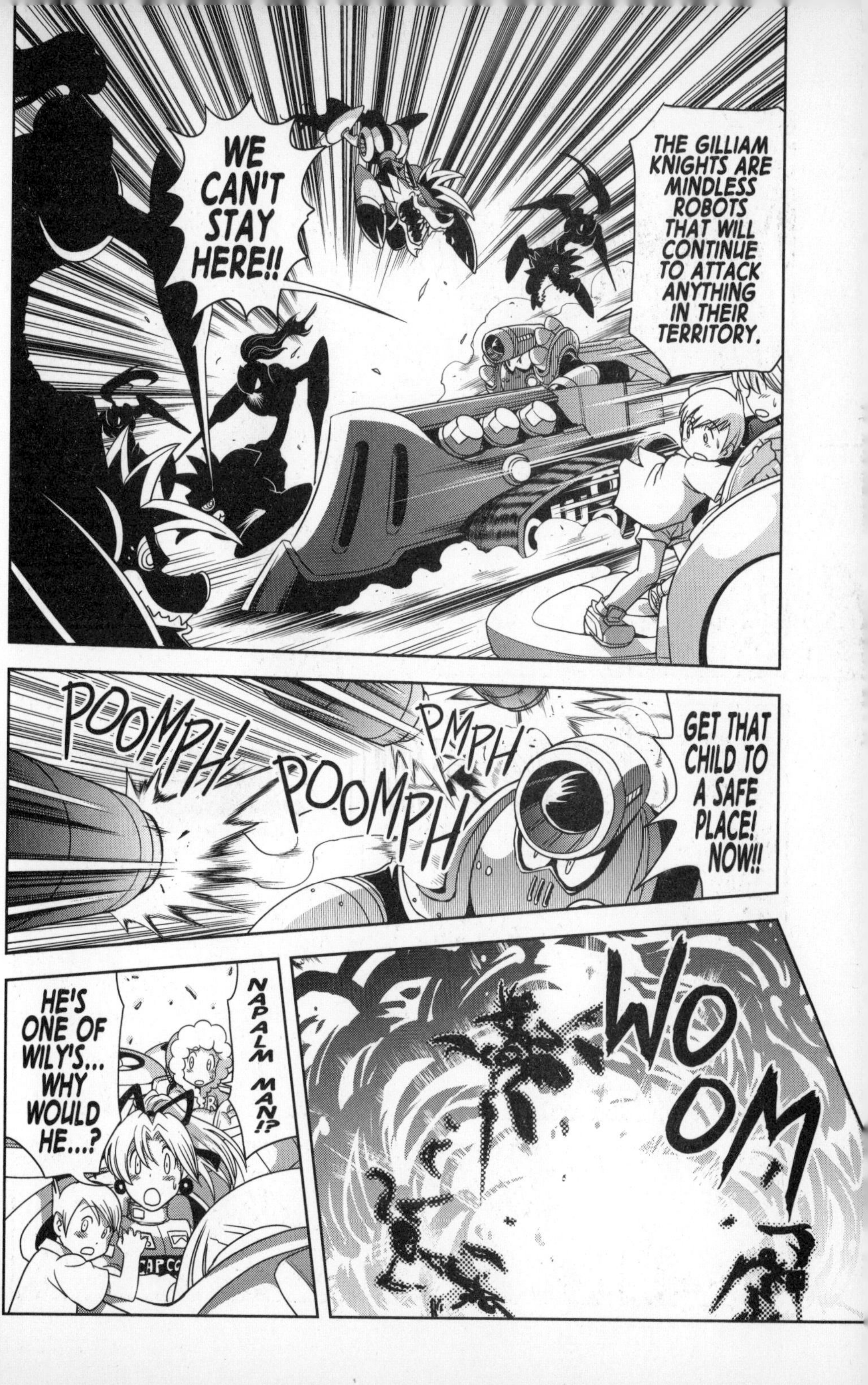
THE GILLIAM KNIGHTS ARE MINDLESS ROBOTS THAT WILL CONTINUE TO ATTACK ANYTHING IN THEIR TERRITORY.
WE CAN'T STAY HERE!!
GET THAT CHILD TO A SAFE PLACE! NOW!!
PMPH
POOMPH
POOMPH
WOOM
NAPALM MAN!?
HE'S ONE OF WILY'S... WHY WOULD HE...?

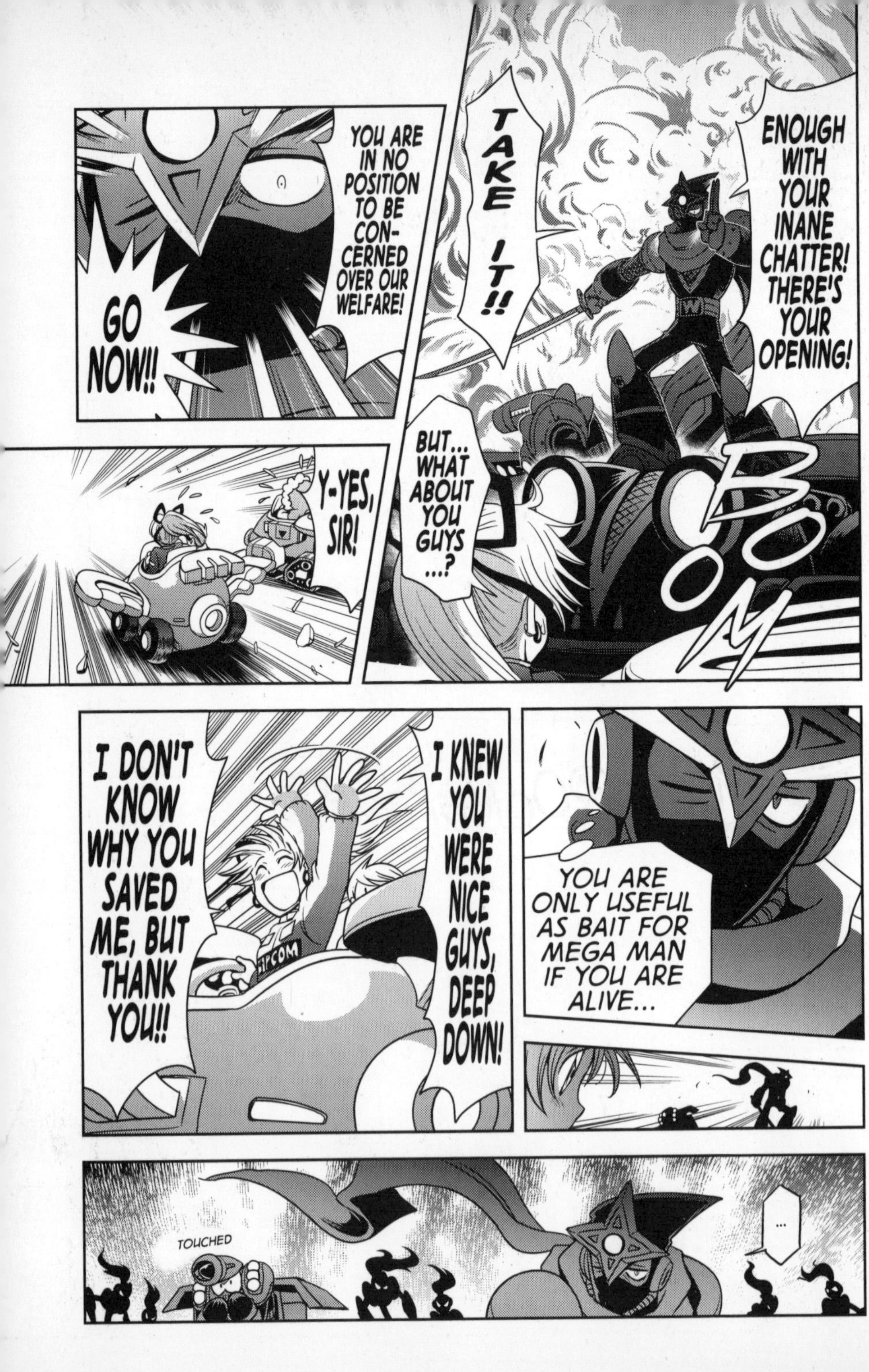
ENOUGH WITH YOUR INANE CHATTER! THERE'S YOUR OPENING!
TAKE IT!!
BUT... WHAT ABOUT YOU GUYS ...?
BOOOM
YOU ARE IN NO POSITION TO BE CON-CERNED OVER OUR WELFARE!
GO NOW!!
Y-YES, SIR!
YOU ARE ONLY USEFUL AS BAIT FOR MEGA MAN IF YOU ARE ALIVE...
I KNEW YOU WERE NICE GUYS, DEEP DOWN!
I DON'T KNOW WHY YOU SAVED ME, BUT THANK YOU!!
...
TOUCHED

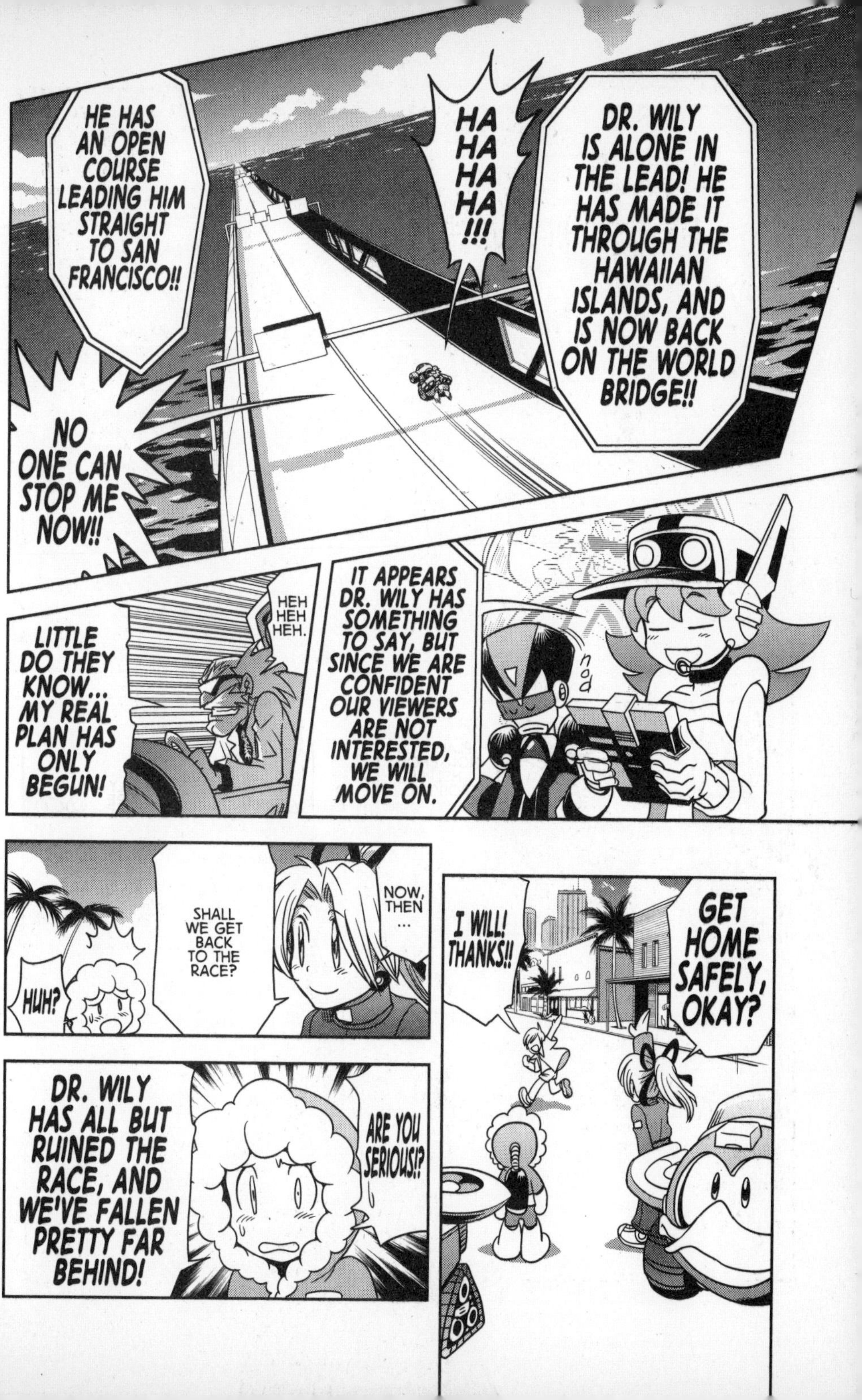
DR. WILY IS ALONE IN THE LEAD! HE HAS MADE IT THROUGH THE HAWAIIAN ISLANDS, AND IS NOW BACK ON THE WORLD BRIDGE!!
HA HA HA HA!!!
HE HAS AN OPEN COURSE LEADING HIM STRAIGHT TO SAN FRANCISCO!!
NO ONE CAN STOP ME NOW!!
IT APPEARS DR. WILY HAS SOMETHING TO SAY, BUT SINCE WE ARE CONFIDENT OUR VIEWERS ARE NOT INTERESTED, WE WILL MOVE ON.
nod
HEH HEH HEH.
LITTLE DO THEY KNOW... MY REAL PLAN HAS ONLY BEGUN!
GET HOME SAFELY, OKAY?
I WILL! THANKS!!
NOW, THEN ...
SHALL WE GET BACK TO THE RACE?
HUH?
ARE YOU SERIOUS!?
DR. WILY HAS ALL BUT RUINED THE RACE, AND WE'VE FALLEN PRETTY FAR BEHIND!

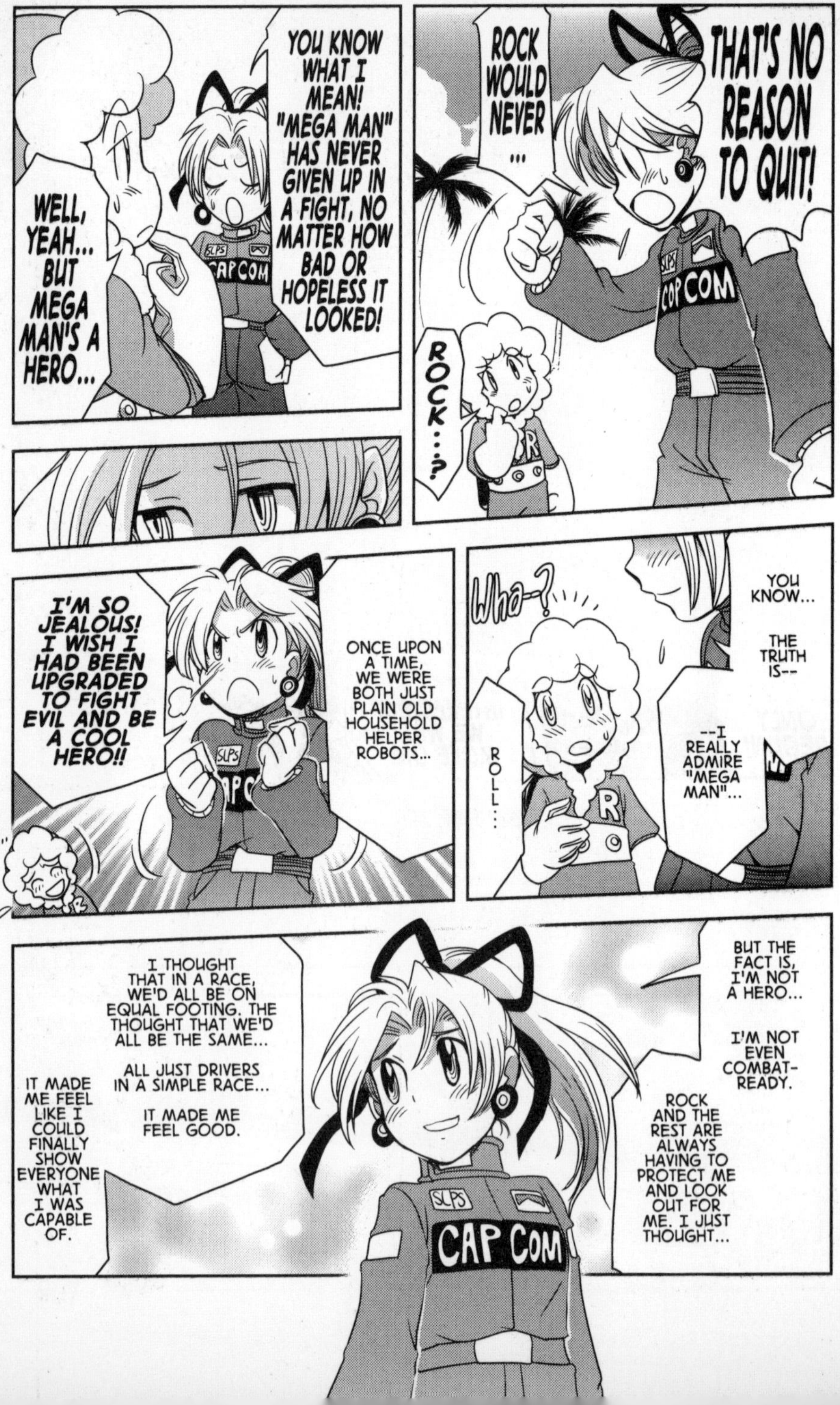
THAT'S NO REASON TO QUIT!
ROCK WOULD NEVER ...
ROCK...?
YOU KNOW WHAT I MEAN! "MEGA MAN" HAS NEVER GIVEN UP IN A FIGHT, NO MATTER HOW BAD OR HOPELESS IT LOOKED!
WELL, YEAH... BUT MEGA MAN'S A HERO...
YOU KNOW...
THE TRUTH IS--
--I REALLY ADMIRE "MEGA MAN"...
Wha--?
ROLL...
ONCE UPON A TIME, WE WERE BOTH JUST PLAIN OLD HOUSEHOLD HELPER ROBOTS...
I'M SO JEALOUS! I WISH I HAD BEEN UPGRADED TO FIGHT EVIL AND BE A COOL HERO!!
UH...
BUT THE FACT IS, I'M NOT A HERO...
I'M NOT EVEN COMBAT-READY.
ROCK AND THE REST ARE ALWAYS HAVING TO PROTECT ME AND LOOK OUT FOR ME. I JUST THOUGHT...
I THOUGHT THAT IN A RACE, WE'D ALL BE ON EQUAL FOOTING. THE THOUGHT THAT WE'D ALL BE THE SAME...
ALL JUST DRIVERS IN A SIMPLE RACE...
IT MADE ME FEEL GOOD.
IT MADE ME FEEL LIKE I COULD FINALLY SHOW EVERYONE WHAT I WAS CAPABLE OF.

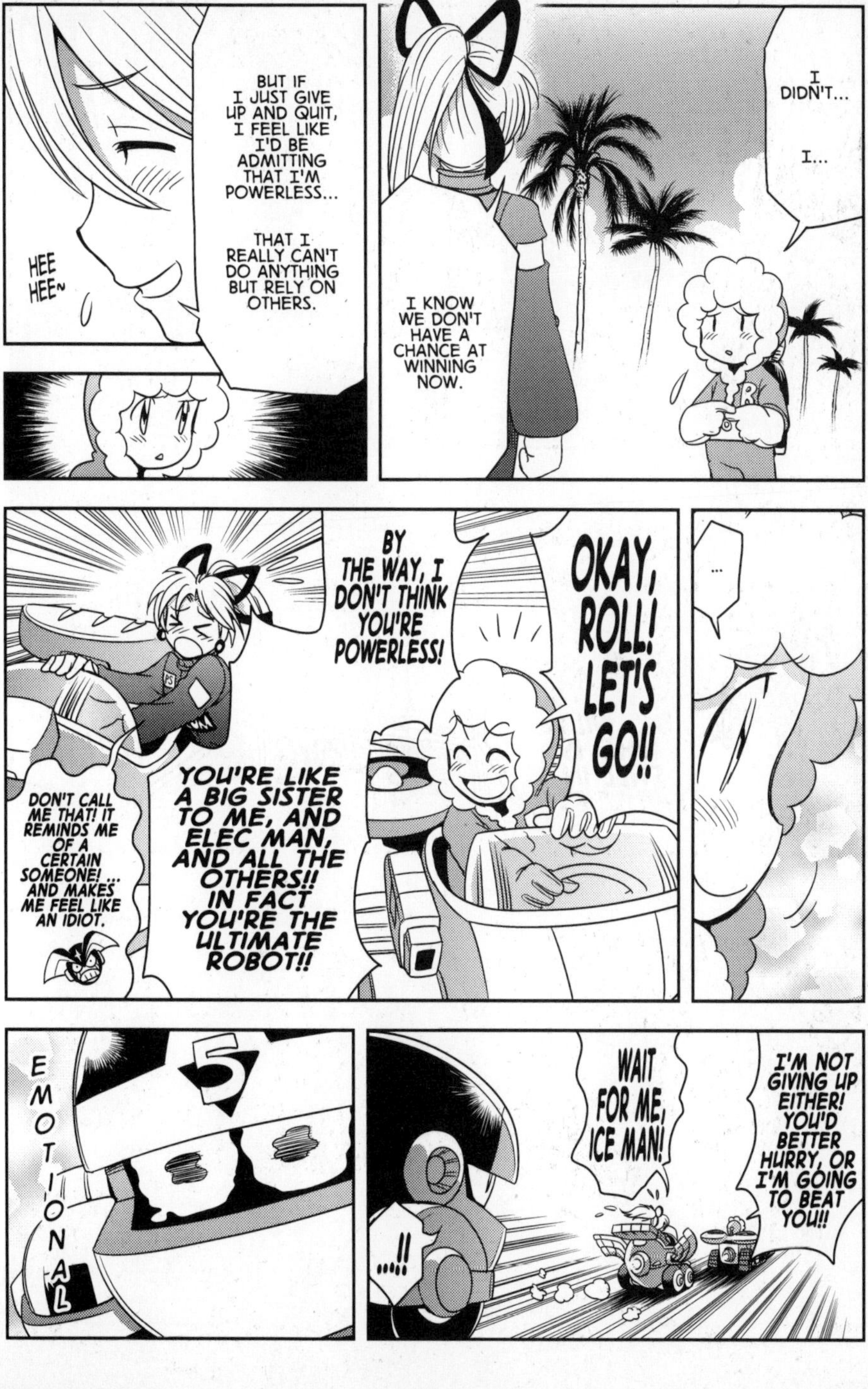
I DIDN'T...
I...
I KNOW WE DON'T HAVE A CHANCE AT WINNING NOW.
BUT IF I JUST GIVE UP AND QUIT, I FEEL LIKE I'D BE ADMITTING THAT I'M POWERLESS...
THAT I REALLY CAN'T DO ANYTHING BUT RELY ON OTHERS.
HEE HEE~
...
OKAY, ROLL! LET'S GO!!
BY THE WAY, I DON'T THINK YOU'RE POWERLESS!
YOU'RE LIKE A BIG SISTER TO ME, AND ELEC MAN, AND ALL THE OTHERS!! IN FACT YOU'RE THE ULTIMATE ROBOT!!
DON'T CALL ME THAT! IT REMINDS ME OF A CERTAIN SOMEONE! ...AND MAKES ME FEEL LIKE AN IDIOT.
I'M NOT GIVING UP EITHER! YOU'D BETTER HURRY, OR I'M GOING TO BEAT YOU!!
WAIT FOR ME, ICE MAN!
...!!
EMOTIONAL

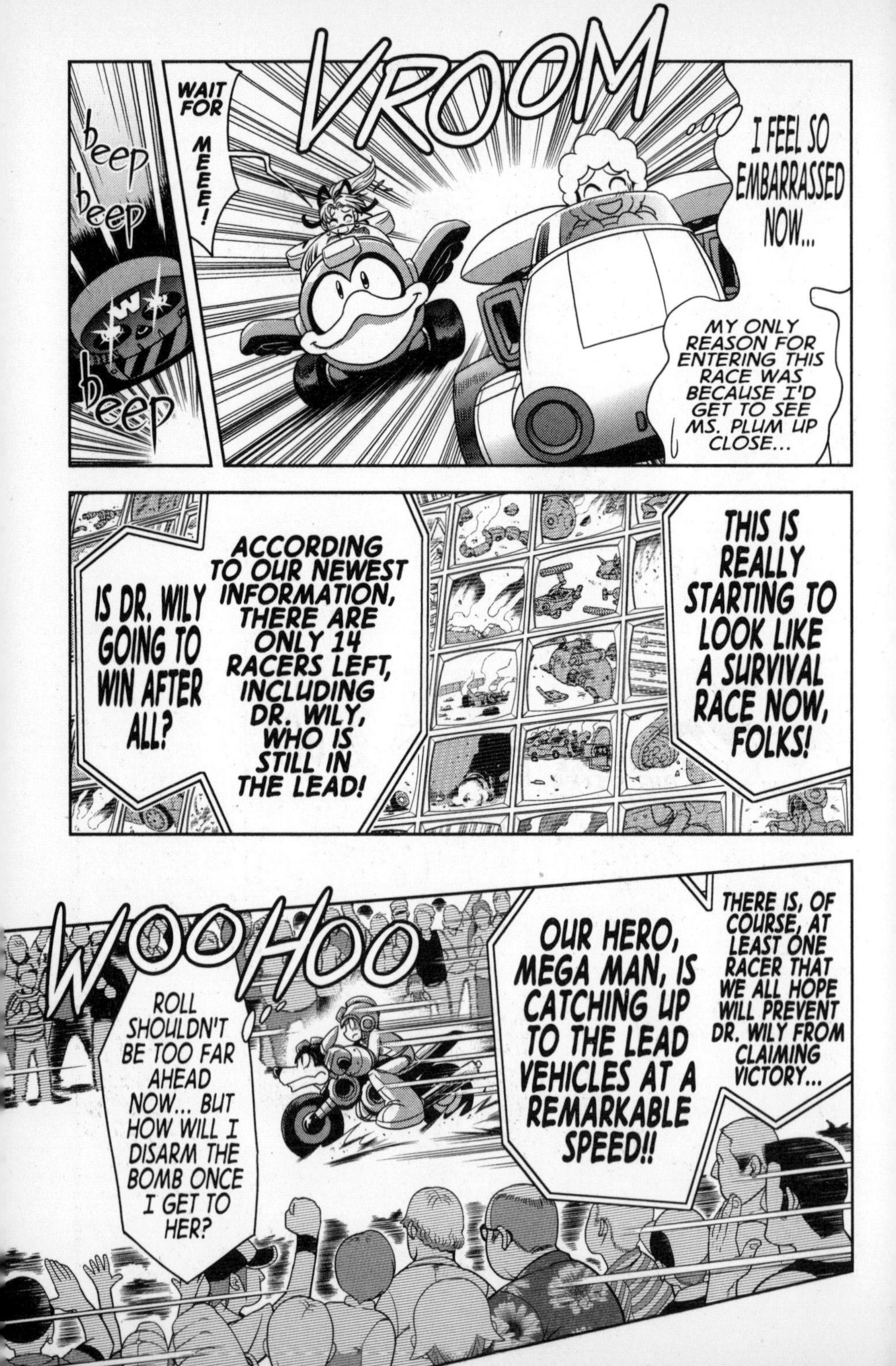
I FEEL SO EMBARRASSED NOW...
MY ONLY REASON FOR ENTERING THIS RACE WAS BECAUSE I'D GET TO SEE MS. PLUM UP CLOSE...
VROOM
WAIT FOR MEEEE!
beep beep beep
THIS IS REALLY STARTING TO LOOK LIKE A SURVIVAL RACE NOW, FOLKS!
ACCORDING TO OUR NEWEST INFORMATION, THERE ARE ONLY 14 RACERS LEFT, INCLUDING DR. WILY, WHO IS STILL IN THE LEAD!
IS DR. WILY GOING TO WIN AFTER ALL?
THERE IS, OF COURSE, AT LEAST ONE RACER THAT WE ALL HOPE WILL PREVENT DR. WILY FROM CLAIMING VICTORY...
OUR HERO, MEGA MAN, IS CATCHING UP TO THE LEAD VEHICLES AT A REMARKABLE SPEED!!
WOO HOO
ROLL SHOULDN'T BE TOO FAR AHEAD NOW... BUT HOW WILL I DISARM THE BOMB ONCE I GET TO HER?

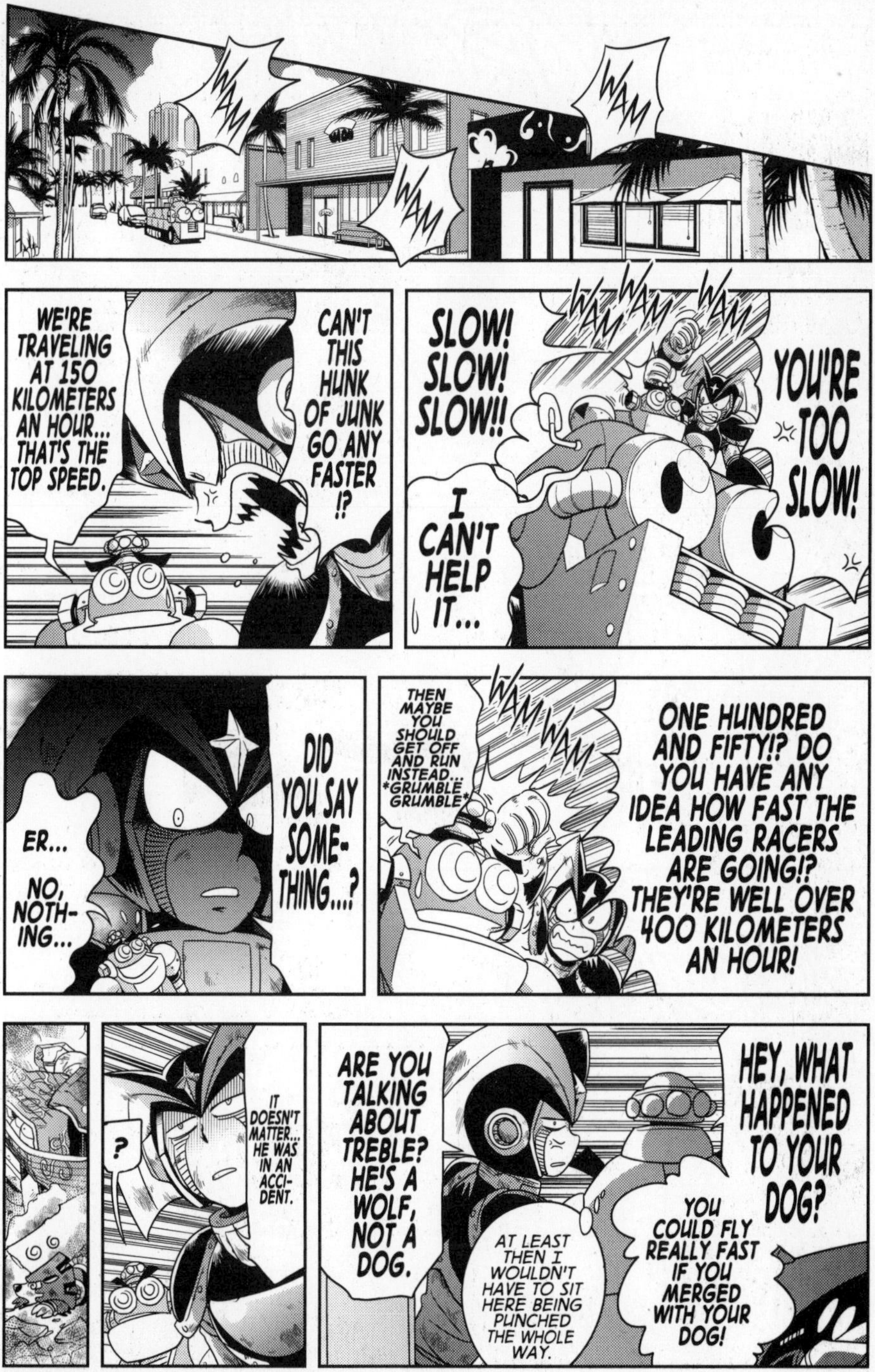
WAM
WAM
WAM
WAM WAM WAM WAM
YOU'RE TOO SLOW!
SLOW! SLOW! SLOW!!
I CAN'T HELP IT...
CAN'T THIS HUNK OF JUNK GO ANY FASTER !?
WE'RE TRAVELING AT 150 KILOMETERS AN HOUR... THAT'S THE TOP SPEED.
ONE HUNDRED AND FIFTY!? DO YOU HAVE ANY IDEA HOW FAST THE LEADING RACERS ARE GOING!? THEY'RE WELL OVER 400 KILOMETERS AN HOUR!
WAM WAM
THEN MAYBE YOU SHOULD GET OFF AND RUN INSTEAD... *GRUMBLE GRUMBLE*
DID YOU SAY SOME-THING...?
ER... NO, NOTH-ING...
HEY, WHAT HAPPENED TO YOUR DOG?
YOU COULD FLY REALLY FAST IF YOU MERGED WITH YOUR DOG!
ARE YOU TALKING ABOUT TREBLE? HE'S A WOLF, NOT A DOG.
AT LEAST THEN I WOULDN'T HAVE TO SIT HERE BEING PUNCHED THE WHOLE WAY.
IT DOESN'T MATTER... HE WAS IN AN ACCI-DENT.
?

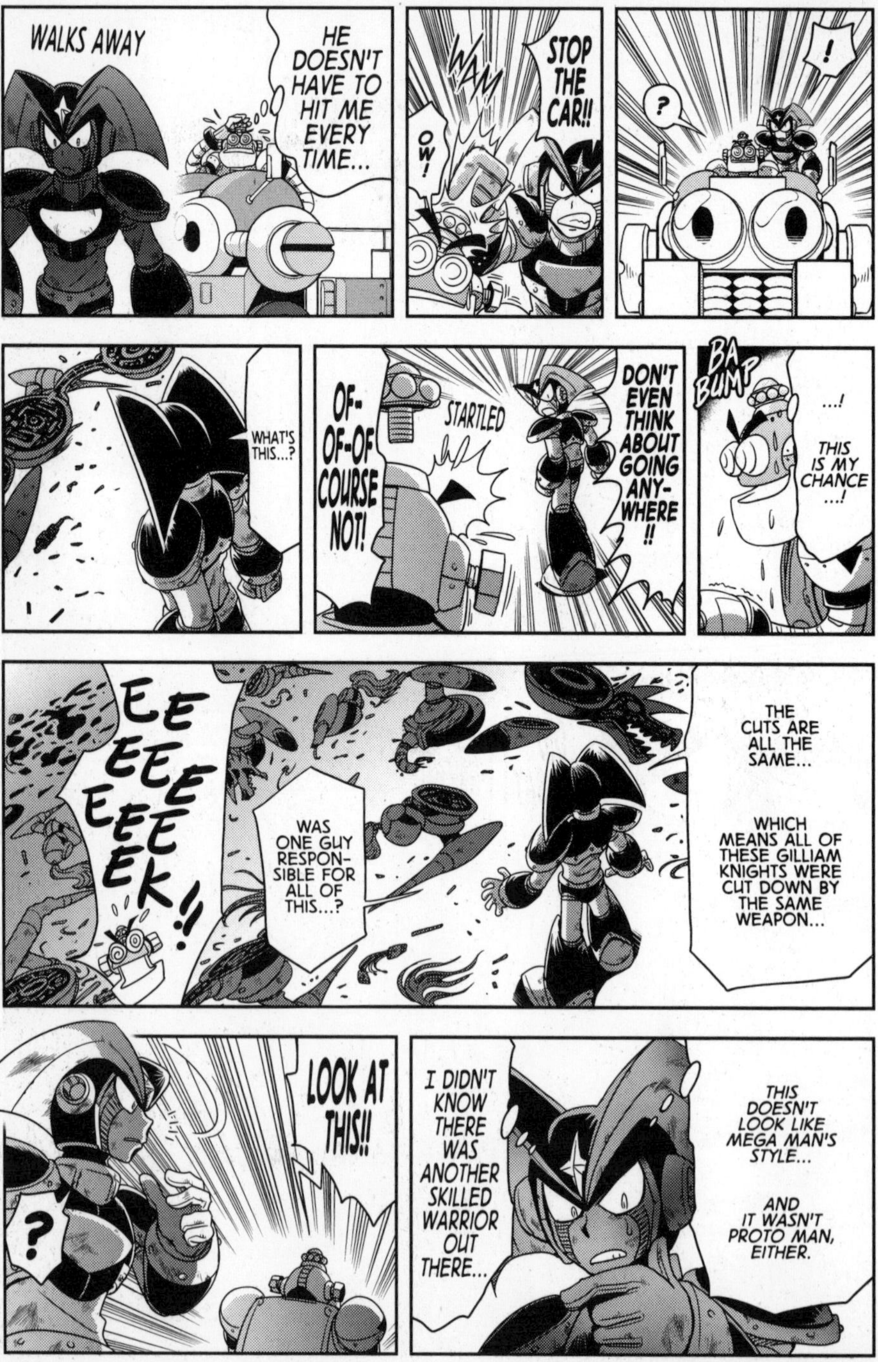
!
?
STOP THE CAR!!
WAM
OW!
HE DOESN'T HAVE TO HIT ME EVERY TIME...
WALKS AWAY
BA BUMP
...!
THIS IS MY CHANCE ...!
DON'T EVEN THINK ABOUT GOING ANY-WHERE!!
STARTLED
OF-OF-OF COURSE NOT!
WHAT'S THIS...?
THE CUTS ARE ALL THE SAME...
WHICH MEANS ALL OF THESE GILLIAM KNIGHTS WERE CUT DOWN BY THE SAME WEAPON...
WAS ONE GUY RESPON-SIBLE FOR ALL OF THIS...?
EEEEEEEEEEK!!
THIS DOESN'T LOOK LIKE MEGA MAN'S STYLE...
AND IT WASN'T PROTO MAN, EITHER.
I DIDN'T KNOW THERE WAS ANOTHER SKILLED WARRIOR OUT THERE...
LOOK AT THIS!!
?

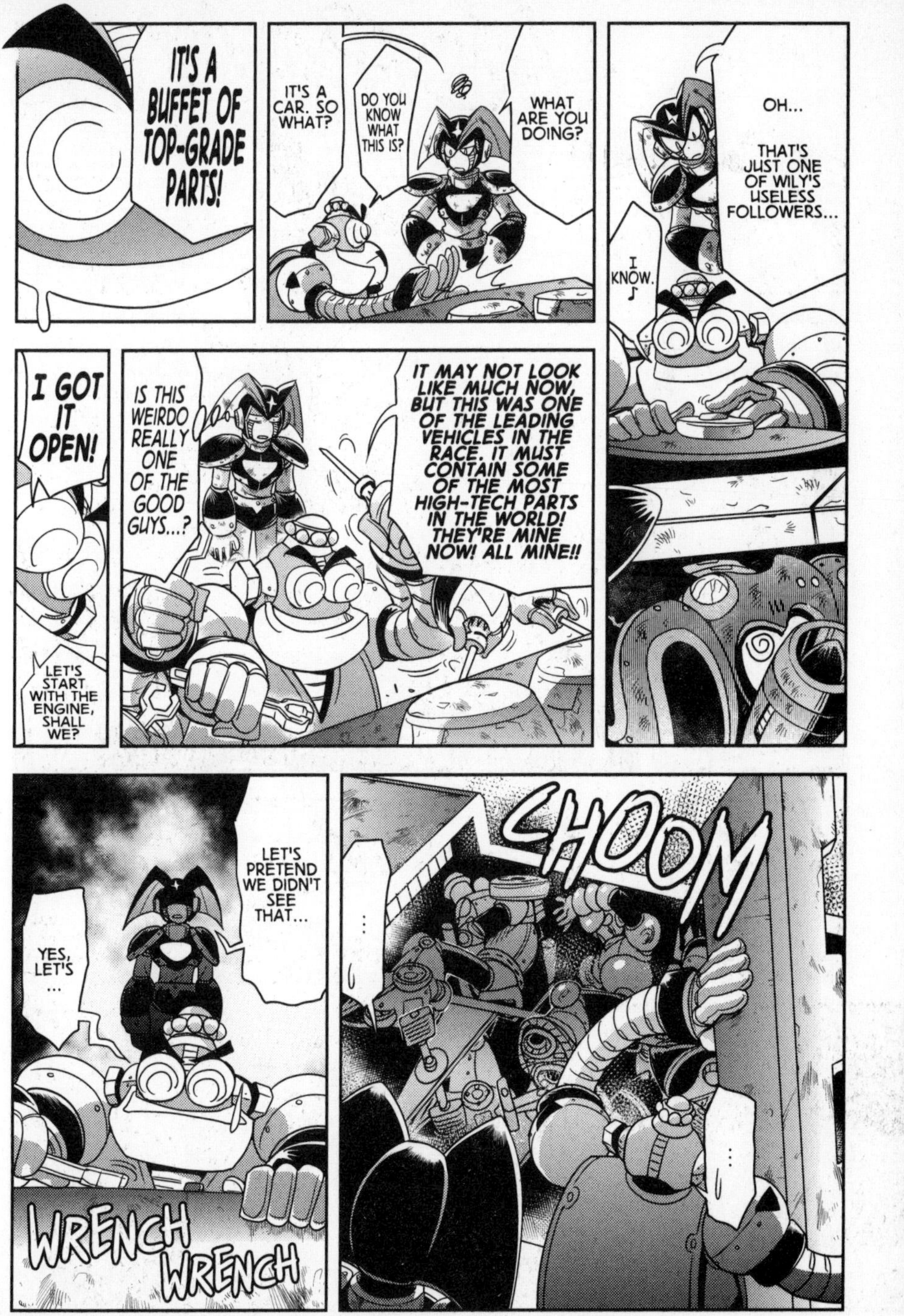
OH...
THAT'S JUST ONE OF WILY'S USELESS FOLLOWERS...
I KNOW. ♪
WHAT ARE YOU DOING?
DO YOU KNOW WHAT THIS IS?
IT'S A CAR. SO WHAT?
IT'S A BUFFET OF TOP-GRADE PARTS!
IT MAY NOT LOOK LIKE MUCH NOW, BUT THIS WAS ONE OF THE LEADING VEHICLES IN THE RACE. IT MUST CONTAIN SOME OF THE MOST HIGH-TECH PARTS IN THE WORLD! THEY'RE MINE NOW! ALL MINE!!
IS THIS WEIRDO REALLY ONE OF THE GOOD GUYS...?
I GOT IT OPEN!
LET'S START WITH THE ENGINE, SHALL WE?
CHOOM
...
...
LET'S PRETEND WE DIDN'T SEE THAT...
YES, LET'S ...
WRENCH WRENCH

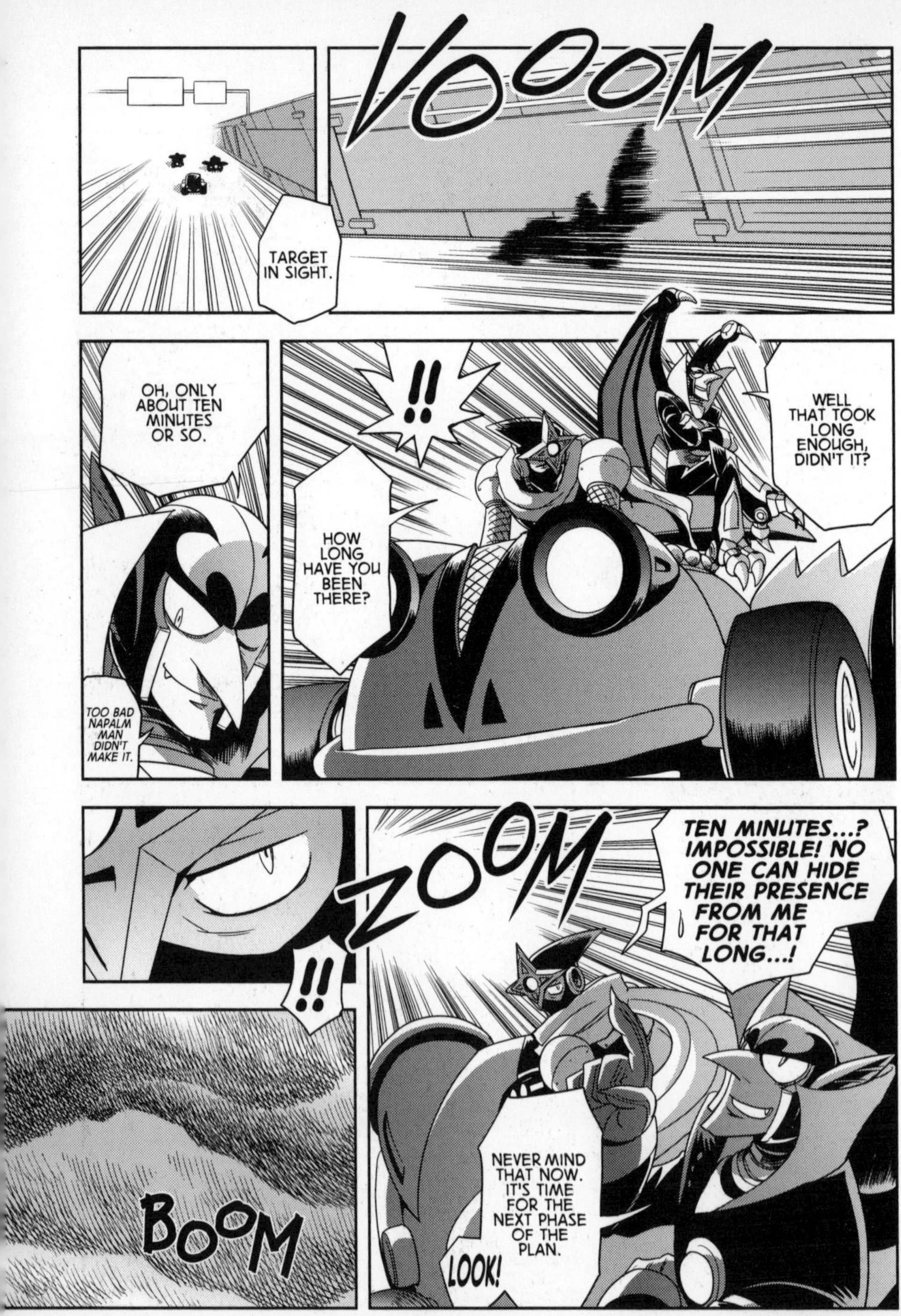
VOOOM
TARGET IN SIGHT.
WELL THAT TOOK LONG ENOUGH, DIDN'T IT?
!!
HOW LONG HAVE YOU BEEN THERE?
OH, ONLY ABOUT TEN MINUTES OR SO.
TOO BAD NAPALM MAN DIDN'T MAKE IT.
TEN MINUTES...? IMPOSSIBLE! NO ONE CAN HIDE THEIR PRESENCE FROM ME FOR THAT LONG...!
ZOOM
NEVER MIND THAT NOW. IT'S TIME FOR THE NEXT PHASE OF THE PLAN.
LOOK!
!!
BOOM

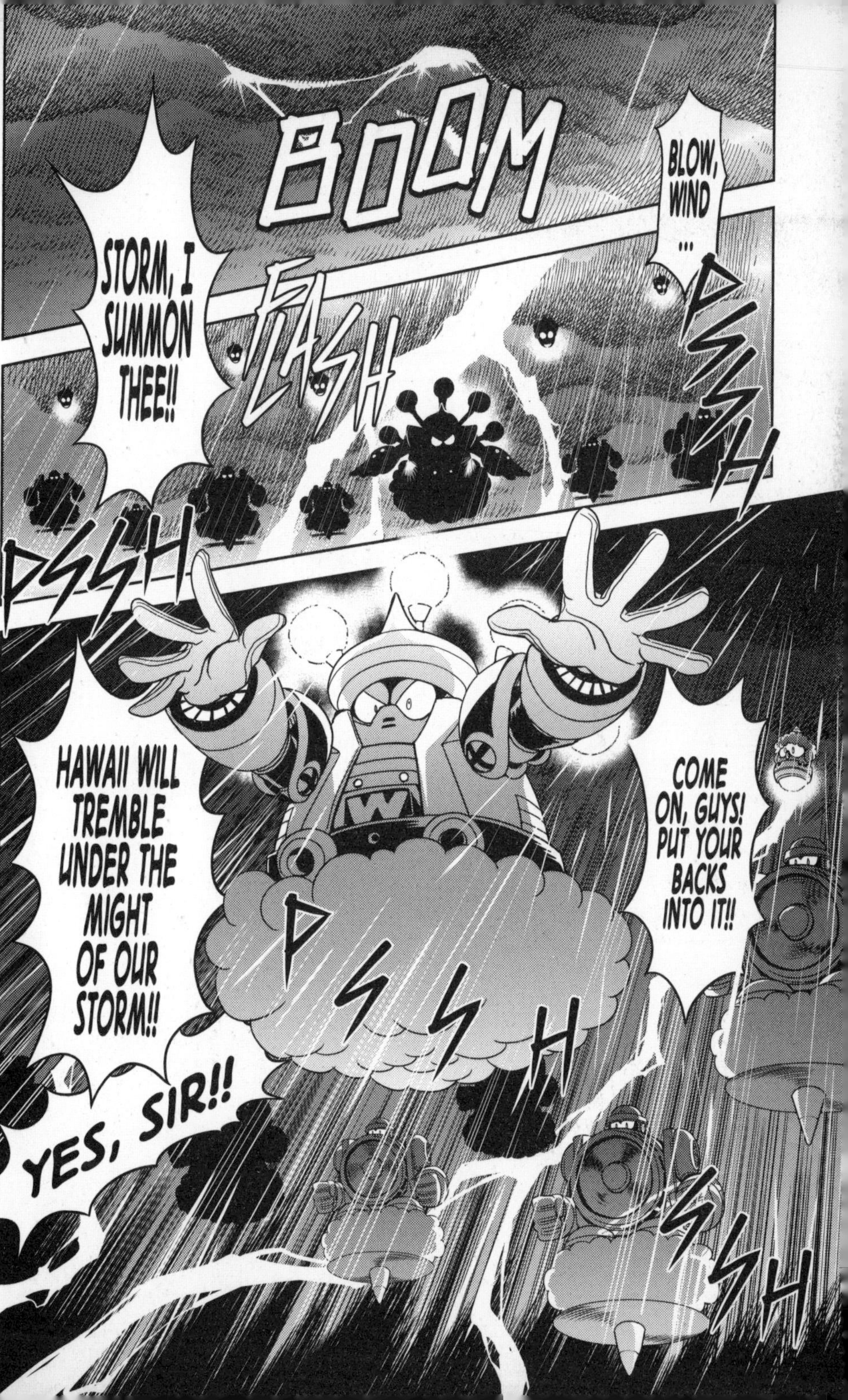
BLOW, WIND ...
BOOM
FLASH
DSSH
STORM, I SUMMON THEE!!
DSSH
COME ON, GUYS! PUT YOUR BACKS INTO IT!!
HAWAII WILL TREMBLE UNDER THE MIGHT OF OUR STORM!!
DSSSH
YES, SIR!!
SSSH

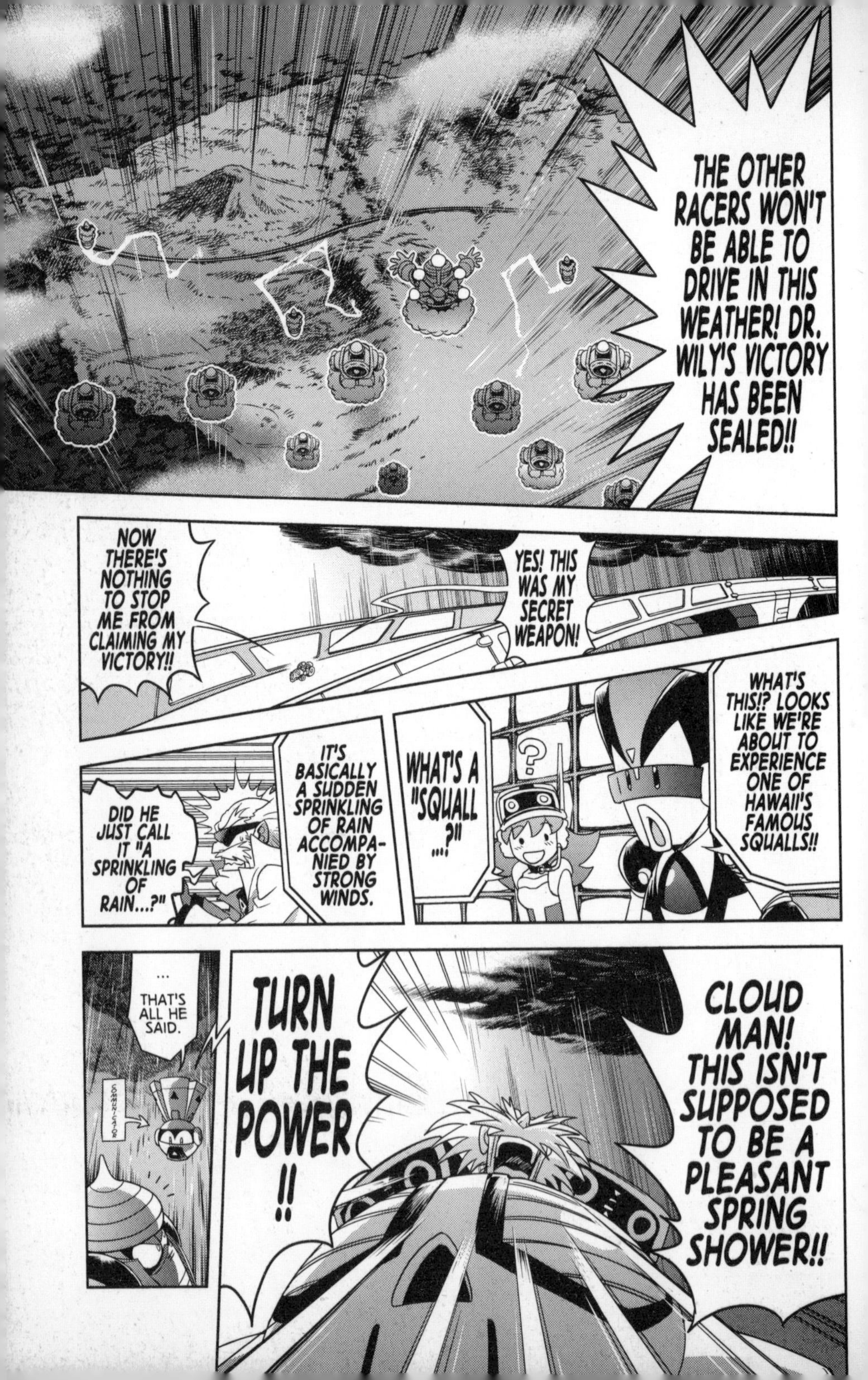
THE OTHER RACERS WON'T BE ABLE TO DRIVE IN THIS WEATHER! DR. WILY'S VICTORY HAS BEEN SEALED!!
YES! THIS WAS MY SECRET WEAPON!
NOW THERE'S NOTHING TO STOP ME FROM CLAIMING MY VICTORY!!
WHAT'S THIS!? LOOKS LIKE WE'RE ABOUT TO EXPERIENCE ONE OF HAWAII'S FAMOUS SQUALLS!!
?
WHAT'S A "SQUALL ...?"
IT'S BASICALLY A SUDDEN SPRINKLING OF RAIN ACCOMPA-NIED BY STRONG WINDS.
DID HE JUST CALL IT "A SPRINKLING OF RAIN...?"
CLOUD MAN! THIS ISN'T SUPPOSED TO BE A PLEASANT SPRING SHOWER!!
TURN UP THE POWER !!
... THAT'S ALL HE SAID.
COMMUNICATOR

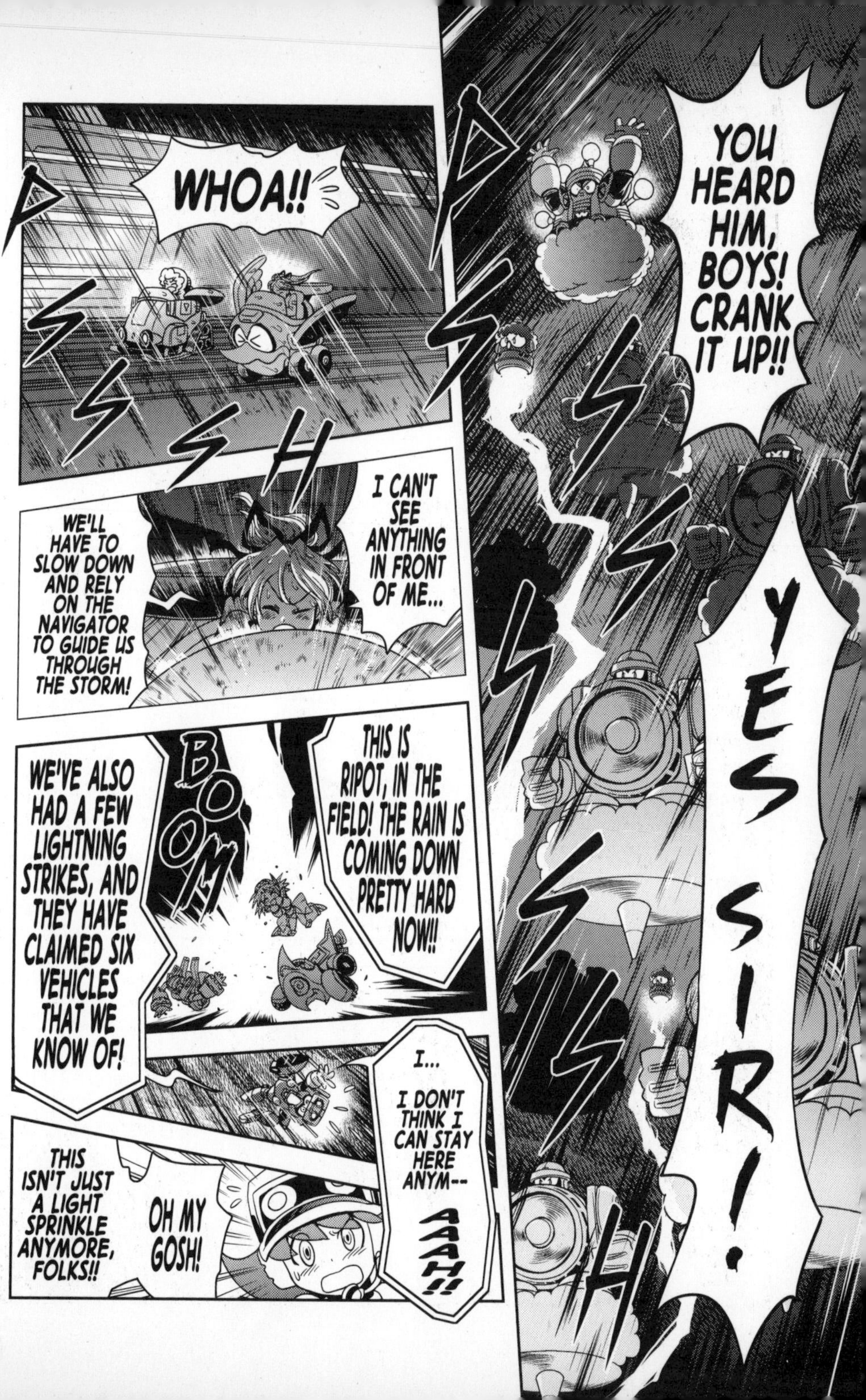
YOU HEARD HIM, BOYS! CRANK IT UP!!
YES SIR!
DSSSSSSSSH
WHOA!!
DSSSH
I CAN'T SEE ANYTHING IN FRONT OF ME...
WE'LL HAVE TO SLOW DOWN AND RELY ON THE NAVIGATOR TO GUIDE US THROUGH THE STORM!
THIS IS RIPOT, IN THE FIELD! THE RAIN IS COMING DOWN PRETTY HARD NOW!!
BOOOM
WE'VE ALSO HAD A FEW LIGHTNING STRIKES, AND THEY HAVE CLAIMED SIX VEHICLES THAT WE KNOW OF!
I... I DON'T THINK I CAN STAY HERE ANYM--
AAAH!!
OH MY GOSH!
THIS ISN'T JUST A LIGHT SPRINKLE ANYMORE, FOLKS!!

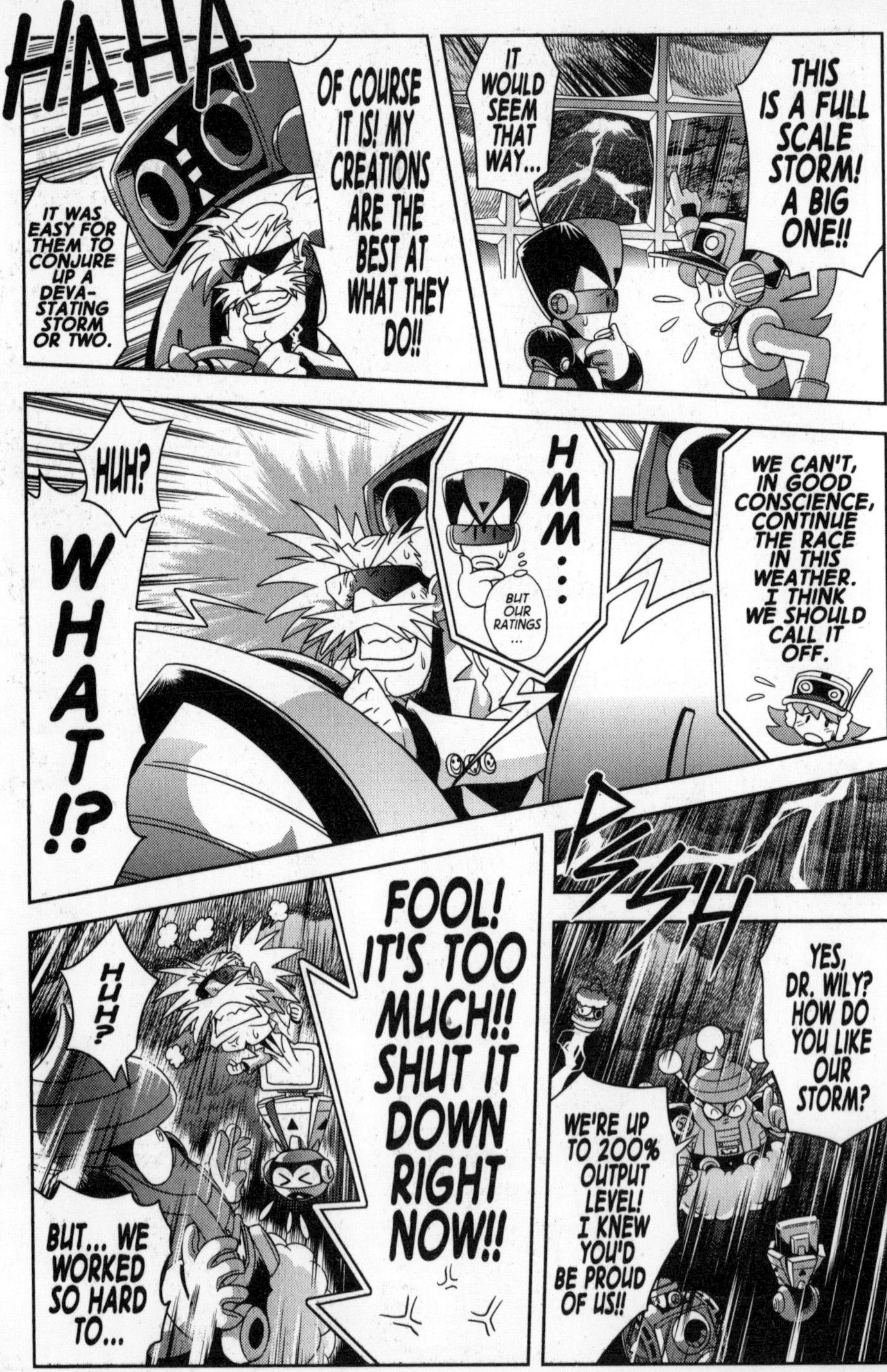
THIS IS A FULL SCALE STORM! A BIG ONE!!
IT WOULD SEEM THAT WAY...
HAHA
OF COURSE IT IS! MY CREATIONS ARE THE BEST AT WHAT THEY DO!!
IT WAS EASY FOR THEM TO CONJURE UP A DEVA-STATING STORM OR TWO.
WE CAN'T, IN GOOD CONSCIENCE, CONTINUE THE RACE IN THIS WEATHER. I THINK WE SHOULD CALL IT OFF.
HMM...
BUT OUR RATINGS ...
HUH?
WHAT!?
BSSH
YES, DR. WILY? HOW DO YOU LIKE OUR STORM?
WE'RE UP TO 200% OUTPUT LEVEL! I KNEW YOU'D BE PROUD OF US!!
FOOL! IT'S TOO MUCH!! SHUT IT DOWN RIGHT NOW!!
HUH?
BUT... WE WORKED SO HARD TO...

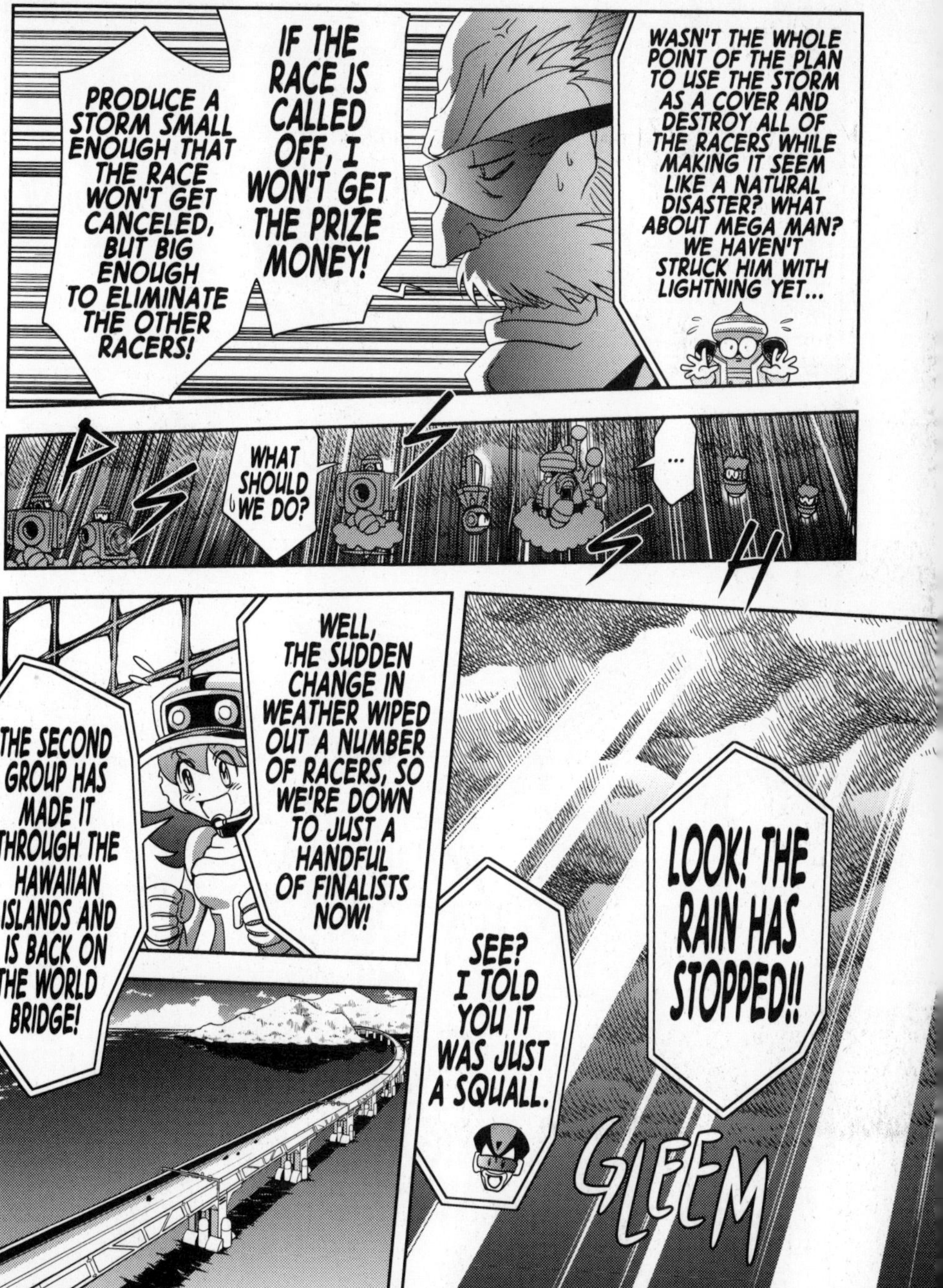
WASN'T THE WHOLE POINT OF THE PLAN TO USE THE STORM AS A COVER AND DESTROY ALL OF THE RACERS WHILE MAKING IT SEEM LIKE A NATURAL DISASTER? WHAT ABOUT MEGA MAN? WE HAVEN'T STRUCK HIM WITH LIGHTNING YET...
IF THE RACE IS CALLED OFF, I WON'T GET THE PRIZE MONEY!
PRODUCE A STORM SMALL ENOUGH THAT THE RACE WON'T GET CANCELED, BUT BIG ENOUGH TO ELIMINATE THE OTHER RACERS!
...
WHAT SHOULD WE DO?
LOOK! THE RAIN HAS STOPPED!!
SEE? I TOLD YOU IT WAS JUST A SQUALL.
GLEEM
WELL, THE SUDDEN CHANGE IN WEATHER WIPED OUT A NUMBER OF RACERS, SO WE'RE DOWN TO JUST A HANDFUL OF FINALISTS NOW!
THE SECOND GROUP HAS MADE IT THROUGH THE HAWAIIAN ISLANDS AND IS BACK ON THE WORLD BRIDGE!

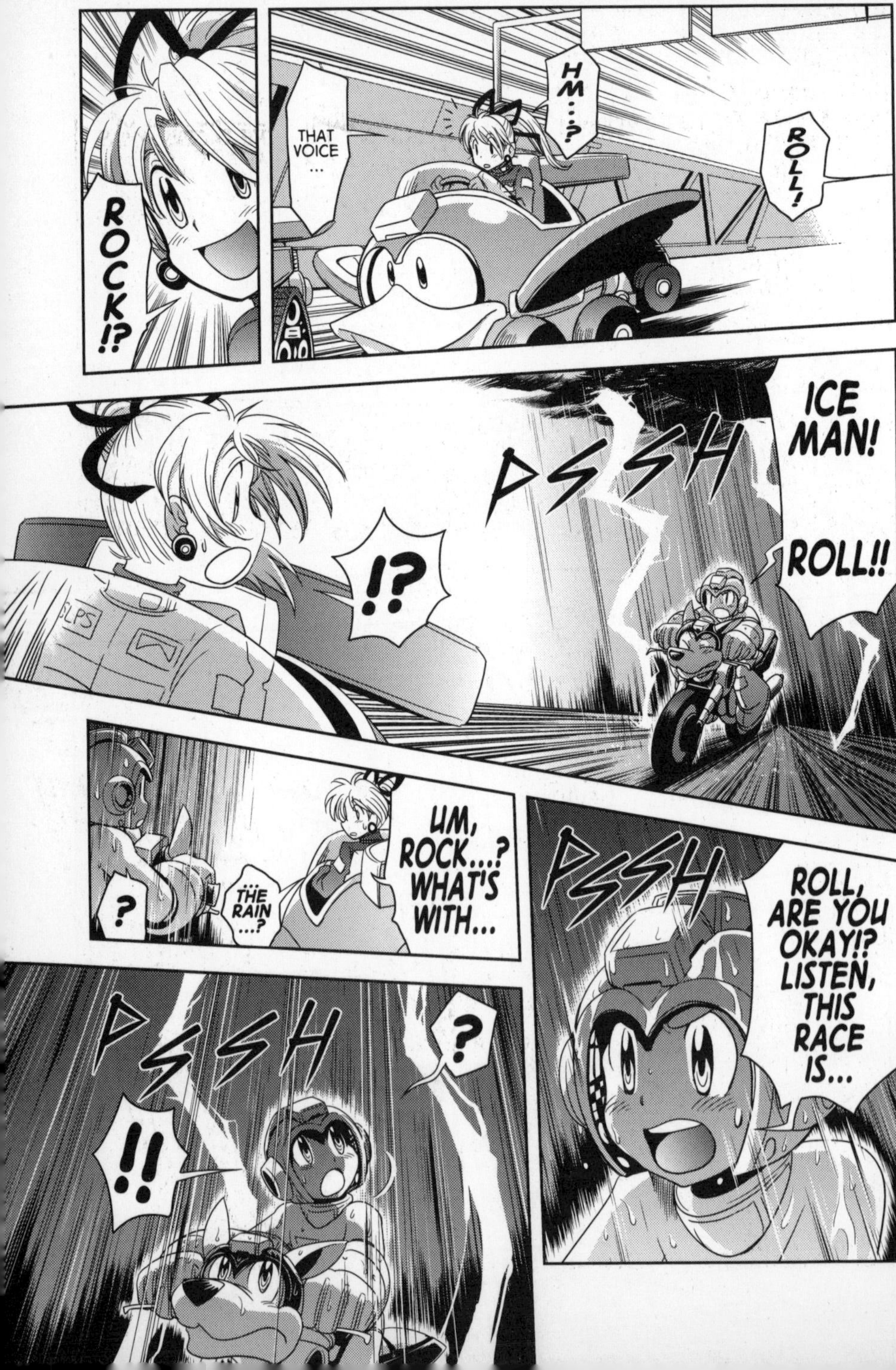
ROLL!
HM...?
THAT VOICE ...
ROCK!?
ICE MAN!
PSSH
ROLL!!
!?
PSSH
ROLL, ARE YOU OKAY!? LISTEN, THIS RACE IS...
UM, ROCK...? WHAT'S WITH...
...THE RAIN ...?
?
PSSH
?
!!

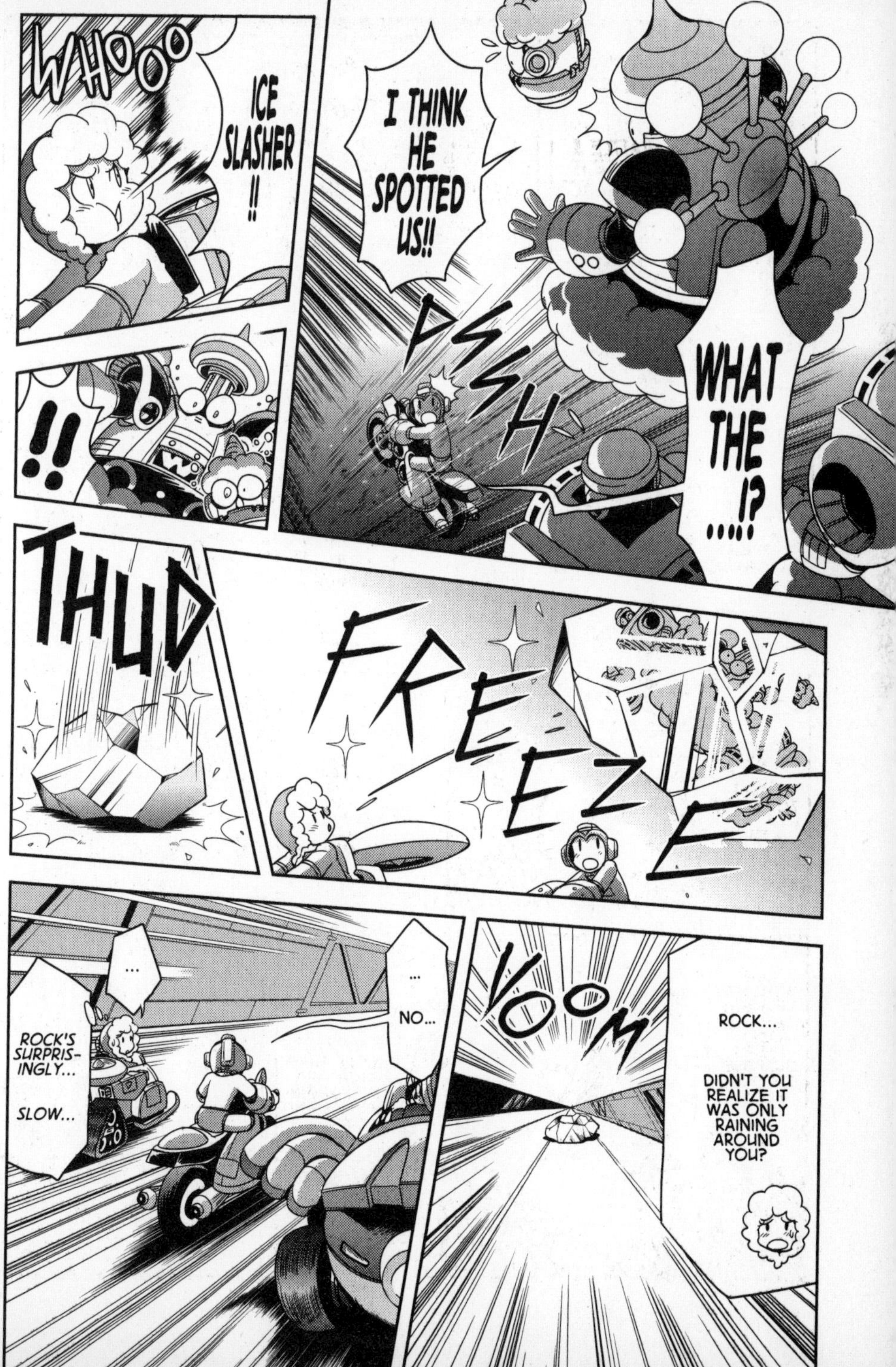
I THINK HE SPOTTED US!!
DSSH
WHAT THE ....!?
WHOOO
ICE SLASHER!!
!!
FREEZE
THUD
VOOM
ROCK...
DIDN'T YOU REALIZE IT WAS ONLY RAINING AROUND YOU?
... NO...
...
ROCK'S SURPRIS-INGLY...
SLOW...

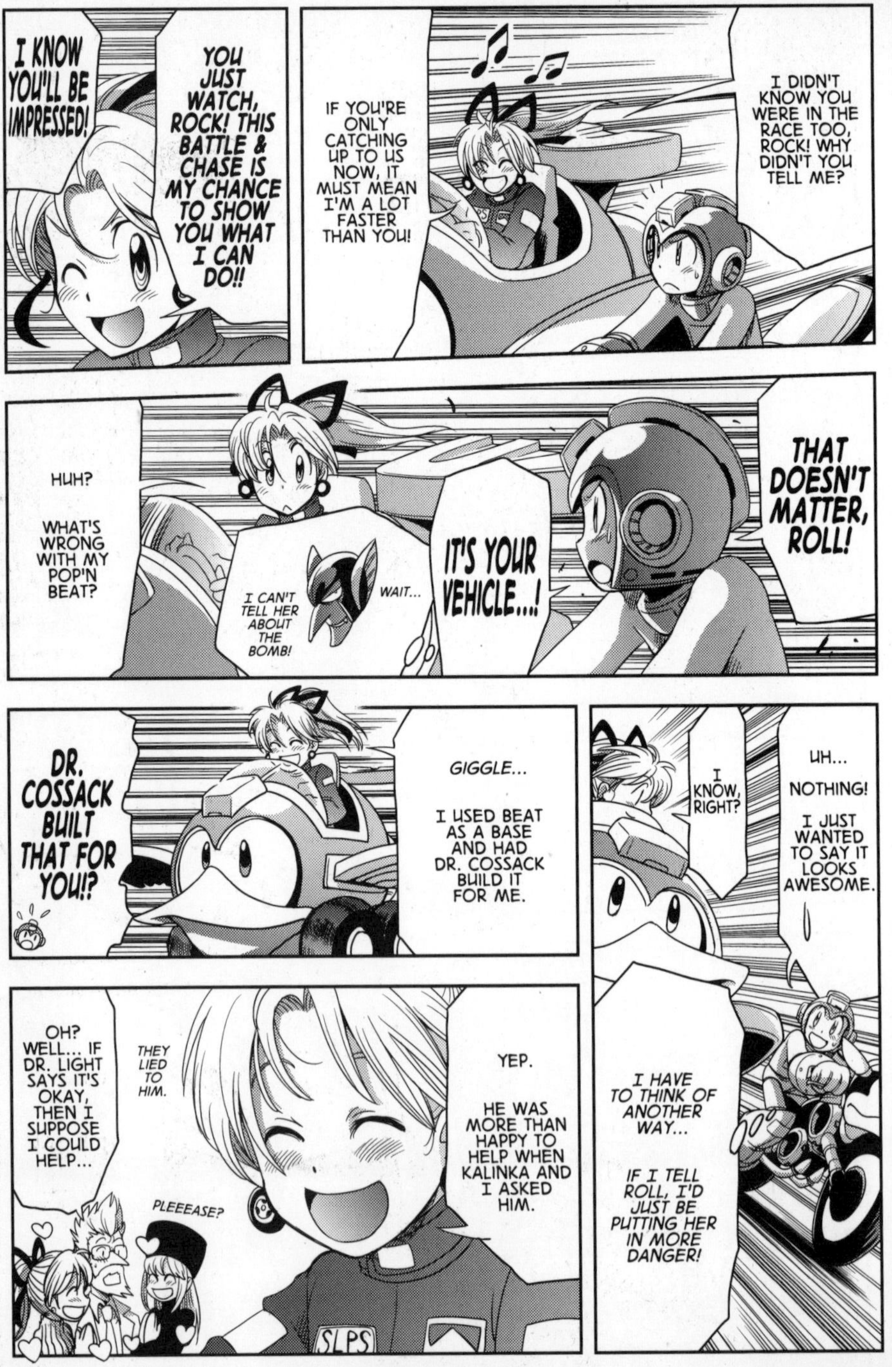
I DIDN'T KNOW YOU WERE IN THE RACE TOO, ROCK! WHY DIDN'T YOU TELL ME?
IF YOU'RE ONLY CATCHING UP TO US NOW, IT MUST MEAN I'M A LOT FASTER THAN YOU!
YOU JUST WATCH, ROCK! THIS BATTLE & CHASE IS MY CHANCE TO SHOW YOU WHAT I CAN DO!!
I KNOW YOU'LL BE IMPRESSED!
THAT DOESN'T MATTER, ROLL!
IT'S YOUR VEHICLE...!
WAIT...
I CAN'T TELL HER ABOUT THE BOMB!
HUH?
WHAT'S WRONG WITH MY POP'N BEAT?
UH...
NOTHING!
I JUST WANTED TO SAY IT LOOKS AWESOME.
I KNOW, RIGHT?
I HAVE TO THINK OF ANOTHER WAY...
IF I TELL ROLL, I'D JUST BE PUTTING HER IN MORE DANGER!
GIGGLE...
I USED BEAT AS A BASE AND HAD DR. COSSACK BUILD IT FOR ME.
DR. COSSACK BUILT THAT FOR YOU!?
YEP.
HE WAS MORE THAN HAPPY TO HELP WHEN KALINKA AND I ASKED HIM.
PLEEEASE?
THEY LIED TO HIM.
OH? WELL... IF DR. LIGHT SAYS IT'S OKAY, THEN I SUPPOSE I COULD HELP...

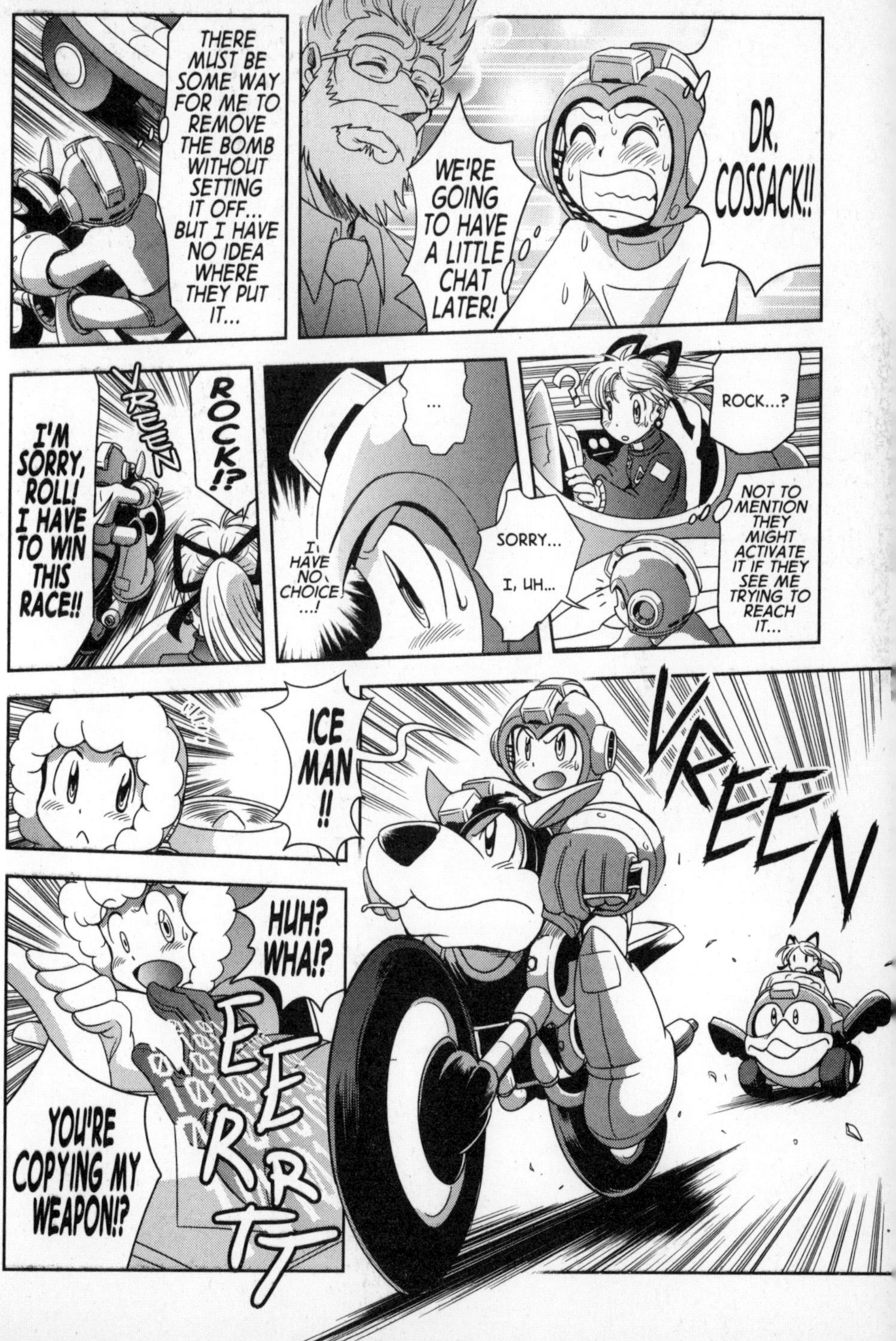
DR. COSSACK!!
WE'RE GOING TO HAVE A LITTLE CHAT LATER!
THERE MUST BE SOME WAY FOR ME TO REMOVE THE BOMB WITHOUT SETTING IT OFF... BUT I HAVE NO IDEA WHERE THEY PUT IT...
ROCK...?
NOT TO MENTION THEY MIGHT ACTIVATE IT IF THEY SEE ME TRYING TO REACH IT...
SORRY...
I, UH...
...
I HAVE NO CHOICE ...!
ROCK!?
VREEN
I'M SORRY, ROLL! I HAVE TO WIN THIS RACE!!
VREEEN
ICE MAN!!
HUH? WHA!?
EEERRRTT
YOU'RE COPYING MY WEAPON!?

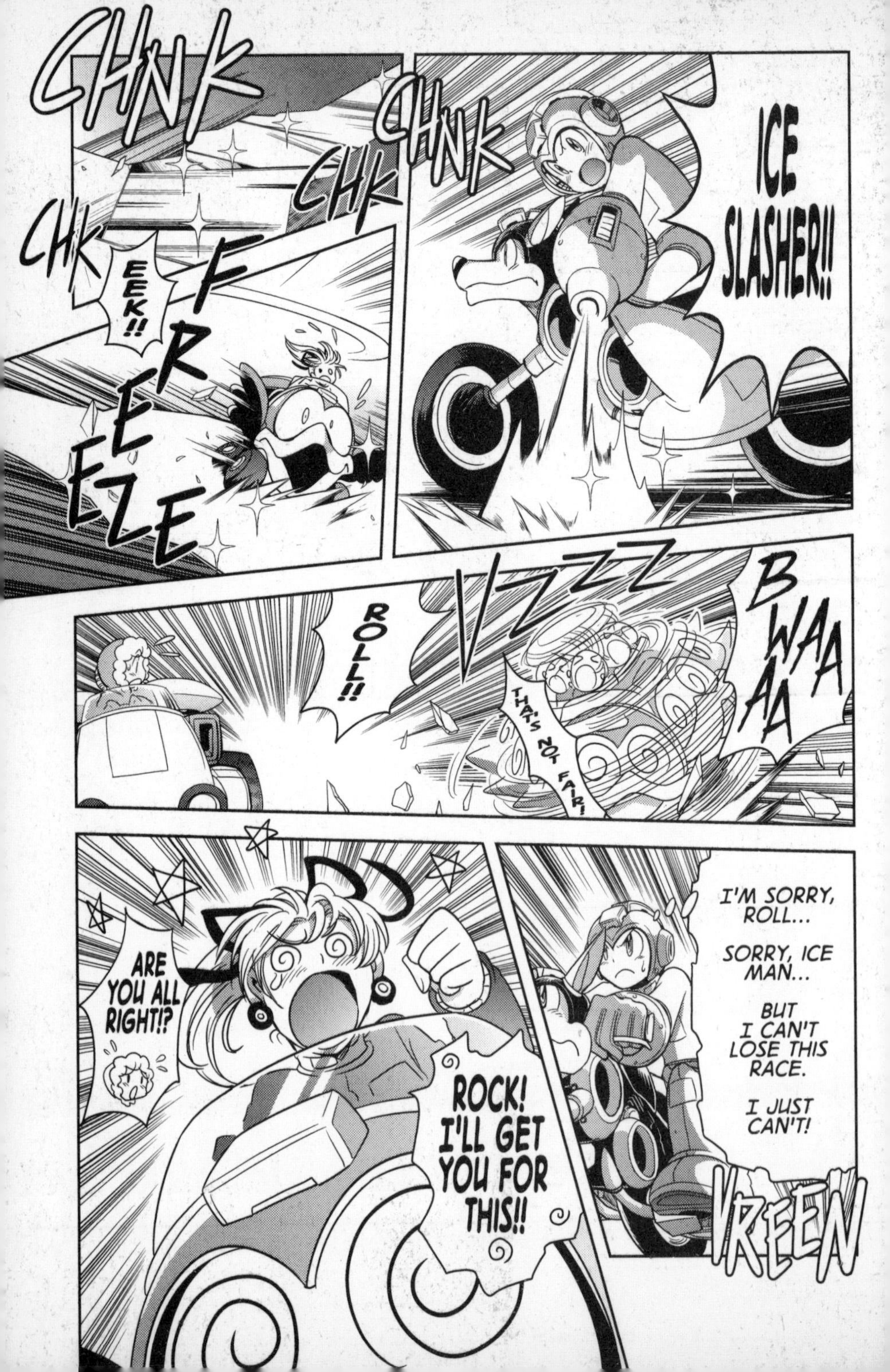
CHNK
ICE SLASHER!!
CHK
CHNK
CHK
EEK!!
FREEZE
BWAAAA
VZZZ
THAT'S NOT FAIR!
ROLL!!
I'M SORRY, ROLL...
SORRY, ICE MAN...
BUT I CAN'T LOSE THIS RACE.
I JUST CAN'T!
VREEN
ARE YOU ALL RIGHT!?
ROCK! I'LL GET YOU FOR THIS!!

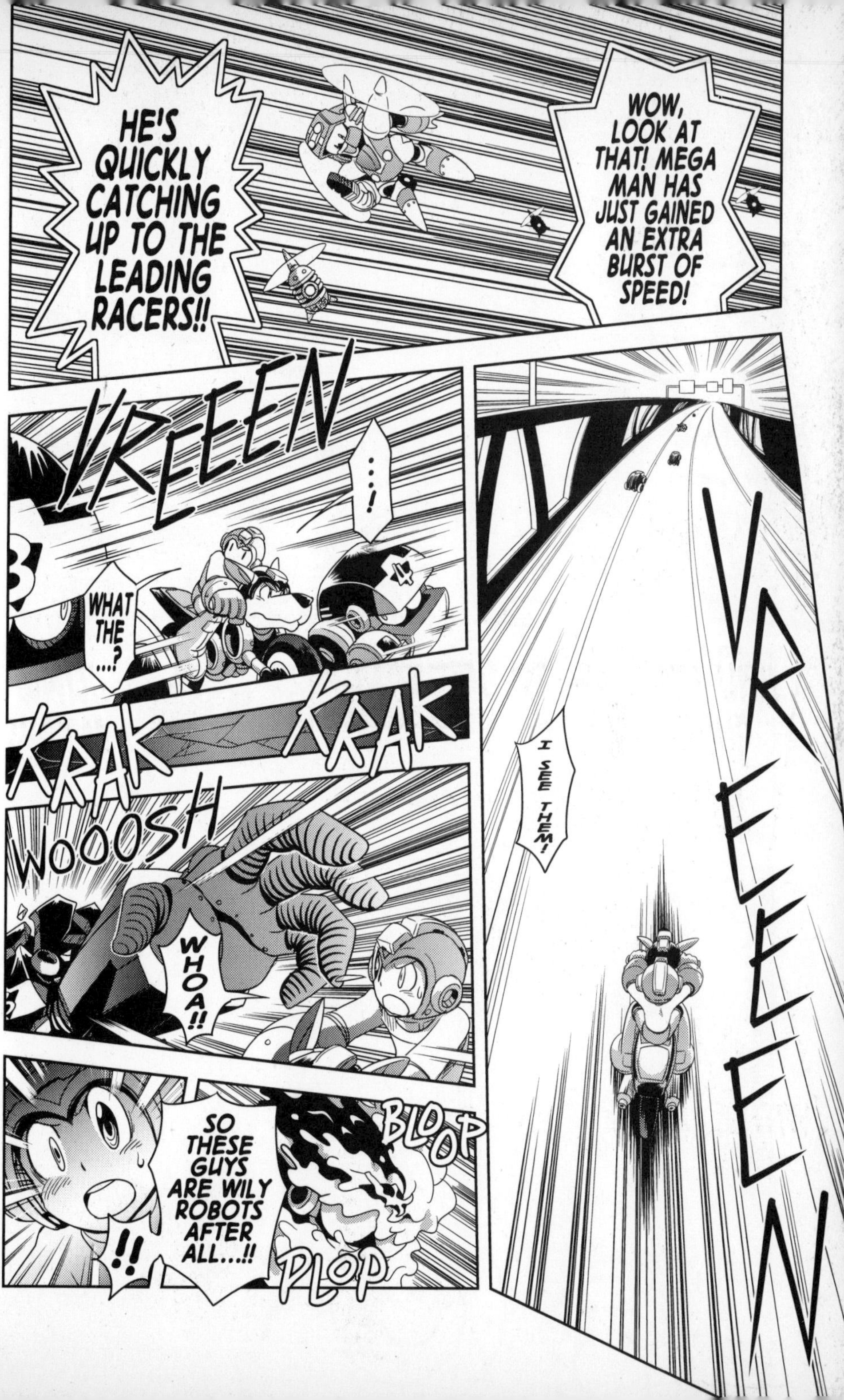
WOW, LOOK AT THAT! MEGA MAN HAS JUST GAINED AN EXTRA BURST OF SPEED!
HE'S QUICKLY CATCHING UP TO THE LEADING RACERS!!
VREEEEN
I SEE THEM!
VREEEEN
...!
WHAT THE ....?
KRAK
KRAK
WOOOSH
WHOA!!
BLOOP
PLOP
SO THESE GUYS ARE WILY ROBOTS AFTER ALL...!!
!!

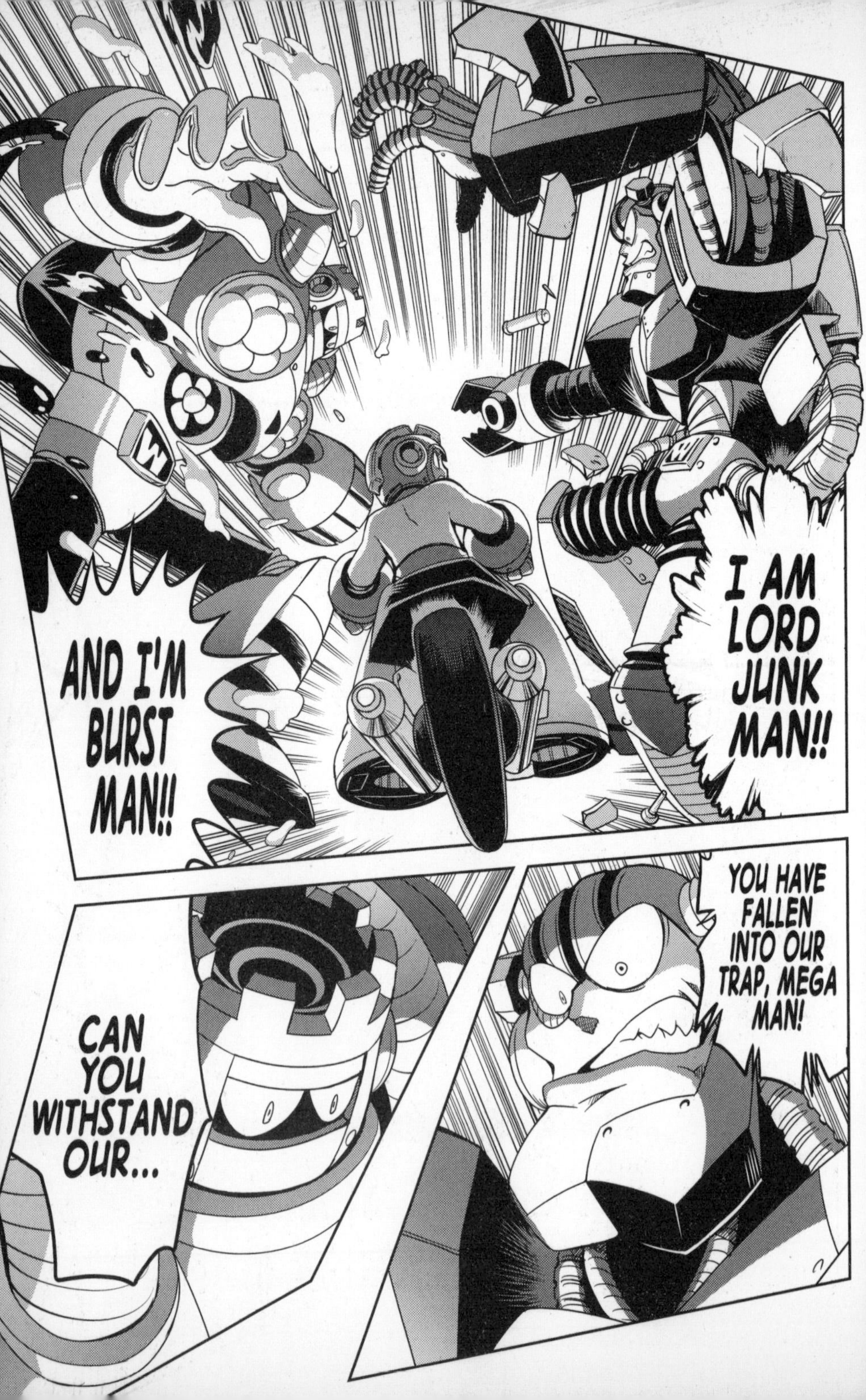
I AM LORD JUNK MAN!!
AND I'M BURST MAN!!
YOU HAVE FALLEN INTO OUR TRAP, MEGA MAN!
CAN YOU WITHSTAND OUR...

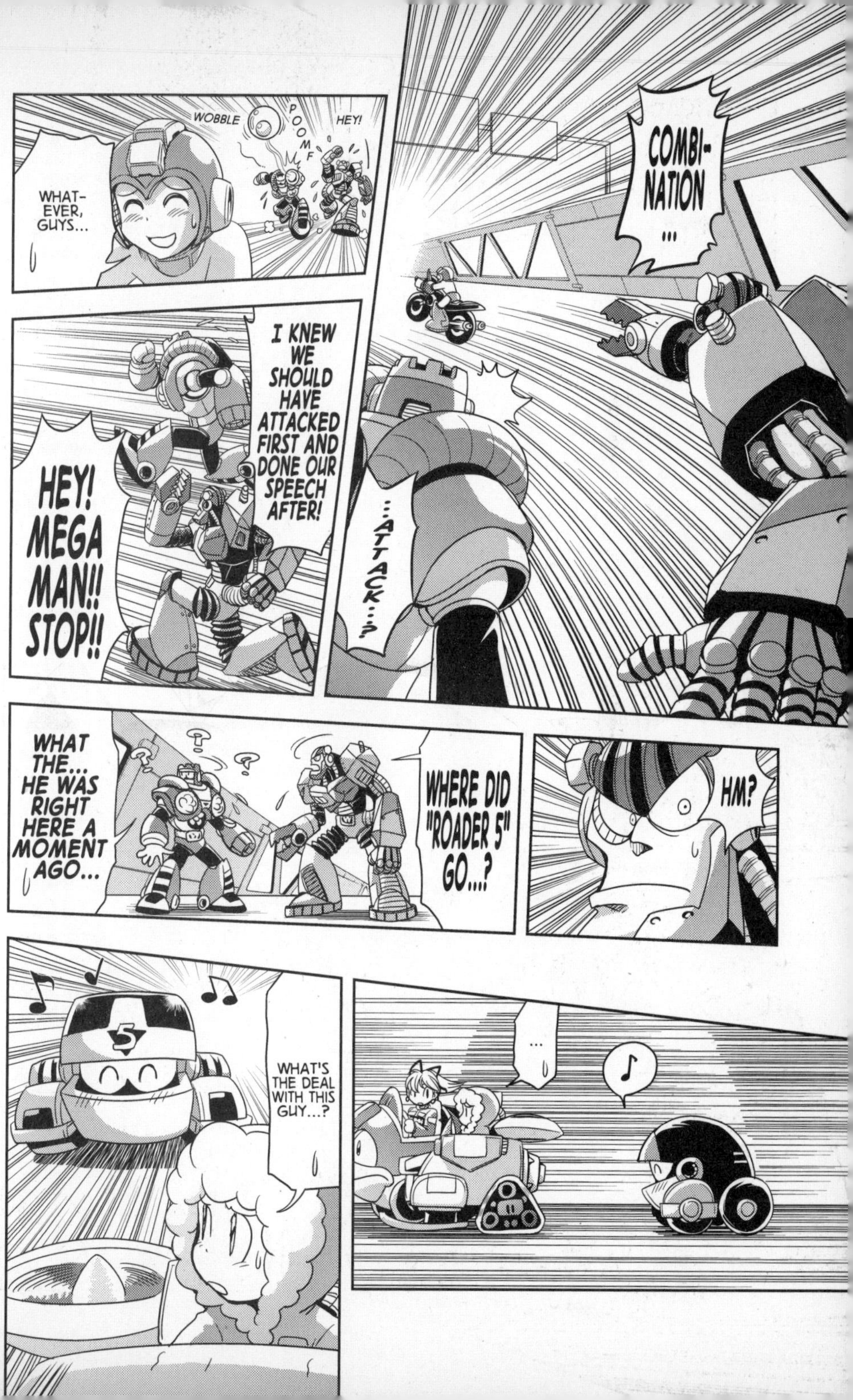
COMBI-NATION ...
...ATTACK...?
HEY!
POOMF
WOBBLE
WHAT-EVER, GUYS...
I KNEW WE SHOULD HAVE ATTACKED FIRST AND DONE OUR SPEECH AFTER!
HEY! MEGA MAN!! STOP!!
HM?
WHERE DID "ROADER 5" GO...?
WHAT THE... HE WAS RIGHT HERE A MOMENT AGO...
...
WHAT'S THE DEAL WITH THIS GUY...?

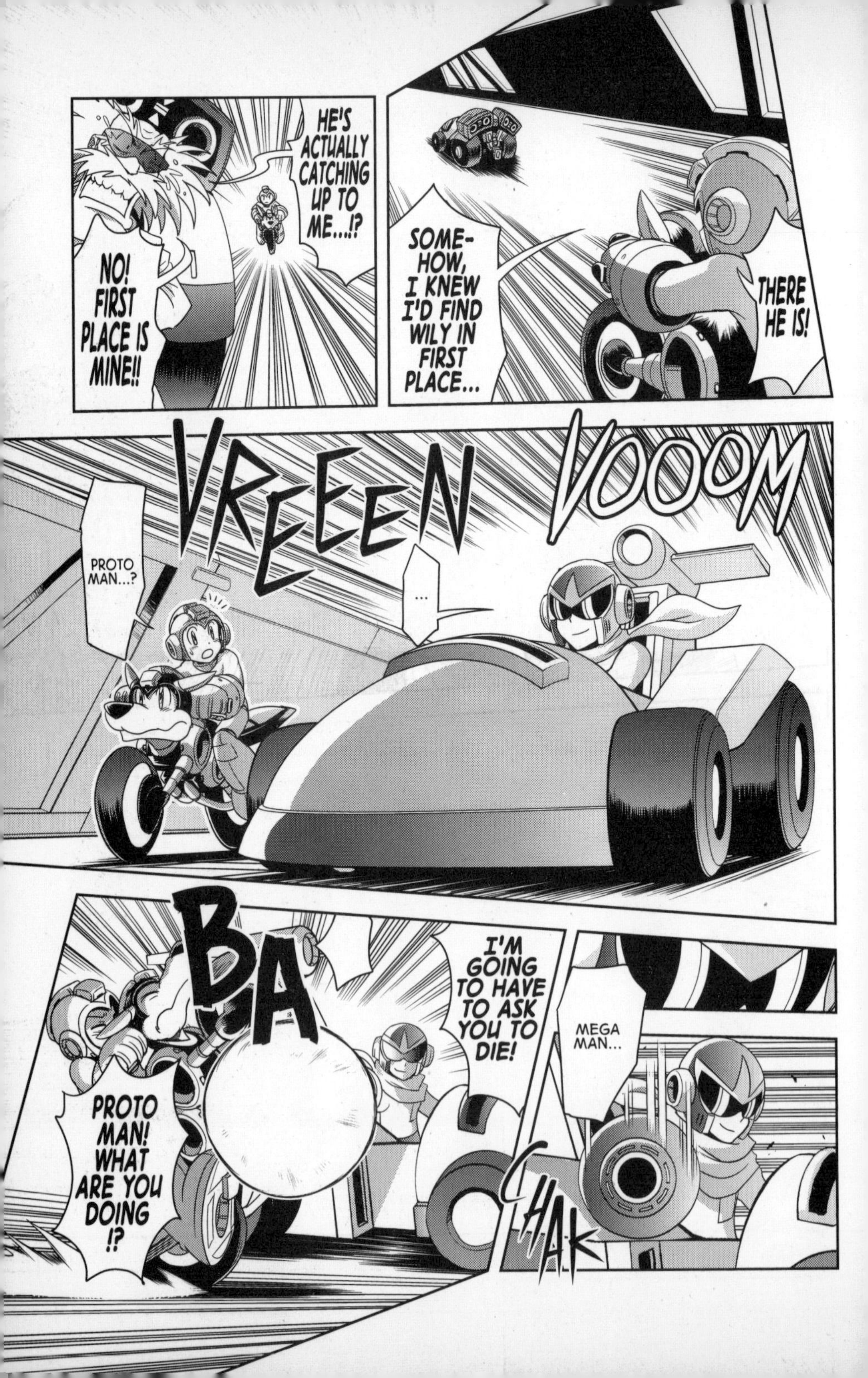
THERE HE IS!
SOME-HOW, I KNEW I'D FIND WILY IN FIRST PLACE...
HE'S ACTUALLY CATCHING UP TO ME...!?
NO! FIRST PLACE IS MINE!!
VOOOM
VREEEN
...
PROTO MAN...?
MEGA MAN...
I'M GOING TO HAVE TO ASK YOU TO DIE!
CHAK
BA
PROTO MAN! WHAT ARE YOU DOING!?

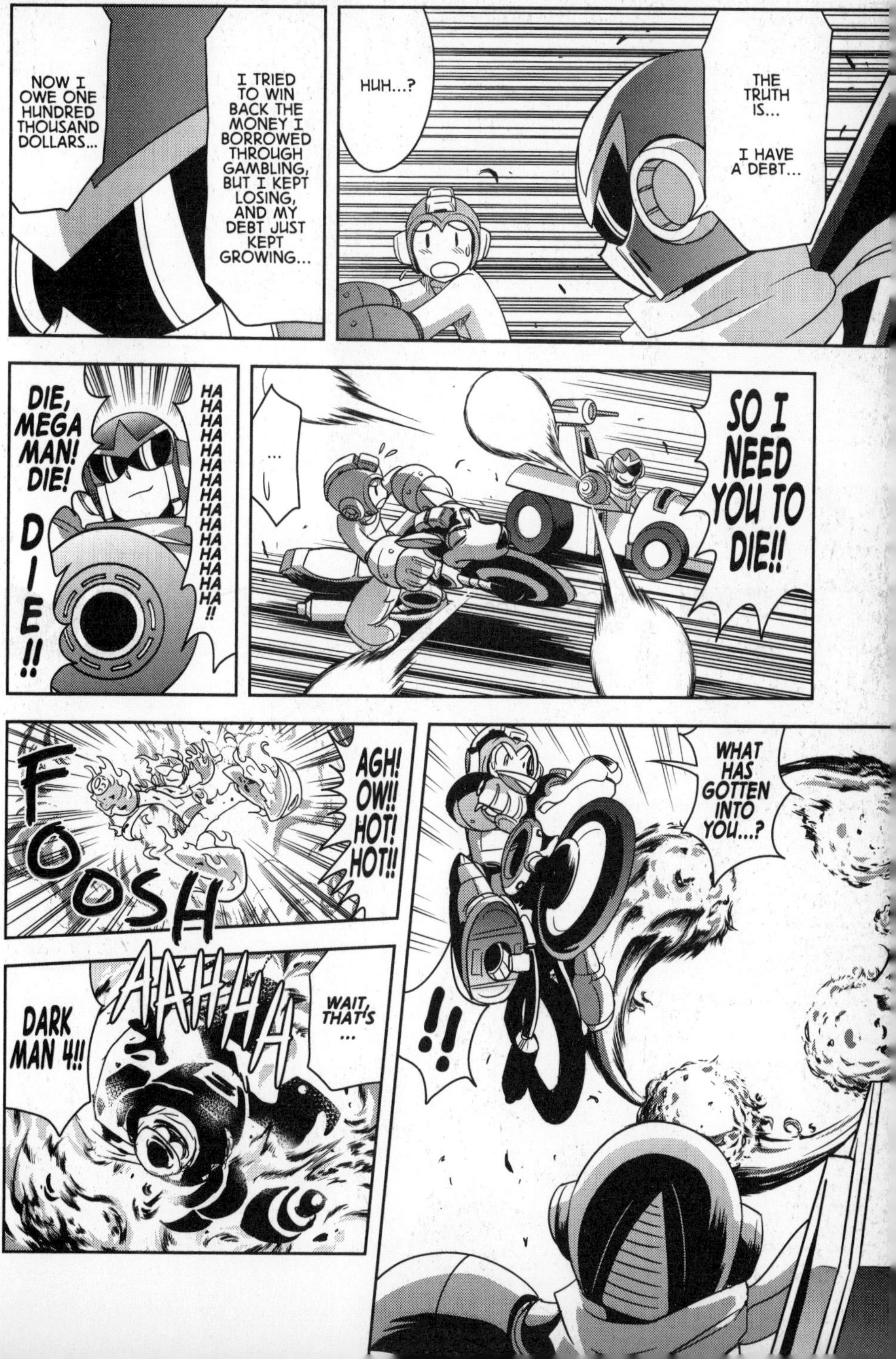
THE TRUTH IS...
I HAVE A DEBT...
HUH...?
I TRIED TO WIN BACK THE MONEY I BORROWED THROUGH GAMBLING, BUT I KEPT LOSING, AND MY DEBT JUST KEPT GROWING...
NOW I OWE ONE HUNDRED THOUSAND DOLLARS...
SO I NEED YOU TO DIE!!
...
HAHAHAHAHAHAHAHAHAHAHAHAHAHAHA!!
DIE, MEGA MAN! DIE!
DIE!!
WHAT HAS GOTTEN INTO YOU...?
!!
AGH! OW!! HOT! HOT!!
FOOSH
AAHHA
WAIT, THAT'S ...
DARK MAN 4!!

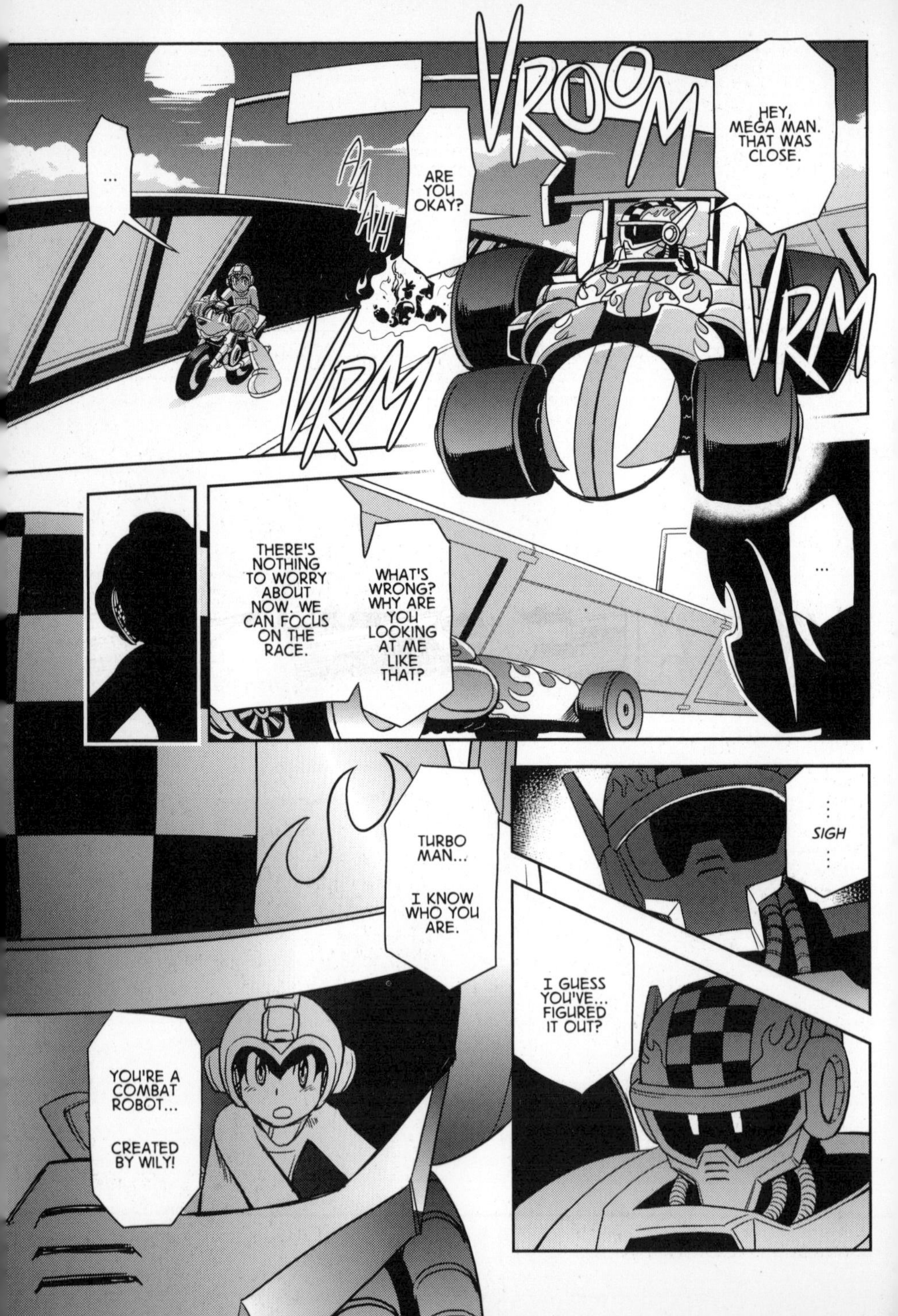
HEY, MEGA MAN. THAT WAS CLOSE.
VROOM
VRM
ARE YOU OKAY?
AAAAH
VRM
...
...
WHAT'S WRONG? WHY ARE YOU LOOKING AT ME LIKE THAT?
THERE'S NOTHING TO WORRY ABOUT NOW. WE CAN FOCUS ON THE RACE.
... SIGH ...
I GUESS YOU'VE... FIGURED IT OUT?
TURBO MAN...
I KNOW WHO YOU ARE.
YOU'RE A COMBAT ROBOT...
CREATED BY WILY!

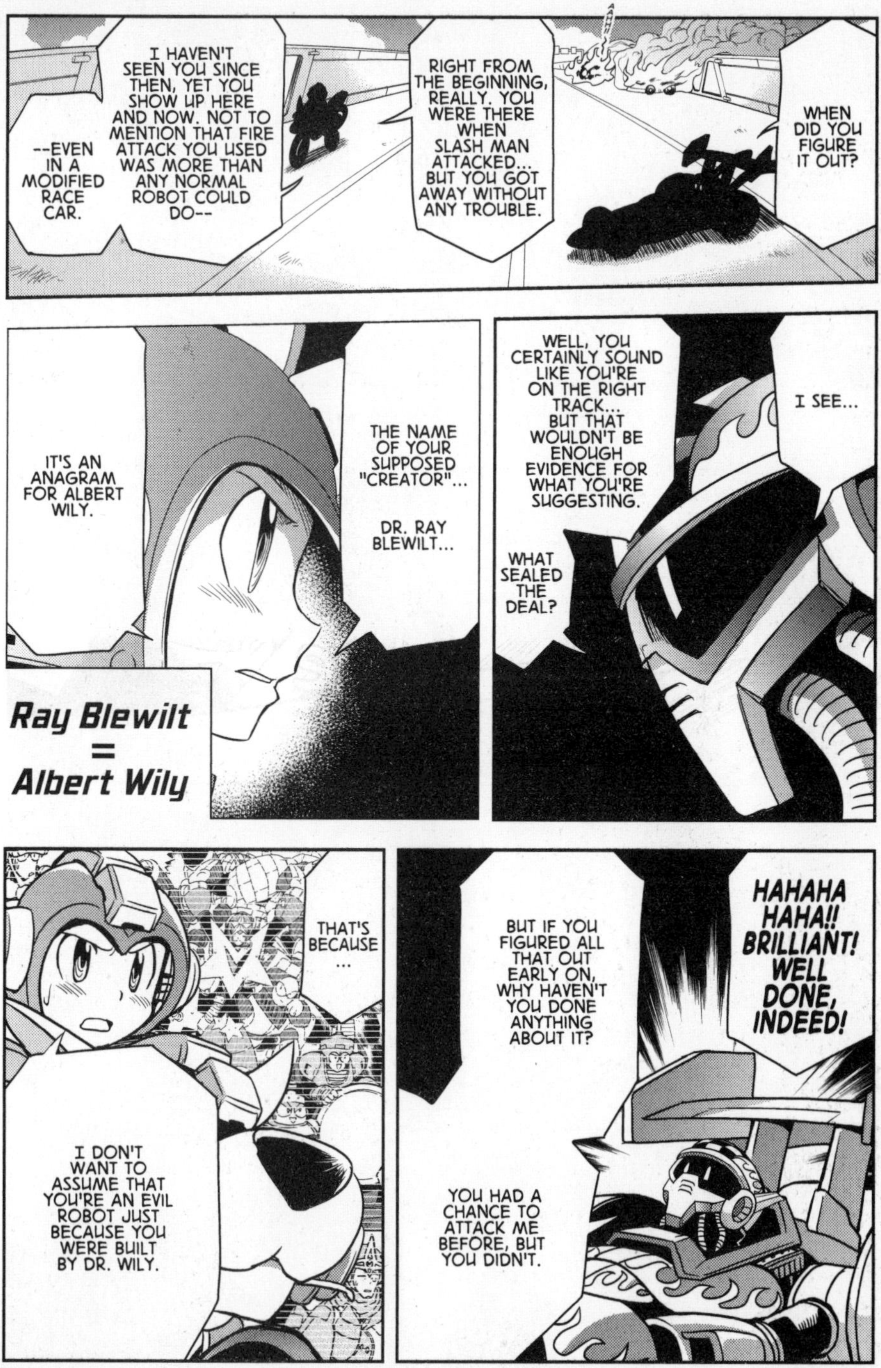
WHEN DID YOU FIGURE IT OUT?
RIGHT FROM THE BEGINNING, REALLY. YOU WERE THERE WHEN SLASH MAN ATTACKED... BUT YOU GOT AWAY WITHOUT ANY TROUBLE.
I HAVEN'T SEEN YOU SINCE THEN, YET YOU SHOW UP HERE AND NOW. NOT TO MENTION THAT FIRE ATTACK YOU USED WAS MORE THAN ANY NORMAL ROBOT COULD DO--
--EVEN IN A MODIFIED RACE CAR.
I SEE...
WELL, YOU CERTAINLY SOUND LIKE YOU'RE ON THE RIGHT TRACK... BUT THAT WOULDN'T BE ENOUGH EVIDENCE FOR WHAT YOU'RE SUGGESTING.
WHAT SEALED THE DEAL?
THE NAME OF YOUR SUPPOSED "CREATOR"...
DR. RAY BLEWILT...
IT'S AN ANAGRAM FOR ALBERT WILY.
Ray Blewilt = Albert Wily
HAHAHA HAHA!! BRILLIANT! WELL DONE, INDEED!
BUT IF YOU FIGURED ALL THAT OUT EARLY ON, WHY HAVEN'T YOU DONE ANYTHING ABOUT IT?
YOU HAD A CHANCE TO ATTACK ME BEFORE, BUT YOU DIDN'T.
THAT'S BECAUSE ...
I DON'T WANT TO ASSUME THAT YOU'RE AN EVIL ROBOT JUST BECAUSE YOU WERE BUILT BY DR. WILY.

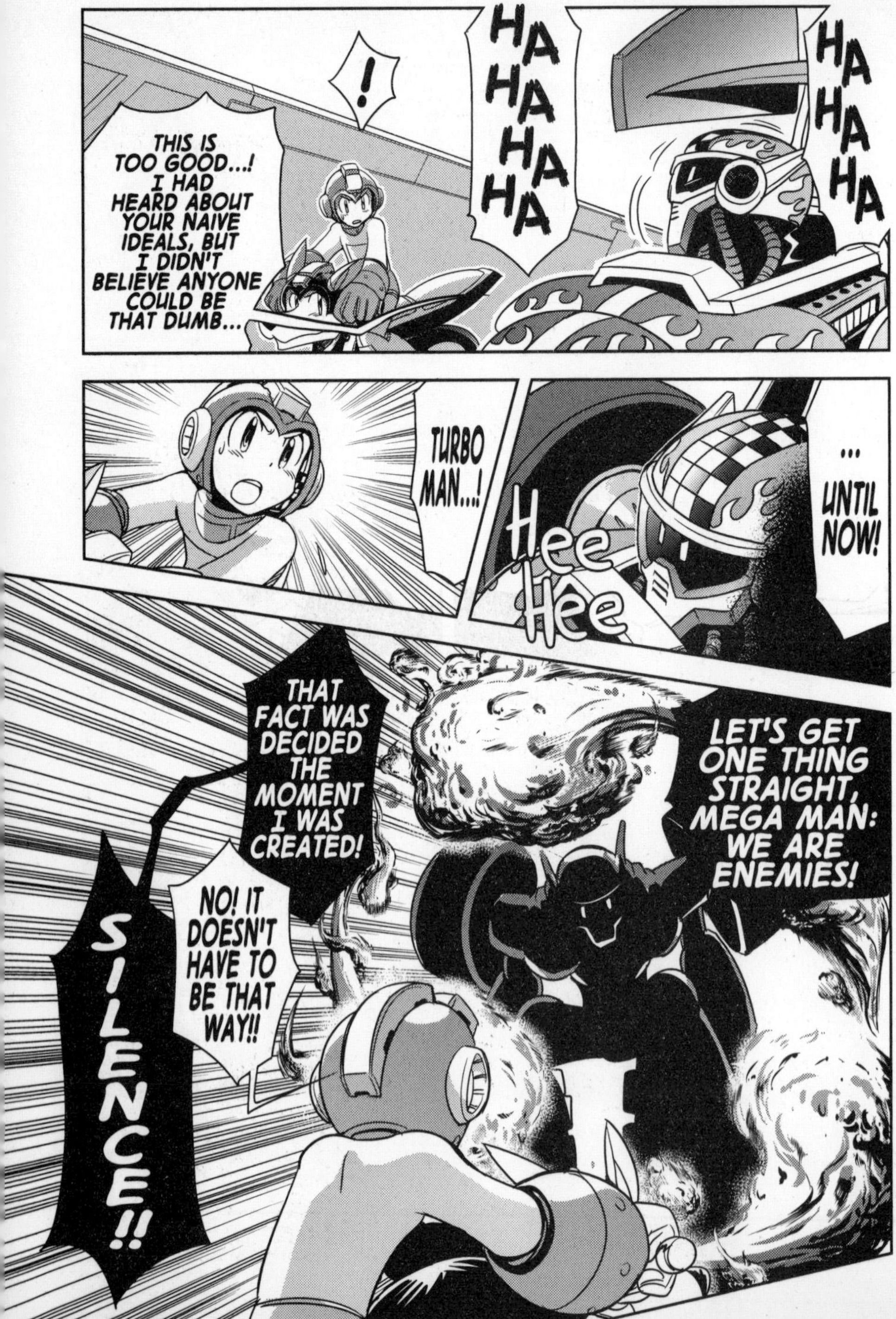
HA HA HA HA HA
HA HA HA HA HA
!
THIS IS TOO GOOD...! I HAD HEARD ABOUT YOUR NAIVE IDEALS, BUT I DIDN'T BELIEVE ANYONE COULD BE THAT DUMB...
... UNTIL NOW!
Hee Hee
TURBO MAN...!
LET'S GET ONE THING STRAIGHT, MEGA MAN: WE ARE ENEMIES!
THAT FACT WAS DECIDED THE MOMENT I WAS CREATED!
NO! IT DOESN'T HAVE TO BE THAT WAY!!
SILENCE!!

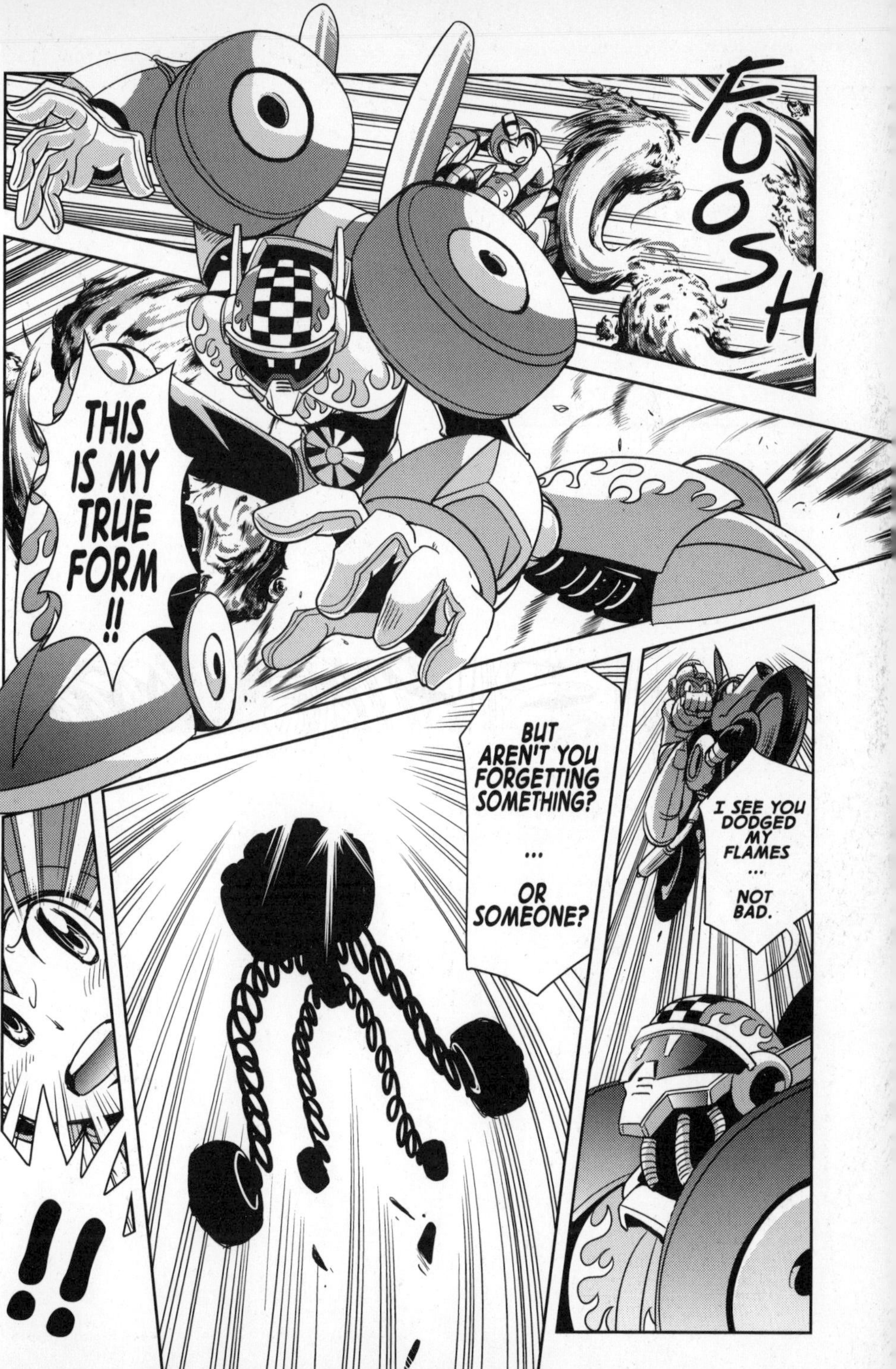
FOOSH
THIS IS MY TRUE FORM !!
I SEE YOU DODGED MY FLAMES ... NOT BAD.
BUT AREN'T YOU FORGETTING SOMETHING? ... OR SOMEONE?
!!

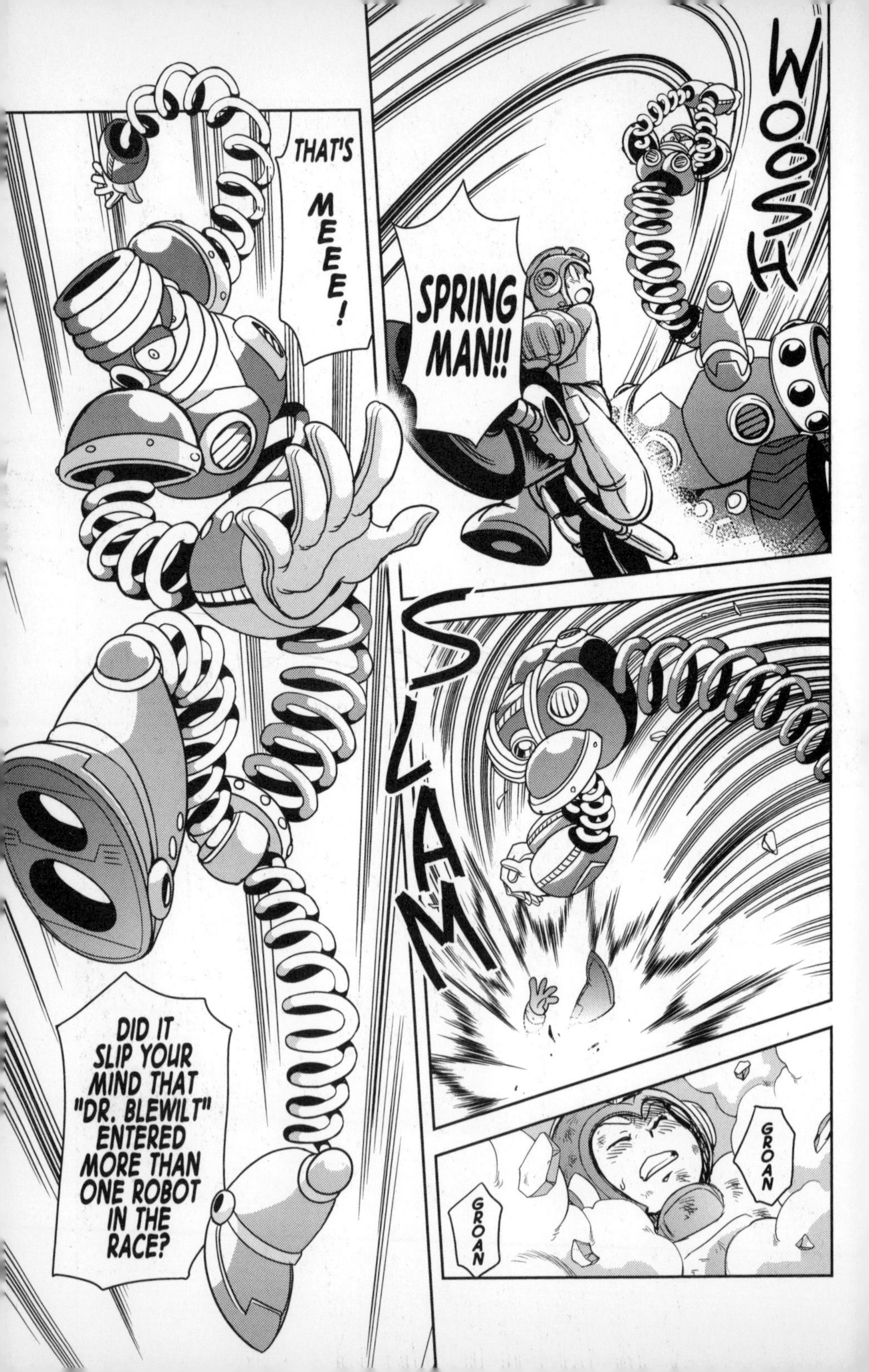
WOOSH
SPRING MAN!!
SLAM
GROAN
GROAN
THAT'S MEEE!
DID IT SLIP YOUR MIND THAT "DR. BLEWILT" ENTERED MORE THAN ONE ROBOT IN THE RACE?

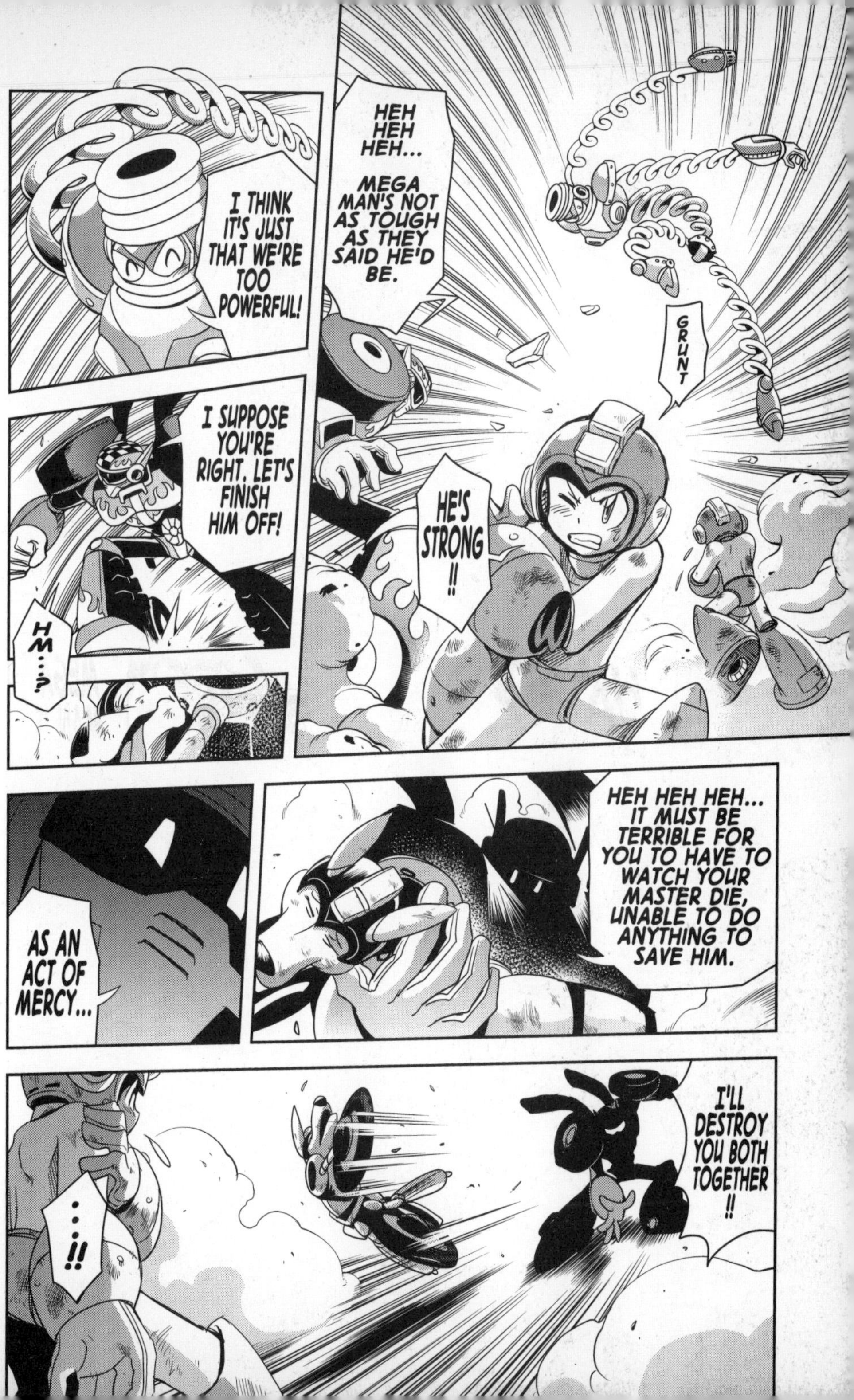
HEH HEH HEH... MEGA MAN'S NOT AS TOUGH AS THEY SAID HE'D BE.
GRUNT
HE'S STRONG!!
I THINK IT'S JUST THAT WE'RE TOO POWERFUL!
I SUPPOSE YOU'RE RIGHT. LET'S FINISH HIM OFF!
HM...?
HEH HEH HEH... IT MUST BE TERRIBLE FOR YOU TO HAVE TO WATCH YOUR MASTER DIE, UNABLE TO DO ANYTHING TO SAVE HIM.
AS AN ACT OF MERCY...
I'LL DESTROY YOU BOTH TOGETHER!!
...!!

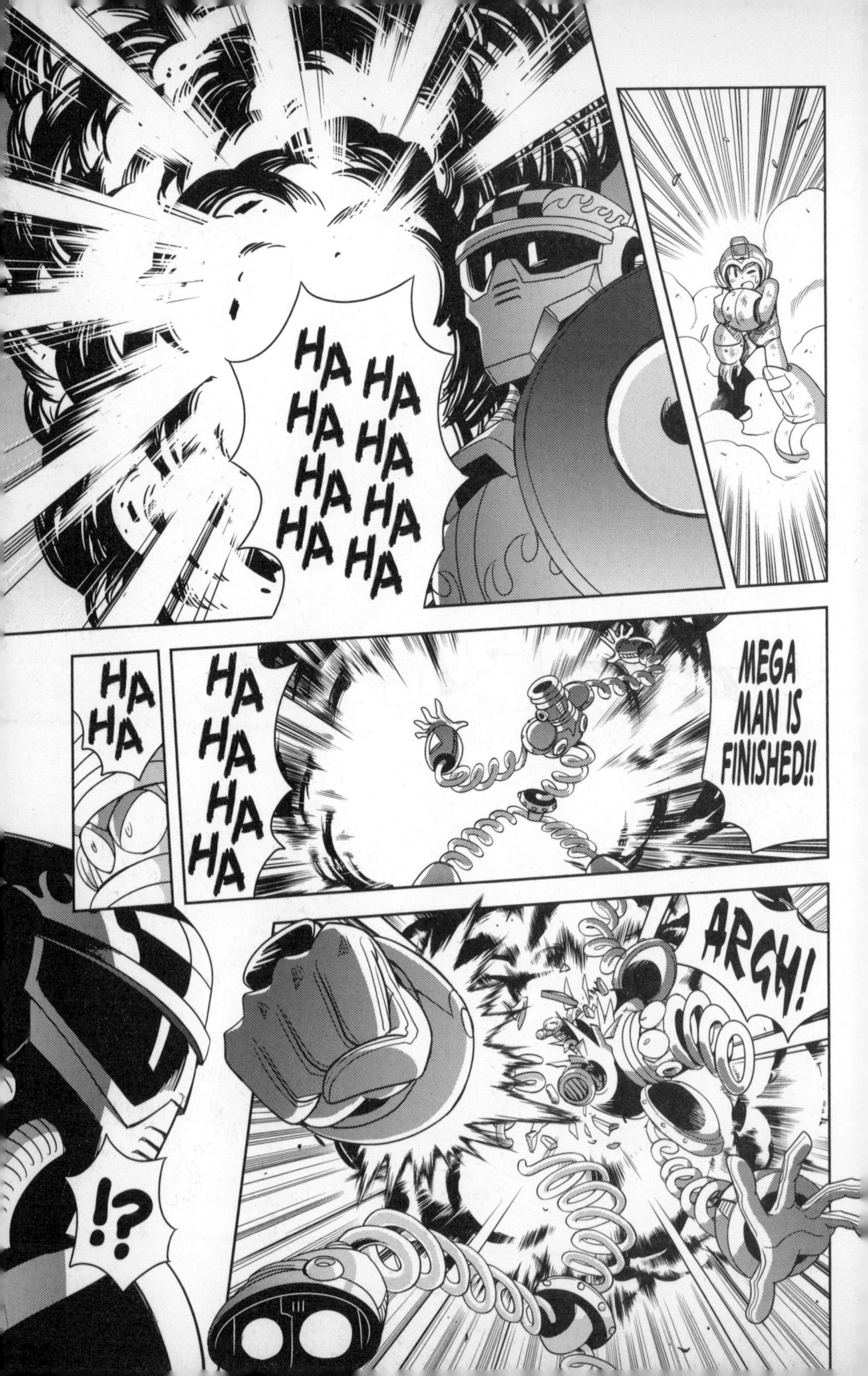
HA HA HA HA HA HA HA HA
MEGA MAN IS FINISHED!!
HA HA HA HA HA
HA HA
ARGH!
!?

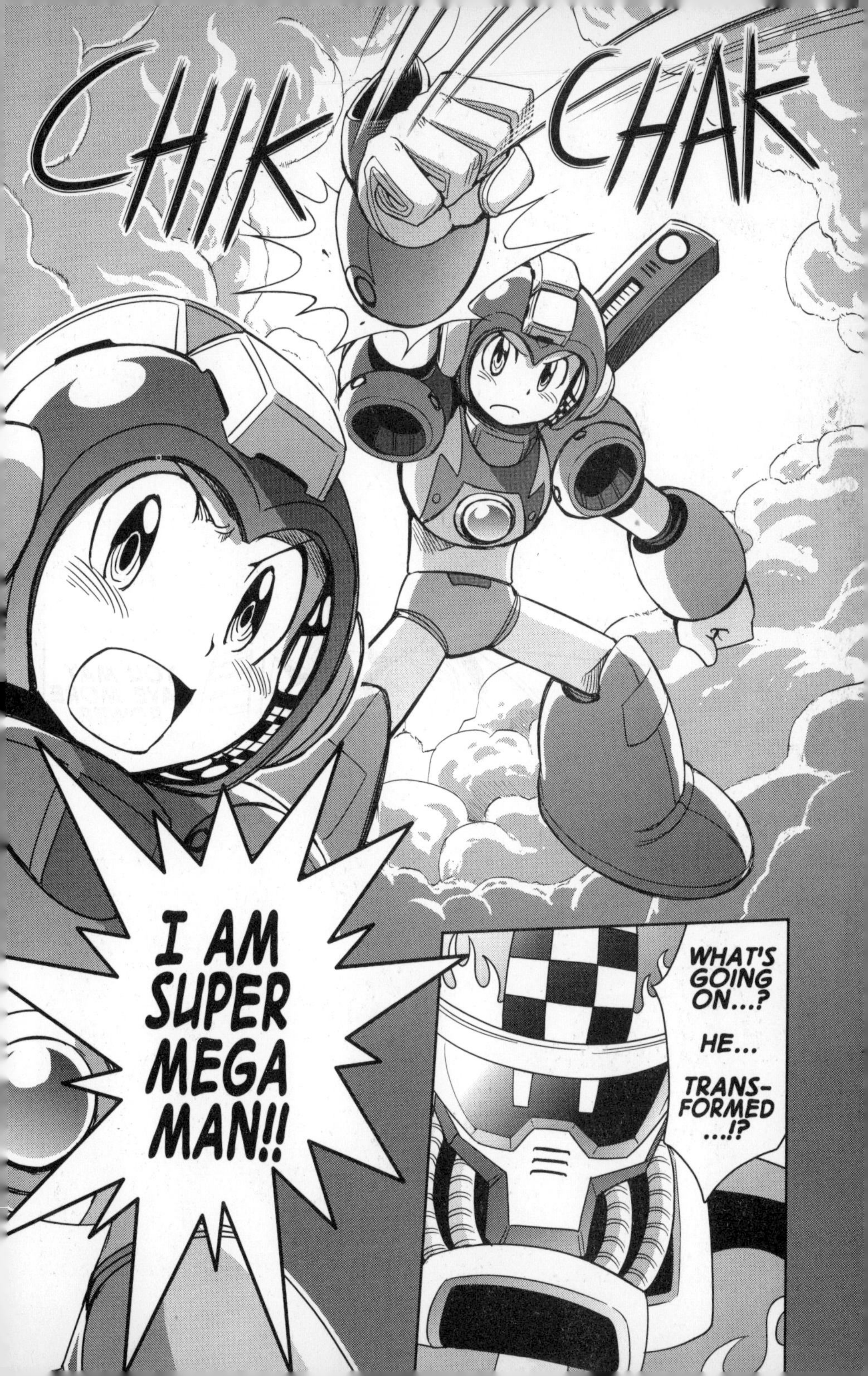
CHIK CHAK
I AM SUPER MEGA MAN!!
WHAT'S GOING ON...?
HE...
TRANS-FORMED ...!?

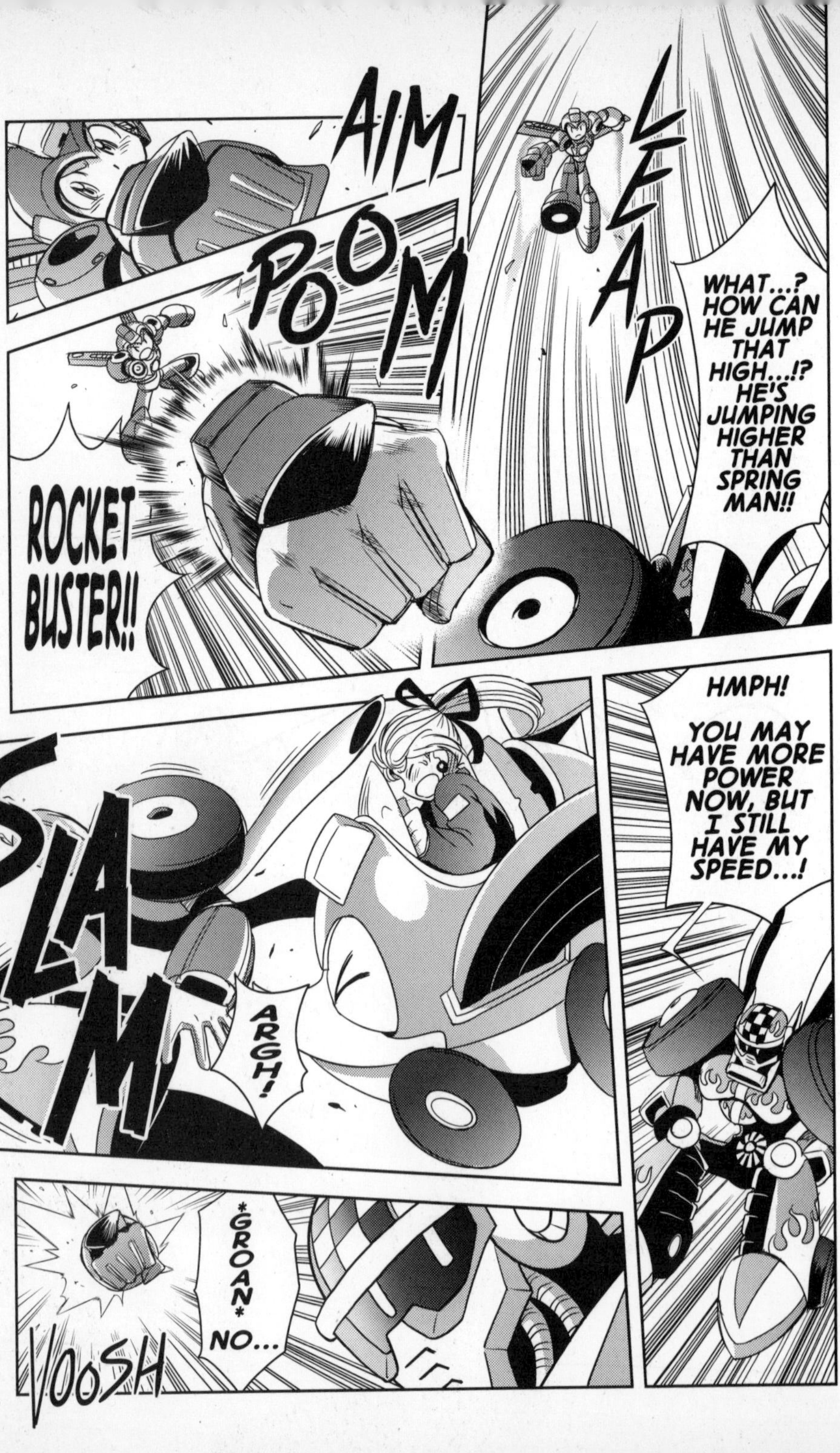
LEAP
WHAT...? HOW CAN HE JUMP THAT HIGH...!? HE'S JUMPING HIGHER THAN SPRING MAN!!
AIM
POOM
ROCKET BUSTER!!
HMPH!
YOU MAY HAVE MORE POWER NOW, BUT I STILL HAVE MY SPEED...!
SLAM
ARGH!
GROAN NO...
VOOSH

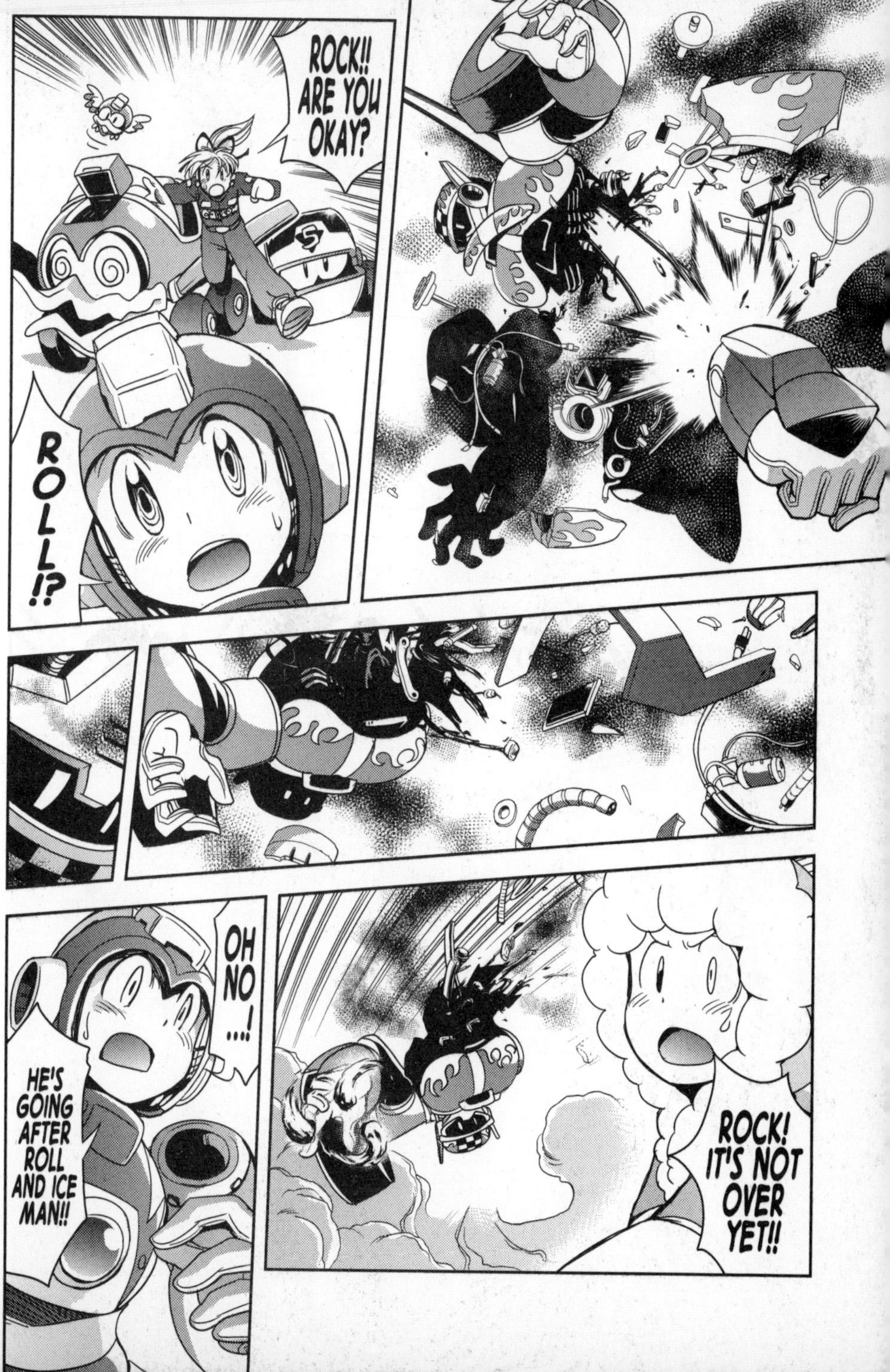
ROCK!! ARE YOU OKAY?
ROLL!?
ROCK! IT'S NOT OVER YET!!
OH NO ...!
HE'S GOING AFTER ROLL AND ICE MAN!!

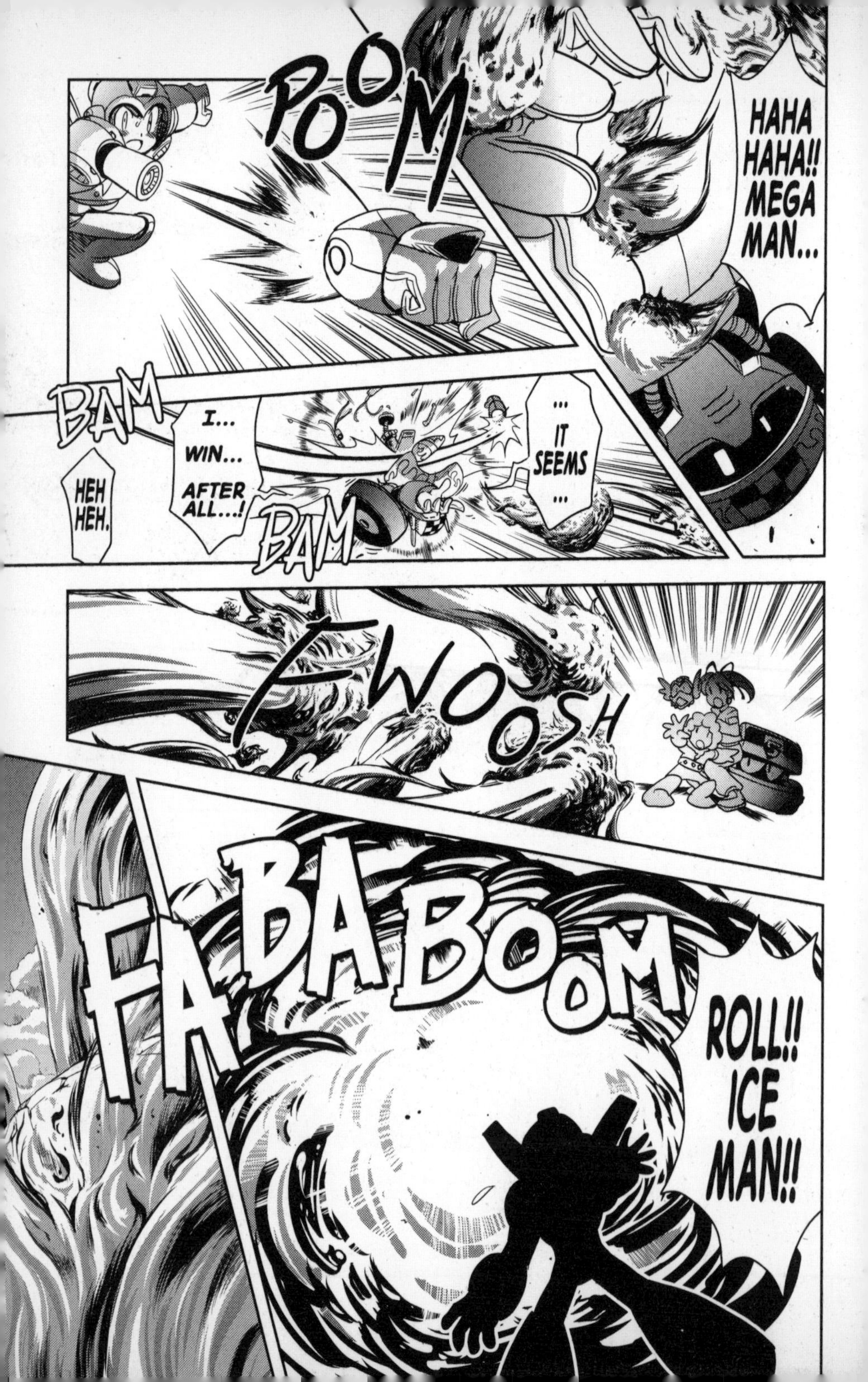
HAHA HAHA!! MEGA MAN...
POOM
... IT SEEMS ...
I... WIN... AFTER ALL...!
BAM
HEH HEH.
BAM
FWOOSH
ROLL!! ICE MAN!!
FABABOOM

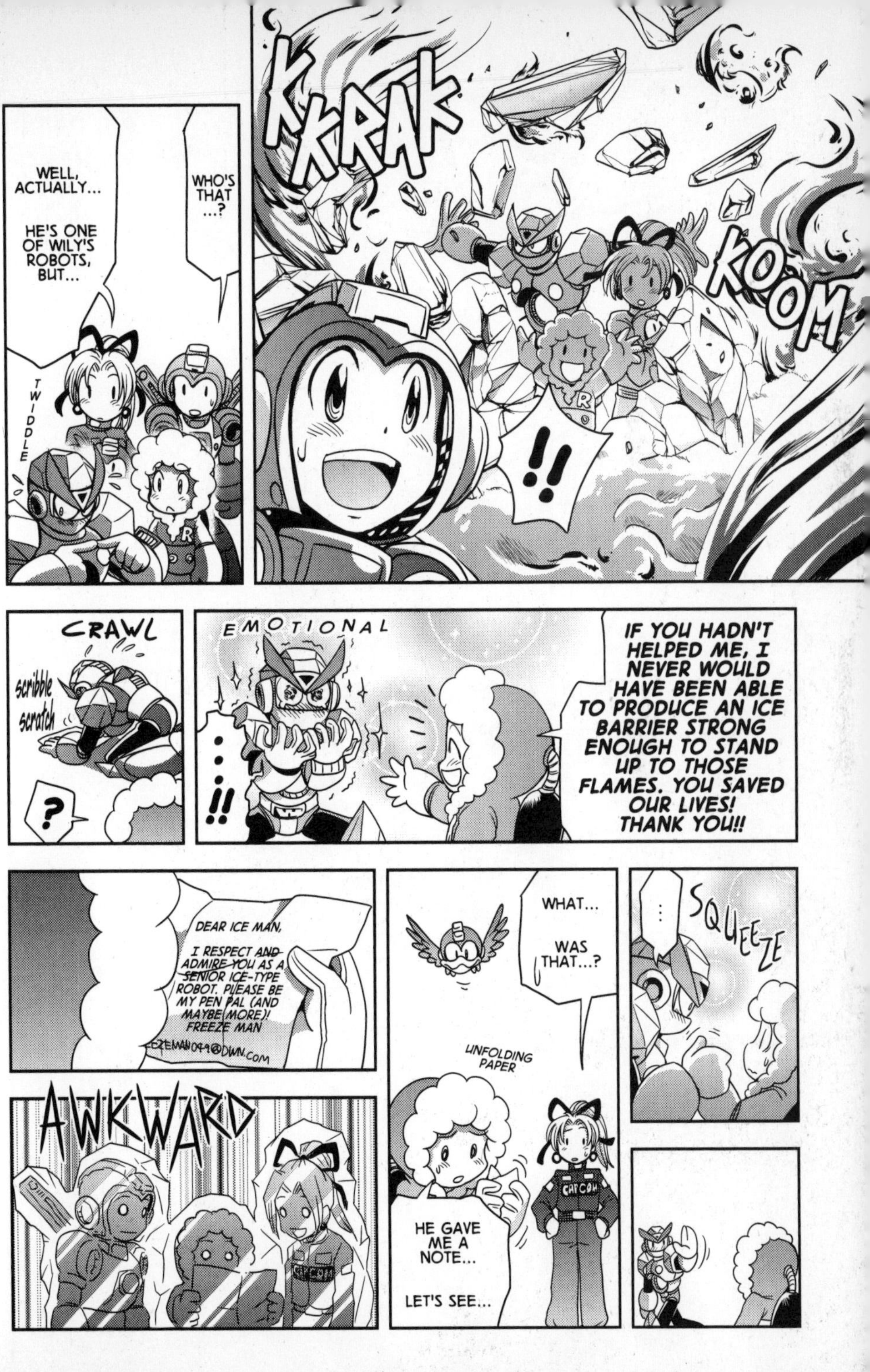
KKRAK
KOOM
!!
WHO'S THAT ...?
WELL, ACTUALLY...
HE'S ONE OF WILY'S ROBOTS, BUT...
TWIDDLE
IF YOU HADN'T HELPED ME, I NEVER WOULD HAVE BEEN ABLE TO PRODUCE AN ICE BARRIER STRONG ENOUGH TO STAND UP TO THOSE FLAMES. YOU SAVED OUR LIVES! THANK YOU!!
EMOTIONAL
...!!
CRAWL
scribble scratch
?
...
SQUEEZE
WHAT...
WAS THAT...?
UNFOLDING PAPER
HE GAVE ME A NOTE...
LET'S SEE...
DEAR ICE MAN,
I RESPECT AND ADMIRE YOU AS A SENIOR ICE-TYPE ROBOT. PLEASE BE MY PEN PAL (AND MAYBE MORE)!
FREEZE MAN
EZEMAN049@DWN.COM
AWKWARD

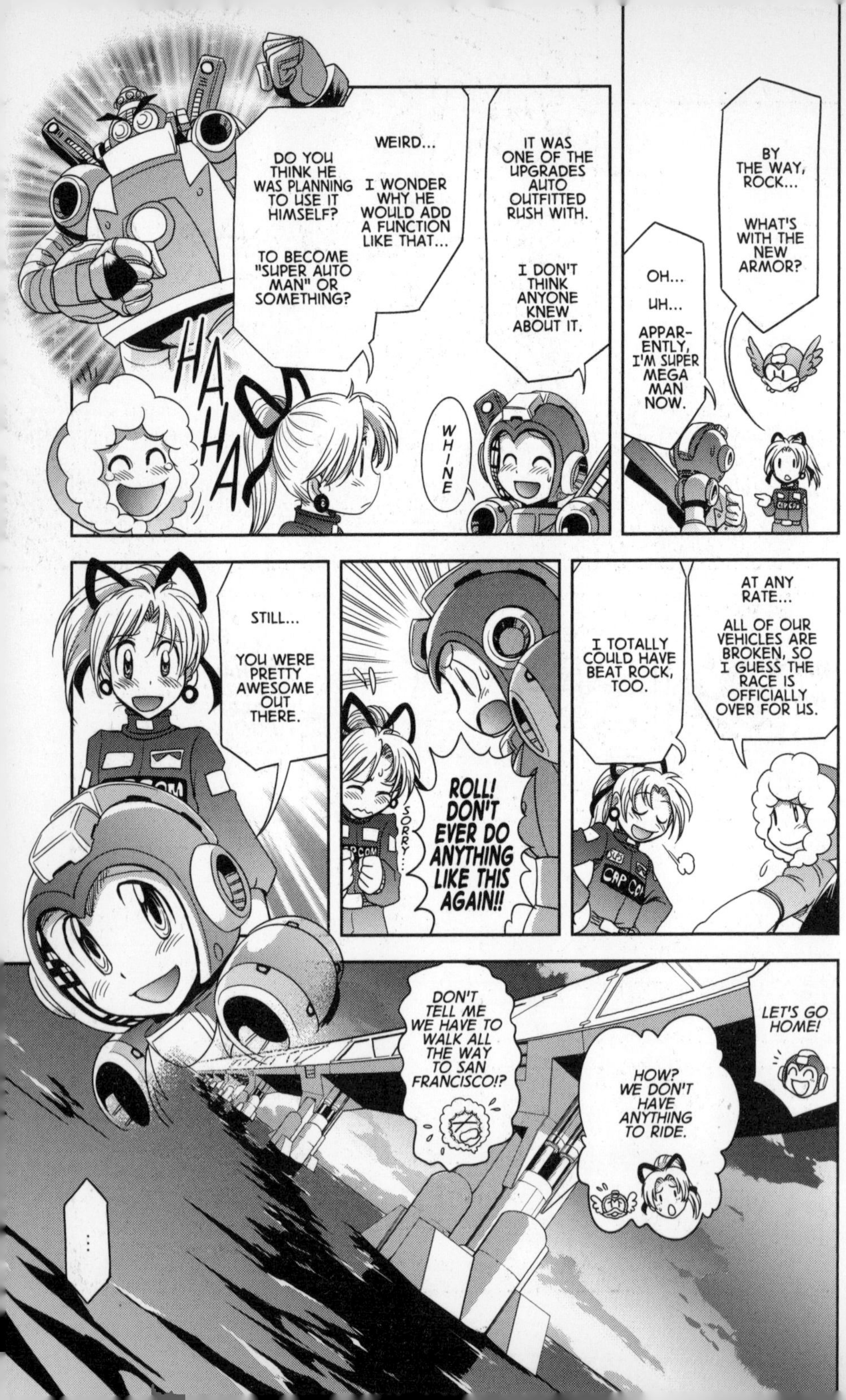
BY THE WAY, ROCK... WHAT'S WITH THE NEW ARMOR?
OH... UH... APPARENTLY, I'M SUPER MEGA MAN NOW.
IT WAS ONE OF THE UPGRADES AUTO OUTFITTED RUSH WITH. I DON'T THINK ANYONE KNEW ABOUT IT.
WHINE
WEIRD... I WONDER WHY HE WOULD ADD A FUNCTION LIKE THAT...
DO YOU THINK HE WAS PLANNING TO USE IT HIMSELF? TO BECOME "SUPER AUTO MAN" OR SOMETHING?
HAHAHA
AT ANY RATE... ALL OF OUR VEHICLES ARE BROKEN, SO I GUESS THE RACE IS OFFICIALLY OVER FOR US.
I TOTALLY COULD HAVE BEAT ROCK, TOO.
ROLL! DON'T EVER DO ANYTHING LIKE THIS AGAIN!!
SORRY...
STILL... YOU WERE PRETTY AWESOME OUT THERE.
LET'S GO HOME!
HOW? WE DON'T HAVE ANYTHING TO RIDE.
DON'T TELL ME WE HAVE TO WALK ALL THE WAY TO SAN FRANCISCO!?
...

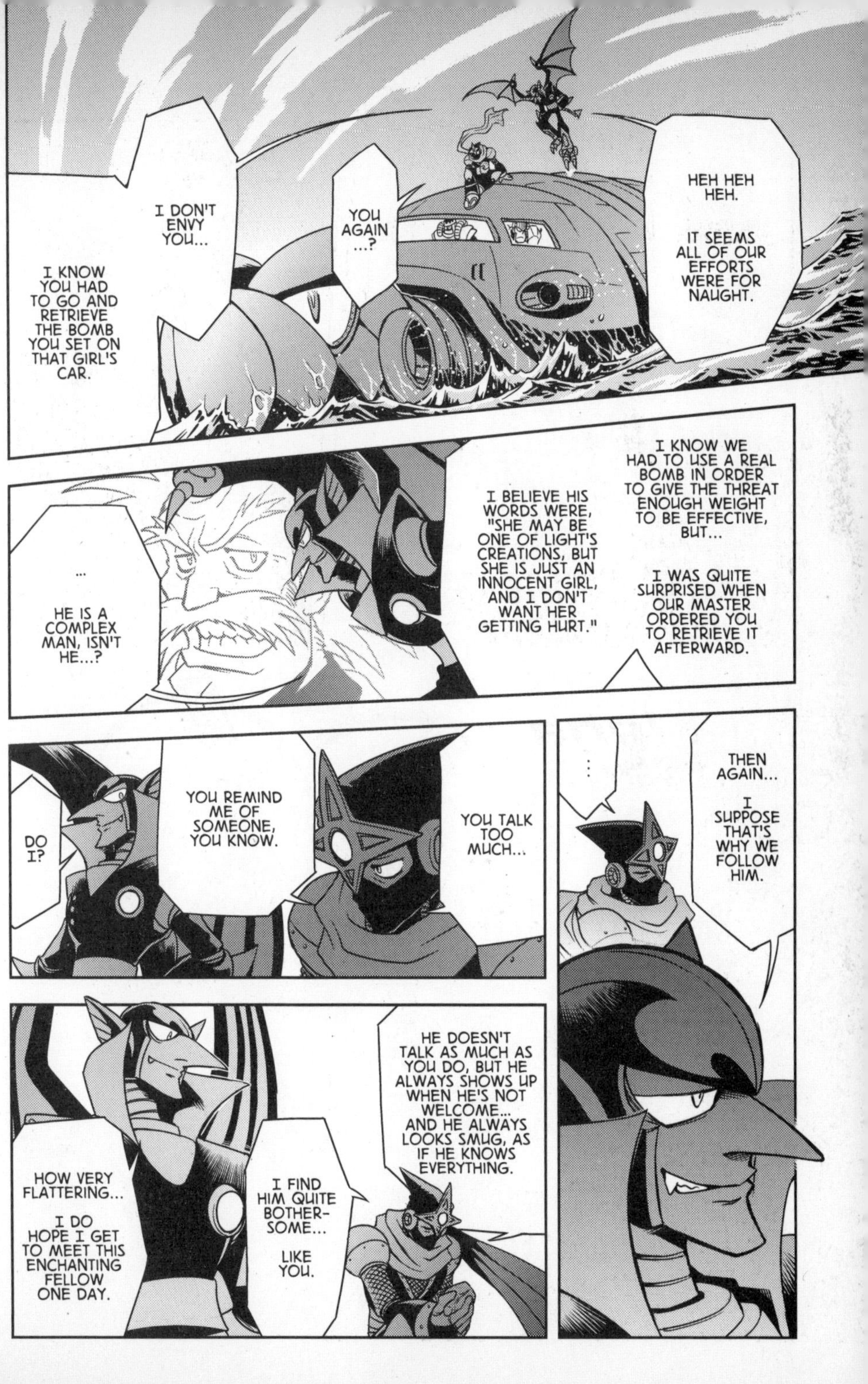
HEH HEH HEH.
IT SEEMS ALL OF OUR EFFORTS WERE FOR NAUGHT.
YOU AGAIN ...?
I DON'T ENVY YOU...
I KNOW YOU HAD TO GO AND RETRIEVE THE BOMB YOU SET ON THAT GIRL'S CAR.
I KNOW WE HAD TO USE A REAL BOMB IN ORDER TO GIVE THE THREAT ENOUGH WEIGHT TO BE EFFECTIVE, BUT...
I WAS QUITE SURPRISED WHEN OUR MASTER ORDERED YOU TO RETRIEVE IT AFTERWARD.
I BELIEVE HIS WORDS WERE, "SHE MAY BE ONE OF LIGHT'S CREATIONS, BUT SHE IS JUST AN INNOCENT GIRL, AND I DON'T WANT HER GETTING HURT."
...
HE IS A COMPLEX MAN, ISN'T HE...?
THEN AGAIN...
I SUPPOSE THAT'S WHY WE FOLLOW HIM.
...
YOU TALK TOO MUCH...
YOU REMIND ME OF SOMEONE, YOU KNOW.
DO I?
HE DOESN'T TALK AS MUCH AS YOU DO, BUT HE ALWAYS SHOWS UP WHEN HE'S NOT WELCOME... AND HE ALWAYS LOOKS SMUG, AS IF HE KNOWS EVERYTHING.
I FIND HIM QUITE BOTHER-SOME...
LIKE YOU.
HOW VERY FLATTERING...
I DO HOPE I GET TO MEET THIS ENCHANTING FELLOW ONE DAY.

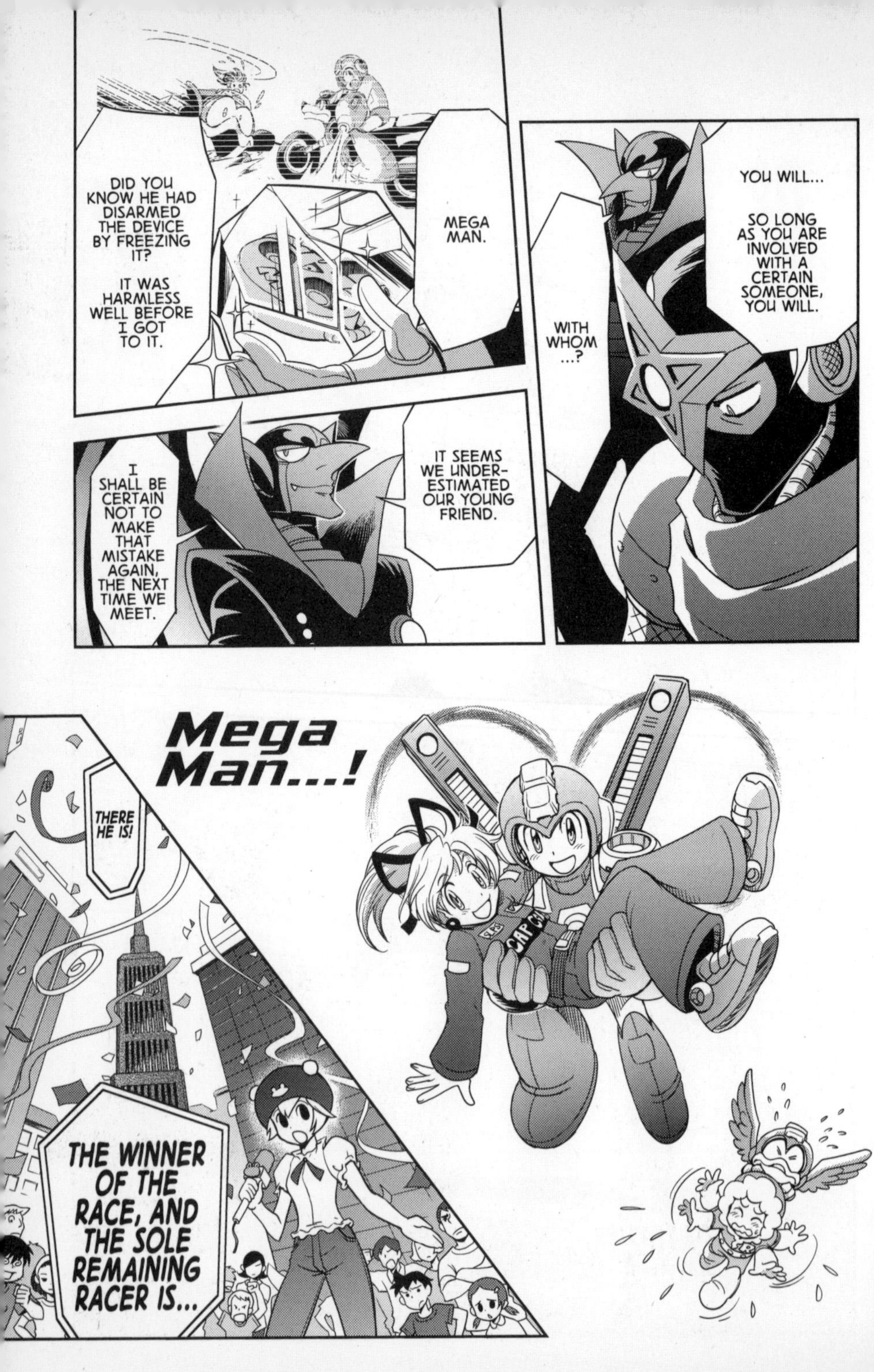
MEGA MAN.
DID YOU KNOW HE HAD DISARMED THE DEVICE BY FREEZING IT?
IT WAS HARMLESS WELL BEFORE I GOT TO IT.
IT SEEMS WE UNDER-ESTIMATED OUR YOUNG FRIEND.
I SHALL BE CERTAIN NOT TO MAKE THAT MISTAKE AGAIN, THE NEXT TIME WE MEET.
YOU WILL...
SO LONG AS YOU ARE INVOLVED WITH A CERTAIN SOMEONE, YOU WILL.
WITH WHOM ...?
THE WINNER OF THE RACE, AND THE SOLE REMAINING RACER IS...
THERE HE IS!
Mega Man...!

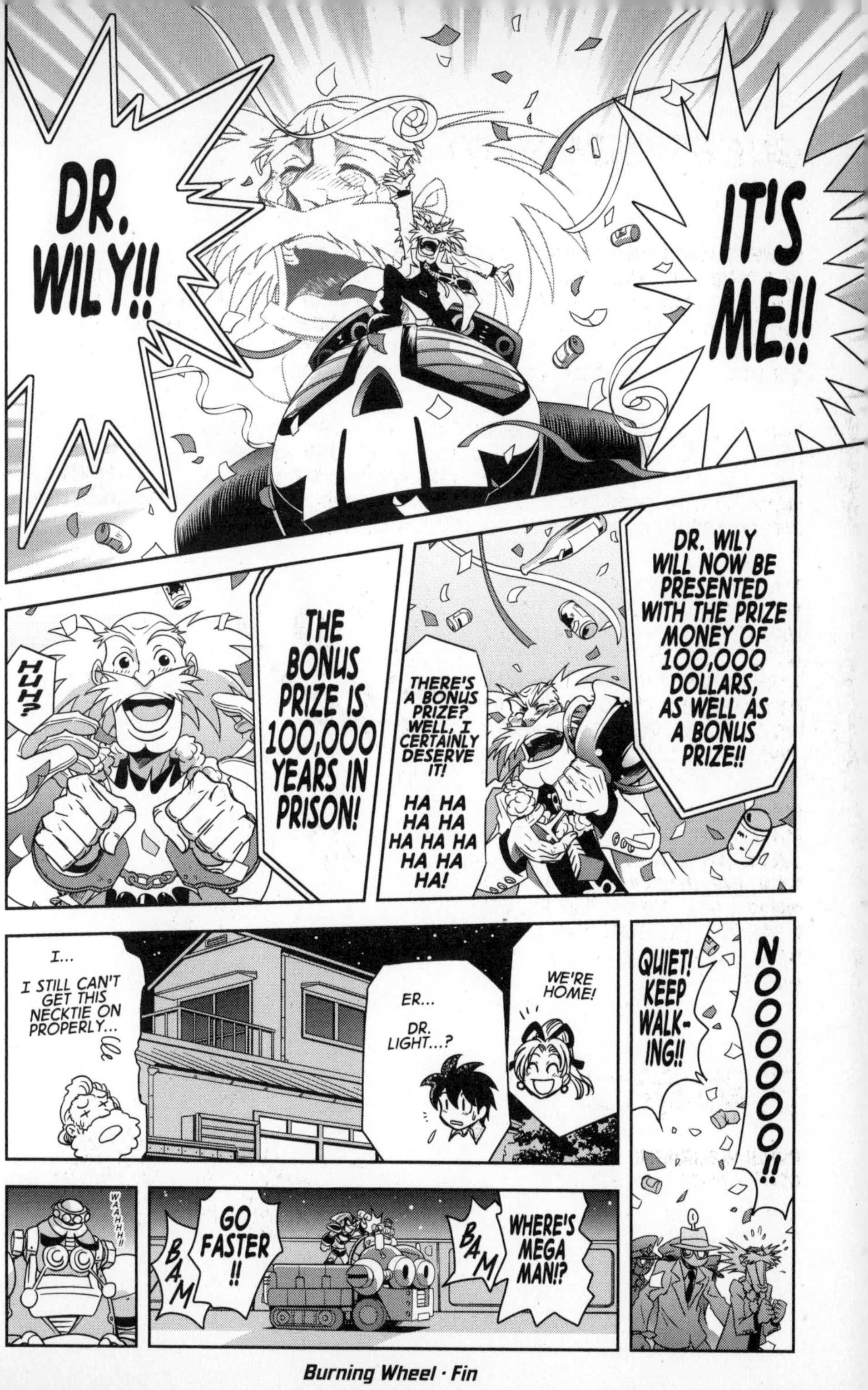
IT'S ME!!
DR. WILY!!
DR. WILY WILL NOW BE PRESENTED WITH THE PRIZE MONEY OF 100,000 DOLLARS, AS WELL AS A BONUS PRIZE!!
THERE'S A BONUS PRIZE? WELL, I CERTAINLY DESERVE IT!
HA HA HA HA HA HA HA HA HA HA HA!
THE BONUS PRIZE IS 100,000 YEARS IN PRISON!
HUH?
NOOOOOOO!!
QUIET! KEEP WALK-ING!!
WE'RE HOME!
ER... DR. LIGHT...?
I... I STILL CAN'T GET THIS NECKTIE ON PROPERLY...
WHERE'S MEGA MAN!?
BAM
GO FASTER!!
BAM
WAAHHH!!

Burning Wheel · Fin

GUEST COMMENT

HONESTLY, YOU NEVER KNOW WHERE LIFE WILL LEAD YOU, OR WHAT IT HAS IN STORE FOR YOU NEXT. I NEVER WOULD HAVE DREAMED THAT I'D ONE DAY NOT ONLY GET TO MEET THE ARTIST BEHIND ONE OF MY FAVORITE CHILDHOOD MANGAS (I STILL HAVE THE PAGES THAT I CUT OUT OF MY BONBON ISSUES), BUT ALSO GET THE OPPORTUNITY TO HAVE MY ILLUSTRATION INCLUDED IN ONE OF HIS MANGA BOOKS.

WHEN YOU TOLD ME THE SUBJECT OF MY ILLUSTRATION HAD TO BE DR. WILY, I ADMIT I WAS A BIT TROUBLED. EVERYONE KNOWS YOU LOVE DR. WILY, AND AS IT HAPPENS, I'VE NEVER DRAWN A "DR. WILY" THAT I'VE BEEN HAPPY WITH. I SUPPOSE YOU COULD SAY THIS IS "A CAPCOM EMPLOYEE'S INTERPRETATION OF ARIGA'S DR. WILY." WHAT DO YOU THINK?!

I KNOW WE HAVEN'T KNOWN EACH OTHER FOR VERY LONG, HAVING ONLY MET WHEN WE WERE WORKING ON "R20"... BUT I SINCERELY HOPE THAT WE WILL GET ANOTHER OPPORTUNITY TO WORK TOGETHER ON A MEGA MAN PROJECT.

WE SHOULD HAVE ANOTHER MATCH IN BATTLE & CHASE SOMEDAY! I WANT A REMATCH FOR THE ROCKBOARD BATTLE WHERE YOU WIPED THE FLOOR WITH ME. I'LL USE THE POP'N BEAT AND LEAVE YOU IN THE DUST!!

日暮竜二

RYUJI HIGURASHI
(CAPCOM DESIGN STUDIO)

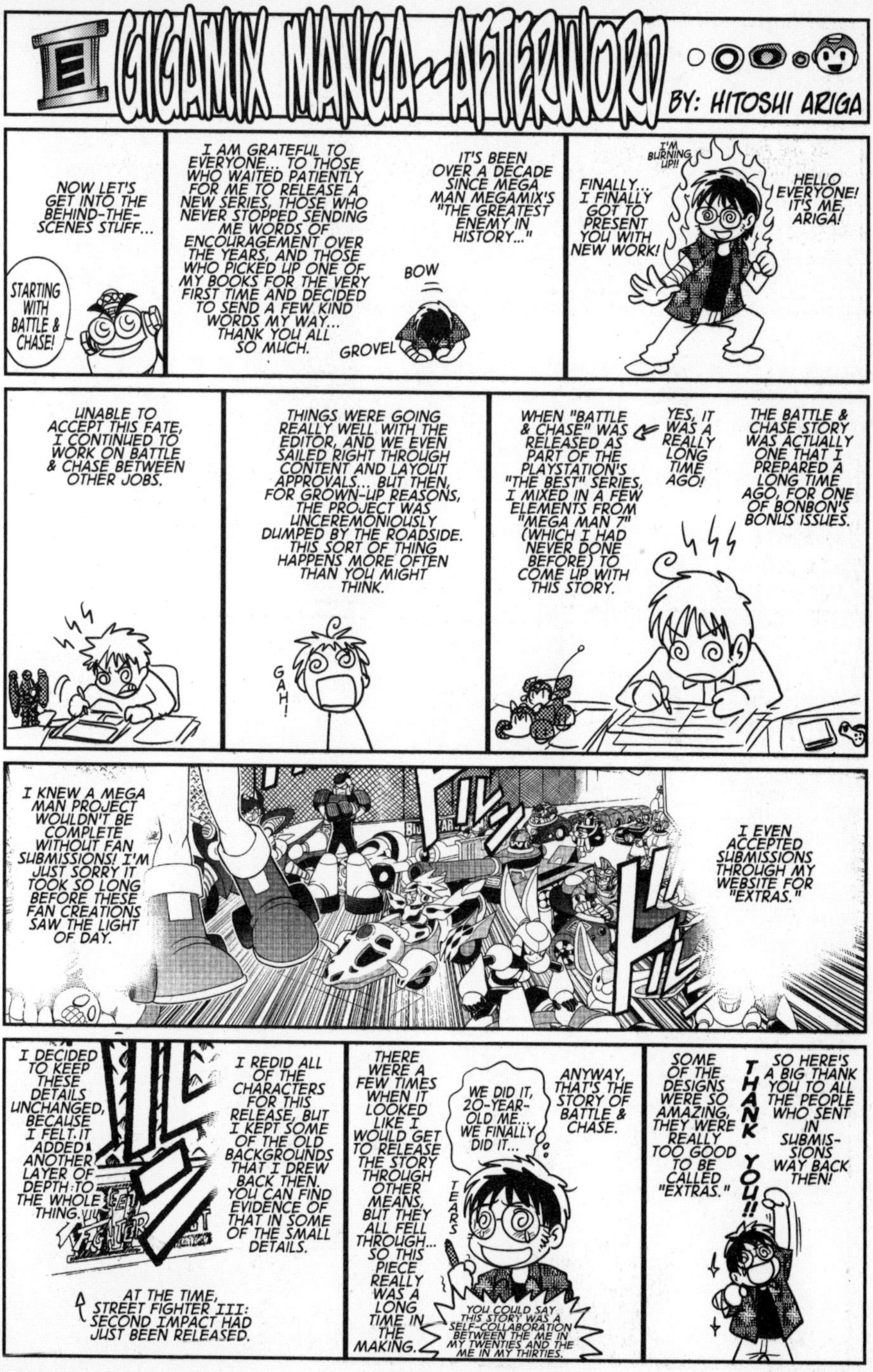
GIGAMIX MANGA--AFTERWORD
BY: HITOSHI ARIGA
HELLO EVERYONE! IT'S ME, ARIGA!
I'M BURNING UP!!
FINALLY... I FINALLY GOT TO PRESENT YOU WITH NEW WORK!
IT'S BEEN OVER A DECADE SINCE MEGA MAN MEGAMIX'S "THE GREATEST ENEMY IN HISTORY..."
I AM GRATEFUL TO EVERYONE... TO THOSE WHO WAITED PATIENTLY FOR ME TO RELEASE A NEW SERIES, THOSE WHO NEVER STOPPED SENDING ME WORDS OF ENCOURAGEMENT OVER THE YEARS, AND THOSE WHO PICKED UP ONE OF MY BOOKS FOR THE VERY FIRST TIME AND DECIDED TO SEND A FEW KIND WORDS MY WAY... THANK YOU ALL SO MUCH.
BOW
GROVEL
NOW LET'S GET INTO THE BEHIND-THE-SCENES STUFF...
STARTING WITH BATTLE & CHASE!
THE BATTLE & CHASE STORY WAS ACTUALLY ONE THAT I PREPARED A LONG TIME AGO, FOR ONE OF BONBON'S BONUS ISSUES.
YES, IT WAS A REALLY LONG TIME AGO!
WHEN "BATTLE & CHASE" WAS RELEASED AS PART OF THE PLAYSTATION'S "THE BEST" SERIES, I MIXED IN A FEW ELEMENTS FROM "MEGA MAN 7" (WHICH I HAD NEVER DONE BEFORE) TO COME UP WITH THIS STORY.
THINGS WERE GOING REALLY WELL WITH THE EDITOR, AND WE EVEN SAILED RIGHT THROUGH CONTENT AND LAYOUT APPROVALS... BUT THEN, FOR GROWN-UP REASONS, THE PROJECT WAS UNCEREMONIOUSLY DUMPED BY THE ROADSIDE. THIS SORT OF THING HAPPENS MORE OFTEN THAN YOU MIGHT THINK.
GAH!
UNABLE TO ACCEPT THIS FATE, I CONTINUED TO WORK ON BATTLE & CHASE BETWEEN OTHER JOBS.
I KNEW A MEGA MAN PROJECT WOULDN'T BE COMPLETE WITHOUT FAN SUBMISSIONS! I'M JUST SORRY IT TOOK SO LONG BEFORE THESE FAN CREATIONS SAW THE LIGHT OF DAY.
I EVEN ACCEPTED SUBMISSIONS THROUGH MY WEBSITE FOR "EXTRAS."
SO HERE'S A BIG THANK YOU TO ALL THE PEOPLE WHO SENT IN SUBMISSIONS WAY BACK THEN!
THANK YOU!!
SOME OF THE DESIGNS WERE SO AMAZING, THEY WERE REALLY TOO GOOD TO BE CALLED "EXTRAS."
ANYWAY, THAT'S THE STORY OF BATTLE & CHASE.
WE DID IT, 20-YEAR-OLD ME... WE FINALLY DID IT...
THERE WERE A FEW TIMES WHEN IT LOOKED LIKE I WOULD GET TO RELEASE THE STORY THROUGH OTHER MEANS, BUT THEY ALL FELL THROUGH... SO THIS PIECE REALLY WAS A LONG TIME IN THE MAKING.
TEARS
YOU COULD SAY THIS STORY WAS A SELF-COLLABORATION BETWEEN THE ME IN MY TWENTIES AND THE ME IN MY THIRTIES.
I REDID ALL OF THE CHARACTERS FOR THIS RELEASE, BUT I KEPT SOME OF THE OLD BACKGROUNDS THAT I DREW BACK THEN. YOU CAN FIND EVIDENCE OF THAT IN SOME OF THE SMALL DETAILS.
I DECIDED TO KEEP THESE DETAILS UNCHANGED, BECAUSE I FELT IT ADDED ANOTHER LAYER OF DEPTH TO THE WHOLE THING.
AT THE TIME, STREET FIGHTER III: SECOND IMPACT HAD JUST BEEN RELEASED.

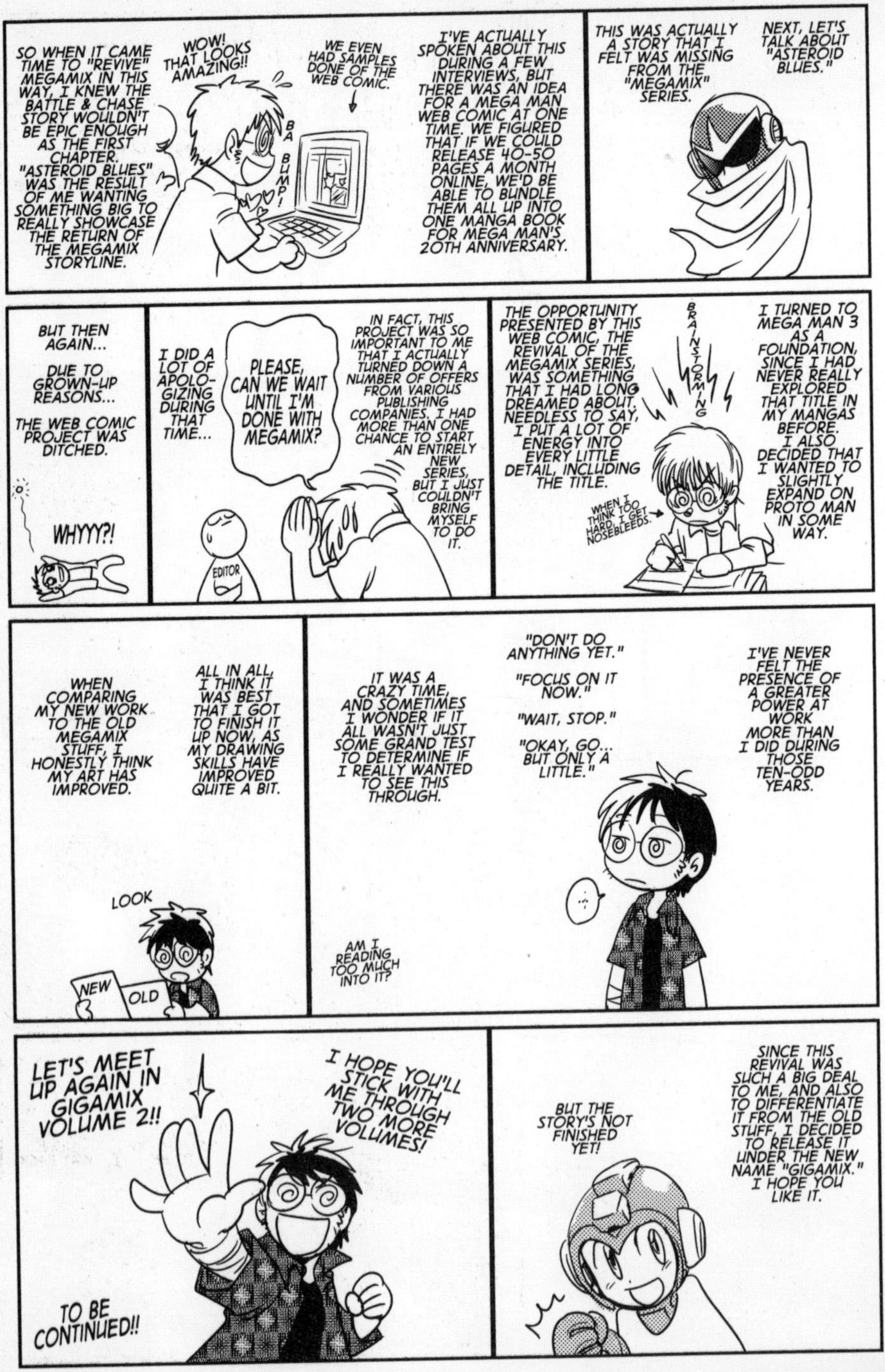
NEXT, LET'S TALK ABOUT "ASTEROID BLUES."
THIS WAS ACTUALLY A STORY THAT I FELT WAS MISSING FROM THE "MEGAMIX" SERIES.
I'VE ACTUALLY SPOKEN ABOUT THIS DURING A FEW INTERVIEWS, BUT THERE WAS AN IDEA FOR A MEGA MAN WEB COMIC AT ONE TIME. WE FIGURED THAT IF WE COULD RELEASE 40-50 PAGES A MONTH ONLINE, WE'D BE ABLE TO BUNDLE THEM ALL UP INTO ONE MANGA BOOK FOR MEGA MAN'S 20TH ANNIVERSARY.
WE EVEN HAD SAMPLES DONE OF THE WEB COMIC.
BA BUMP!
WOW! THAT LOOKS AMAZING!!
SO WHEN IT CAME TIME TO "REVIVE" MEGAMIX IN THIS WAY, I KNEW THE BATTLE & CHASE STORY WOULDN'T BE EPIC ENOUGH AS THE FIRST CHAPTER. "ASTEROID BLUES" WAS THE RESULT OF ME WANTING SOMETHING BIG TO REALLY SHOWCASE THE RETURN OF THE MEGAMIX STORYLINE.
I TURNED TO MEGA MAN 3 AS A FOUNDATION, SINCE I HAD NEVER REALLY EXPLORED THAT TITLE IN MY MANGAS BEFORE. I ALSO DECIDED THAT I WANTED TO SLIGHTLY EXPAND ON PROTO MAN IN SOME WAY.
BRAINSTORMING
THE OPPORTUNITY PRESENTED BY THIS WEB COMIC, THE REVIVAL OF THE MEGAMIX SERIES, WAS SOMETHING THAT I HAD LONG DREAMED ABOUT. NEEDLESS TO SAY, I PUT A LOT OF ENERGY INTO EVERY LITTLE DETAIL, INCLUDING THE TITLE.
WHEN I THINK TOO HARD, I GET NOSEBLEEDS.
IN FACT, THIS PROJECT WAS SO IMPORTANT TO ME THAT I ACTUALLY TURNED DOWN A NUMBER OF OFFERS FROM VARIOUS PUBLISHING COMPANIES. I HAD MORE THAN ONE CHANCE TO START AN ENTIRELY NEW SERIES, BUT I JUST COULDN'T BRING MYSELF TO DO IT.
PLEASE, CAN WE WAIT UNTIL I'M DONE WITH MEGAMIX?
I DID A LOT OF APOLOGIZING DURING THAT TIME...
EDITOR
BUT THEN AGAIN...
DUE TO GROWN-UP REASONS...
THE WEB COMIC PROJECT WAS DITCHED.
WHYYY?!
I'VE NEVER FELT THE PRESENCE OF A GREATER POWER AT WORK MORE THAN I DID DURING THOSE TEN-ODD YEARS.
"DON'T DO ANYTHING YET."
"FOCUS ON IT NOW."
"WAIT, STOP."
"OKAY, GO... BUT ONLY A LITTLE."
IT WAS A CRAZY TIME, AND SOMETIMES I WONDER IF IT ALL WASN'T JUST SOME GRAND TEST TO DETERMINE IF I REALLY WANTED TO SEE THIS THROUGH.
AM I READING TOO MUCH INTO IT?
ALL IN ALL, I THINK IT WAS BEST THAT I GOT TO FINISH IT UP NOW, AS MY DRAWING SKILLS HAVE IMPROVED QUITE A BIT.
WHEN COMPARING MY NEW WORK TO THE OLD MEGAMIX STUFF, I HONESTLY THINK MY ART HAS IMPROVED.
LOOK
NEW
OLD
SINCE THIS REVIVAL WAS SUCH A BIG DEAL TO ME, AND ALSO TO DIFFERENTIATE IT FROM THE OLD STUFF, I DECIDED TO RELEASE IT UNDER THE NEW NAME "GIGAMIX." I HOPE YOU LIKE IT.
BUT THE STORY'S NOT FINISHED YET!
I HOPE YOU'LL STICK WITH ME THROUGH TWO MORE VOLUMES!
LET'S MEET UP AGAIN IN GIGAMIX VOLUME 2!!
TO BE CONTINUED!!

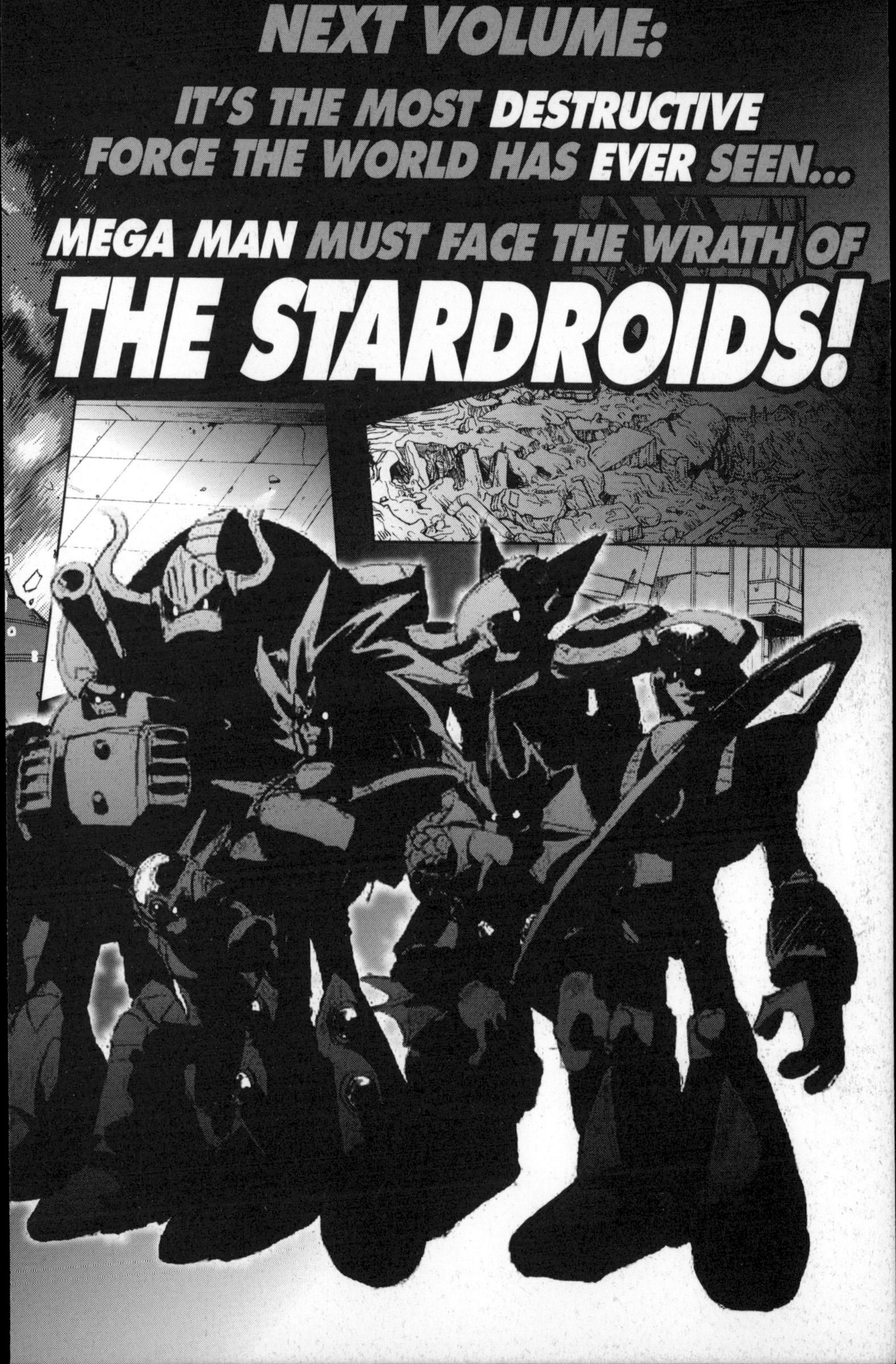
NEXT VOLUME:
IT'S THE MOST DESTRUCTIVE FORCE THE WORLD HAS EVER SEEN...
MEGA MAN MUST FACE THE WRATH OF
THE STARDROIDS!

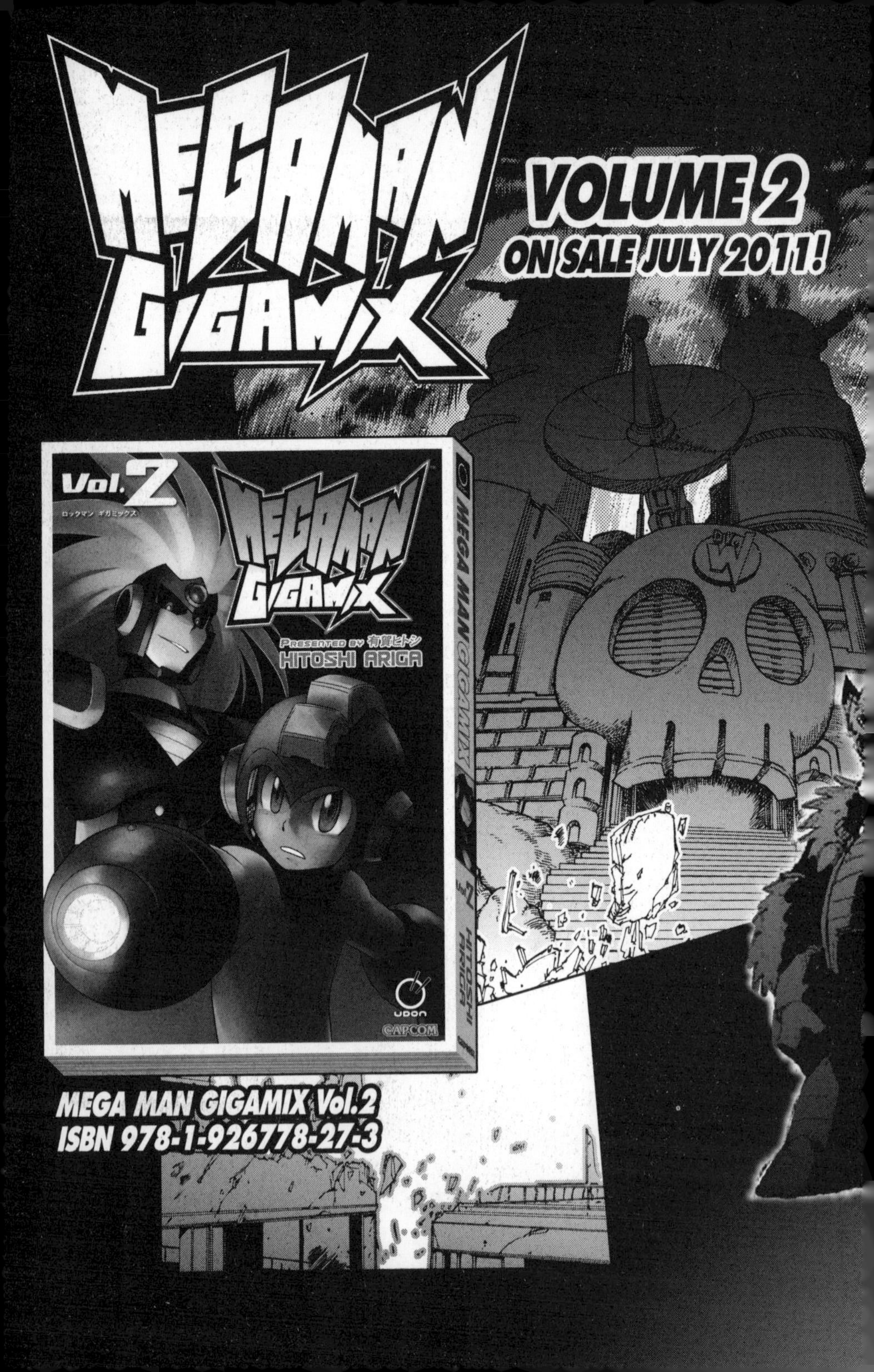

MEGAMAN GIGAMIX
VOLUME 2
ON SALE JULY 2011!
Vol.2
ロックマン ギガミックス
MEGAMAN GIGAMIX
PRESENTED BY 有賀ヒトシ
HITOSHI ARIGA
MEGA MAN GIGAMIX
HITOSHI ARIGA
UDON
CAPCOM
MEGA MAN GIGAMIX Vol.2
ISBN 978-1-926778-27-3

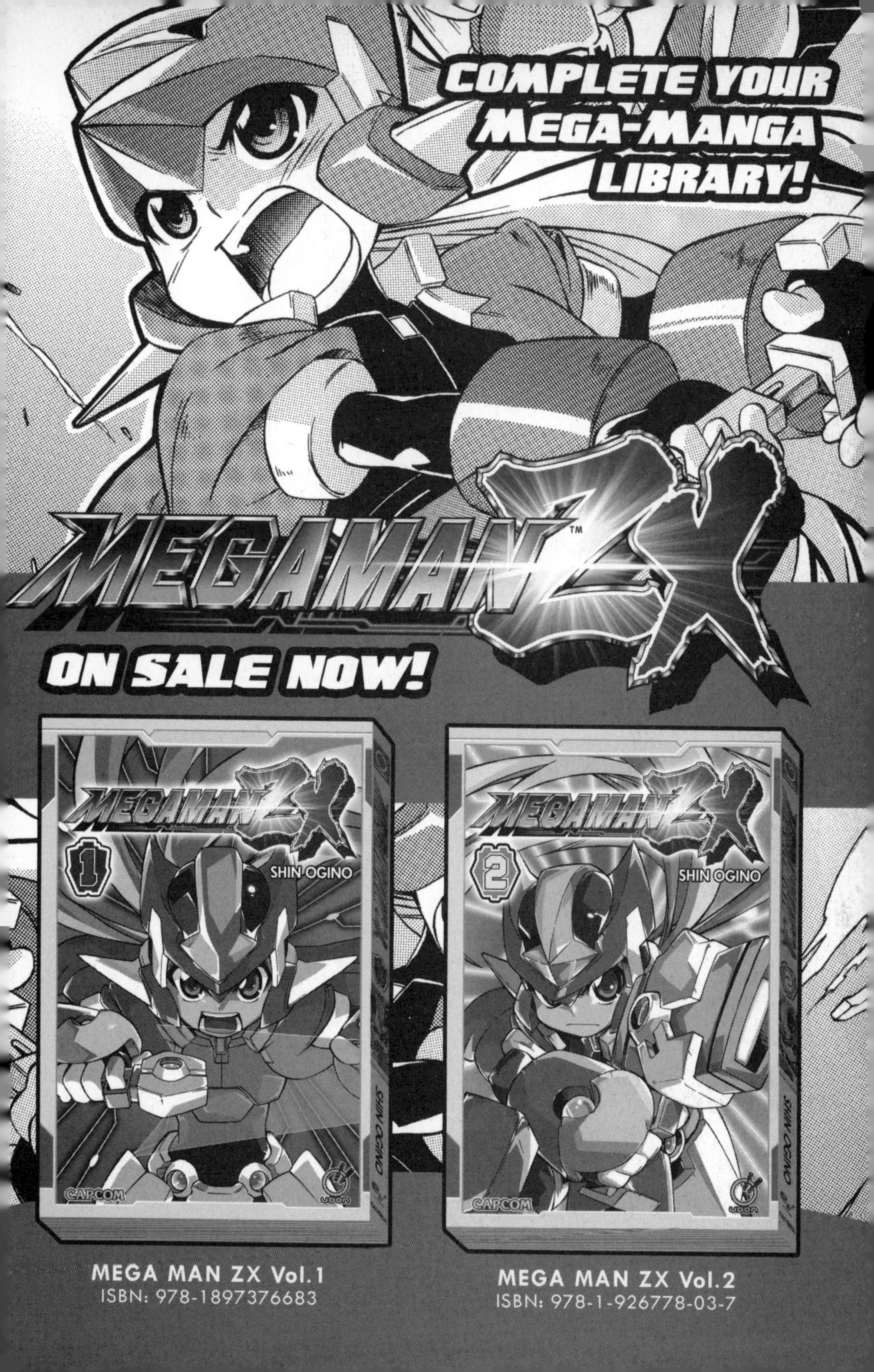
COMPLETE YOUR MEGA-MANGA LIBRARY!
MEGAMAN ZX™
ON SALE NOW!
MEGAMAN ZX
1
SHIN OGINO
CAPCOM
MEGAMAN ZX
2
SHIN OGINO
CAPCOM
MEGA MAN ZX Vol.1
ISBN: 978-1897376683
MEGA MAN ZX Vol.2
ISBN: 978-1-926778-03-7